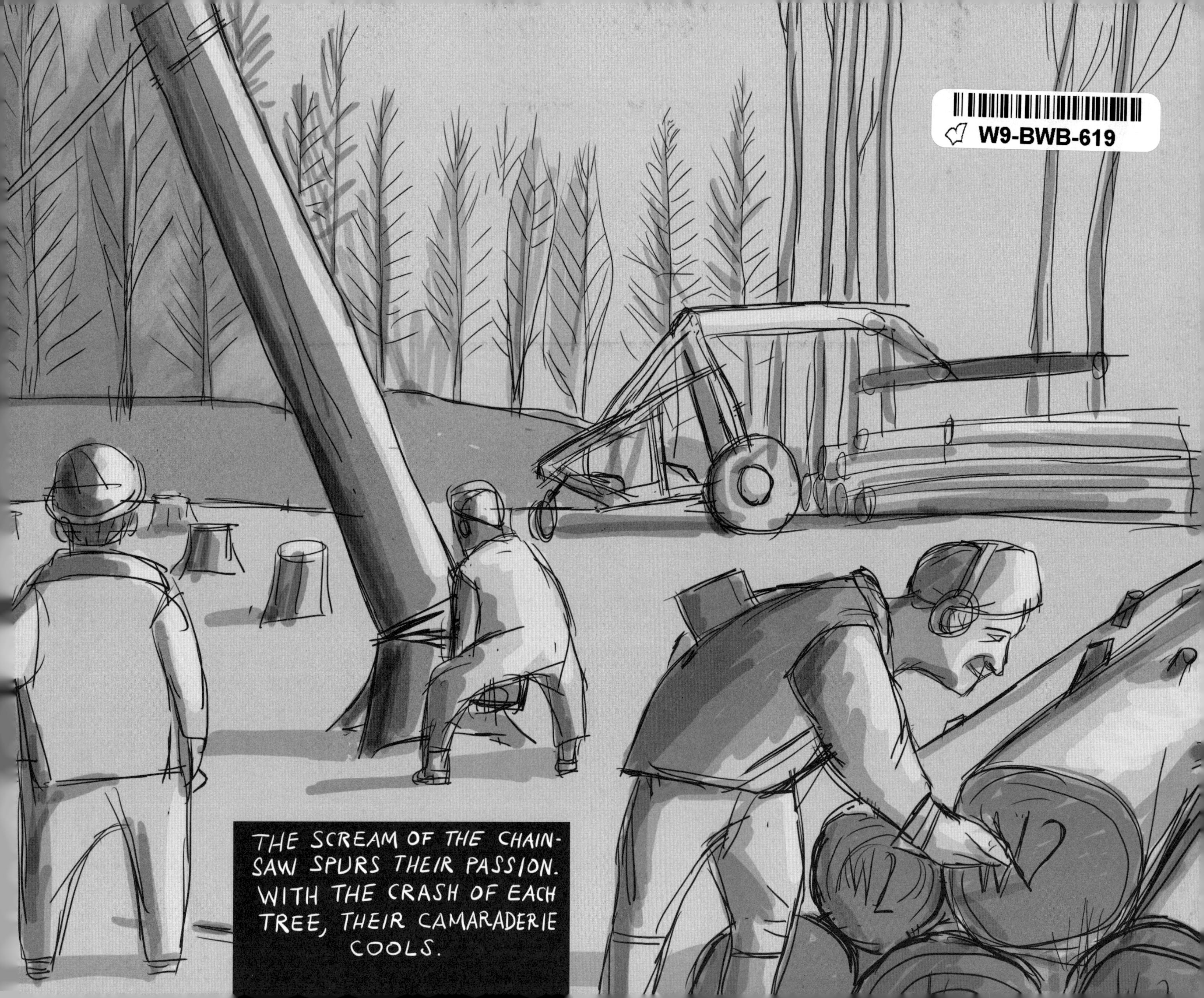
THE SCREAM OF THE CHAIN-SAW SPURS THEIR PASSION. WITH THE CRASH OF EACH TREE, THEIR CAMARADERIE COOLS.

TWO AVID READERS COPULATE
IN THE SHADOW OF THE
NANCHANTZ PAPER PLANT
IN OUTER CANTHUS.

Copyright © 2011 by Ben Katchor

All rights reserved. Published in the United States by Pantheon Books, a division of Random House, Inc., New York, and in Canada by Random House of Canada Limited, Toronto.

Pantheon Books and colophon are registered trademarks of Random House, Inc.

Portions of this work originally appeared in different form in Baltimore *City Paper*, *The Forward*, Miami *New Times*, Chicago *Newcity*, Philadelphia *City Paper*, San Diego *Reader*, San Francisco *Weekly*, and Washington *City Paper*.

Library of Congress Cataloging-in-Publication Data
Katchor, Ben.
The cardboard valise / Ben Katchor.
p. cm.
ISBN 978-0-375-42114-3
1. Graphic novels. I. Title.
PN6733.K38C37 2011   741.5'973—dc22   2010022967

www.pantheonbooks.com
Printed in Singapore

First Edition

2 4 6 8 9 7 5 3 1

The Cardboard Valise

Ben Katchor

Pantheon Books, New York

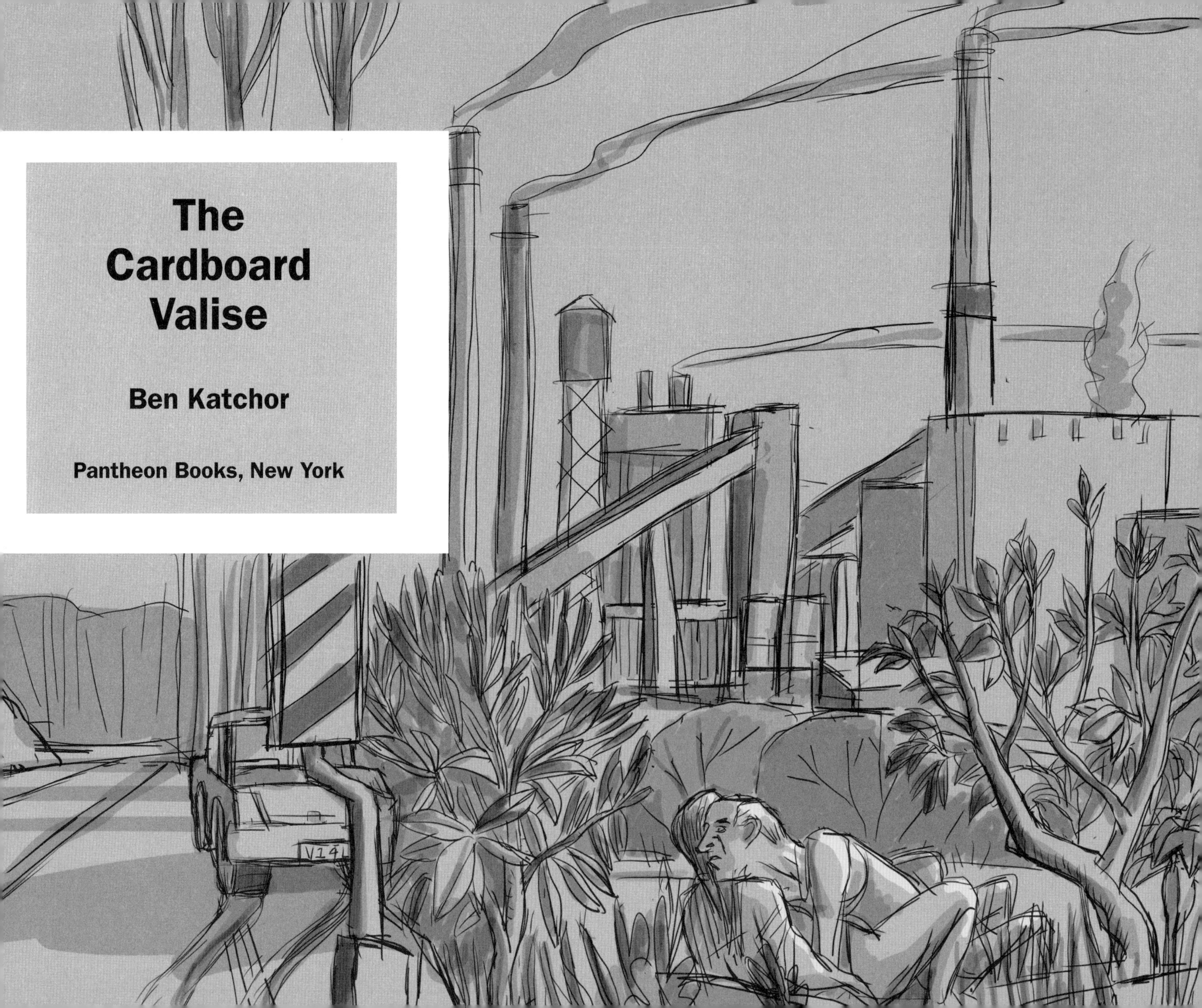
V14

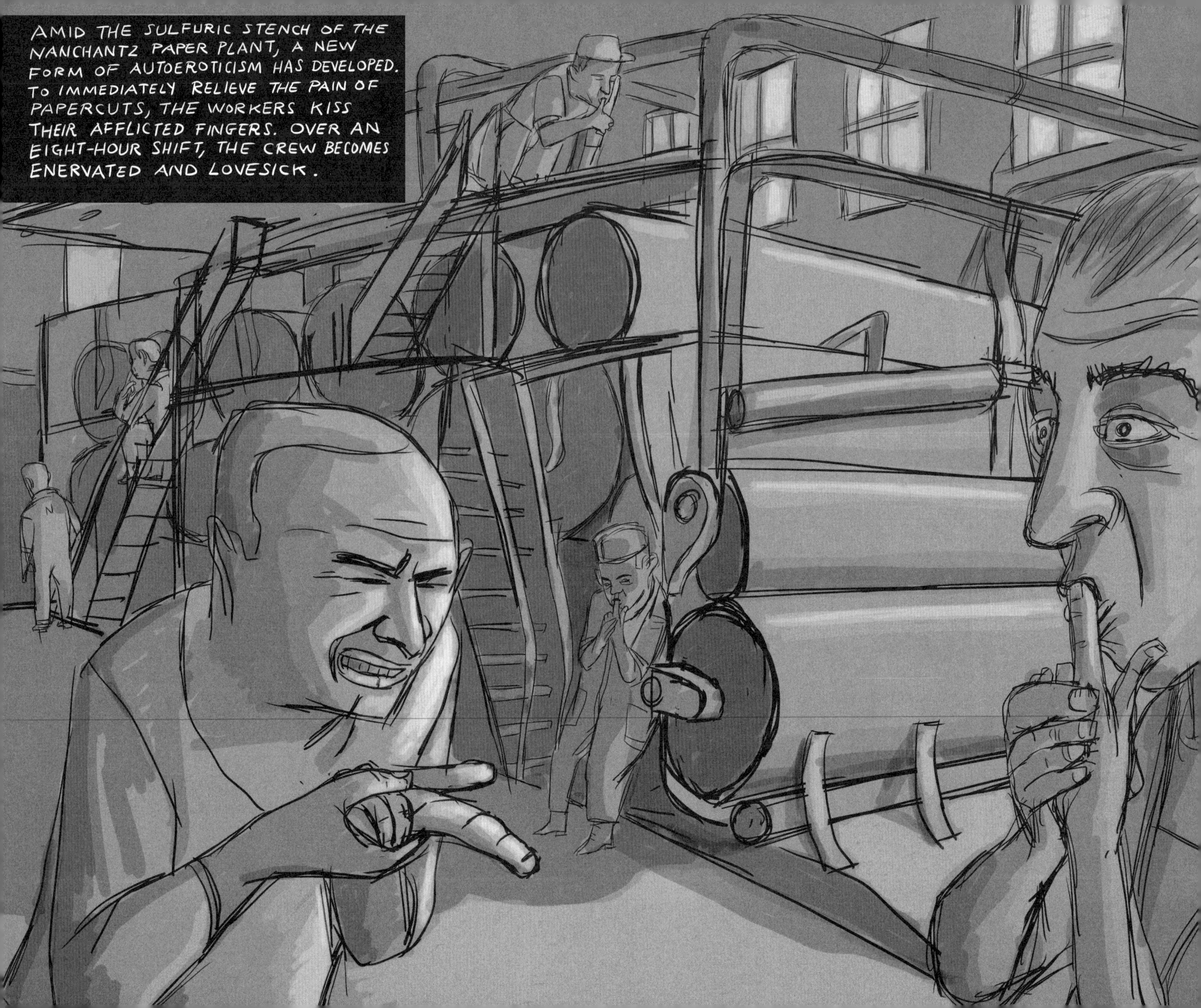
AMID THE SULFURIC STENCH OF THE NANCHANTZ PAPER PLANT, A NEW FORM OF AUTOEROTICISM HAS DEVELOPED. TO IMMEDIATELY RELIEVE THE PAIN OF PAPERCUTS, THE WORKERS KISS THEIR AFFLICTED FINGERS. OVER AN EIGHT-HOUR SHIFT, THE CREW BECOMES ENERVATED AND LOVESICK.

A PRINTER IN GAZOGENE CITY CHECKS THE REGISTRATION OF COLOR — RED OVER A LINE DRAWING OF A DISEASED AORTA — IN A SMALL, SELF-PUBLISHED EDITION OF LOVE POEMS.

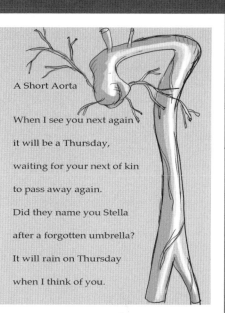

A Short Aorta

When I see you next again
it will be a Thursday,
waiting for your next of kin
to pass away again.
Did they name you Stella
after a forgotten umbrella?
It will rain on Thursday
when I think of you.

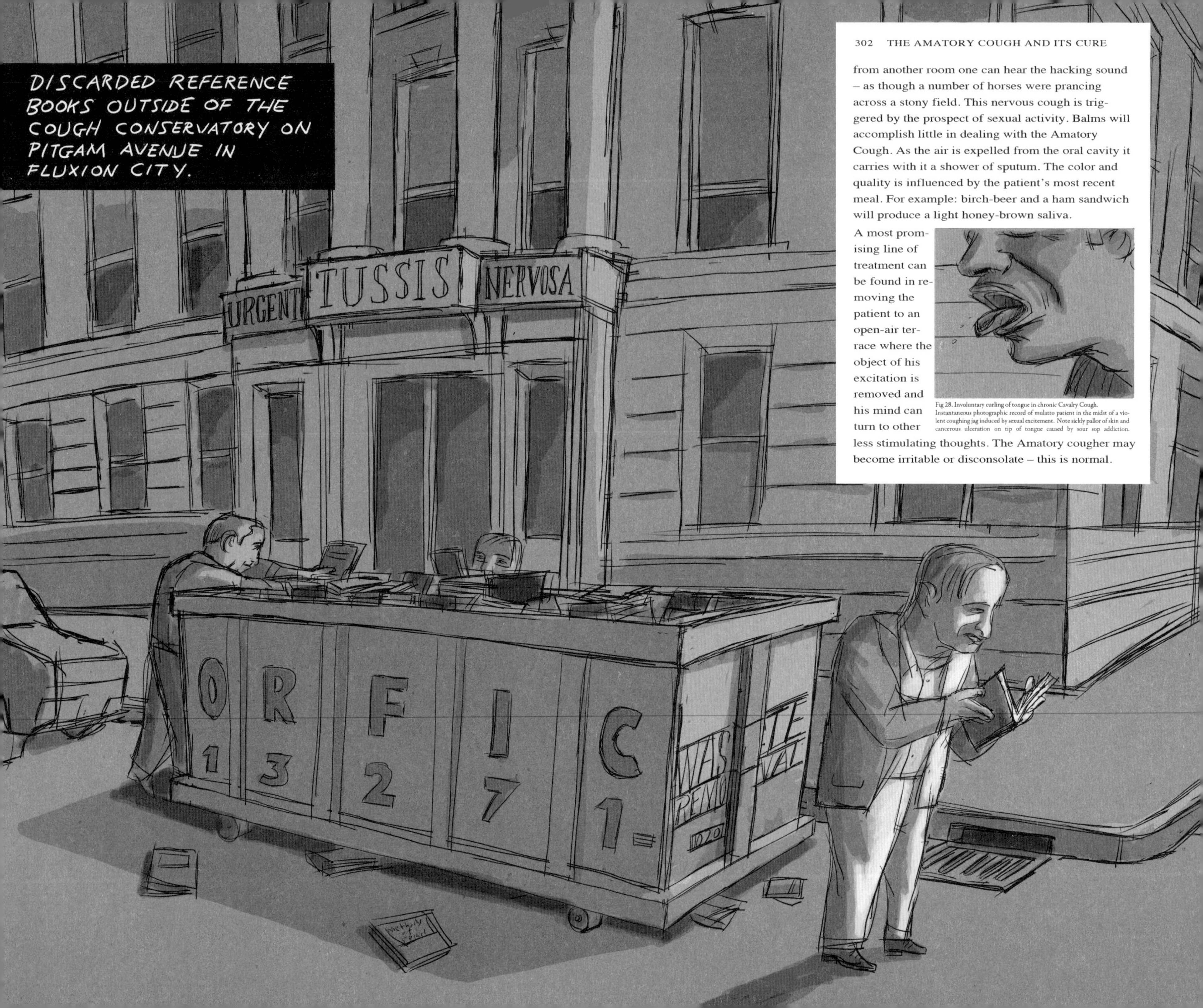
DISCARDED REFERENCE BOOKS OUTSIDE OF THE COUGH CONSERVATORY ON PITGAM AVENUE IN FLUXION CITY.
URGENT
TUSSIS
NERVOSA
ORFIC
1 3 2 7 1

from another room one can hear the hacking sound – as though a number of horses were prancing across a stony field. This nervous cough is triggered by the prospect of sexual activity. Balms will accomplish little in dealing with the Amatory Cough. As the air is expelled from the oral cavity it carries with it a shower of sputum. The color and quality is influenced by the patient's most recent meal. For example: birch-beer and a ham sandwich will produce a light honey-brown saliva.

Fig 28. Involuntary curling of tongue in chronic Cavalry Cough. Instantaneous photographic record of mulatto patient in the midst of a violent coughing jag induced by sexual excitement. Note sickly pallor of skin and cancerous ulceration on tip of tongue caused by sour sop addiction.

A most promising line of treatment can be found in removing the patient to an open-air terrace where the object of his excitation is removed and his mind can turn to other less stimulating thoughts. The Amatory cougher may become irritable or disconsolate – this is normal.

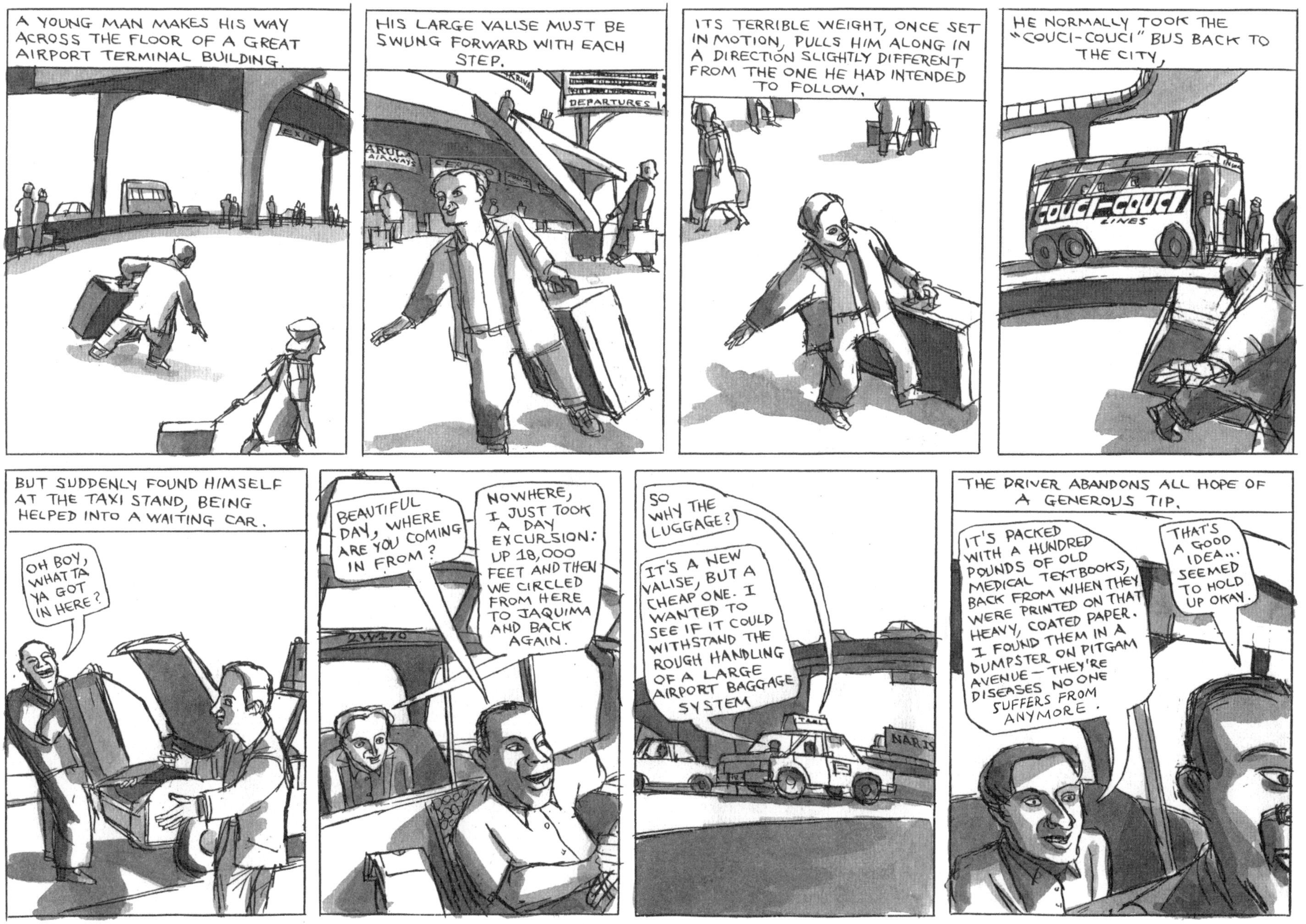
A YOUNG MAN MAKES HIS WAY ACROSS THE FLOOR OF A GREAT AIRPORT TERMINAL BUILDING.
EXIT
HIS LARGE VALISE MUST BE SWUNG FORWARD WITH EACH STEP.
DEPARTURES
ARULA AIRWAYS
ITS TERRIBLE WEIGHT, ONCE SET IN MOTION, PULLS HIM ALONG IN A DIRECTION SLIGHTLY DIFFERENT FROM THE ONE HE HAD INTENDED TO FOLLOW.
HE NORMALLY TOOK THE "COUCI-COUCI" BUS BACK TO THE CITY,
COUCI-COUCI
LINES
BUT SUDDENLY FOUND HIMSELF AT THE TAXI STAND, BEING HELPED INTO A WAITING CAR.
OH BOY, WHATTA YA GOT IN HERE?
BEAUTIFUL DAY, WHERE ARE YOU COMING IN FROM?
NOWHERE, I JUST TOOK A DAY EXCURSION: UP 18,000 FEET AND THEN WE CIRCLED FROM HERE TO JAQUIMA AND BACK AGAIN.
SO WHY THE LUGGAGE?
IT'S A NEW VALISE, BUT A CHEAP ONE. I WANTED TO SEE IF IT COULD WITHSTAND THE ROUGH HANDLING OF A LARGE AIRPORT BAGGAGE SYSTEM
TAXI
NARIS
THE DRIVER ABANDONS ALL HOPE OF A GENEROUS TIP.
IT'S PACKED WITH A HUNDRED POUNDS OF OLD MEDICAL TEXTBOOKS, BACK FROM WHEN THEY WERE PRINTED ON THAT HEAVY, COATED PAPER. I FOUND THEM IN A DUMPSTER ON PITGAM AVENUE — THEY'RE DISEASES NO ONE SUFFERS FROM ANYMORE.
THAT'S A GOOD IDEA... SEEMED TO HOLD UP OKAY.

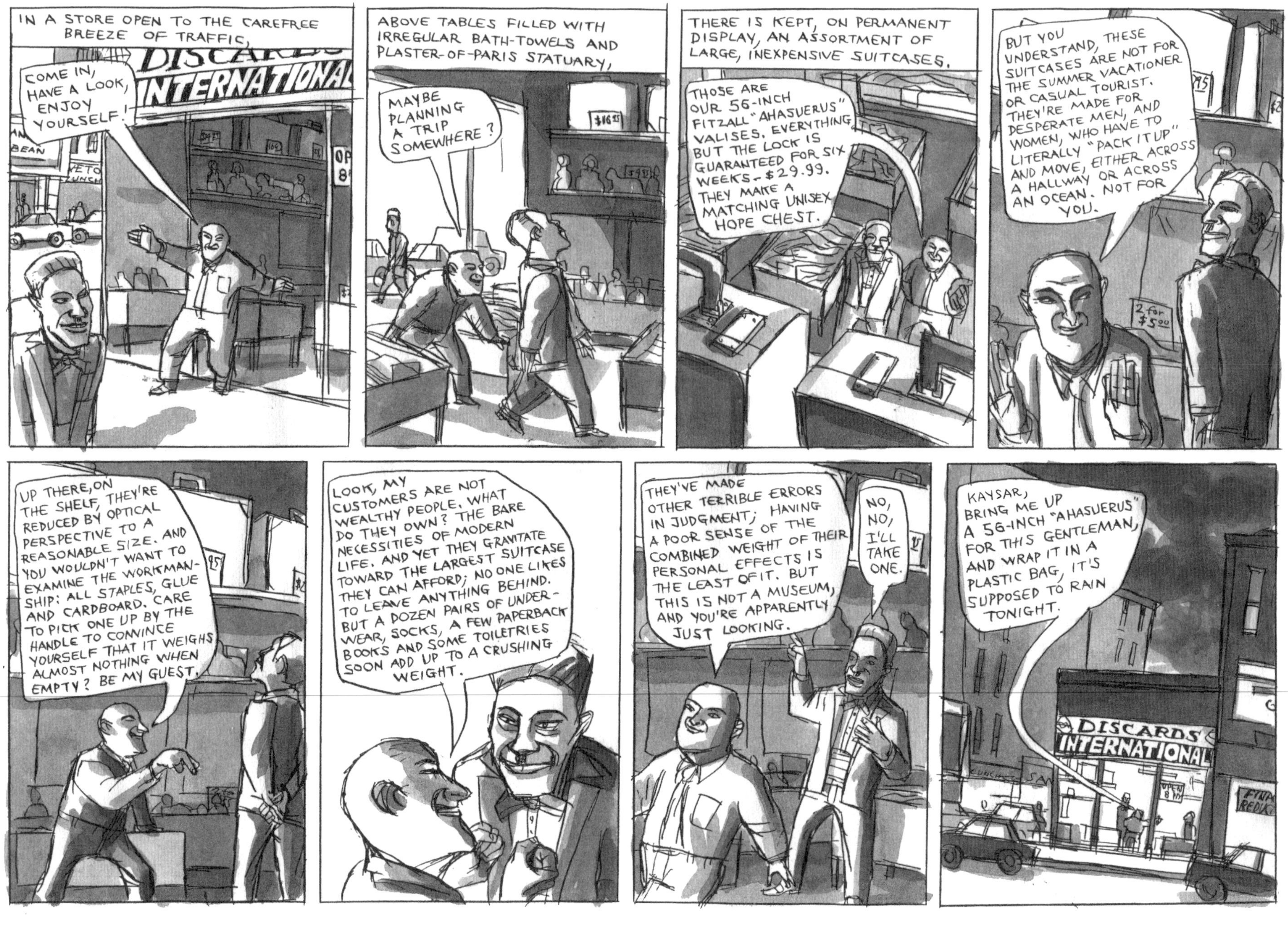
IN A STORE OPEN TO THE CAREFREE BREEZE OF TRAFFIC,
DISCARDS INTERNATIONAL
COME IN, HAVE A LOOK, ENJOY YOURSELF!
ABOVE TABLES FILLED WITH IRREGULAR BATH-TOWELS AND PLASTER-OF-PARIS STATUARY,
MAYBE PLANNING A TRIP SOMEWHERE?
THERE IS KEPT, ON PERMANENT DISPLAY, AN ASSORTMENT OF LARGE, INEXPENSIVE SUITCASES.
THOSE ARE OUR 56-INCH FITZALL "AHASUERUS" VALISES. EVERYTHING BUT THE LOCK IS GUARANTEED FOR SIX WEEKS - $29.99. THEY MAKE A MATCHING UNISEX HOPE CHEST.
BUT YOU UNDERSTAND, THESE SUITCASES ARE NOT FOR THE SUMMER VACATIONER OR CASUAL TOURIST. THEY'RE MADE FOR DESPERATE MEN, AND WOMEN, WHO HAVE TO LITERALLY "PACK IT UP" AND MOVE, EITHER ACROSS A HALLWAY OR ACROSS AN OCEAN. NOT FOR YOU.
2 for $5.00
UP THERE, ON THE SHELF, THEY'RE REDUCED BY OPTICAL PERSPECTIVE TO A REASONABLE SIZE. AND YOU WOULDN'T WANT TO EXAMINE THE WORKMANSHIP: ALL STAPLES, GLUE AND CARDBOARD. CARE TO PICK ONE UP BY THE HANDLE TO CONVINCE YOURSELF THAT IT WEIGHS ALMOST NOTHING WHEN EMPTY? BE MY GUEST.
LOOK, MY CUSTOMERS ARE NOT WEALTHY PEOPLE. WHAT DO THEY OWN? THE BARE NECESSITIES OF MODERN LIFE. AND YET THEY GRAVITATE TOWARD THE LARGEST SUITCASE THEY CAN AFFORD; NO ONE LIKES TO LEAVE ANYTHING BEHIND. BUT A DOZEN PAIRS OF UNDERWEAR, SOCKS, A FEW PAPERBACK BOOKS AND SOME TOILETRIES SOON ADD UP TO A CRUSHING WEIGHT.
THEY'VE MADE OTHER TERRIBLE ERRORS IN JUDGMENT; HAVING A POOR SENSE OF THE COMBINED WEIGHT OF THEIR PERSONAL EFFECTS IS THE LEAST OF IT. BUT THIS IS NOT A MUSEUM, AND YOU'RE APPARENTLY JUST LOOKING.
NO, NO, I'LL TAKE ONE.
KAYSAR, BRING ME UP A 56-INCH "AHASUERUS" FOR THIS GENTLEMAN, AND WRAP IT IN A PLASTIC BAG, IT'S SUPPOSED TO RAIN TONIGHT.
DISCARDS INTERNATIONAL

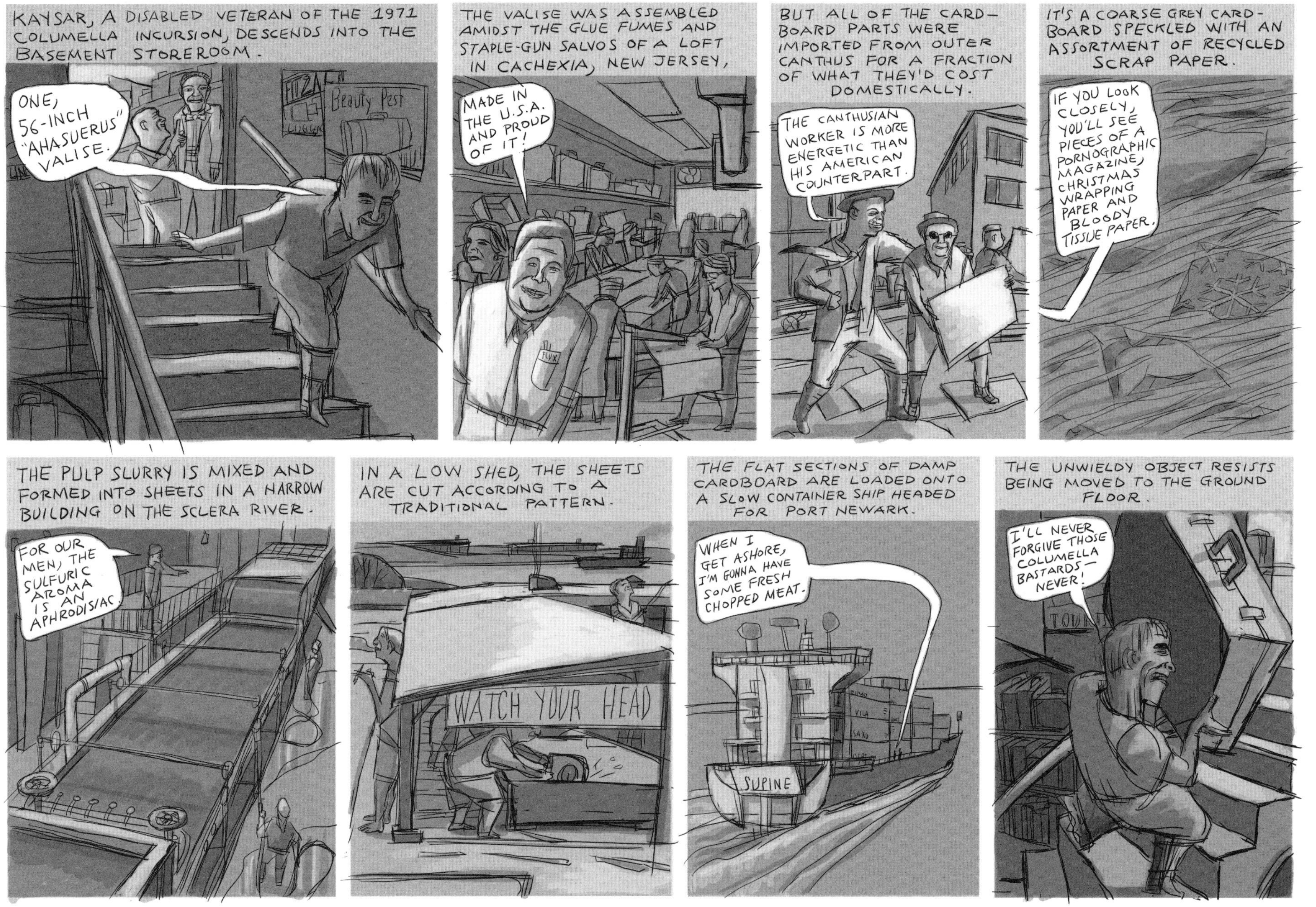
KAYSAR, A DISABLED VETERAN OF THE 1971 COLUMELLA INCURSION, DESCENDS INTO THE BASEMENT STOREROOM.
ONE, 56-INCH "AHASUERUS" VALISE.
Beauty Pest
THE VALISE WAS ASSEMBLED AMIDST THE GLUE FUMES AND STAPLE-GUN SALVOS OF A LOFT IN CACHEXIA, NEW JERSEY,
MADE IN THE U.S.A. AND PROUD OF IT!
BUT ALL OF THE CARD-BOARD PARTS WERE IMPORTED FROM OUTER CANTHUS FOR A FRACTION OF WHAT THEY'D COST DOMESTICALLY.
THE CANTHUSIAN WORKER IS MORE ENERGETIC THAN HIS AMERICAN COUNTERPART.
IT'S A COARSE GREY CARD-BOARD SPECKLED WITH AN ASSORTMENT OF RECYCLED SCRAP PAPER.
IF YOU LOOK CLOSELY, YOU'LL SEE PIECES OF A PORNOGRAPHIC MAGAZINE, CHRISTMAS WRAPPING PAPER AND BLOODY TISSUE PAPER.
THE PULP SLURRY IS MIXED AND FORMED INTO SHEETS IN A NARROW BUILDING ON THE SCLERA RIVER.
FOR OUR MEN, THE SULFURIC AROMA IS AN APHRODISIAC.
IN A LOW SHED, THE SHEETS ARE CUT ACCORDING TO A TRADITIONAL PATTERN.
WATCH YOUR HEAD
THE FLAT SECTIONS OF DAMP CARDBOARD ARE LOADED ONTO A SLOW CONTAINER SHIP HEADED FOR PORT NEWARK.
WHEN I GET ASHORE, I'M GONNA HAVE SOME FRESH CHOPPED MEAT.
SUPINE
THE UNWIELDY OBJECT RESISTS BEING MOVED TO THE GROUND FLOOR.
I'LL NEVER FORGIVE THOSE COLUMELLA BASTARDS— NEVER!

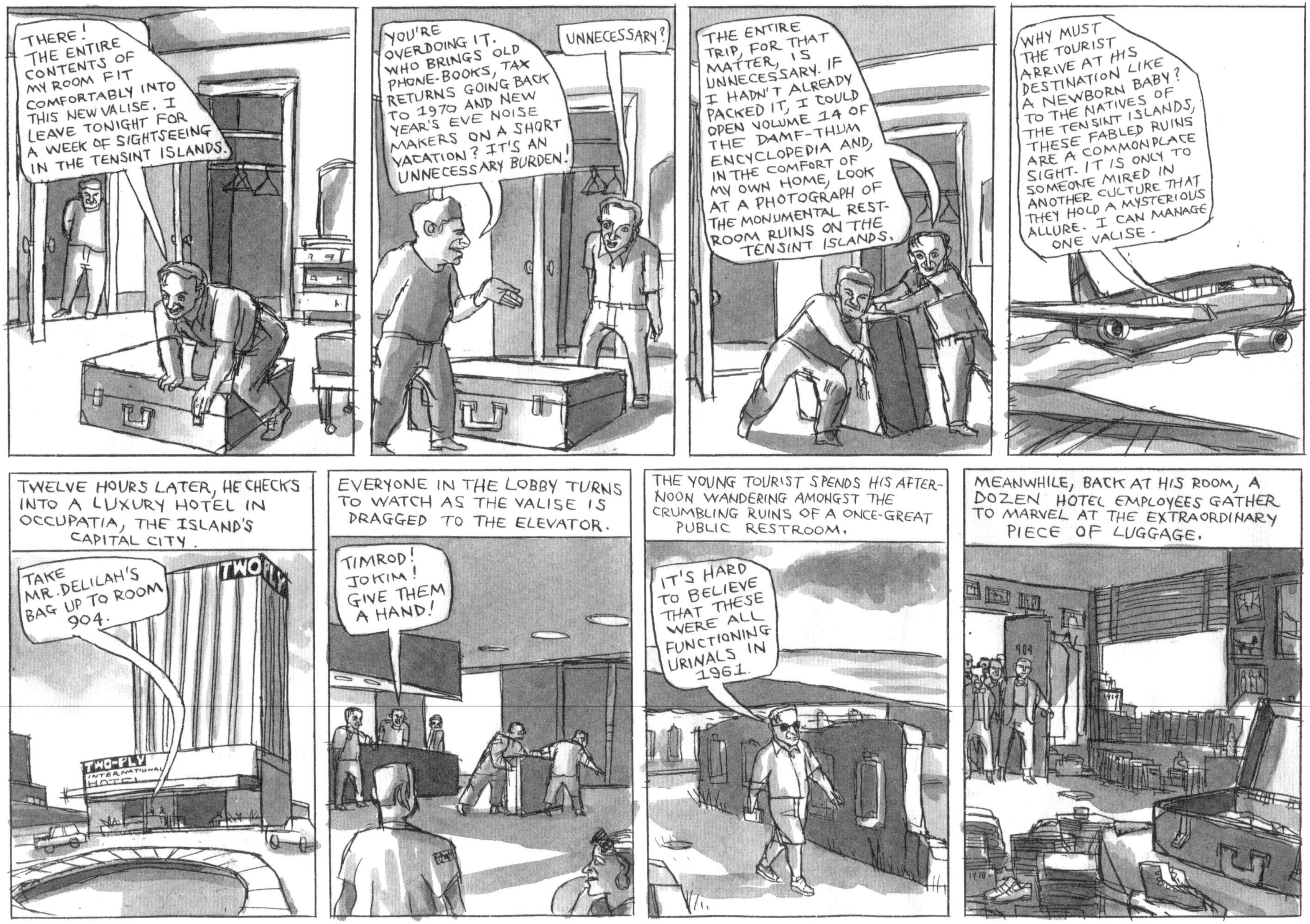
THERE! THE ENTIRE CONTENTS OF MY ROOM FIT COMFORTABLY INTO THIS NEW VALISE. I LEAVE TONIGHT FOR A WEEK OF SIGHTSEEING IN THE TENSINT ISLANDS.
YOU'RE OVERDOING IT. WHO BRINGS OLD PHONE-BOOKS, TAX RETURNS GOING BACK TO 1970 AND NEW YEAR'S EVE NOISE MAKERS ON A SHORT VACATION? IT'S AN UNNECESSARY BURDEN!
UNNECESSARY?
THE ENTIRE TRIP, FOR THAT MATTER, IS UNNECESSARY. IF I HADN'T ALREADY PACKED IT, I COULD OPEN VOLUME 14 OF THE DAMF-THUM ENCYCLOPEDIA AND, IN THE COMFORT OF MY OWN HOME, LOOK AT A PHOTOGRAPH OF THE MONUMENTAL REST-ROOM RUINS ON THE TENSINT ISLANDS.
WHY MUST THE TOURIST ARRIVE AT HIS DESTINATION LIKE A NEWBORN BABY? TO THE NATIVES OF THE TENSINT ISLANDS, THESE FABLED RUINS ARE A COMMONPLACE SIGHT. IT IS ONLY TO SOMEONE MIRED IN ANOTHER CULTURE THAT THEY HOLD A MYSTERIOUS ALLURE. I CAN MANAGE ONE VALISE.
TWELVE HOURS LATER, HE CHECKS INTO A LUXURY HOTEL IN OCCUPATIA, THE ISLAND'S CAPITAL CITY.
TWO PLY
TAKE MR. DELILAH'S BAG UP TO ROOM 904.
TWO-PLY INTERNATIONAL
EVERYONE IN THE LOBBY TURNS TO WATCH AS THE VALISE IS DRAGGED TO THE ELEVATOR.
TIMROD! JOKIM! GIVE THEM A HAND!
THE YOUNG TOURIST SPENDS HIS AFTERNOON WANDERING AMONGST THE CRUMBLING RUINS OF A ONCE-GREAT PUBLIC RESTROOM.
IT'S HARD TO BELIEVE THAT THESE WERE ALL FUNCTIONING URINALS IN 1961.
MEANWHILE, BACK AT HIS ROOM, A DOZEN HOTEL EMPLOYEES GATHER TO MARVEL AT THE EXTRAORDINARY PIECE OF LUGGAGE.
904

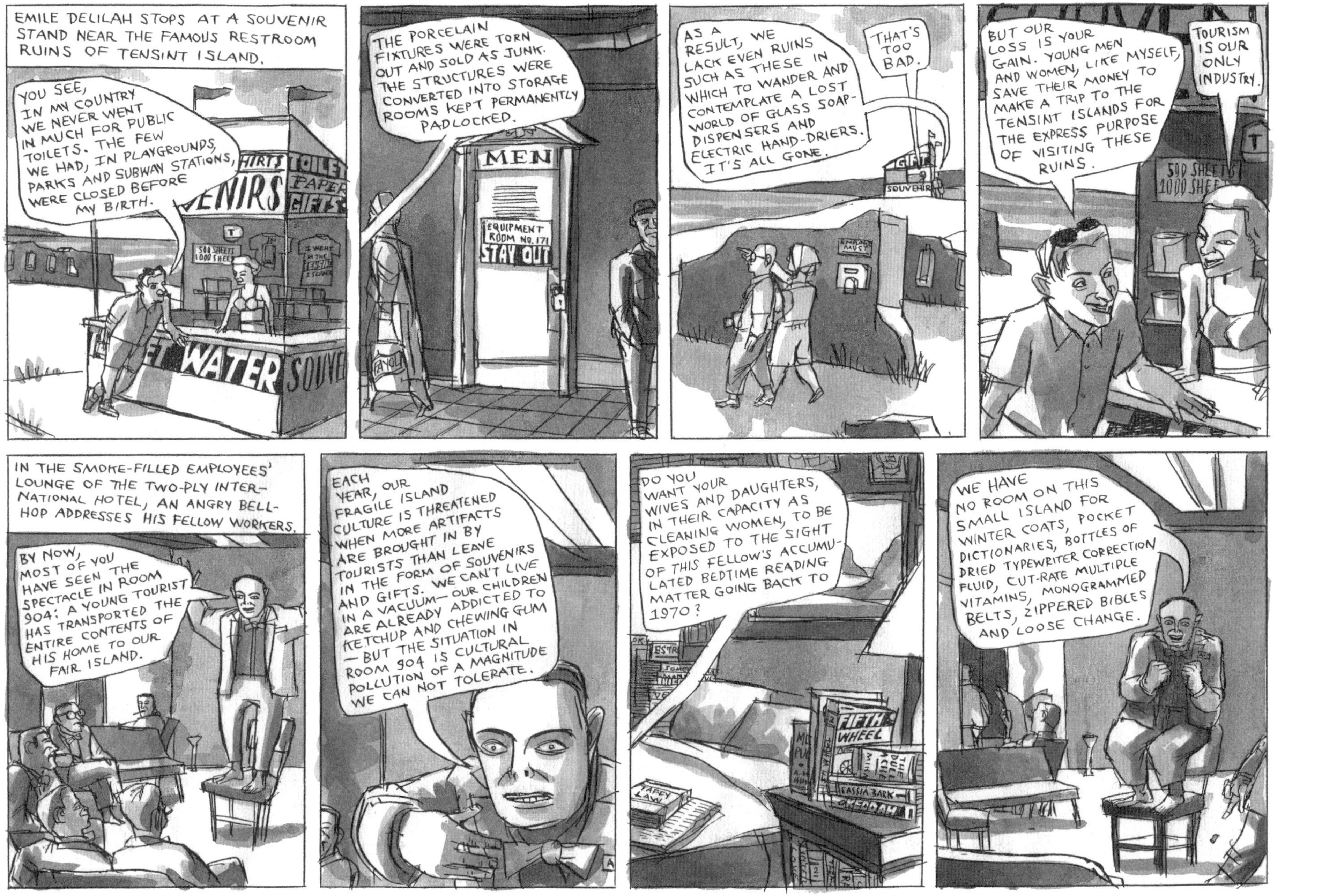
EMILE DELILAH STOPS AT A SOUVENIR STAND NEAR THE FAMOUS RESTROOM RUINS OF TENSINT ISLAND.
YOU SEE, IN MY COUNTRY WE NEVER WENT IN MUCH FOR PUBLIC TOILETS. THE FEW WE HAD, IN PLAYGROUNDS, PARKS AND SUBWAY STATIONS, WERE CLOSED BEFORE MY BIRTH.
WATER
THE PORCELAIN FIXTURES WERE TORN OUT AND SOLD AS JUNK. THE STRUCTURES WERE CONVERTED INTO STORAGE ROOMS KEPT PERMANENTLY PADLOCKED.
MEN
EQUIPMENT ROOM NO. 171
STAY OUT
AS A RESULT, WE LACK EVEN RUINS SUCH AS THESE IN WHICH TO WANDER AND CONTEMPLATE A LOST WORLD OF GLASS SOAP-DISPENSERS AND ELECTRIC HAND-DRIERS. IT'S ALL GONE.
THAT'S TOO BAD.
BUT OUR LOSS IS YOUR GAIN. YOUNG MEN AND WOMEN, LIKE MYSELF, SAVE THEIR MONEY TO MAKE A TRIP TO THE TENSINT ISLANDS FOR THE EXPRESS PURPOSE OF VISITING THESE RUINS.
TOURISM IS OUR ONLY INDUSTRY.
IN THE SMOKE-FILLED EMPLOYEES' LOUNGE OF THE TWO-PLY INTERNATIONAL HOTEL, AN ANGRY BELL-HOP ADDRESSES HIS FELLOW WORKERS.
BY NOW, MOST OF YOU HAVE SEEN THE SPECTACLE IN ROOM 904: A YOUNG TOURIST HAS TRANSPORTED THE ENTIRE CONTENTS OF HIS HOME TO OUR FAIR ISLAND.
EACH YEAR, OUR FRAGILE ISLAND CULTURE IS THREATENED WHEN MORE ARTIFACTS ARE BROUGHT IN BY TOURISTS THAN LEAVE IN THE FORM OF SOUVENIRS AND GIFTS. WE CAN'T LIVE IN A VACUUM— OUR CHILDREN ARE ALREADY ADDICTED TO KETCHUP AND CHEWING GUM —BUT THE SITUATION IN ROOM 904 IS CULTURAL POLLUTION OF A MAGNITUDE WE CAN NOT TOLERATE.
DO YOU WANT YOUR WIVES AND DAUGHTERS, IN THEIR CAPACITY AS CLEANING WOMEN, TO BE EXPOSED TO THE SIGHT OF THIS FELLOW'S ACCUMULATED BEDTIME READING MATTER GOING BACK TO 1970?
FIFTH WHEEL
CASSIA BARK
TAFFY LAW
WE HAVE NO ROOM ON THIS SMALL ISLAND FOR WINTER COATS, POCKET DICTIONARIES, BOTTLES OF DRIED TYPEWRITER CORRECTION FLUID, CUT-RATE MULTIPLE VITAMINS, MONOGRAMMED BELTS, ZIPPERED BIBLES AND LOOSE CHANGE.

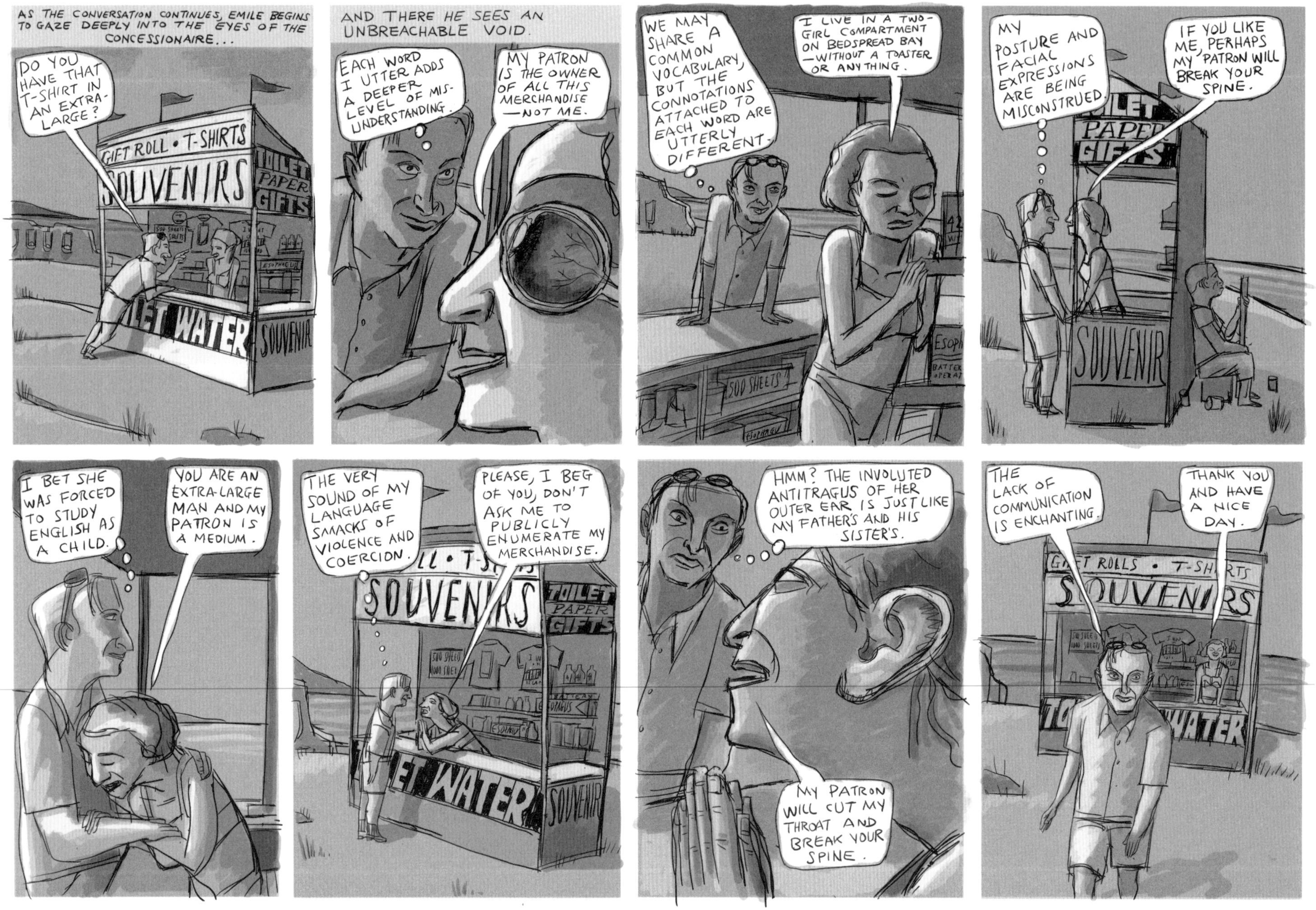
AS THE CONVERSATION CONTINUES, EMILE BEGINS TO GAZE DEEPLY INTO THE EYES OF THE CONCESSIONAIRE...
DO YOU HAVE THAT T-SHIRT IN AN EXTRA-LARGE?
GIFT ROLL • T-SHIRTS
SOUVENIRS
TOILET PAPER GIFTS
ILET WATER
SOUVENIR
AND THERE HE SEES AN UNBREACHABLE VOID.
EACH WORD I UTTER ADDS A DEEPER LEVEL OF MISUNDERSTANDING.
MY PATRON IS THE OWNER OF ALL THIS MERCHANDISE —NOT ME.
WE MAY SHARE A COMMON VOCABULARY, BUT THE CONNOTATIONS ATTACHED TO EACH WORD ARE UTTERLY DIFFERENT.
I LIVE IN A TWO-GIRL COMPARTMENT ON BEDSPREAD BAY —WITHOUT A TOASTER OR ANYTHING.
500 SHEETS
MY POSTURE AND FACIAL EXPRESSIONS ARE BEING MISCONSTRUED.
IF YOU LIKE ME, PERHAPS MY PATRON WILL BREAK YOUR SPINE.
SOUVENIR
I BET SHE WAS FORCED TO STUDY ENGLISH AS A CHILD.
YOU ARE AN EXTRA-LARGE MAN AND MY PATRON IS A MEDIUM.
THE VERY SOUND OF MY LANGUAGE SMACKS OF VIOLENCE AND COERCION.
PLEASE, I BEG OF YOU, DON'T ASK ME TO PUBLICLY ENUMERATE MY MERCHANDISE.
SOUVENIRS
TOILET PAPER GIFTS
ET WATER
SOUVENIR
HMM? THE INVOLUTED ANTITRAGUS OF HER OUTER EAR IS JUST LIKE MY FATHER'S AND HIS SISTER'S.
MY PATRON WILL CUT MY THROAT AND BREAK YOUR SPINE.
THE LACK OF COMMUNICATION IS ENCHANTING.
THANK YOU AND HAVE A NICE DAY.
GIFT ROLLS • T-SHIRTS
SOUVENIRS
WATER

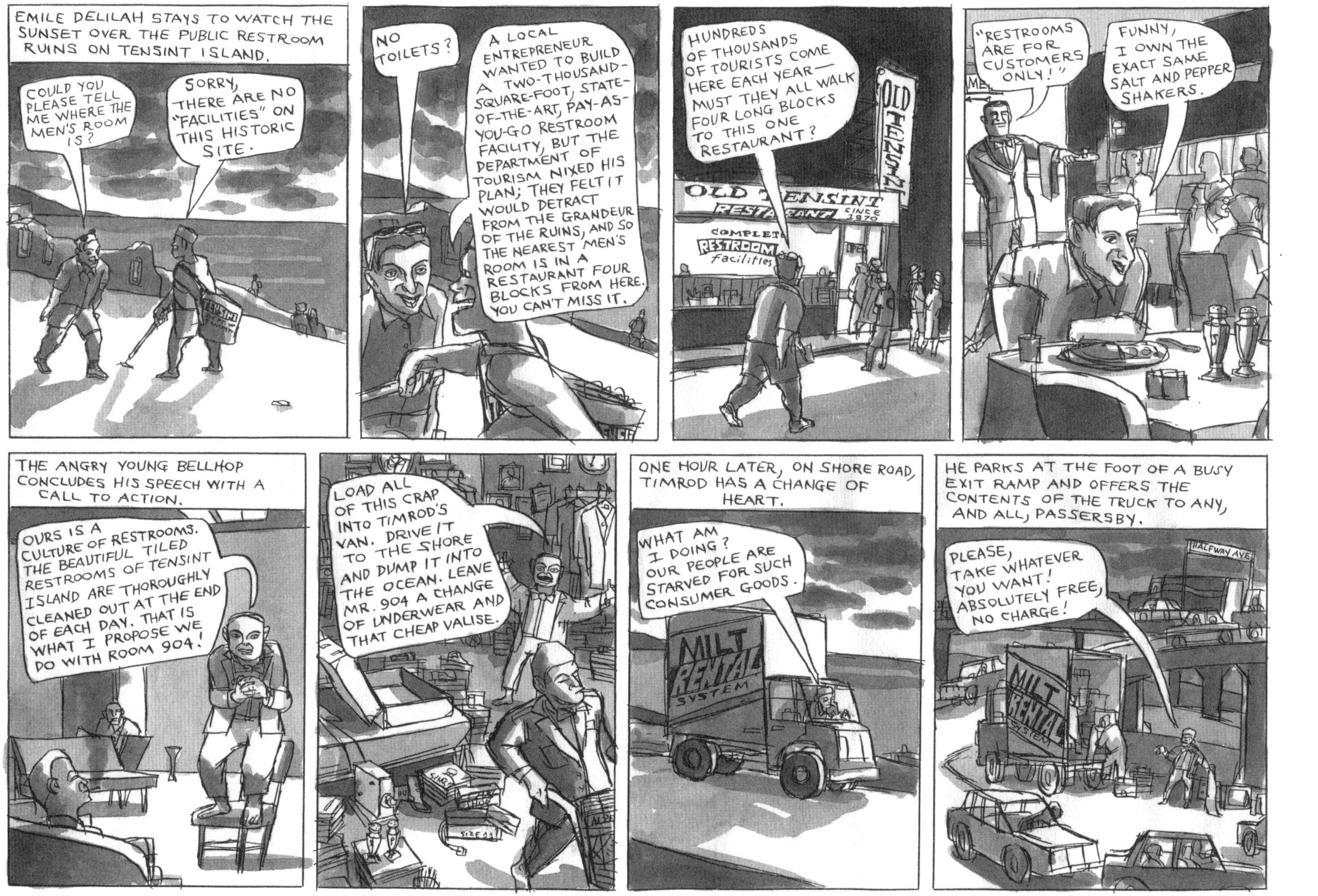
EMILE DELILAH STAYS TO WATCH THE SUNSET OVER THE PUBLIC RESTROOM RUINS ON TENSINT ISLAND.
COULD YOU PLEASE TELL ME WHERE THE MEN'S ROOM IS?
SORRY, THERE ARE NO "FACILITIES" ON THIS HISTORIC SITE.
NO TOILETS?
A LOCAL ENTREPRENEUR WANTED TO BUILD A TWO-THOUSAND-SQUARE-FOOT, STATE-OF-THE-ART, PAY-AS-YOU-GO RESTROOM FACILITY, BUT THE DEPARTMENT OF TOURISM NIXED HIS PLAN; THEY FELT IT WOULD DETRACT FROM THE GRANDEUR OF THE RUINS, AND SO THE NEAREST MEN'S ROOM IS IN A RESTAURANT FOUR BLOCKS FROM HERE. YOU CAN'T MISS IT.
HUNDREDS OF THOUSANDS OF TOURISTS COME HERE EACH YEAR— MUST THEY ALL WALK FOUR LONG BLOCKS TO THIS ONE RESTAURANT?
OLD TENSINT
RESTAURANT SINCE 1970
COMPLETE RESTROOM Facilities
"RESTROOMS ARE FOR CUSTOMERS ONLY!"
FUNNY, I OWN THE EXACT SAME SALT AND PEPPER SHAKERS.
THE ANGRY YOUNG BELLHOP CONCLUDES HIS SPEECH WITH A CALL TO ACTION.
OURS IS A CULTURE OF RESTROOMS. THE BEAUTIFUL TILED RESTROOMS OF TENSINT ISLAND ARE THOROUGHLY CLEANED OUT AT THE END OF EACH DAY. THAT IS WHAT I PROPOSE WE DO WITH ROOM 904!
LOAD ALL OF THIS CRAP INTO TIMROD'S VAN. DRIVE IT TO THE SHORE AND DUMP IT INTO THE OCEAN. LEAVE MR. 904 A CHANGE OF UNDERWEAR AND THAT CHEAP VALISE.
ONE HOUR LATER, ON SHORE ROAD, TIMROD HAS A CHANGE OF HEART.
WHAT AM I DOING? OUR PEOPLE ARE STARVED FOR SUCH CONSUMER GOODS.
MILT RENTAL SYSTEM
HE PARKS AT THE FOOT OF A BUSY EXIT RAMP AND OFFERS THE CONTENTS OF THE TRUCK TO ANY, AND ALL, PASSERSBY.
HALFWAY AVE
PLEASE, TAKE WHATEVER YOU WANT! ABSOLUTELY FREE, NO CHARGE!
MILT RENTAL SYSTEM

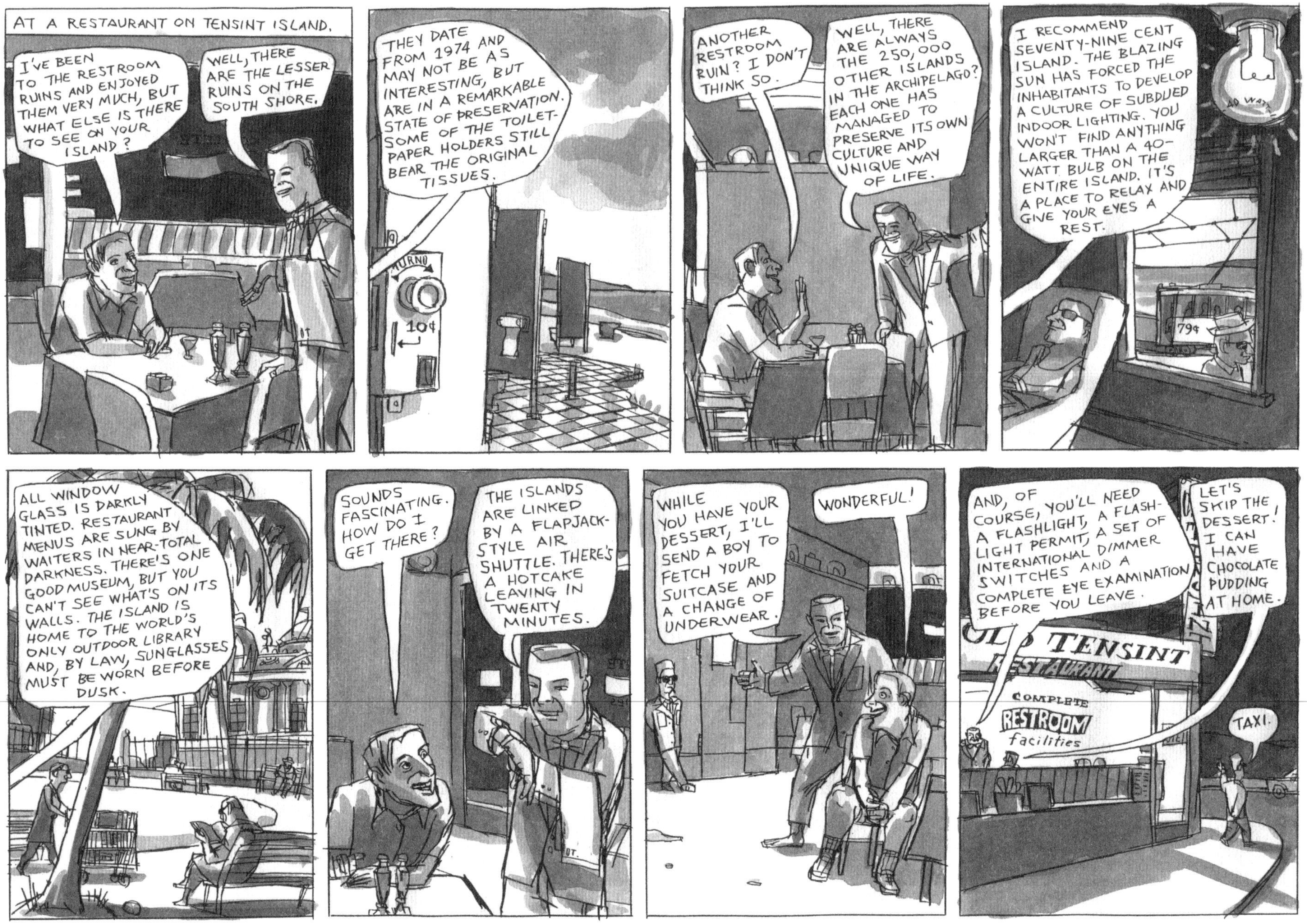
AT A RESTAURANT ON TENSINT ISLAND.
I'VE BEEN TO THE RESTROOM RUINS AND ENJOYED THEM VERY MUCH, BUT WHAT ELSE IS THERE TO SEE ON YOUR ISLAND?
WELL, THERE ARE THE LESSER RUINS ON THE SOUTH SHORE.
THEY DATE FROM 1974 AND MAY NOT BE AS INTERESTING, BUT ARE IN A REMARKABLE STATE OF PRESERVATION. SOME OF THE TOILET-PAPER HOLDERS STILL BEAR THE ORIGINAL TISSUES.
10¢
ANOTHER RESTROOM RUIN? I DON'T THINK SO.
WELL, THERE ARE ALWAYS THE 250,000 OTHER ISLANDS IN THE ARCHIPELAGO? EACH ONE HAS MANAGED TO PRESERVE ITS OWN CULTURE AND UNIQUE WAY OF LIFE.
I RECOMMEND SEVENTY-NINE CENT ISLAND. THE BLAZING SUN HAS FORCED THE INHABITANTS TO DEVELOP A CULTURE OF SUBDUED INDOOR LIGHTING. YOU WON'T FIND ANYTHING LARGER THAN A 40-WATT BULB ON THE ENTIRE ISLAND. IT'S A PLACE TO RELAX AND GIVE YOUR EYES A REST.
79¢
ALL WINDOW GLASS IS DARKLY TINTED. RESTAURANT MENUS ARE SUNG BY WAITERS IN NEAR-TOTAL DARKNESS. THERE'S ONE GOOD MUSEUM, BUT YOU CAN'T SEE WHAT'S ON ITS WALLS. THE ISLAND IS HOME TO THE WORLD'S ONLY OUTDOOR LIBRARY AND, BY LAW, SUNGLASSES MUST BE WORN BEFORE DUSK.
SOUNDS FASCINATING. HOW DO I GET THERE?
THE ISLANDS ARE LINKED BY A FLAPJACK-STYLE AIR SHUTTLE. THERE'S A HOTCAKE LEAVING IN TWENTY MINUTES.
WHILE YOU HAVE YOUR DESSERT, I'LL SEND A BOY TO FETCH YOUR SUITCASE AND A CHANGE OF UNDERWEAR.
WONDERFUL!
AND, OF COURSE, YOU'LL NEED A FLASHLIGHT, A FLASH-LIGHT PERMIT, A SET OF INTERNATIONAL DIMMER SWITCHES AND A COMPLETE EYE EXAMINATION BEFORE YOU LEAVE.
LET'S SKIP THE DESSERT! I CAN HAVE CHOCOLATE PUDDING AT HOME.
OLD TENSINT
RESTAURANT
COMPLETE
RESTROOM
facilities
TAXI.

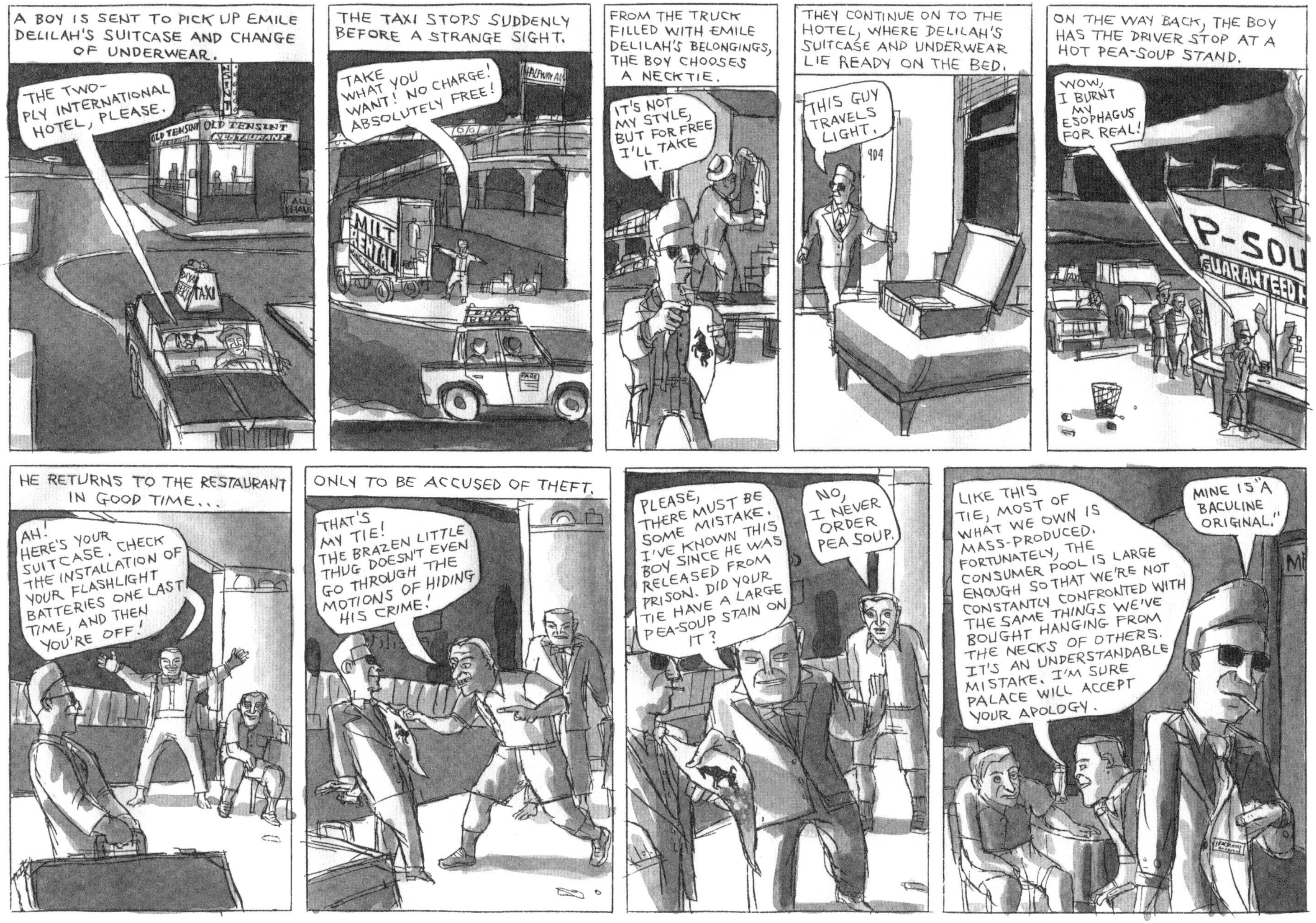
A BOY IS SENT TO PICK UP EMILE DELILAH'S SUITCASE AND CHANGE OF UNDERWEAR.
THE TWO-PLY INTERNATIONAL HOTEL, PLEASE.
OLD TENSINT RESTAURANT
TAXI
THE TAXI STOPS SUDDENLY BEFORE A STRANGE SIGHT.
TAKE WHAT YOU WANT! NO CHARGE! ABSOLUTELY FREE!
MILT RENTAL
FROM THE TRUCK FILLED WITH EMILE DELILAH'S BELONGINGS, THE BOY CHOOSES A NECKTIE.
IT'S NOT MY STYLE, BUT FOR FREE I'LL TAKE IT.
THEY CONTINUE ON TO THE HOTEL, WHERE DELILAH'S SUITCASE AND UNDERWEAR LIE READY ON THE BED.
THIS GUY TRAVELS LIGHT.
904
ON THE WAY BACK, THE BOY HAS THE DRIVER STOP AT A HOT PEA-SOUP STAND.
WOW, I BURNT MY ESOPHAGUS FOR REAL!
P-SOU
GUARANTEED H
HE RETURNS TO THE RESTAURANT IN GOOD TIME...
AH! HERE'S YOUR SUITCASE. CHECK THE INSTALLATION OF YOUR FLASHLIGHT BATTERIES ONE LAST TIME, AND THEN YOU'RE OFF!
ONLY TO BE ACCUSED OF THEFT.
THAT'S MY TIE! THE BRAZEN LITTLE THUG DOESN'T EVEN GO THROUGH THE MOTIONS OF HIDING HIS CRIME!
PLEASE, THERE MUST BE SOME MISTAKE. I'VE KNOWN THIS BOY SINCE HE WAS RELEASED FROM PRISON. DID YOUR TIE HAVE A LARGE PEA-SOUP STAIN ON IT?
NO, I NEVER ORDER PEA SOUP.
LIKE THIS TIE, MOST OF WHAT WE OWN IS MASS-PRODUCED. FORTUNATELY, THE CONSUMER POOL IS LARGE ENOUGH SO THAT WE'RE NOT CONSTANTLY CONFRONTED WITH THE SAME THINGS WE'VE BOUGHT HANGING FROM THE NECKS OF OTHERS. IT'S AN UNDERSTANDABLE MISTAKE. I'M SURE PALACE WILL ACCEPT YOUR APOLOGY.
MINE IS "A BACULINE ORIGINAL."

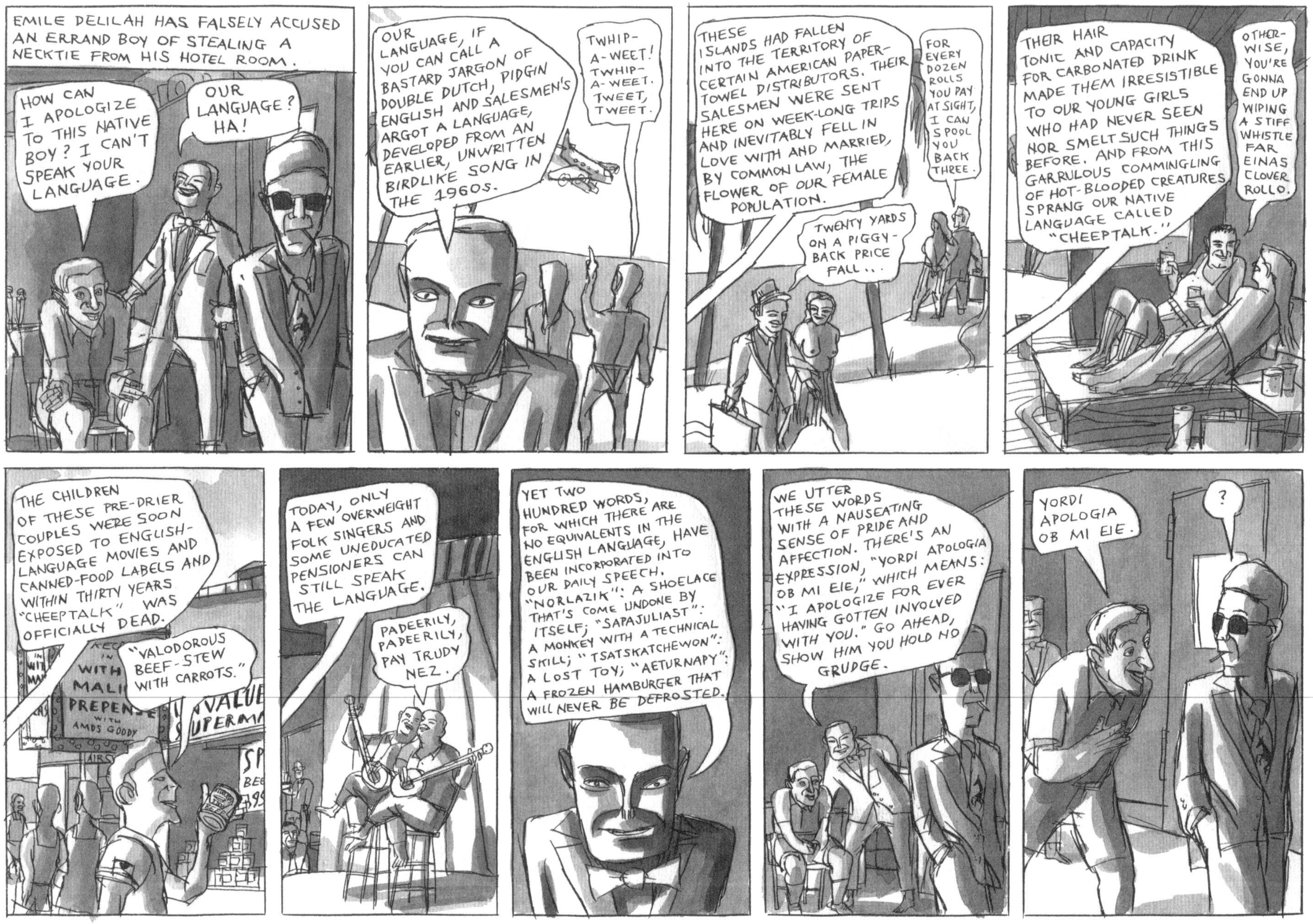
EMILE DELILAH HAS FALSELY ACCUSED AN ERRAND BOY OF STEALING A NECKTIE FROM HIS HOTEL ROOM.
HOW CAN I APOLOGIZE TO THIS NATIVE BOY? I CAN'T SPEAK YOUR LANGUAGE.
OUR LANGUAGE? HA!
OUR LANGUAGE, IF YOU CAN CALL A BASTARD JARGON OF DOUBLE DUTCH, PIDGIN ENGLISH AND SALESMEN'S ARGOT A LANGUAGE, DEVELOPED FROM AN EARLIER, UNWRITTEN BIRDLIKE SONG IN THE 1960s.
TWHIP-A-WEET! TWHIP-A-WEET. TWEET, TWEET.
THESE ISLANDS HAD FALLEN INTO THE TERRITORY OF CERTAIN AMERICAN PAPER-TOWEL DISTRIBUTORS. THEIR SALESMEN WERE SENT HERE ON WEEK-LONG TRIPS AND INEVITABLY FELL IN LOVE WITH AND MARRIED, BY COMMON LAW, THE FLOWER OF OUR FEMALE POPULATION.
FOR EVERY DOZEN ROLLS YOU PAY AT SIGHT, I CAN SPOOL YOU BACK THREE.
TWENTY YARDS ON A PIGGY-BACK PRICE FALL...
THEIR HAIR TONIC AND CAPACITY FOR CARBONATED DRINK MADE THEM IRRESISTIBLE TO OUR YOUNG GIRLS WHO HAD NEVER SEEN NOR SMELT SUCH THINGS BEFORE. AND FROM THIS GARRULOUS COMMINGLING OF HOT-BLOODED CREATURES SPRANG OUR NATIVE LANGUAGE CALLED "CHEEPTALK."
OTHER-WISE, YOU'RE GONNA END UP WIPING A STIFF WHISTLE FAR EINAS CLOVER ROLLO.
THE CHILDREN OF THESE PRE-DRIER COUPLES WERE SOON EXPOSED TO ENGLISH-LANGUAGE MOVIES AND CANNED-FOOD LABELS AND WITHIN THIRTY YEARS "CHEEPTALK" WAS OFFICIALLY DEAD.
"VALODOROUS BEEF-STEW WITH CARROTS."
PREPENSE
TODAY, ONLY A FEW OVERWEIGHT FOLK SINGERS AND SOME UNEDUCATED PENSIONERS CAN STILL SPEAK THE LANGUAGE.
PADEERILY, PADEERILY, PAY TRUDY NEZ.
YET TWO HUNDRED WORDS, FOR WHICH THERE ARE NO EQUIVALENTS IN THE ENGLISH LANGUAGE, HAVE BEEN INCORPORATED INTO OUR DAILY SPEECH. "NORLAZIK": A SHOELACE THAT'S COME UNDONE BY ITSELF; "SAPAJULIAST": A MONKEY WITH A TECHNICAL SKILL; "TSATSKATCHEWON": A LOST TOY; "AETURNAPY": A FROZEN HAMBURGER THAT WILL NEVER BE DEFROSTED.
WE UTTER THESE WORDS WITH A NAUSEATING SENSE OF PRIDE AND AFFECTION. THERE'S AN EXPRESSION, "YORDI APOLOGIA OB MI EIE," WHICH MEANS: "I APOLOGIZE FOR EVER HAVING GOTTEN INVOLVED WITH YOU." GO AHEAD, SHOW HIM YOU HOLD NO GRUDGE.
YORDI APOLOGIA OB MI EIE.
?

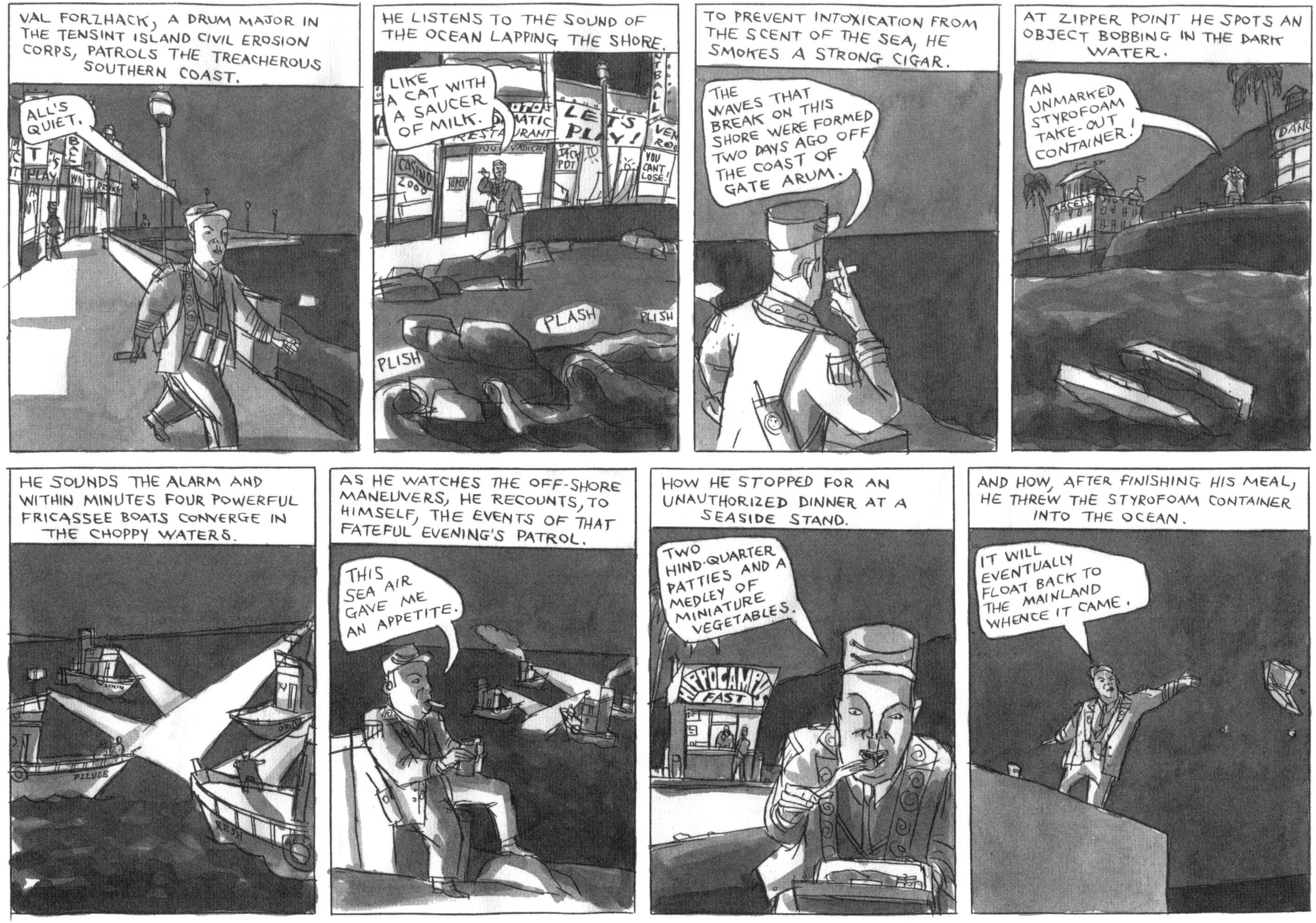
VAL FORZHACK, A DRUM MAJOR IN THE TENSINT ISLAND CIVIL EROSION CORPS, PATROLS THE TREACHEROUS SOUTHERN COAST.
ALL'S QUIET.
HE LISTENS TO THE SOUND OF THE OCEAN LAPPING THE SHORE.
LIKE A CAT WITH A SAUCER OF MILK.
LET'S PLAY!
YOU CAN'T LOSE!
PLASH
PLISH
PLISH
TO PREVENT INTOXICATION FROM THE SCENT OF THE SEA, HE SMOKES A STRONG CIGAR.
THE WAVES THAT BREAK ON THIS SHORE WERE FORMED TWO DAYS AGO OFF THE COAST OF GATE ARUM.
AT ZIPPER POINT HE SPOTS AN OBJECT BOBBING IN THE DARK WATER.
AN UNMARKED STYROFOAM TAKE-OUT CONTAINER!
HE SOUNDS THE ALARM AND WITHIN MINUTES FOUR POWERFUL FRICASSEE BOATS CONVERGE IN THE CHOPPY WATERS.
AS HE WATCHES THE OFF-SHORE MANEUVERS, HE RECOUNTS, TO HIMSELF, THE EVENTS OF THAT FATEFUL EVENING'S PATROL.
THIS SEA AIR GAVE ME AN APPETITE.
HOW HE STOPPED FOR AN UNAUTHORIZED DINNER AT A SEASIDE STAND.
TWO HIND-QUARTER PATTIES AND A MEDLEY OF MINIATURE VEGETABLES.
FAST
AND HOW, AFTER FINISHING HIS MEAL, HE THREW THE STYROFOAM CONTAINER INTO THE OCEAN.
IT WILL EVENTUALLY FLOAT BACK TO THE MAINLAND WHENCE IT CAME.

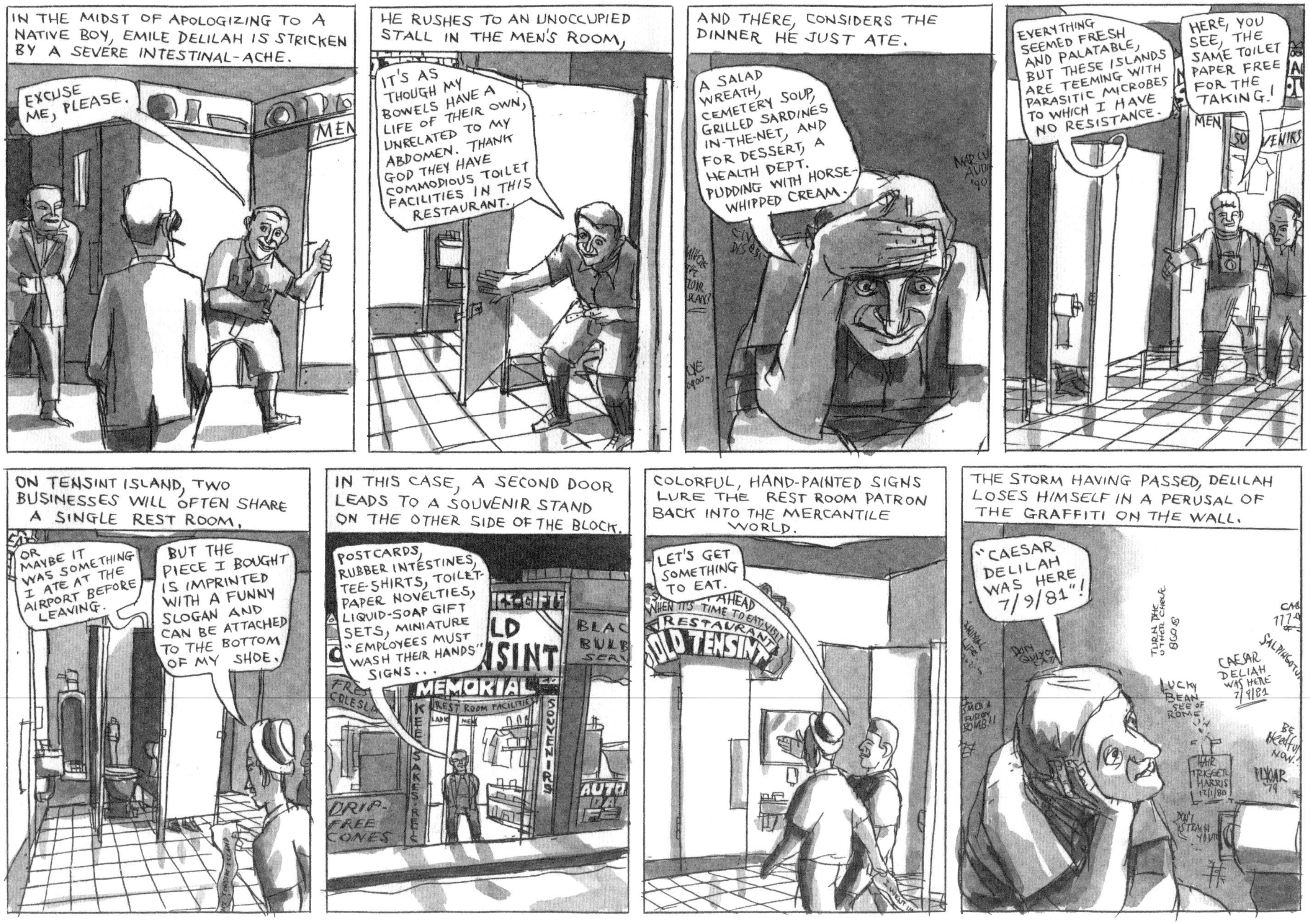
IN THE MIDST OF APOLOGIZING TO A NATIVE BOY, EMILE DELILAH IS STRICKEN BY A SEVERE INTESTINAL-ACHE.
EXCUSE ME, PLEASE.
MEN
HE RUSHES TO AN UNOCCUPIED STALL IN THE MEN'S ROOM,
IT'S AS THOUGH MY BOWELS HAVE A LIFE OF THEIR OWN, UNRELATED TO MY ABDOMEN. THANK GOD THEY HAVE COMMODIOUS TOILET FACILITIES IN THIS RESTAURANT.
AND THERE, CONSIDERS THE DINNER HE JUST ATE.
A SALAD WREATH, CEMETERY SOUP, GRILLED SARDINES IN-THE-NET, AND FOR DESSERT, A HEALTH DEPT. PUDDING WITH HORSE-WHIPPED CREAM.
EVERYTHING SEEMED FRESH AND PALATABLE, BUT THESE ISLANDS ARE TEEMING WITH PARASITIC MICROBES TO WHICH I HAVE NO RESISTANCE.
HERE, YOU SEE, THE SAME TOILET PAPER FREE FOR THE TAKING!
MEN
SOUVENIRS
ON TENSINT ISLAND, TWO BUSINESSES WILL OFTEN SHARE A SINGLE REST ROOM,
OR MAYBE IT WAS SOMETHING I ATE AT THE AIRPORT BEFORE LEAVING.
BUT THE PIECE I BOUGHT IS IMPRINTED WITH A FUNNY SLOGAN AND CAN BE ATTACHED TO THE BOTTOM OF MY SHOE.
IN THIS CASE, A SECOND DOOR LEADS TO A SOUVENIR STAND ON THE OTHER SIDE OF THE BLOCK.
POSTCARDS, RUBBER INTESTINES, TEE-SHIRTS, TOILET-PAPER NOVELTIES, LIQUID-SOAP GIFT SETS, MINIATURE "EMPLOYEES MUST WASH THEIR HANDS" SIGNS...
MEMORIAL
REST ROOM FACILITIES
SOUVENIRS
DRIP-FREE CONES
COLORFUL, HAND-PAINTED SIGNS LURE THE REST ROOM PATRON BACK INTO THE MERCANTILE WORLD.
LET'S GET SOMETHING TO EAT.
WHEN IT'S TIME TO EAT, VISIT
RESTAURANT
OLD TENSINT
THE STORM HAVING PASSED, DELILAH LOSES HIMSELF IN A PERUSAL OF THE GRAFFITI ON THE WALL.
"CAESAR DELILAH WAS HERE 7/9/81"!
TURN THE OTHER CHEEK
LUCKY BEAN
CAESAR DELIAH WAS HERE 7/9/81

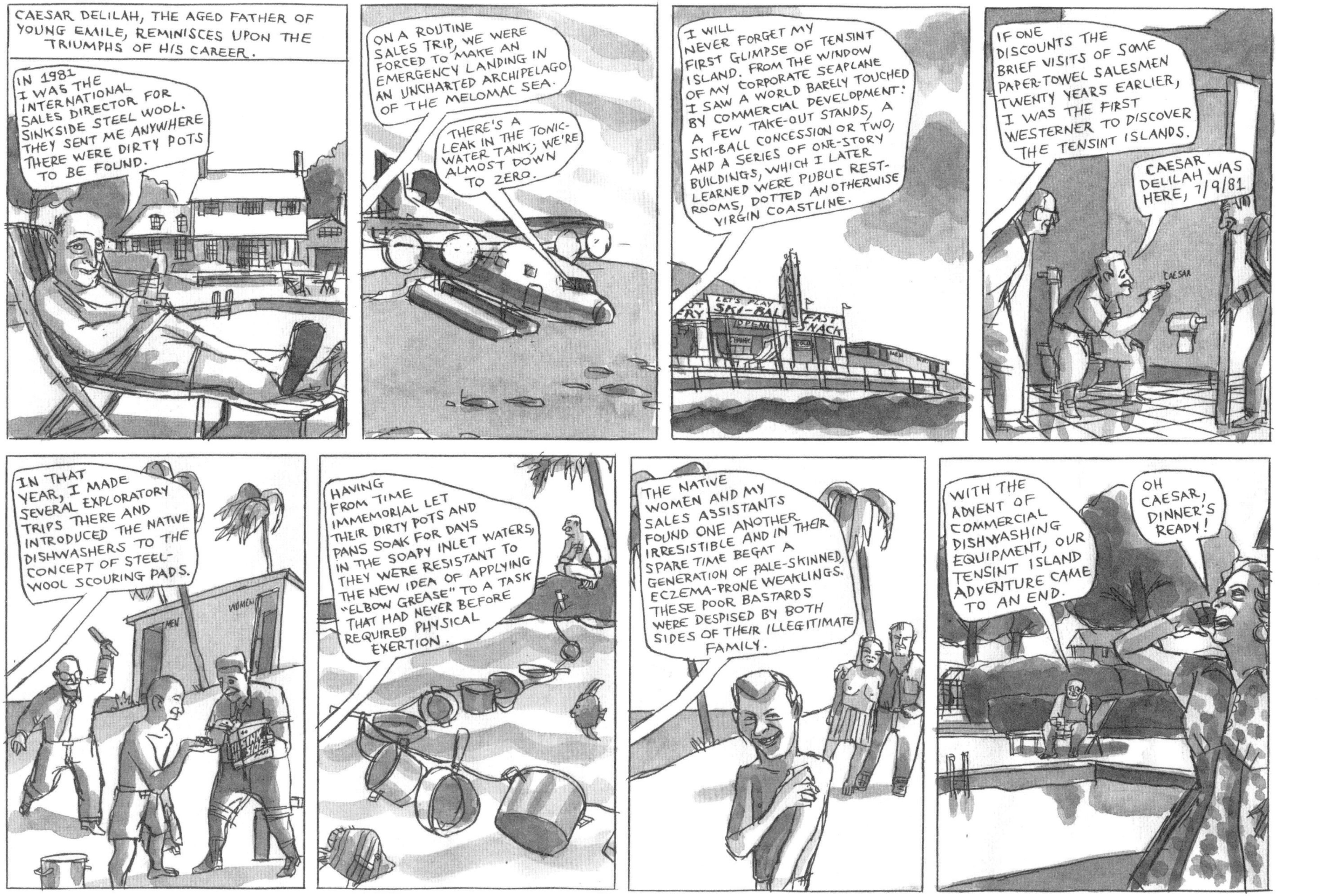

CAESAR DELILAH, THE AGED FATHER OF YOUNG EMILE, REMINISCES UPON THE TRIUMPHS OF HIS CAREER.
IN 1981 I WAS THE INTERNATIONAL SALES DIRECTOR FOR SINKSIDE STEEL WOOL. THEY SENT ME ANYWHERE THERE WERE DIRTY POTS TO BE FOUND.
ON A ROUTINE SALES TRIP, WE WERE FORCED TO MAKE AN EMERGENCY LANDING IN AN UNCHARTED ARCHIPELAGO OF THE MELOMAC SEA.
THERE'S A LEAK IN THE TONIC-WATER TANK; WE'RE ALMOST DOWN TO ZERO.
I WILL NEVER FORGET MY FIRST GLIMPSE OF TENSINT ISLAND. FROM THE WINDOW OF MY CORPORATE SEAPLANE I SAW A WORLD BARELY TOUCHED BY COMMERCIAL DEVELOPMENT: A FEW TAKE-OUT STANDS, A SKI-BALL CONCESSION OR TWO, AND A SERIES OF ONE-STORY BUILDINGS, WHICH I LATER LEARNED WERE PUBLIC REST-ROOMS, DOTTED AN OTHERWISE VIRGIN COASTLINE.
LET'S PLAY SKI-BALL
SNACK
IF ONE DISCOUNTS THE BRIEF VISITS OF SOME PAPER-TOWEL SALESMEN TWENTY YEARS EARLIER, I WAS THE FIRST WESTERNER TO DISCOVER THE TENSINT ISLANDS.
CAESAR DELILAH WAS HERE, 7/9/81
CAESAR
IN THAT YEAR, I MADE SEVERAL EXPLORATORY TRIPS THERE AND INTRODUCED THE NATIVE DISHWASHERS TO THE CONCEPT OF STEEL-WOOL SCOURING PADS.
MEN
WOMEN
HAVING FROM TIME IMMEMORIAL LET THEIR DIRTY POTS AND PANS SOAK FOR DAYS IN THE SOAPY INLET WATERS, THEY WERE RESISTANT TO THE NEW IDEA OF APPLYING "ELBOW GREASE" TO A TASK THAT HAD NEVER BEFORE REQUIRED PHYSICAL EXERTION.
THE NATIVE WOMEN AND MY SALES ASSISTANTS FOUND ONE ANOTHER IRRESISTIBLE AND IN THEIR SPARE TIME BEGAT A GENERATION OF PALE-SKINNED, ECZEMA-PRONE WEAKLINGS. THESE POOR BASTARDS WERE DESPISED BY BOTH SIDES OF THEIR ILLEGITIMATE FAMILY.
WITH THE ADVENT OF COMMERCIAL DISHWASHING EQUIPMENT, OUR TENSINT ISLAND ADVENTURE CAME TO AN END.
OH CAESAR, DINNER'S READY!

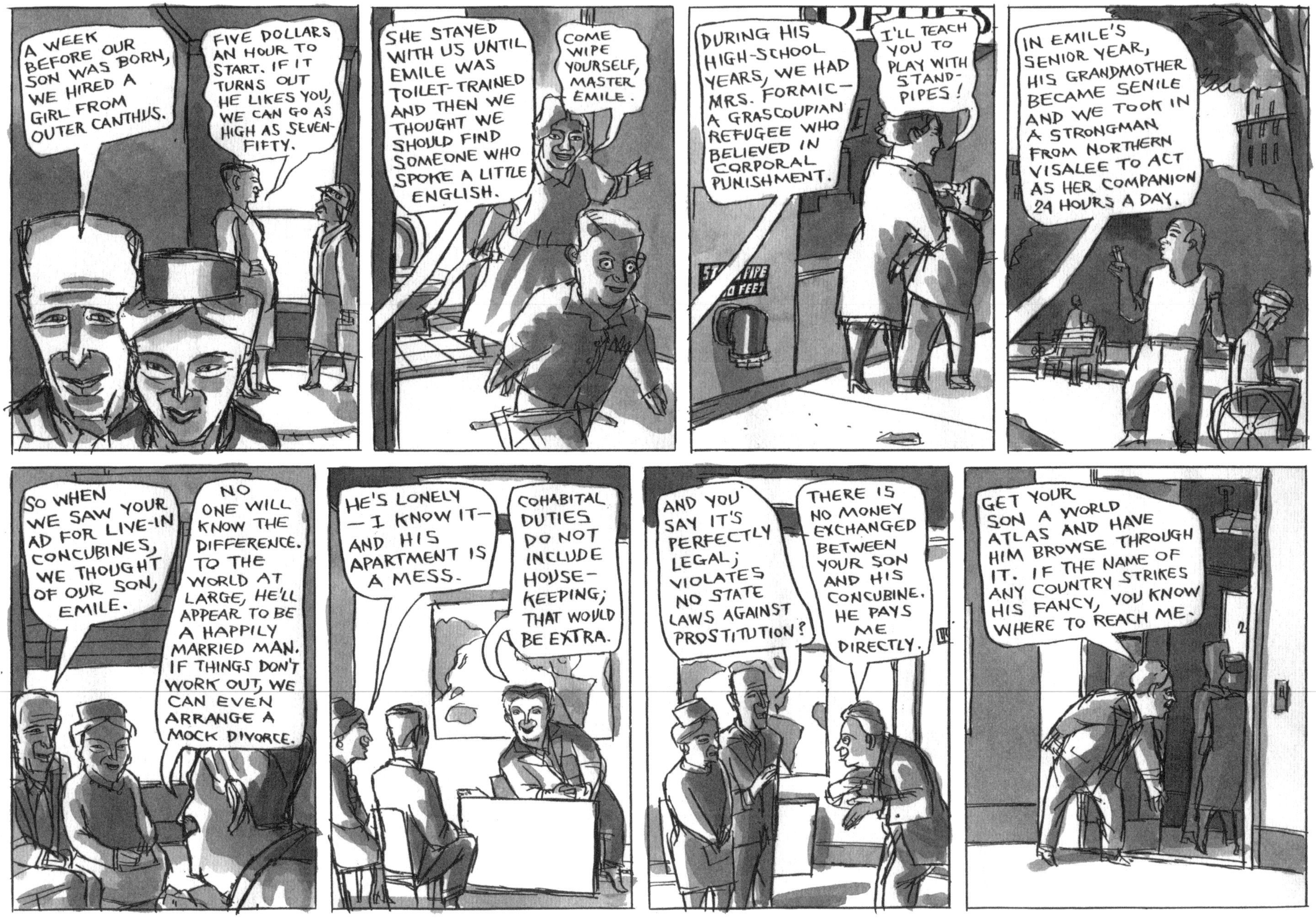
A WEEK BEFORE OUR SON WAS BORN, WE HIRED A GIRL FROM OUTER CANTHUS.
FIVE DOLLARS AN HOUR TO START. IF IT TURNS OUT HE LIKES YOU, WE CAN GO AS HIGH AS SEVEN-FIFTY.
SHE STAYED WITH US UNTIL EMILE WAS TOILET-TRAINED AND THEN WE THOUGHT WE SHOULD FIND SOMEONE WHO SPOKE A LITTLE ENGLISH.
COME WIPE YOURSELF, MASTER EMILE.
DURING HIS HIGH-SCHOOL YEARS, WE HAD MRS. FORMIC— A GRASCOUPIAN REFUGEE WHO BELIEVED IN CORPORAL PUNISHMENT.
I'LL TEACH YOU TO PLAY WITH STAND-PIPES!
IN EMILE'S SENIOR YEAR, HIS GRANDMOTHER BECAME SENILE AND WE TOOK IN A STRONGMAN FROM NORTHERN VISALEE TO ACT AS HER COMPANION 24 HOURS A DAY.
SO WHEN WE SAW YOUR AD FOR LIVE-IN CONCUBINES, WE THOUGHT OF OUR SON, EMILE.
NO ONE WILL KNOW THE DIFFERENCE. TO THE WORLD AT LARGE, HE'LL APPEAR TO BE A HAPPILY MARRIED MAN. IF THINGS DON'T WORK OUT, WE CAN EVEN ARRANGE A MOCK DIVORCE.
HE'S LONELY —I KNOW IT— AND HIS APARTMENT IS A MESS.
COHABITAL DUTIES DO NOT INCLUDE HOUSE-KEEPING; THAT WOULD BE EXTRA.
AND YOU SAY IT'S PERFECTLY LEGAL; VIOLATES NO STATE LAWS AGAINST PROSTITUTION?
THERE IS NO MONEY EXCHANGED BETWEEN YOUR SON AND HIS CONCUBINE. HE PAYS ME DIRECTLY.
GET YOUR SON A WORLD ATLAS AND HAVE HIM BROWSE THROUGH IT. IF THE NAME OF ANY COUNTRY STRIKES HIS FANCY, YOU KNOW WHERE TO REACH ME.

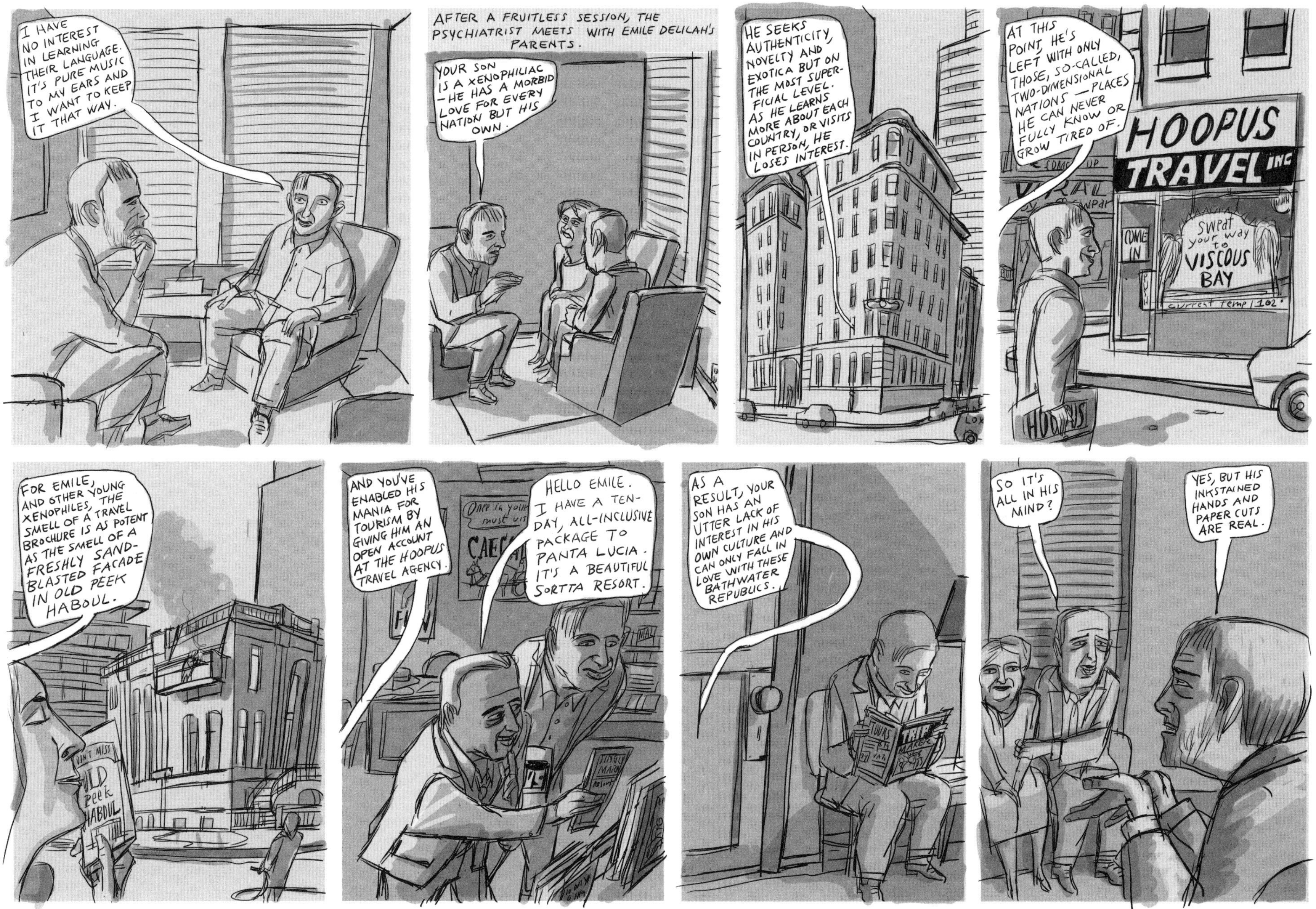
I HAVE NO INTEREST IN LEARNING THEIR LANGUAGE. IT'S PURE MUSIC TO MY EARS AND I WANT TO KEEP IT THAT WAY.
AFTER A FRUITLESS SESSION, THE PSYCHIATRIST MEETS WITH EMILE DELILAH'S PARENTS.
YOUR SON IS A XENOPHILIAC —HE HAS A MORBID LOVE FOR EVERY NATION BUT HIS OWN.
HE SEEKS AUTHENTICITY, NOVELTY AND EXOTICA BUT ON THE MOST SUPER-FICIAL LEVEL. AS HE LEARNS MORE ABOUT EACH COUNTRY, OR VISITS IN PERSON, HE LOSES INTEREST.
AT THIS POINT, HE'S LEFT WITH ONLY THOSE, SO-CALLED, TWO-DIMENSIONAL NATIONS —PLACES HE CAN NEVER FULLY KNOW OR GROW TIRED OF.
HOOPUS TRAVEL INC
COME IN
Sweat your way to VISCOUS BAY
current temp / 102°
FOR EMILE, AND OTHER YOUNG XENOPHILES, THE SMELL OF A TRAVEL BROCHURE IS AS POTENT AS THE SMELL OF A FRESHLY SAND-BLASTED FACADE IN OLD PEEK HABOUL.
DON'T MISS OLD Peek HABOUL
AND YOU'VE ENABLED HIS MANIA FOR TOURISM BY GIVING HIM AN OPEN ACCOUNT AT THE HOOPUS TRAVEL AGENCY.
HELLO EMILE. I HAVE A TEN-DAY, ALL-INCLUSIVE PACKAGE TO PANTA LUCIA. IT'S A BEAUTIFUL SORTTA RESORT.
AS A RESULT, YOUR SON HAS AN UTTER LACK OF INTEREST IN HIS OWN CULTURE AND CAN ONLY FALL IN LOVE WITH THESE BATHWATER REPUBLICS.
TOURS
TRIP MAKER
SO IT'S ALL IN HIS MIND?
YES, BUT HIS INKSTAINED HANDS AND PAPER CUTS ARE REAL.

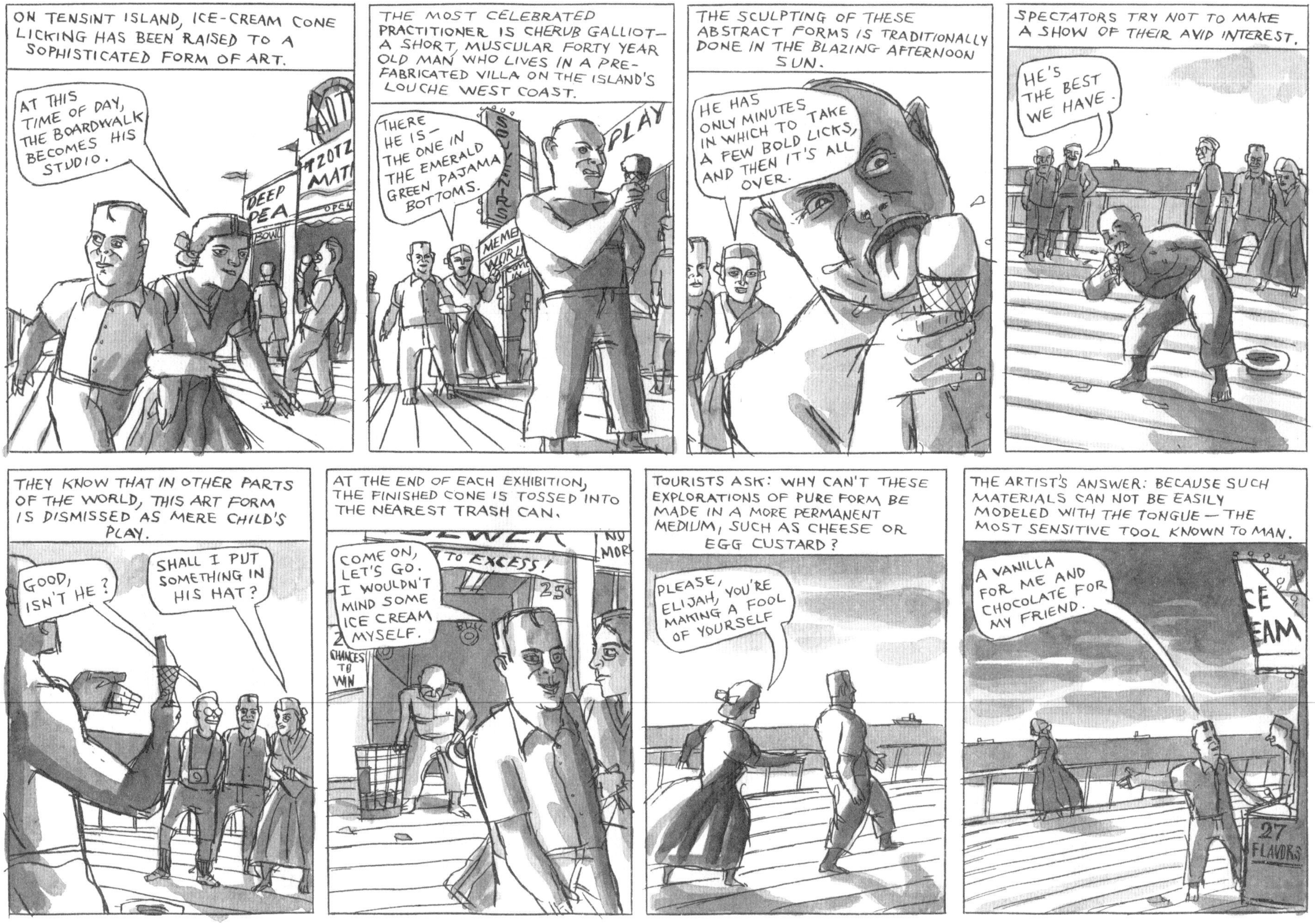
ON TENSINT ISLAND, ICE-CREAM CONE LICKING HAS BEEN RAISED TO A SOPHISTICATED FORM OF ART.
AT THIS TIME OF DAY, THE BOARDWALK BECOMES HIS STUDIO.
THE MOST CELEBRATED PRACTITIONER IS CHERUB GALLIOT— A SHORT, MUSCULAR FORTY YEAR OLD MAN WHO LIVES IN A PRE-FABRICATED VILLA ON THE ISLAND'S LOUCHE WEST COAST.
THERE HE IS— THE ONE IN THE EMERALD GREEN PAJAMA BOTTOMS.
PLAY
THE SCULPTING OF THESE ABSTRACT FORMS IS TRADITIONALLY DONE IN THE BLAZING AFTERNOON SUN.
HE HAS ONLY MINUTES IN WHICH TO TAKE A FEW BOLD LICKS, AND THEN IT'S ALL OVER.
SPECTATORS TRY NOT TO MAKE A SHOW OF THEIR AVID INTEREST.
HE'S THE BEST WE HAVE.
THEY KNOW THAT IN OTHER PARTS OF THE WORLD, THIS ART FORM IS DISMISSED AS MERE CHILD'S PLAY.
GOOD, ISN'T HE ?
SHALL I PUT SOMETHING IN HIS HAT?
AT THE END OF EACH EXHIBITION, THE FINISHED CONE IS TOSSED INTO THE NEAREST TRASH CAN.
COME ON, LET'S GO. I WOULDN'T MIND SOME ICE CREAM MYSELF.
TO EXCESS!
25¢
CHANCES TO WIN
TOURISTS ASK: WHY CAN'T THESE EXPLORATIONS OF PURE FORM BE MADE IN A MORE PERMANENT MEDIUM, SUCH AS CHEESE OR EGG CUSTARD?
PLEASE, ELIJAH, YOU'RE MAKING A FOOL OF YOURSELF
THE ARTIST'S ANSWER: BECAUSE SUCH MATERIALS CAN NOT BE EASILY MODELED WITH THE TONGUE — THE MOST SENSITIVE TOOL KNOWN TO MAN.
A VANILLA FOR ME AND CHOCOLATE FOR MY FRIEND.
27 FLAVORS

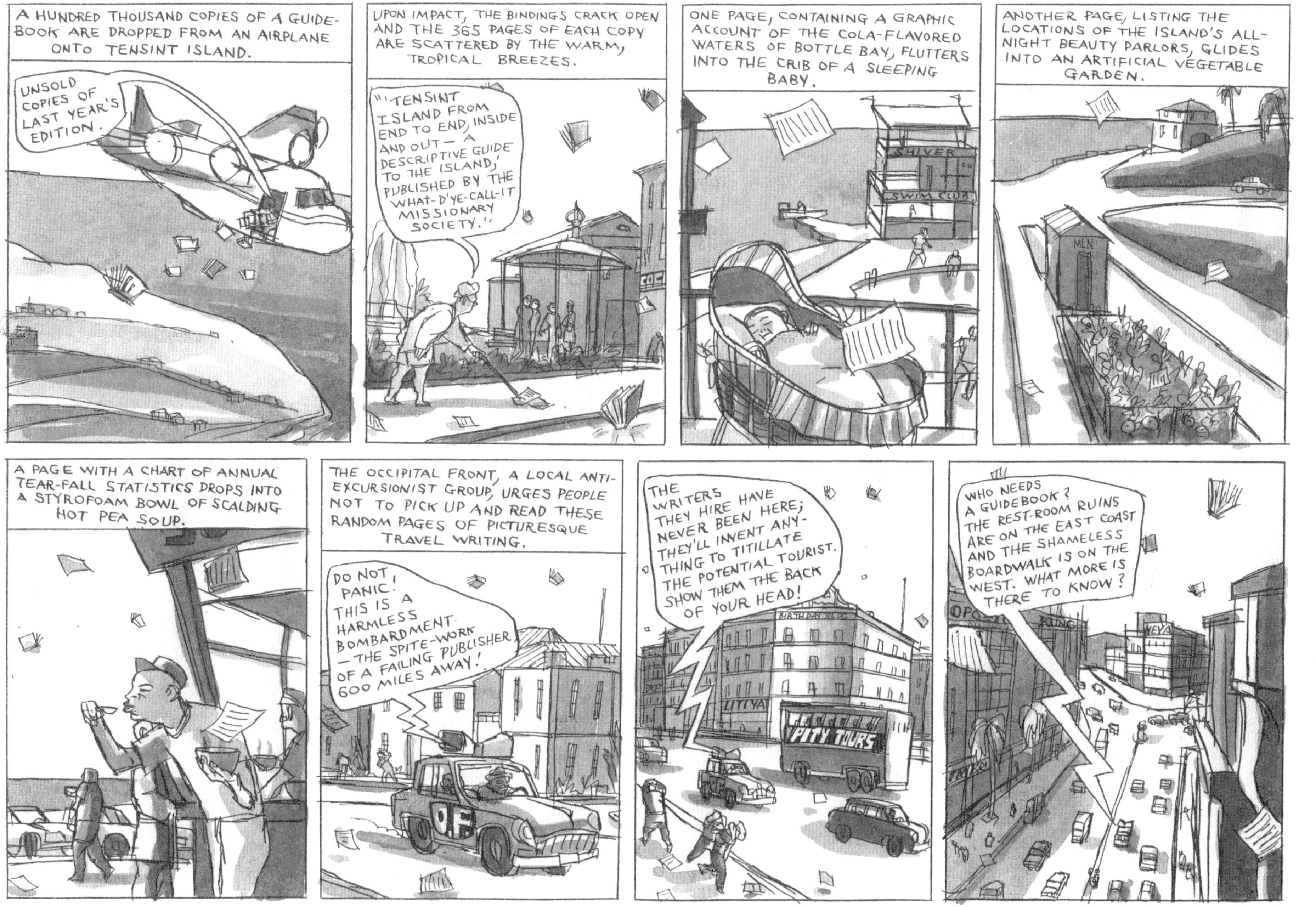
A HUNDRED THOUSAND COPIES OF A GUIDE-BOOK ARE DROPPED FROM AN AIRPLANE ONTO TENSINT ISLAND.
UNSOLD COPIES OF LAST YEAR'S EDITION.
UPON IMPACT, THE BINDINGS CRACK OPEN AND THE 365 PAGES OF EACH COPY ARE SCATTERED BY THE WARM, TROPICAL BREEZES.
"'TENSINT ISLAND FROM END TO END, INSIDE AND OUT— A DESCRIPTIVE GUIDE TO THE ISLAND,' PUBLISHED BY THE WHAT-D'YE-CALL-IT MISSIONARY SOCIETY."
ONE PAGE, CONTAINING A GRAPHIC ACCOUNT OF THE COLA-FLAVORED WATERS OF BOTTLE BAY, FLUTTERS INTO THE CRIB OF A SLEEPING BABY.
SHIVER
SWIM CLUB
ANOTHER PAGE, LISTING THE LOCATIONS OF THE ISLAND'S ALL-NIGHT BEAUTY PARLORS, GLIDES INTO AN ARTIFICIAL VEGETABLE GARDEN.
MEN
A PAGE WITH A CHART OF ANNUAL TEAR-FALL STATISTICS DROPS INTO A STYROFOAM BOWL OF SCALDING HOT PEA SOUP.
THE OCCIPITAL FRONT, A LOCAL ANTI-EXCURSIONIST GROUP, URGES PEOPLE NOT TO PICK UP AND READ THESE RANDOM PAGES OF PICTURESQUE TRAVEL WRITING.
DO NOT PANIC! THIS IS A HARMLESS BOMBARDMENT. —THE SPITE-WORK OF A FAILING PUBLISHER, 600 MILES AWAY!
O.F.
THE WRITERS THEY HIRE HAVE NEVER BEEN HERE; THEY'LL INVENT ANY-THING TO TITILLATE THE POTENTIAL TOURIST. SHOW THEM THE BACK OF YOUR HEAD!
BIRTHDAY BLDG.
LITIYA
PITY TOURS
WHO NEEDS A GUIDEBOOK? THE REST-ROOM RUINS ARE ON THE EAST COAST AND THE SHAMELESS BOARDWALK IS ON THE WEST. WHAT MORE IS THERE TO KNOW?

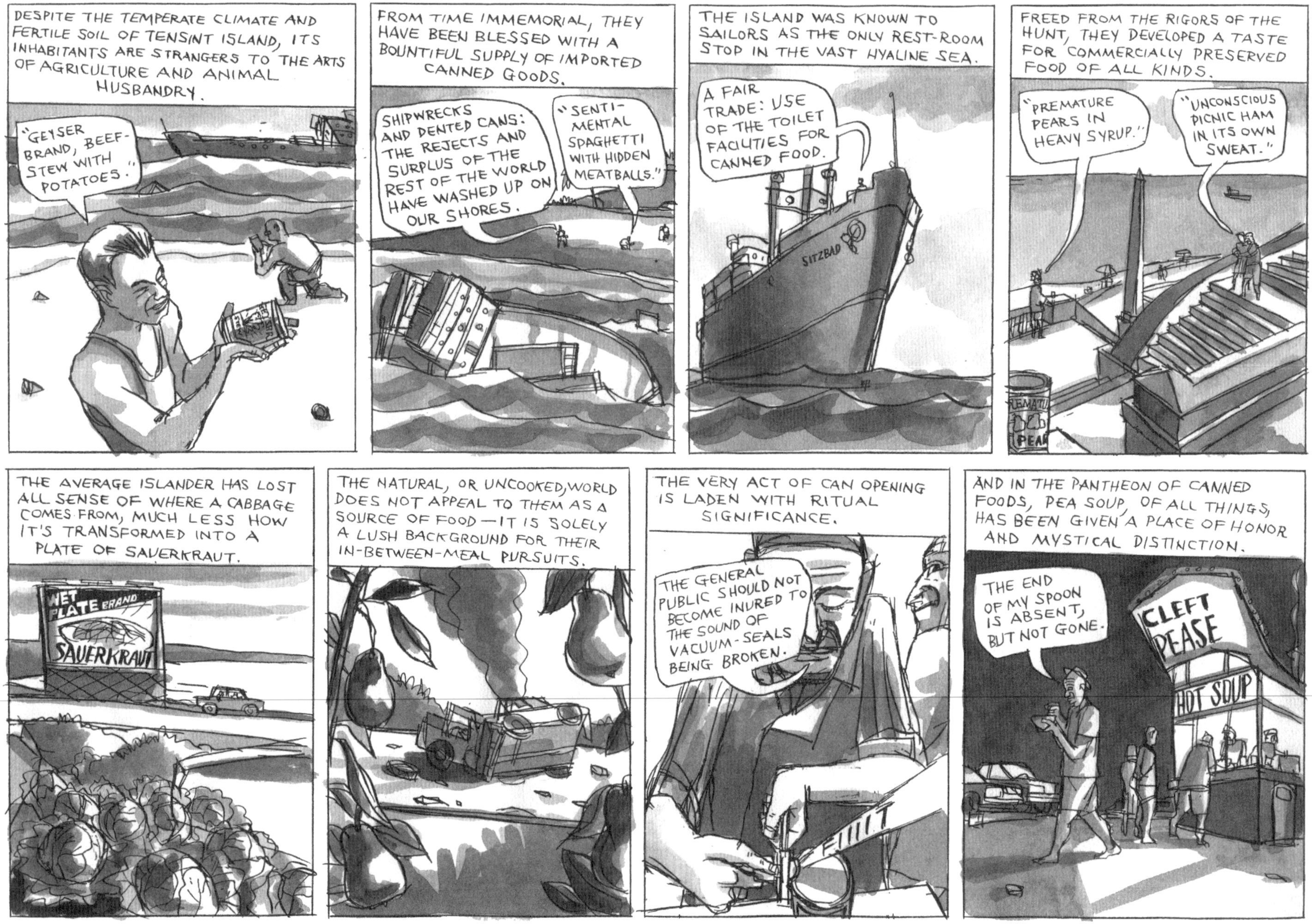
DESPITE THE TEMPERATE CLIMATE AND FERTILE SOIL OF TENSINT ISLAND, ITS INHABITANTS ARE STRANGERS TO THE ARTS OF AGRICULTURE AND ANIMAL HUSBANDRY.
"GEYSER BRAND, BEEF-STEW WITH POTATOES."
FROM TIME IMMEMORIAL, THEY HAVE BEEN BLESSED WITH A BOUNTIFUL SUPPLY OF IMPORTED CANNED GOODS.
SHIPWRECKS AND DENTED CANS: THE REJECTS AND SURPLUS OF THE REST OF THE WORLD HAVE WASHED UP ON OUR SHORES.
"SENTI-MENTAL SPAGHETTI WITH HIDDEN MEATBALLS."
THE ISLAND WAS KNOWN TO SAILORS AS THE ONLY REST-ROOM STOP IN THE VAST HYALINE SEA.
A FAIR TRADE: USE OF THE TOILET FACILITIES FOR CANNED FOOD.
SITZBAD
FREED FROM THE RIGORS OF THE HUNT, THEY DEVELOPED A TASTE FOR COMMERCIALLY PRESERVED FOOD OF ALL KINDS.
"PREMATURE PEARS IN HEAVY SYRUP."
"UNCONSCIOUS PICNIC HAM IN ITS OWN SWEAT."
THE AVERAGE ISLANDER HAS LOST ALL SENSE OF WHERE A CABBAGE COMES FROM, MUCH LESS HOW IT'S TRANSFORMED INTO A PLATE OF SAUERKRAUT.
WET PLATE BRAND
SAUERKRAUT
THE NATURAL, OR UNCOOKED, WORLD DOES NOT APPEAL TO THEM AS A SOURCE OF FOOD—IT IS SOLELY A LUSH BACKGROUND FOR THEIR IN-BETWEEN-MEAL PURSUITS.
THE VERY ACT OF CAN OPENING IS LADEN WITH RITUAL SIGNIFICANCE.
THE GENERAL PUBLIC SHOULD NOT BECOME INURED TO THE SOUND OF VACUUM-SEALS BEING BROKEN.
AND IN THE PANTHEON OF CANNED FOODS, PEA SOUP, OF ALL THINGS, HAS BEEN GIVEN A PLACE OF HONOR AND MYSTICAL DISTINCTION.
THE END OF MY SPOON IS ABSENT, BUT NOT GONE.
CLEFT PEASE
HOT SOUP

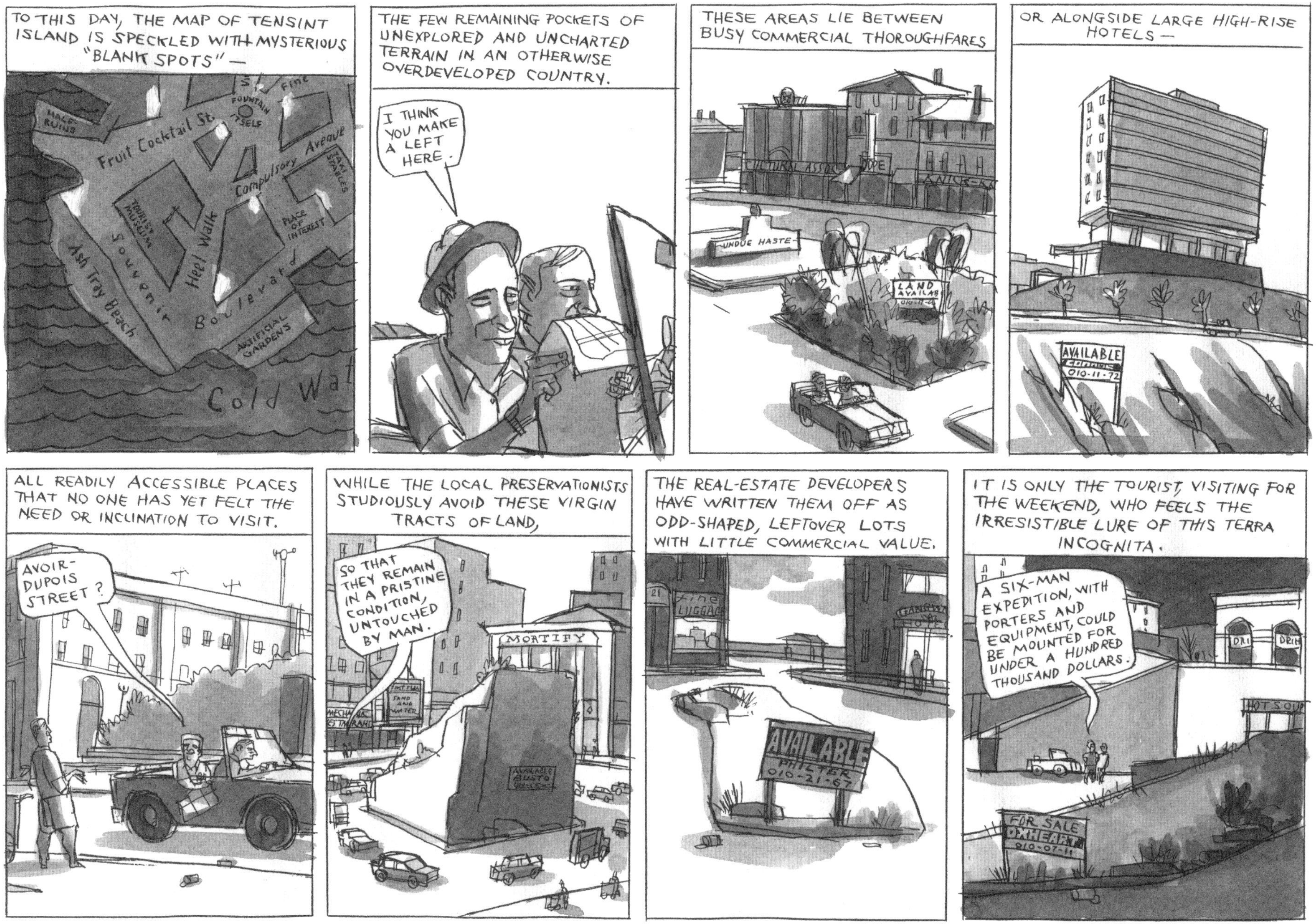
TO THIS DAY, THE MAP OF TENSINT ISLAND IS SPECKLED WITH MYSTERIOUS "BLANK SPOTS" —
Fruit Cocktail St.
Compulsory Avenue
Heel Walk
Souvenir Boulevard
Ash Tray Beach
Tourist Museum
Place of Interest
Artificial Gardens
Cold Wat
THE FEW REMAINING POCKETS OF UNEXPLORED AND UNCHARTED TERRAIN IN AN OTHERWISE OVERDEVELOPED COUNTRY.
I THINK YOU MAKE A LEFT HERE.
THESE AREAS LIE BETWEEN BUSY COMMERCIAL THOROUGHFARES
UNDUE HASTE
OR ALONGSIDE LARGE HIGH-RISE HOTELS —
AVAILABLE
010-11-72
ALL READILY ACCESSIBLE PLACES THAT NO ONE HAS YET FELT THE NEED OR INCLINATION TO VISIT.
AVOIR-DUPOIS STREET?
WHILE THE LOCAL PRESERVATIONISTS STUDIOUSLY AVOID THESE VIRGIN TRACTS OF LAND,
SO THAT THEY REMAIN IN A PRISTINE CONDITION, UNTOUCHED BY MAN.
MORTIFY
SAND AND WATER
THE REAL-ESTATE DEVELOPERS HAVE WRITTEN THEM OFF AS ODD-SHAPED, LEFTOVER LOTS WITH LITTLE COMMERCIAL VALUE.
AVAILABLE
PHILTER
010-21-67
IT IS ONLY THE TOURIST, VISITING FOR THE WEEKEND, WHO FEELS THE IRRESISTIBLE LURE OF THIS TERRA INCOGNITA.
A SIX-MAN EXPEDITION, WITH PORTERS AND EQUIPMENT, COULD BE MOUNTED FOR UNDER A HUNDRED THOUSAND DOLLARS.
FOR SALE
OXHEART
010-07-11

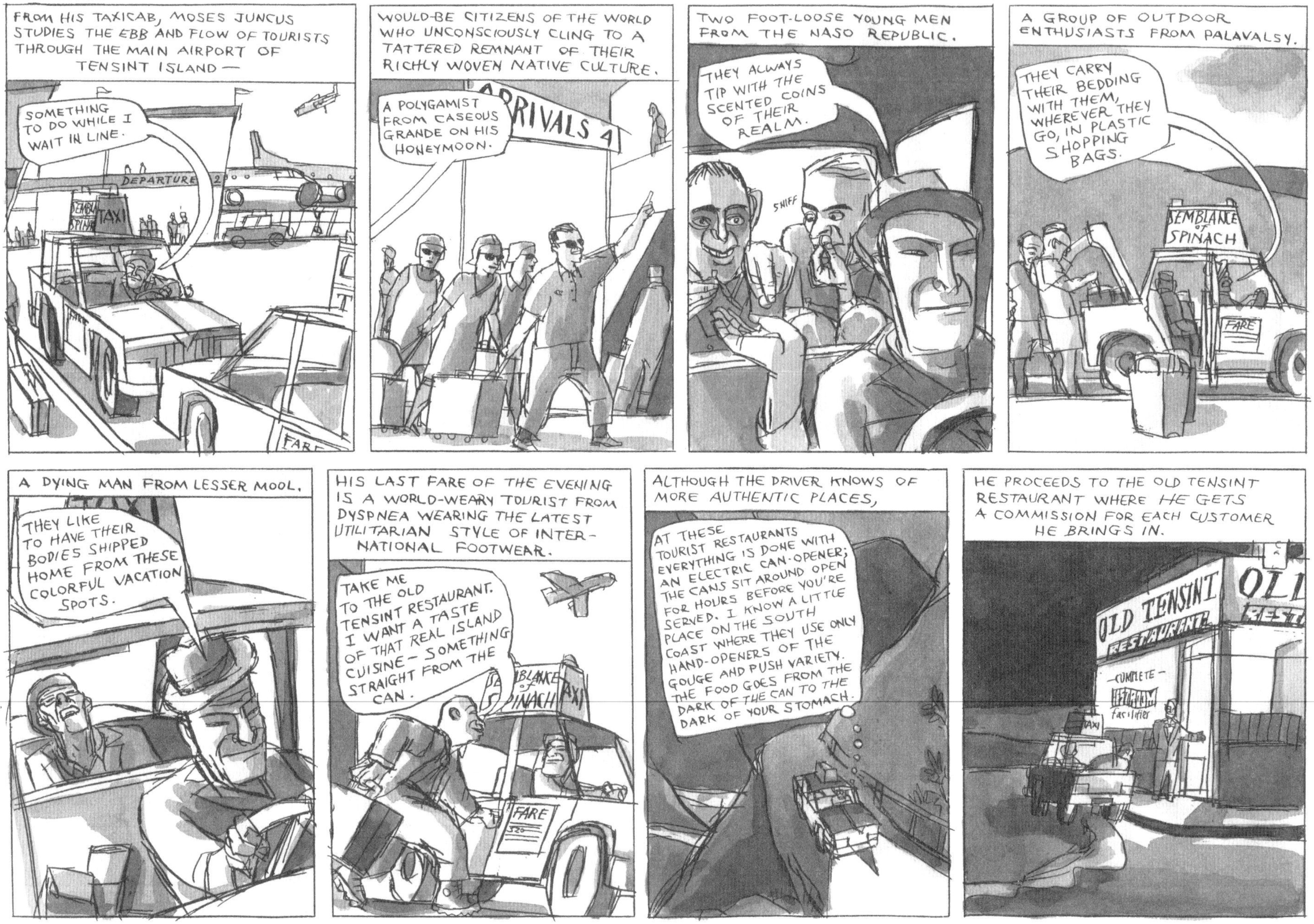
FROM HIS TAXICAB, MOSES JUNCUS STUDIES THE EBB AND FLOW OF TOURISTS THROUGH THE MAIN AIRPORT OF TENSINT ISLAND —
SOMETHING TO DO WHILE I WAIT IN LINE.
DEPARTURE 2
TAXI
WOULD-BE CITIZENS OF THE WORLD WHO UNCONSCIOUSLY CLING TO A TATTERED REMNANT OF THEIR RICHLY WOVEN NATIVE CULTURE.
A POLYGAMIST FROM CASEOUS GRANDE ON HIS HONEYMOON.
ARRIVALS 4
TWO FOOT-LOOSE YOUNG MEN FROM THE NASO REPUBLIC.
THEY ALWAYS TIP WITH THE SCENTED COINS OF THEIR REALM.
SNIFF
A GROUP OF OUTDOOR ENTHUSIASTS FROM PALAVALSY.
THEY CARRY THEIR BEDDING WITH THEM, WHEREVER THEY GO, IN PLASTIC SHOPPING BAGS.
SEMBLANCE of SPINACH
FARE
A DYING MAN FROM LESSER MOOL.
THEY LIKE TO HAVE THEIR BODIES SHIPPED HOME FROM THESE COLORFUL VACATION SPOTS.
HIS LAST FARE OF THE EVENING IS A WORLD-WEARY TOURIST FROM DYSPNEA WEARING THE LATEST UTILITARIAN STYLE OF INTERNATIONAL FOOTWEAR.
TAKE ME TO THE OLD TENSINT RESTAURANT. I WANT A TASTE OF THAT REAL ISLAND CUISINE — SOMETHING STRAIGHT FROM THE CAN.
SEMBLANCE of SPINACH TAXI
FARE
ALTHOUGH THE DRIVER KNOWS OF MORE AUTHENTIC PLACES,
AT THESE TOURIST RESTAURANTS EVERYTHING IS DONE WITH AN ELECTRIC CAN-OPENER; THE CANS SIT AROUND OPEN FOR HOURS BEFORE YOU'RE SERVED. I KNOW A LITTLE PLACE ON THE SOUTH COAST WHERE THEY USE ONLY HAND-OPENERS OF THE GOUGE AND PUSH VARIETY. THE FOOD GOES FROM THE DARK OF THE CAN TO THE DARK OF YOUR STOMACH.
HE PROCEEDS TO THE OLD TENSINT RESTAURANT WHERE HE GETS A COMMISSION FOR EACH CUSTOMER HE BRINGS IN.
OLD TENSINT RESTAURANT
— COMPLETE —
fasilifier
TAXI

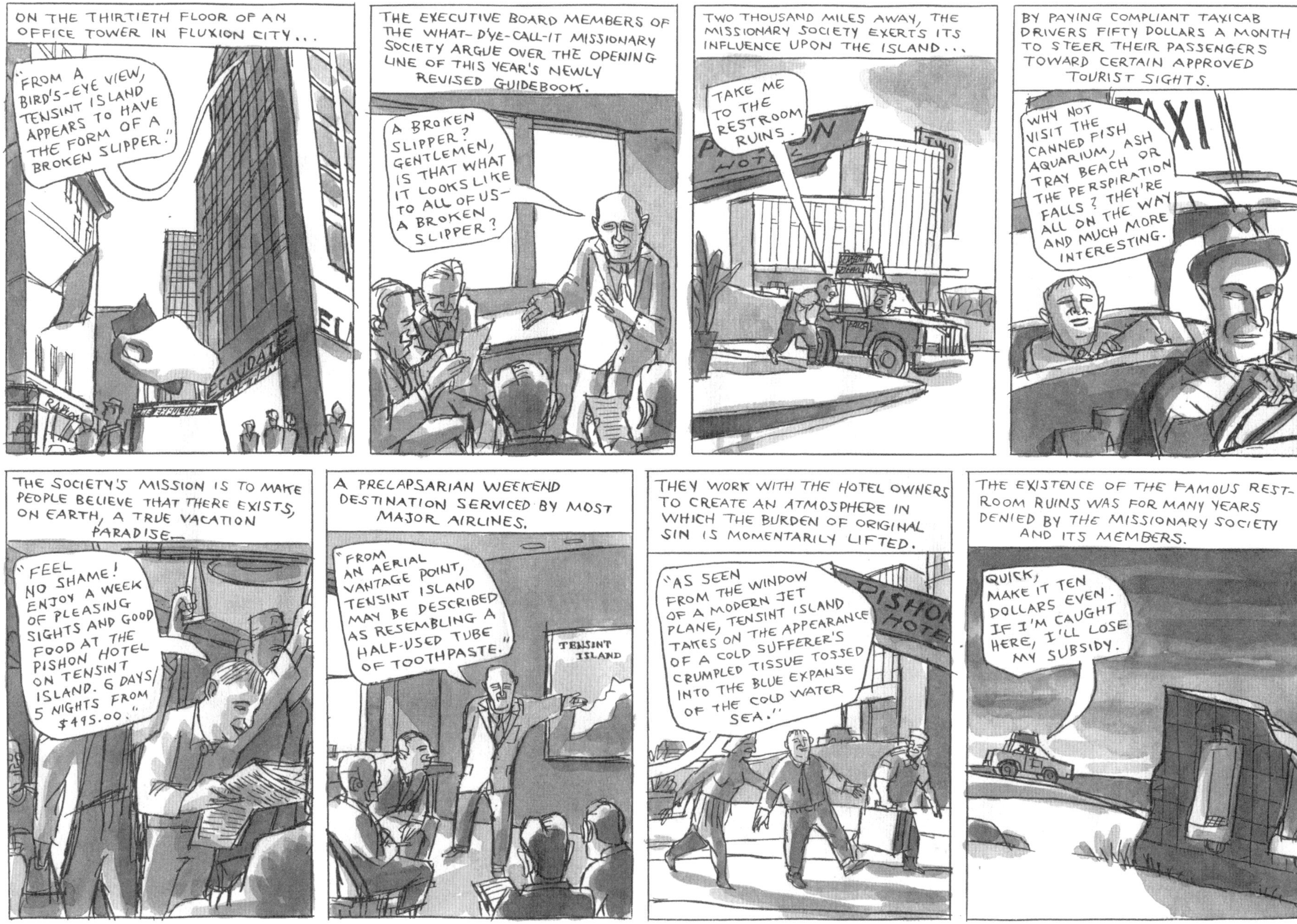
ON THE THIRTIETH FLOOR OF AN OFFICE TOWER IN FLUXION CITY...
"FROM A BIRD'S-EYE VIEW, TENSINT ISLAND APPEARS TO HAVE THE FORM OF A BROKEN SLIPPER."
THE EXECUTIVE BOARD MEMBERS OF THE WHAT-D'YE-CALL-IT MISSIONARY SOCIETY ARGUE OVER THE OPENING LINE OF THIS YEAR'S NEWLY REVISED GUIDEBOOK.
A BROKEN SLIPPER? GENTLEMEN, IS THAT WHAT IT LOOKS LIKE TO ALL OF US- A BROKEN SLIPPER?
TWO THOUSAND MILES AWAY, THE MISSIONARY SOCIETY EXERTS ITS INFLUENCE UPON THE ISLAND...
TAKE ME TO THE RESTROOM RUINS.
BY PAYING COMPLIANT TAXICAB DRIVERS FIFTY DOLLARS A MONTH TO STEER THEIR PASSENGERS TOWARD CERTAIN APPROVED TOURIST SIGHTS.
WHY NOT VISIT THE CANNED FISH AQUARIUM, ASH TRAY BEACH OR THE PERSPIRATION FALLS? THEY'RE ALL ON THE WAY AND MUCH MORE INTERESTING.
THE SOCIETY'S MISSION IS TO MAKE PEOPLE BELIEVE THAT THERE EXISTS, ON EARTH, A TRUE VACATION PARADISE–
"FEEL NO SHAME! ENJOY A WEEK OF PLEASING SIGHTS AND GOOD FOOD AT THE PISHON HOTEL ON TENSINT ISLAND. 6 DAYS/5 NIGHTS FROM $495.00."
A PRELAPSARIAN WEEKEND DESTINATION SERVICED BY MOST MAJOR AIRLINES.
"FROM AN AERIAL VANTAGE POINT, TENSINT ISLAND MAY BE DESCRIBED AS RESEMBLING A HALF-USED TUBE OF TOOTHPASTE."
TENSINT ISLAND
THEY WORK WITH THE HOTEL OWNERS TO CREATE AN ATMOSPHERE IN WHICH THE BURDEN OF ORIGINAL SIN IS MOMENTARILY LIFTED.
"AS SEEN FROM THE WINDOW OF A MODERN JET PLANE, TENSINT ISLAND TAKES ON THE APPEARANCE OF A COLD SUFFERER'S CRUMPLED TISSUE TOSSED INTO THE BLUE EXPANSE OF THE COLD WATER SEA."
THE EXISTENCE OF THE FAMOUS REST-ROOM RUINS WAS FOR MANY YEARS DENIED BY THE MISSIONARY SOCIETY AND ITS MEMBERS.
QUICK, MAKE IT TEN DOLLARS EVEN. IF I'M CAUGHT HERE, I'LL LOSE MY SUBSIDY.

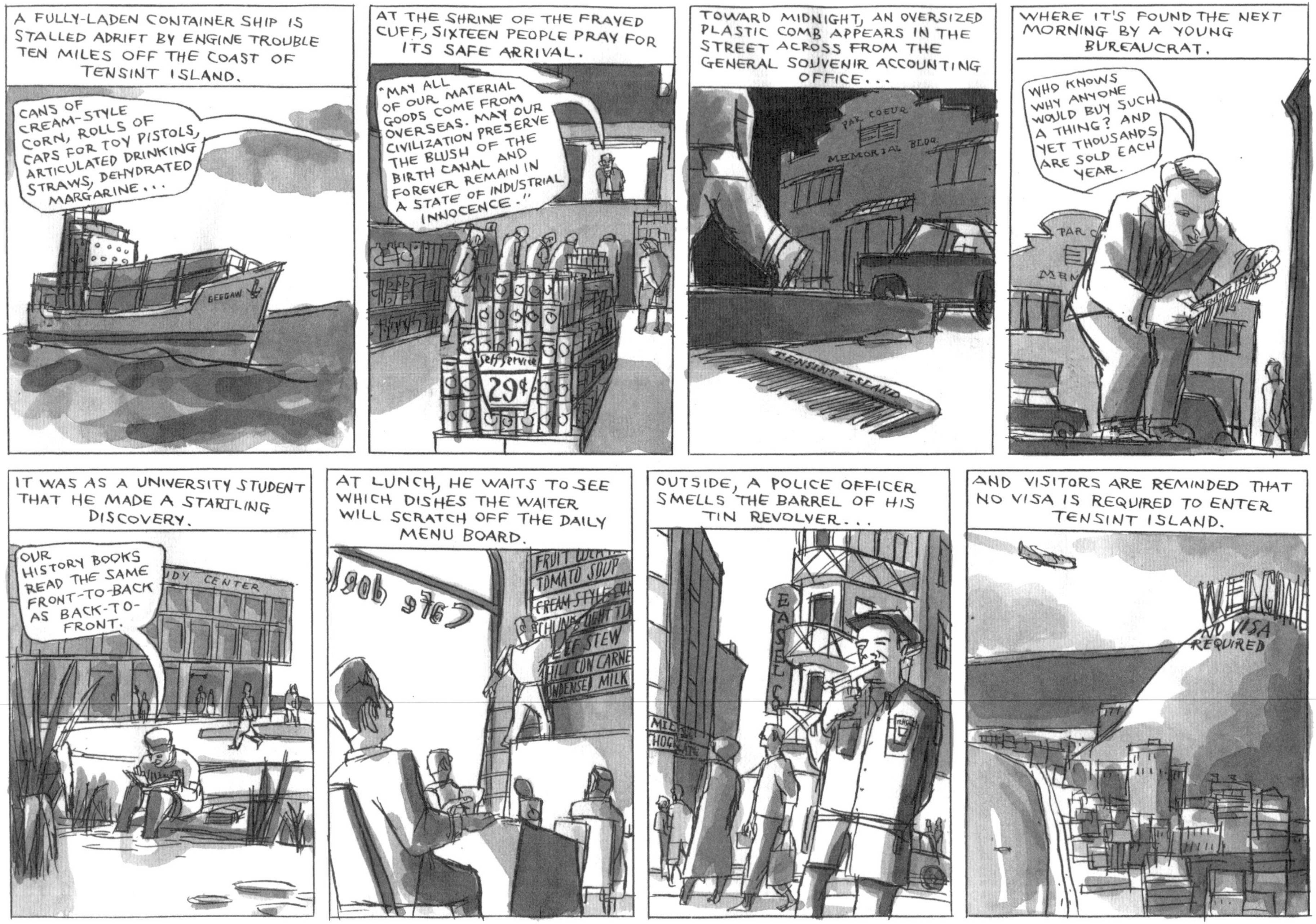
A FULLY-LADEN CONTAINER SHIP IS STALLED ADRIFT BY ENGINE TROUBLE TEN MILES OFF THE COAST OF TENSINT ISLAND.
CANS OF CREAM-STYLE CORN, ROLLS OF CAPS FOR TOY PISTOLS, ARTICULATED DRINKING STRAWS, DEHYDRATED MARGARINE...
BEEGAW
AT THE SHRINE OF THE FRAYED CUFF, SIXTEEN PEOPLE PRAY FOR ITS SAFE ARRIVAL.
"MAY ALL OF OUR MATERIAL GOODS COME FROM OVERSEAS. MAY OUR CIVILIZATION PRESERVE THE BLUSH OF THE BIRTH CANAL AND FOREVER REMAIN IN A STATE OF INDUSTRIAL INNOCENCE."
Self Service
29¢
TOWARD MIDNIGHT, AN OVERSIZED PLASTIC COMB APPEARS IN THE STREET ACROSS FROM THE GENERAL SOUVENIR ACCOUNTING OFFICE...
PAR COEUR
MEMORIAL BLDG.
TENSINT ISLAND
WHERE IT'S FOUND THE NEXT MORNING BY A YOUNG BUREAUCRAT.
WHO KNOWS WHY ANYONE WOULD BUY SUCH A THING? AND YET THOUSANDS ARE SOLD EACH YEAR.
IT WAS AS A UNIVERSITY STUDENT THAT HE MADE A STARTLING DISCOVERY.
OUR HISTORY BOOKS READ THE SAME FRONT-TO-BACK AS BACK-TO-FRONT.
AT LUNCH, HE WAITS TO SEE WHICH DISHES THE WAITER WILL SCRATCH OFF THE DAILY MENU BOARD.
TOMATO SOUP
OUTSIDE, A POLICE OFFICER SMELLS THE BARREL OF HIS TIN REVOLVER...
AND VISITORS ARE REMINDED THAT NO VISA IS REQUIRED TO ENTER TENSINT ISLAND.
NO VISA REQUIRED

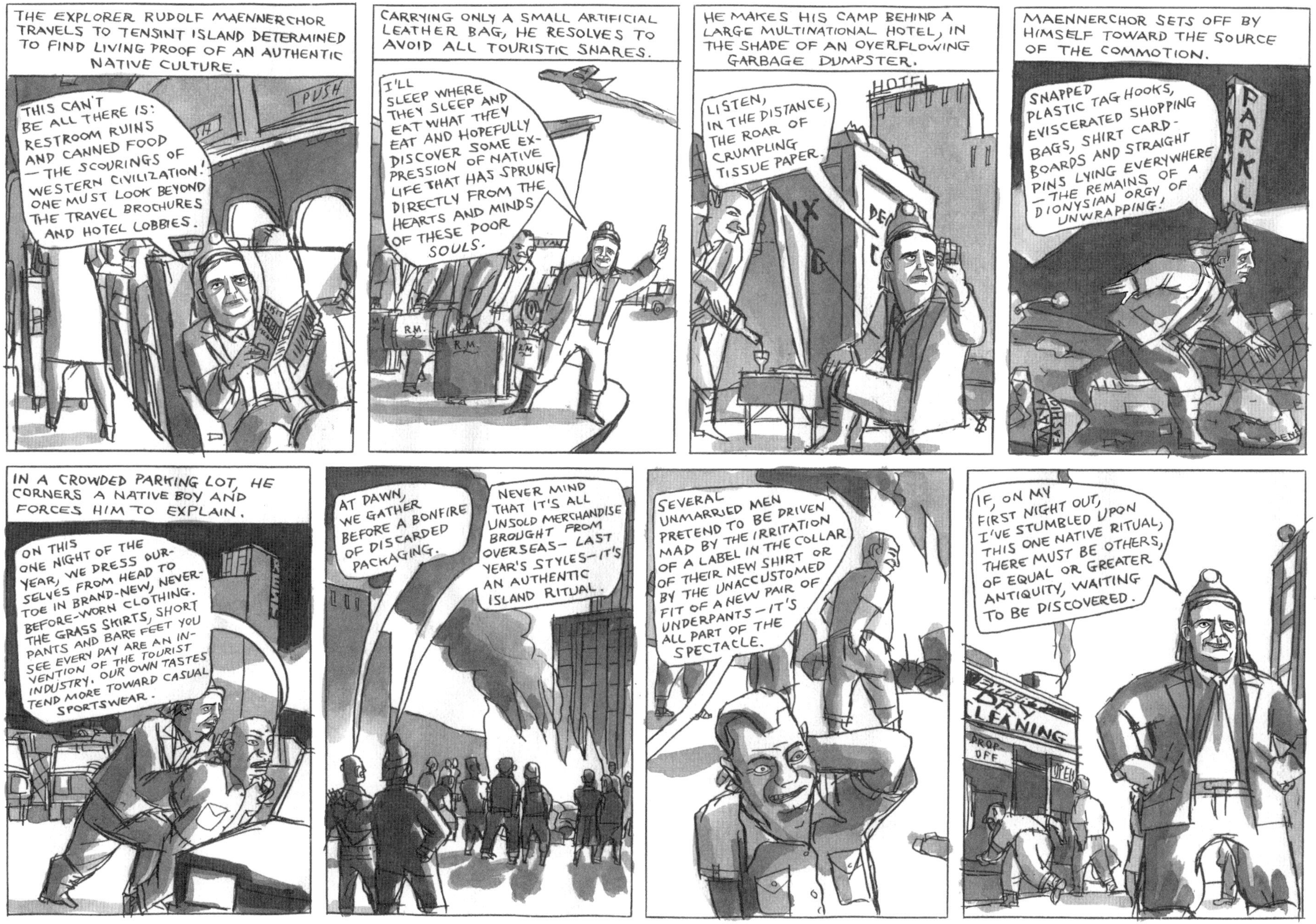
THE EXPLORER RUDOLF MAENNERCHOR TRAVELS TO TENSINT ISLAND DETERMINED TO FIND LIVING PROOF OF AN AUTHENTIC NATIVE CULTURE.
PUSH
THIS CAN'T BE ALL THERE IS: RESTROOM RUINS AND CANNED FOOD — THE SCOURINGS OF WESTERN CIVILIZATION! ONE MUST LOOK BEYOND THE TRAVEL BROCHURES AND HOTEL LOBBIES.
CARRYING ONLY A SMALL ARTIFICIAL LEATHER BAG, HE RESOLVES TO AVOID ALL TOURISTIC SNARES.
I'LL SLEEP WHERE THEY SLEEP AND EAT WHAT THEY EAT AND HOPEFULLY DISCOVER SOME EXPRESSION OF NATIVE LIFE THAT HAS SPRUNG DIRECTLY FROM THE HEARTS AND MINDS OF THESE POOR SOULS.
HE MAKES HIS CAMP BEHIND A LARGE MULTINATIONAL HOTEL, IN THE SHADE OF AN OVERFLOWING GARBAGE DUMPSTER.
HOTEL
LISTEN, IN THE DISTANCE, THE ROAR OF CRUMPLING TISSUE PAPER.
MAENNERCHOR SETS OFF BY HIMSELF TOWARD THE SOURCE OF THE COMMOTION.
SNAPPED PLASTIC TAG HOOKS, EVISCERATED SHOPPING BAGS, SHIRT CARDBOARDS AND STRAIGHT PINS LYING EVERYWHERE — THE REMAINS OF A DIONYSIAN ORGY OF UNWRAPPING!
PARK
IN A CROWDED PARKING LOT, HE CORNERS A NATIVE BOY AND FORCES HIM TO EXPLAIN.
ON THIS ONE NIGHT OF THE YEAR, WE DRESS OURSELVES FROM HEAD TO TOE IN BRAND-NEW, NEVER-BEFORE-WORN CLOTHING. THE GRASS SKIRTS, SHORT PANTS AND BARE FEET YOU SEE EVERY DAY ARE AN INVENTION OF THE TOURIST INDUSTRY. OUR OWN TASTES TEND MORE TOWARD CASUAL SPORTSWEAR.
AT DAWN, WE GATHER BEFORE A BONFIRE OF DISCARDED PACKAGING.
NEVER MIND THAT IT'S ALL UNSOLD MERCHANDISE BROUGHT FROM OVERSEAS— LAST YEAR'S STYLES— IT'S AN AUTHENTIC ISLAND RITUAL.
SEVERAL UNMARRIED MEN PRETEND TO BE DRIVEN MAD BY THE IRRITATION OF A LABEL IN THE COLLAR OF THEIR NEW SHIRT OR BY THE UNACCUSTOMED FIT OF A NEW PAIR OF UNDERPANTS — IT'S ALL PART OF THE SPECTACLE.
IF, ON MY FIRST NIGHT OUT, I'VE STUMBLED UPON THIS ONE NATIVE RITUAL, THERE MUST BE OTHERS, OF EQUAL OR GREATER ANTIQUITY, WAITING TO BE DISCOVERED.
DRY CLEANING
DROP-OFF
OPEN

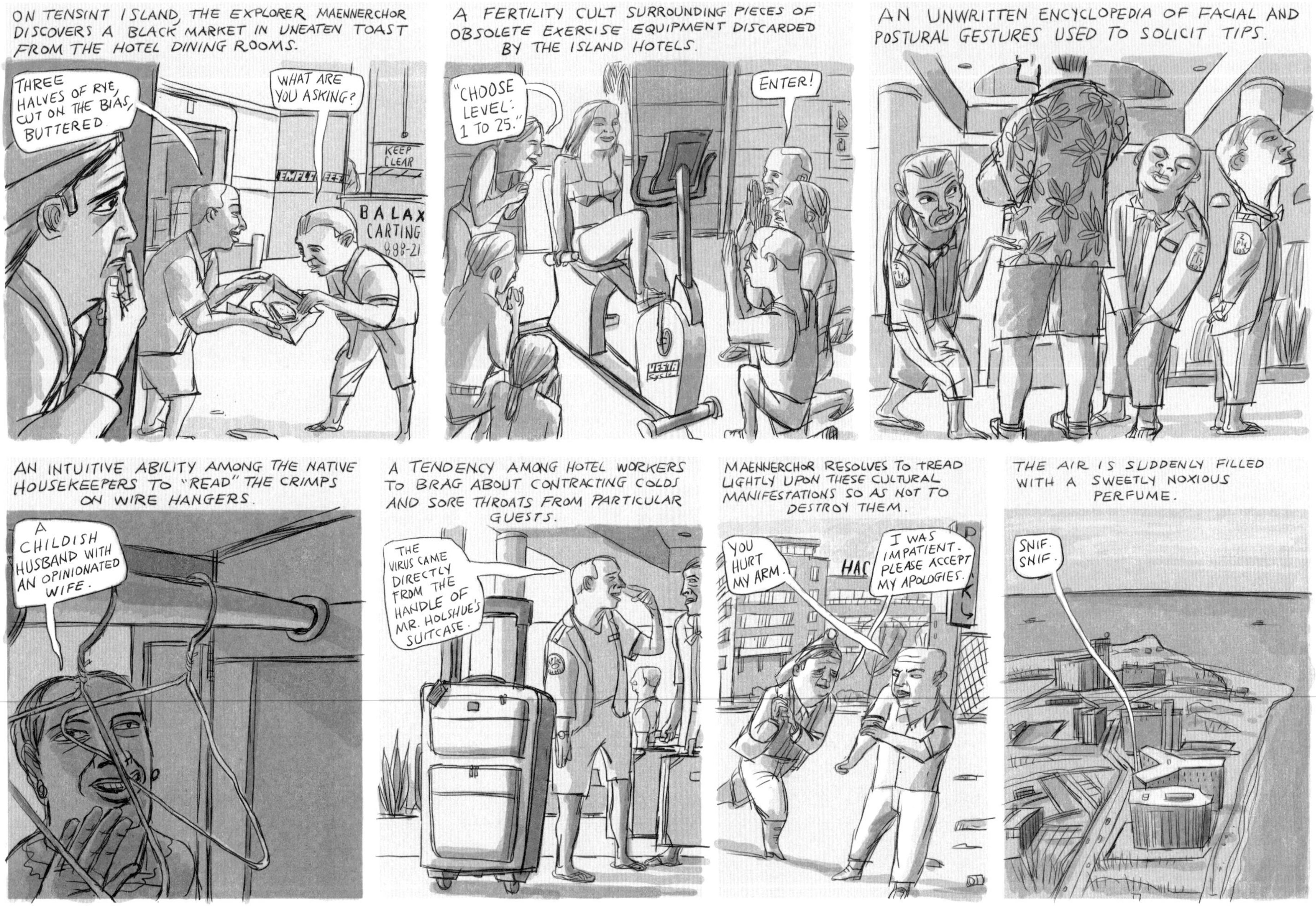
ON TENSINT ISLAND, THE EXPLORER MAENNERCHOR DISCOVERS A BLACK MARKET IN UNEATEN TOAST FROM THE HOTEL DINING ROOMS.
THREE HALVES OF RYE, CUT ON THE BIAS, BUTTERED.
WHAT ARE YOU ASKING?
KEEP CLEAR
BALAX CARTING
A FERTILITY CULT SURROUNDING PIECES OF OBSOLETE EXERCISE EQUIPMENT DISCARDED BY THE ISLAND HOTELS.
"CHOOSE LEVEL: 1 TO 25."
ENTER!
VESTA
AN UNWRITTEN ENCYCLOPEDIA OF FACIAL AND POSTURAL GESTURES USED TO SOLICIT TIPS.
AN INTUITIVE ABILITY AMONG THE NATIVE HOUSEKEEPERS TO "READ" THE CRIMPS ON WIRE HANGERS.
A CHILDISH HUSBAND WITH AN OPINIONATED WIFE.
A TENDENCY AMONG HOTEL WORKERS TO BRAG ABOUT CONTRACTING COLDS AND SORE THROATS FROM PARTICULAR GUESTS.
THE VIRUS CAME DIRECTLY FROM THE HANDLE OF MR. HOLSHUE'S SUITCASE.
MAENNERCHOR RESOLVES TO TREAD LIGHTLY UPON THESE CULTURAL MANIFESTATIONS SO AS NOT TO DESTROY THEM.
YOU HURT MY ARM.
I WAS IMPATIENT. PLEASE ACCEPT MY APOLOGIES.
THE AIR IS SUDDENLY FILLED WITH A SWEETLY NOXIOUS PERFUME.
SNIF. SNIF.

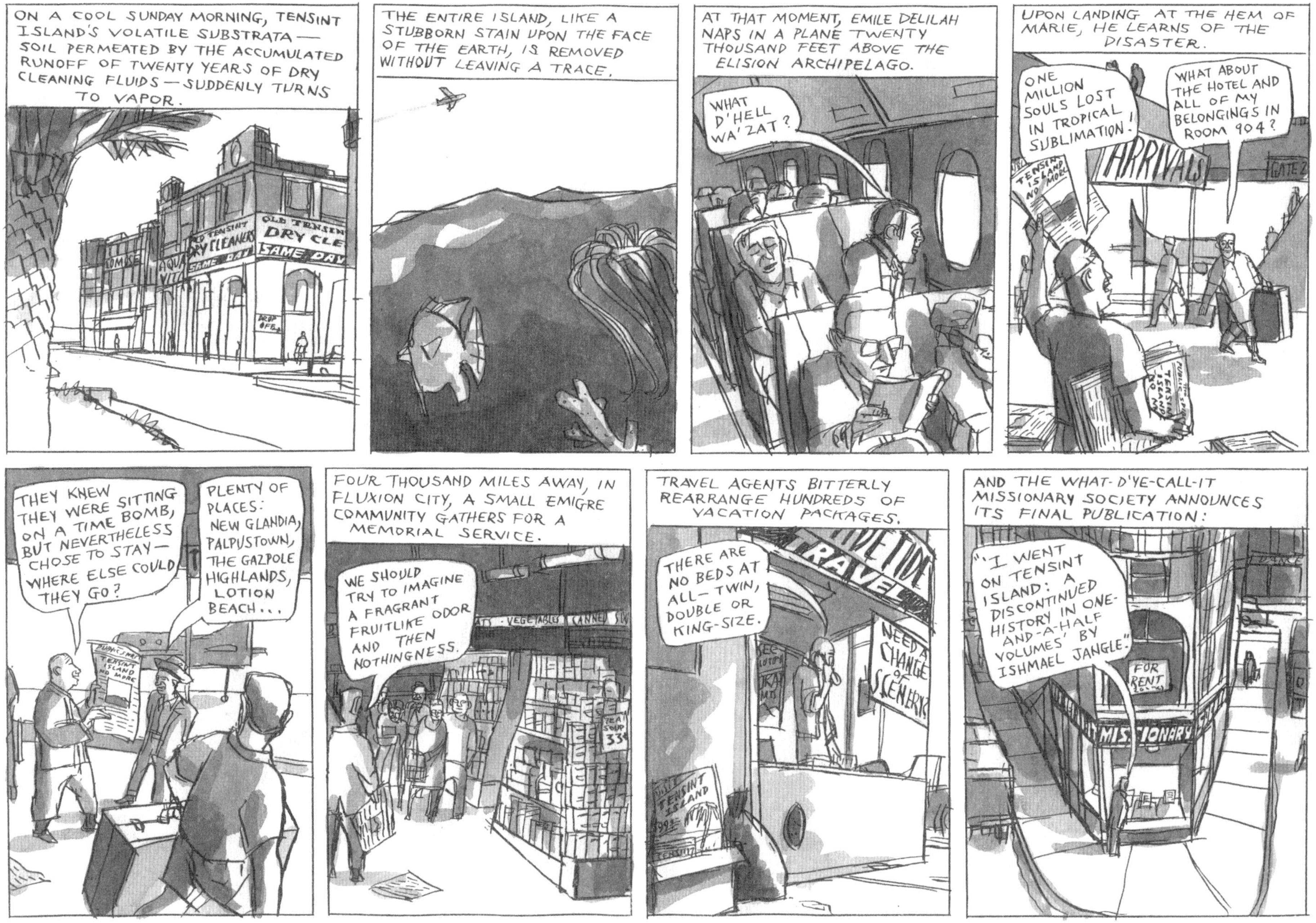
ON A COOL SUNDAY MORNING, TENSINT ISLAND'S VOLATILE SUBSTRATA — SOIL PERMEATED BY THE ACCUMULATED RUNOFF OF TWENTY YEARS OF DRY CLEANING FLUIDS — SUDDENLY TURNS TO VAPOR.
DRY CLEANERS
SAME DAY
THE ENTIRE ISLAND, LIKE A STUBBORN STAIN UPON THE FACE OF THE EARTH, IS REMOVED WITHOUT LEAVING A TRACE.
AT THAT MOMENT, EMILE DELILAH NAPS IN A PLANE TWENTY THOUSAND FEET ABOVE THE ELISION ARCHIPELAGO.
WHAT D'HELL WA'ZAT?
UPON LANDING AT THE HEM OF MARIE, HE LEARNS OF THE DISASTER.
ONE MILLION SOULS LOST IN TROPICAL SUBLIMATION!
WHAT ABOUT THE HOTEL AND ALL OF MY BELONGINGS IN ROOM 904?
ARRIVALS
GATE 2
THEY KNEW THEY WERE SITTING ON A TIME BOMB, BUT NEVERTHELESS CHOSE TO STAY— WHERE ELSE COULD THEY GO?
PLENTY OF PLACES: NEW GLANDIA, PALPUSTOWN, THE GAZPOLE HIGHLANDS, LOTION BEACH...
TENSINT ISLAND NO MORE
FOUR THOUSAND MILES AWAY, IN FLUXION CITY, A SMALL EMIGRE COMMUNITY GATHERS FOR A MEMORIAL SERVICE.
WE SHOULD TRY TO IMAGINE A FRAGRANT FRUITLIKE ODOR AND THEN NOTHINGNESS.
VEGETABLES
CANNED
TRAVEL AGENTS BITTERLY REARRANGE HUNDREDS OF VACATION PACKAGES.
THERE ARE NO BEDS AT ALL— TWIN, DOUBLE OR KING-SIZE.
TRAVEL
NEED A CHANGE OF SCENERY?
TENSINT ISLAND
AND THE WHAT-D'YE-CALL-IT MISSIONARY SOCIETY ANNOUNCES ITS FINAL PUBLICATION:
"'I WENT ON TENSINT ISLAND: A DISCONTINUED HISTORY IN ONE-AND-A-HALF VOLUMES' BY ISHMAEL JANGLE."
FOR RENT
MISSIONARY

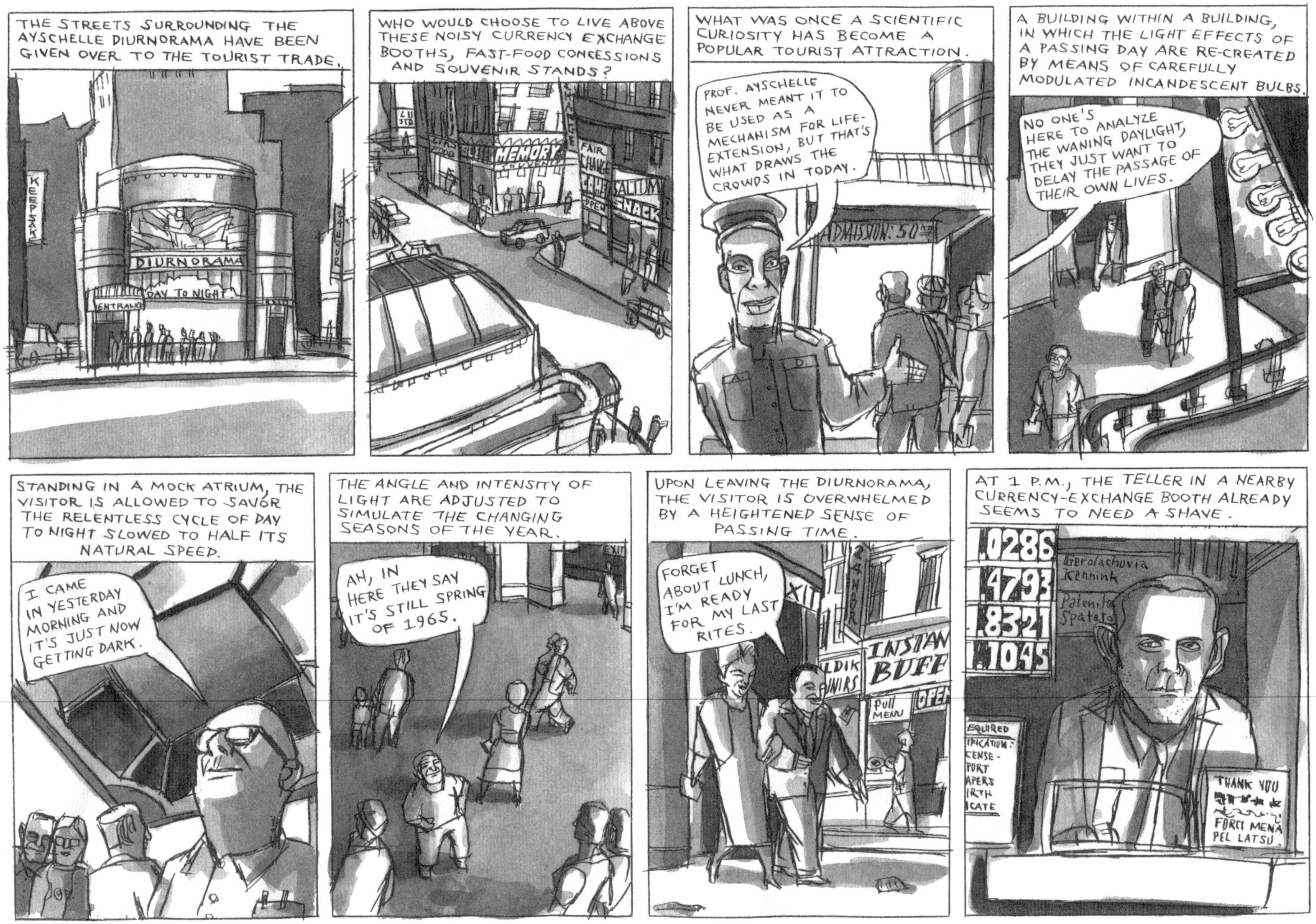
THE STREETS SURROUNDING THE AYSCHELLE DIURNORAMA HAVE BEEN GIVEN OVER TO THE TOURIST TRADE.
KEEPSAKE
DIURNORAMA
DAY TO NIGHT
ENTRANCE
WHO WOULD CHOOSE TO LIVE ABOVE THESE NOISY CURRENCY EXCHANGE BOOTHS, FAST-FOOD CONCESSIONS AND SOUVENIR STANDS?
MEMORY
WHAT WAS ONCE A SCIENTIFIC CURIOSITY HAS BECOME A POPULAR TOURIST ATTRACTION.
PROF. AYSCHELLE NEVER MEANT IT TO BE USED AS A MECHANISM FOR LIFE-EXTENSION, BUT THAT'S WHAT DRAWS THE CROWDS IN TODAY.
ADMISSION: 50¢
A BUILDING WITHIN A BUILDING, IN WHICH THE LIGHT EFFECTS OF A PASSING DAY ARE RE-CREATED BY MEANS OF CAREFULLY MODULATED INCANDESCENT BULBS.
NO ONE'S HERE TO ANALYZE THE WANING DAYLIGHT, THEY JUST WANT TO DELAY THE PASSAGE OF THEIR OWN LIVES.
STANDING IN A MOCK ATRIUM, THE VISITOR IS ALLOWED TO SAVOR THE RELENTLESS CYCLE OF DAY TO NIGHT SLOWED TO HALF ITS NATURAL SPEED.
I CAME IN YESTERDAY MORNING AND IT'S JUST NOW GETTING DARK.
THE ANGLE AND INTENSITY OF LIGHT ARE ADJUSTED TO SIMULATE THE CHANGING SEASONS OF THE YEAR.
AH, IN HERE THEY SAY IT'S STILL SPRING OF 1965.
UPON LEAVING THE DIURNORAMA, THE VISITOR IS OVERWHELMED BY A HEIGHTENED SENSE OF PASSING TIME.
FORGET ABOUT LUNCH, I'M READY FOR MY LAST RITES.
INSTAN BUFF
AT 1 P.M., THE TELLER IN A NEARBY CURRENCY-EXCHANGE BOOTH ALREADY SEEMS TO NEED A SHAVE.
.0286
.4793
.8321
.1045
THANK YOU
FORCI MENA PEL LATSU

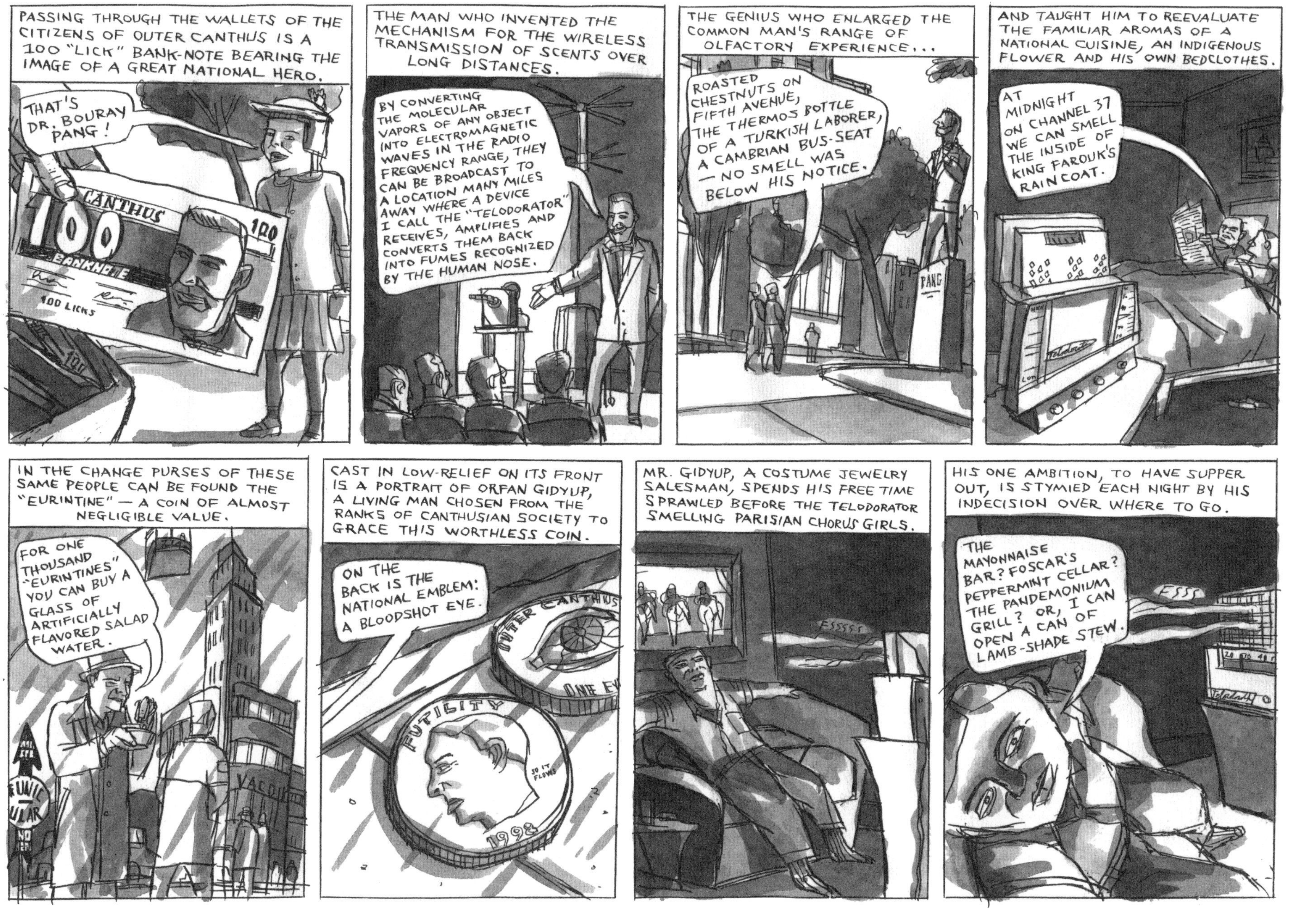
PASSING THROUGH THE WALLETS OF THE CITIZENS OF OUTER CANTHUS IS A 100 "LICK" BANK-NOTE BEARING THE IMAGE OF A GREAT NATIONAL HERO.
THAT'S DR. BOURAY PANG!
CANTHUS
100
BANKNOTE
100 LICKS
THE MAN WHO INVENTED THE MECHANISM FOR THE WIRELESS TRANSMISSION OF SCENTS OVER LONG DISTANCES.
BY CONVERTING THE MOLECULAR VAPORS OF ANY OBJECT INTO ELECTROMAGNETIC WAVES IN THE RADIO FREQUENCY RANGE, THEY CAN BE BROADCAST TO A LOCATION MANY MILES AWAY WHERE A DEVICE I CALL THE "TELODORATOR" RECEIVES, AMPLIFIES AND CONVERTS THEM BACK INTO FUMES RECOGNIZED BY THE HUMAN NOSE.
THE GENIUS WHO ENLARGED THE COMMON MAN'S RANGE OF OLFACTORY EXPERIENCE...
ROASTED CHESTNUTS ON FIFTH AVENUE, THE THERMOS BOTTLE OF A TURKISH LABORER, A CAMBRIAN BUS-SEAT — NO SMELL WAS BELOW HIS NOTICE.
PANG
AND TAUGHT HIM TO REEVALUATE THE FAMILIAR AROMAS OF A NATIONAL CUISINE, AN INDIGENOUS FLOWER AND HIS OWN BEDCLOTHES.
AT MIDNIGHT ON CHANNEL 37 WE CAN SMELL THE INSIDE OF KING FAROUK'S RAIN COAT.
IN THE CHANGE PURSES OF THESE SAME PEOPLE CAN BE FOUND THE "EURINTINE" — A COIN OF ALMOST NEGLIGIBLE VALUE.
FOR ONE THOUSAND "EURINTINES" YOU CAN BUY A GLASS OF ARTIFICIALLY FLAVORED SALAD WATER.
FUNICULAR
CAST IN LOW-RELIEF ON ITS FRONT IS A PORTRAIT OF ORFAN GIDYUP, A LIVING MAN CHOSEN FROM THE RANKS OF CANTHUSIAN SOCIETY TO GRACE THIS WORTHLESS COIN.
ON THE BACK IS THE NATIONAL EMBLEM: A BLOODSHOT EYE.
FUTILITY
SO IT FLOWS
1998
MR. GIDYUP, A COSTUME JEWELRY SALESMAN, SPENDS HIS FREE TIME SPRAWLED BEFORE THE TELODORATOR SMELLING PARISIAN CHORUS GIRLS.
ESSSS
HIS ONE AMBITION, TO HAVE SUPPER OUT, IS STYMIED EACH NIGHT BY HIS INDECISION OVER WHERE TO GO.
THE MAYONNAISE BAR? FOSCAR'S PEPPERMINT CELLAR? THE PANDEMONIUM GRILL? OR, I CAN OPEN A CAN OF LAMB-SHADE STEW.
ESSS

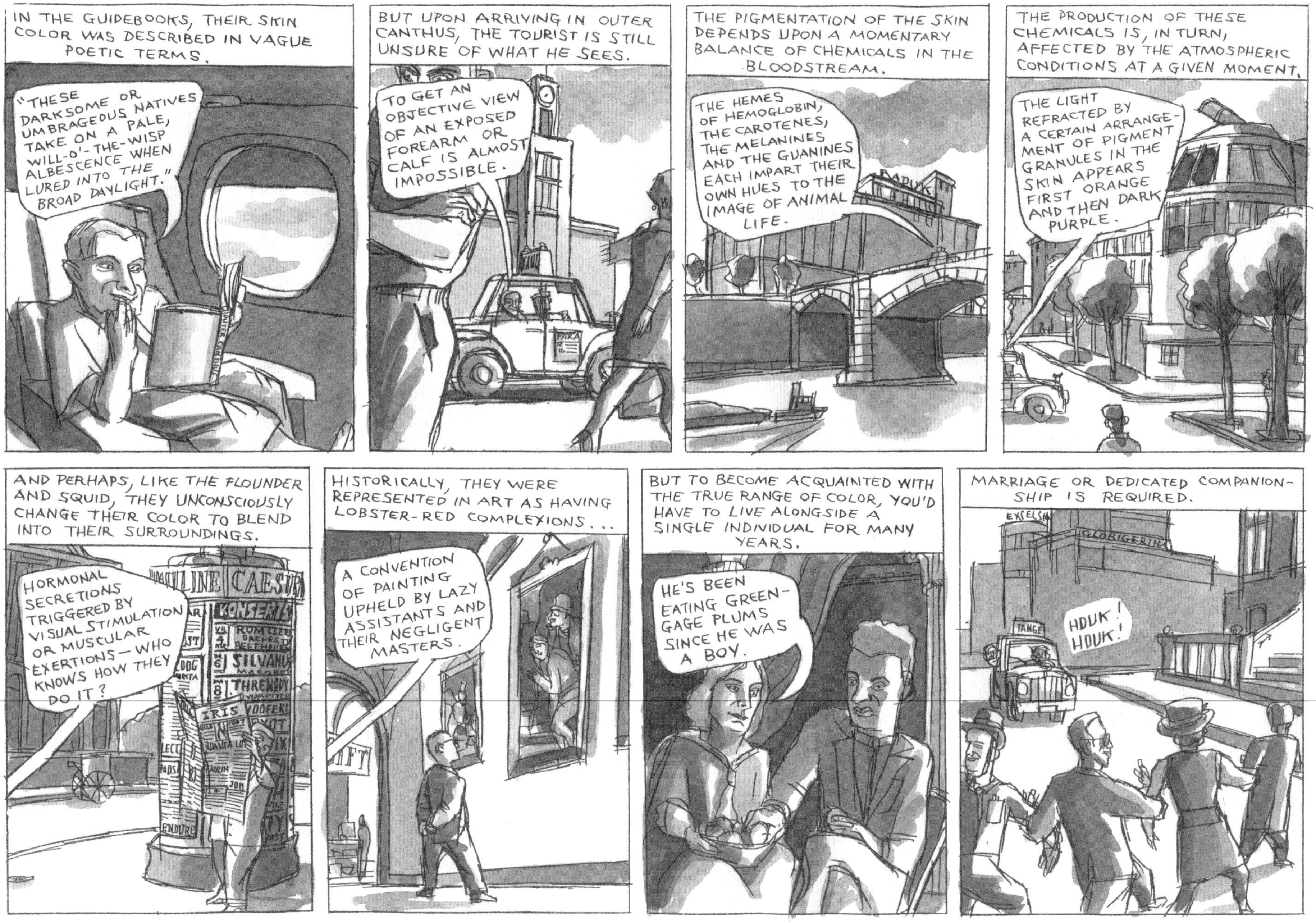
IN THE GUIDEBOOKS, THEIR SKIN COLOR WAS DESCRIBED IN VAGUE POETIC TERMS.
"THESE DARKSOME OR UMBRAGEOUS NATIVES TAKE ON A PALE, WILL-O'-THE-WISP ALBESCENCE WHEN LURED INTO THE BROAD DAYLIGHT."
BUT UPON ARRIVING IN OUTER CANTHUS, THE TOURIST IS STILL UNSURE OF WHAT HE SEES.
TO GET AN OBJECTIVE VIEW OF AN EXPOSED FOREARM OR CALF IS ALMOST IMPOSSIBLE.
THE PIGMENTATION OF THE SKIN DEPENDS UPON A MOMENTARY BALANCE OF CHEMICALS IN THE BLOODSTREAM.
THE HEMES OF HEMOGLOBIN, THE CAROTENES, THE MELANINES AND THE GUANINES EACH IMPART THEIR OWN HUES TO THE IMAGE OF ANIMAL LIFE.
THE PRODUCTION OF THESE CHEMICALS IS, IN TURN, AFFECTED BY THE ATMOSPHERIC CONDITIONS AT A GIVEN MOMENT.
THE LIGHT REFRACTED BY A CERTAIN ARRANGEMENT OF PIGMENT GRANULES IN THE SKIN APPEARS FIRST ORANGE AND THEN DARK PURPLE.
AND PERHAPS, LIKE THE FLOUNDER AND SQUID, THEY UNCONSCIOUSLY CHANGE THEIR COLOR TO BLEND INTO THEIR SURROUNDINGS.
HORMONAL SECRETIONS TRIGGERED BY VISUAL STIMULATION OR MUSCULAR EXERTIONS—WHO KNOWS HOW THEY DO IT?
HISTORICALLY, THEY WERE REPRESENTED IN ART AS HAVING LOBSTER-RED COMPLEXIONS...
A CONVENTION OF PAINTING UPHELD BY LAZY ASSISTANTS AND THEIR NEGLIGENT MASTERS.
BUT TO BECOME ACQUAINTED WITH THE TRUE RANGE OF COLOR, YOU'D HAVE TO LIVE ALONGSIDE A SINGLE INDIVIDUAL FOR MANY YEARS.
HE'S BEEN EATING GREENGAGE PLUMS SINCE HE WAS A BOY.
MARRIAGE OR DEDICATED COMPANIONSHIP IS REQUIRED.
HOUK! HOUK!

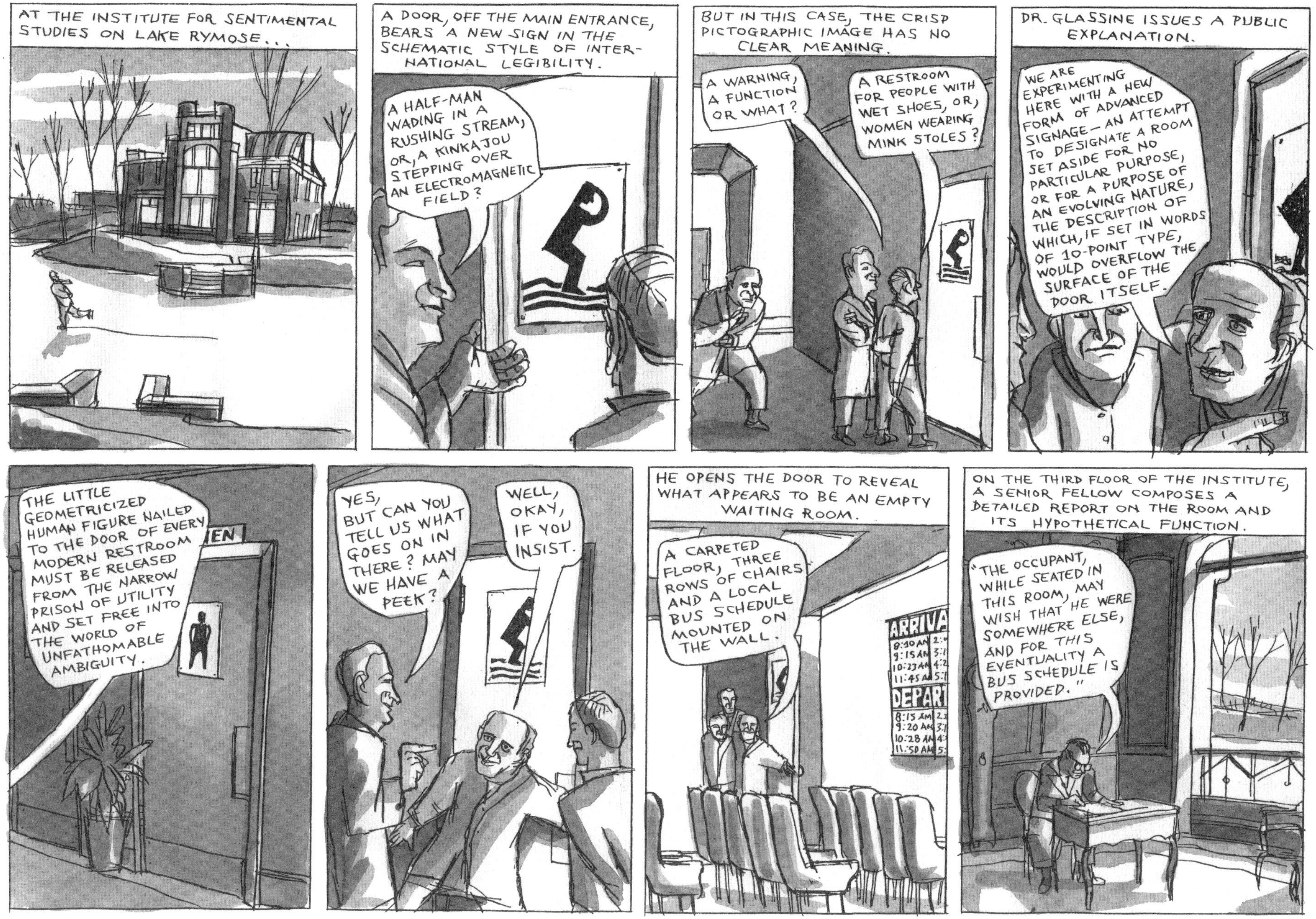

AT THE INSTITUTE FOR SENTIMENTAL STUDIES ON LAKE RYMOSE...
A DOOR, OFF THE MAIN ENTRANCE, BEARS A NEW SIGN IN THE SCHEMATIC STYLE OF INTERNATIONAL LEGIBILITY.
A HALF-MAN WADING IN A RUSHING STREAM, OR, A KINKAJOU STEPPING OVER AN ELECTROMAGNETIC FIELD?
BUT IN THIS CASE, THE CRISP PICTOGRAPHIC IMAGE HAS NO CLEAR MEANING.
A WARNING, A FUNCTION OR WHAT?
A RESTROOM FOR PEOPLE WITH WET SHOES, OR, WOMEN WEARING MINK STOLES?
DR. GLASSINE ISSUES A PUBLIC EXPLANATION.
WE ARE EXPERIMENTING HERE WITH A NEW FORM OF ADVANCED SIGNAGE—AN ATTEMPT TO DESIGNATE A ROOM SET ASIDE FOR NO PARTICULAR PURPOSE, OR FOR A PURPOSE OF AN EVOLVING NATURE, THE DESCRIPTION OF WHICH, IF SET IN WORDS OF 10-POINT TYPE, WOULD OVERFLOW THE SURFACE OF THE DOOR ITSELF.
THE LITTLE GEOMETRICIZED HUMAN FIGURE NAILED TO THE DOOR OF EVERY MODERN RESTROOM MUST BE RELEASED FROM THE NARROW PRISON OF UTILITY AND SET FREE INTO THE WORLD OF UNFATHOMABLE AMBIGUITY.
YES, BUT CAN YOU TELL US WHAT GOES ON IN THERE? MAY WE HAVE A PEEK?
WELL, OKAY, IF YOU INSIST.
HE OPENS THE DOOR TO REVEAL WHAT APPEARS TO BE AN EMPTY WAITING ROOM.
A CARPETED FLOOR, THREE ROWS OF CHAIRS AND A LOCAL BUS SCHEDULE MOUNTED ON THE WALL.
ON THE THIRD FLOOR OF THE INSTITUTE, A SENIOR FELLOW COMPOSES A DETAILED REPORT ON THE ROOM AND ITS HYPOTHETICAL FUNCTION.
"THE OCCUPANT, WHILE SEATED IN THIS ROOM, MAY WISH THAT HE WERE SOMEWHERE ELSE, AND FOR THIS EVENTUALITY A BUS SCHEDULE IS PROVIDED."

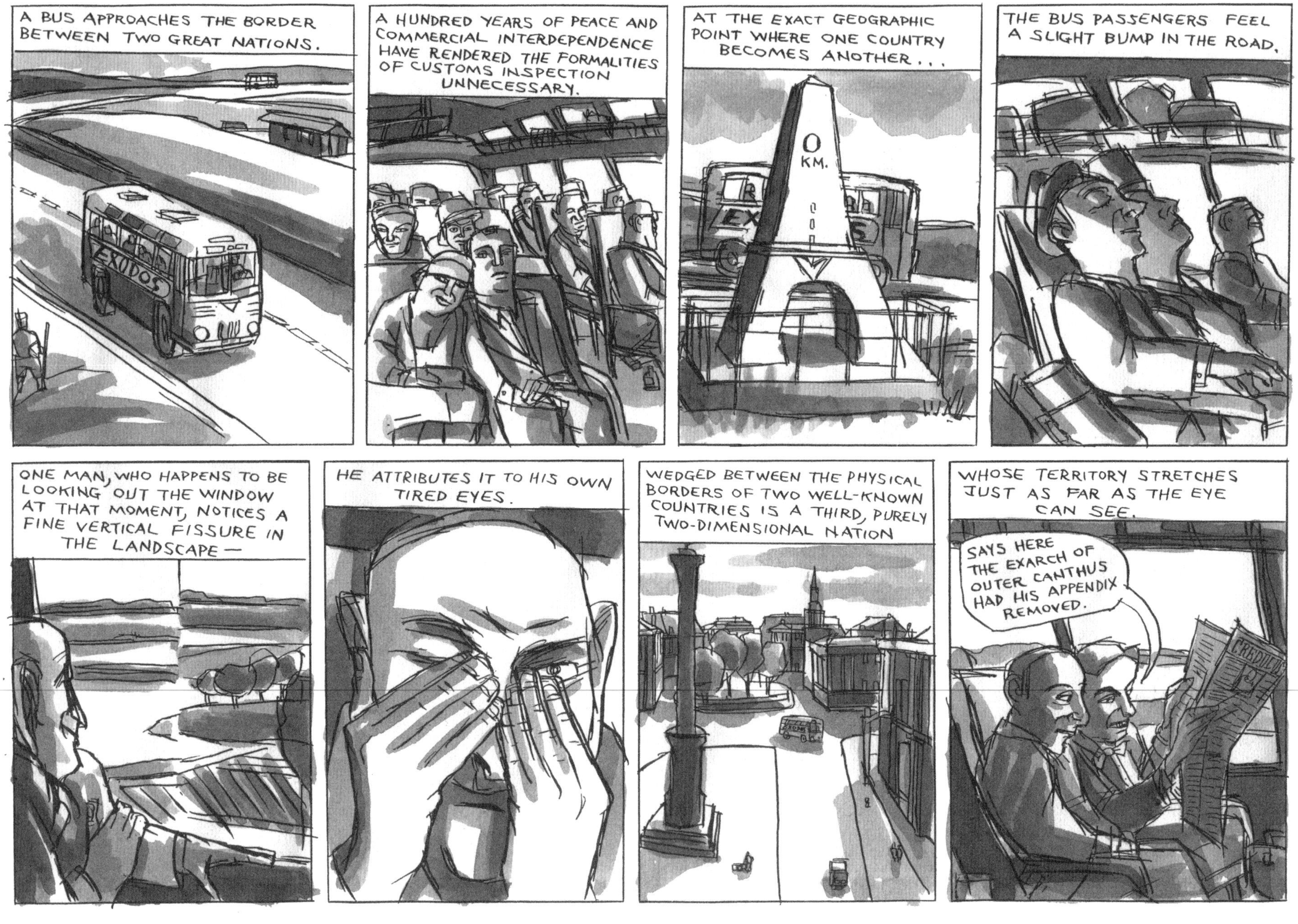
A BUS APPROACHES THE BORDER BETWEEN TWO GREAT NATIONS.
EXODOS
A HUNDRED YEARS OF PEACE AND COMMERCIAL INTERDEPENDENCE HAVE RENDERED THE FORMALITIES OF CUSTOMS INSPECTION UNNECESSARY.
AT THE EXACT GEOGRAPHIC POINT WHERE ONE COUNTRY BECOMES ANOTHER . . .
0 KM.
THE BUS PASSENGERS FEEL A SLIGHT BUMP IN THE ROAD.
ONE MAN, WHO HAPPENS TO BE LOOKING OUT THE WINDOW AT THAT MOMENT, NOTICES A FINE VERTICAL FISSURE IN THE LANDSCAPE —
HE ATTRIBUTES IT TO HIS OWN TIRED EYES.
WEDGED BETWEEN THE PHYSICAL BORDERS OF TWO WELL-KNOWN COUNTRIES IS A THIRD, PURELY TWO-DIMENSIONAL NATION
WHOSE TERRITORY STRETCHES JUST AS FAR AS THE EYE CAN SEE.
SAYS HERE THE EXARCH OF OUTER CANTHUS HAD HIS APPENDIX REMOVED.

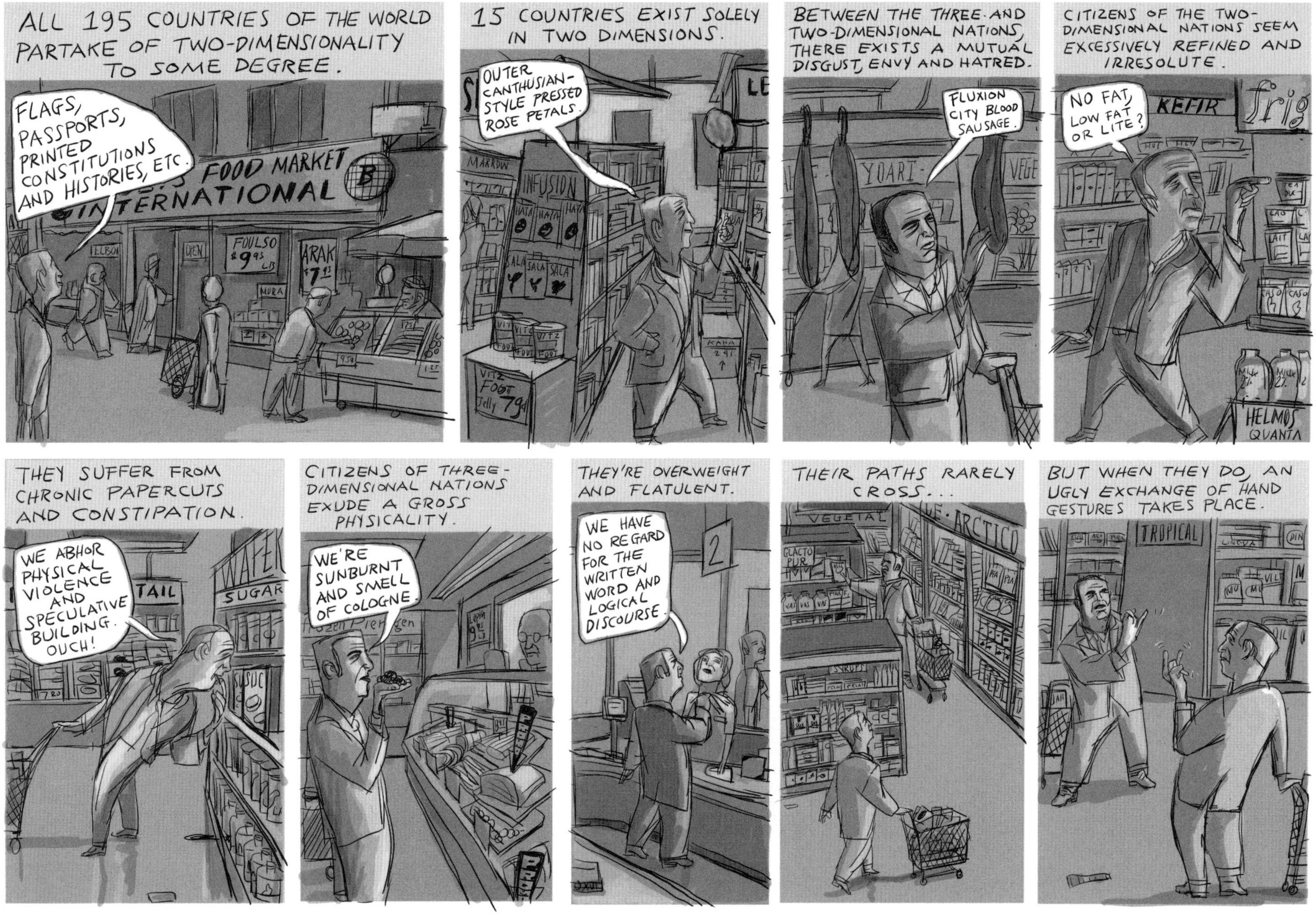
ALL 195 COUNTRIES OF THE WORLD PARTAKE OF TWO-DIMENSIONALITY TO SOME DEGREE.
FLAGS, PASSPORTS, PRINTED CONSTITUTIONS AND HISTORIES, ETC.
FOOD MARKET INTERNATIONAL
15 COUNTRIES EXIST SOLELY IN TWO DIMENSIONS.
OUTER CANTHUSIAN-STYLE PRESSED ROSE PETALS.
BETWEEN THE THREE- AND TWO-DIMENSIONAL NATIONS, THERE EXISTS A MUTUAL DISGUST, ENVY AND HATRED.
FLUXION CITY BLOOD SAUSAGE.
CITIZENS OF THE TWO-DIMENSIONAL NATIONS SEEM EXCESSIVELY REFINED AND IRRESOLUTE.
NO FAT, LOW FAT OR LITE?
THEY SUFFER FROM CHRONIC PAPERCUTS AND CONSTIPATION.
WE ABHOR PHYSICAL VIOLENCE AND SPECULATIVE BUILDING. OUCH!
CITIZENS OF THREE-DIMENSIONAL NATIONS EXUDE A GROSS PHYSICALITY.
WE'RE SUNBURNT AND SMELL OF COLOGNE.
THEY'RE OVERWEIGHT AND FLATULENT.
WE HAVE NO REGARD FOR THE WRITTEN WORD AND LOGICAL DISCOURSE.
THEIR PATHS RARELY CROSS...
BUT WHEN THEY DO, AN UGLY EXCHANGE OF HAND GESTURES TAKES PLACE.

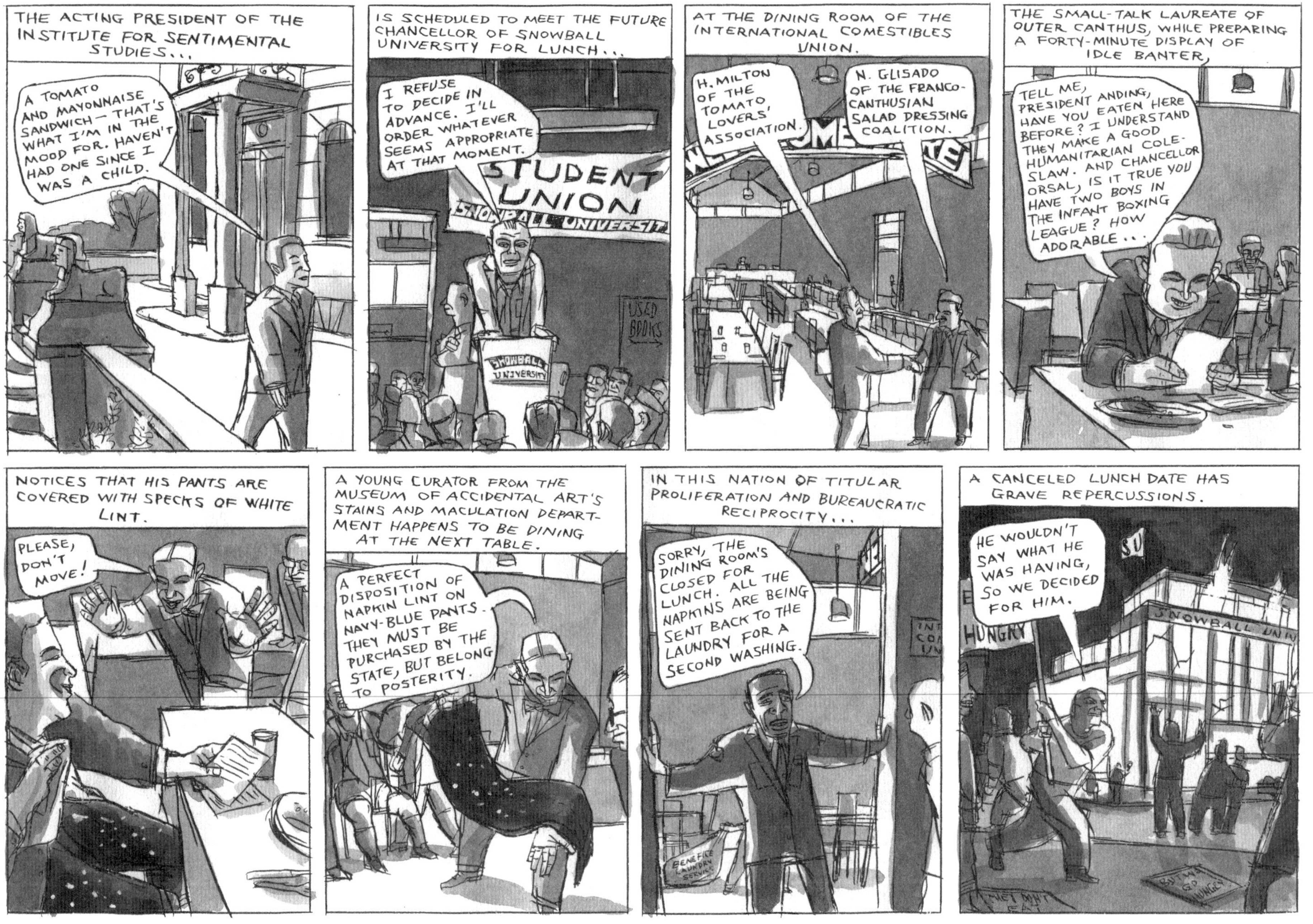
THE ACTING PRESIDENT OF THE INSTITUTE FOR SENTIMENTAL STUDIES...
A TOMATO AND MAYONNAISE SANDWICH — THAT'S WHAT I'M IN THE MOOD FOR. HAVEN'T HAD ONE SINCE I WAS A CHILD.
IS SCHEDULED TO MEET THE FUTURE CHANCELLOR OF SNOWBALL UNIVERSITY FOR LUNCH...
I REFUSE TO DECIDE IN ADVANCE. I'LL ORDER WHATEVER SEEMS APPROPRIATE AT THAT MOMENT.
STUDENT UNION
SNOWBALL UNIVERSITY
USED BOOKS
AT THE DINING ROOM OF THE INTERNATIONAL COMESTIBLES UNION.
H. MILTON OF THE TOMATO LOVERS' ASSOCIATION.
N. GLISADO OF THE FRANCO-CANTHUSIAN SALAD DRESSING COALITION.
THE SMALL-TALK LAUREATE OF OUTER CANTHUS, WHILE PREPARING A FORTY-MINUTE DISPLAY OF IDLE BANTER,
TELL ME, PRESIDENT ANDING, HAVE YOU EATEN HERE BEFORE? I UNDERSTAND THEY MAKE A GOOD HUMANITARIAN COLE-SLAW. AND CHANCELLOR ORSAL, IS IT TRUE YOU HAVE TWO BOYS IN THE INFANT BOXING LEAGUE? HOW ADORABLE...
NOTICES THAT HIS PANTS ARE COVERED WITH SPECKS OF WHITE LINT.
PLEASE, DON'T MOVE!
A YOUNG CURATOR FROM THE MUSEUM OF ACCIDENTAL ART'S STAINS AND MACULATION DEPART-MENT HAPPENS TO BE DINING AT THE NEXT TABLE.
A PERFECT DISPOSITION OF NAPKIN LINT ON NAVY-BLUE PANTS. THEY MUST BE PURCHASED BY THE STATE, BUT BELONG TO POSTERITY.
IN THIS NATION OF TITULAR PROLIFERATION AND BUREAUCRATIC RECIPROCITY...
SORRY, THE DINING ROOM'S CLOSED FOR LUNCH. ALL THE NAPKINS ARE BEING SENT BACK TO THE LAUNDRY FOR A SECOND WASHING.
BENEFICE LAUNDRY SERVICE
A CANCELED LUNCH DATE HAS GRAVE REPERCUSSIONS.
HE WOULDN'T SAY WHAT HE WAS HAVING, SO WE DECIDED FOR HIM.
HUNGRY
SNOWBALL UNIV

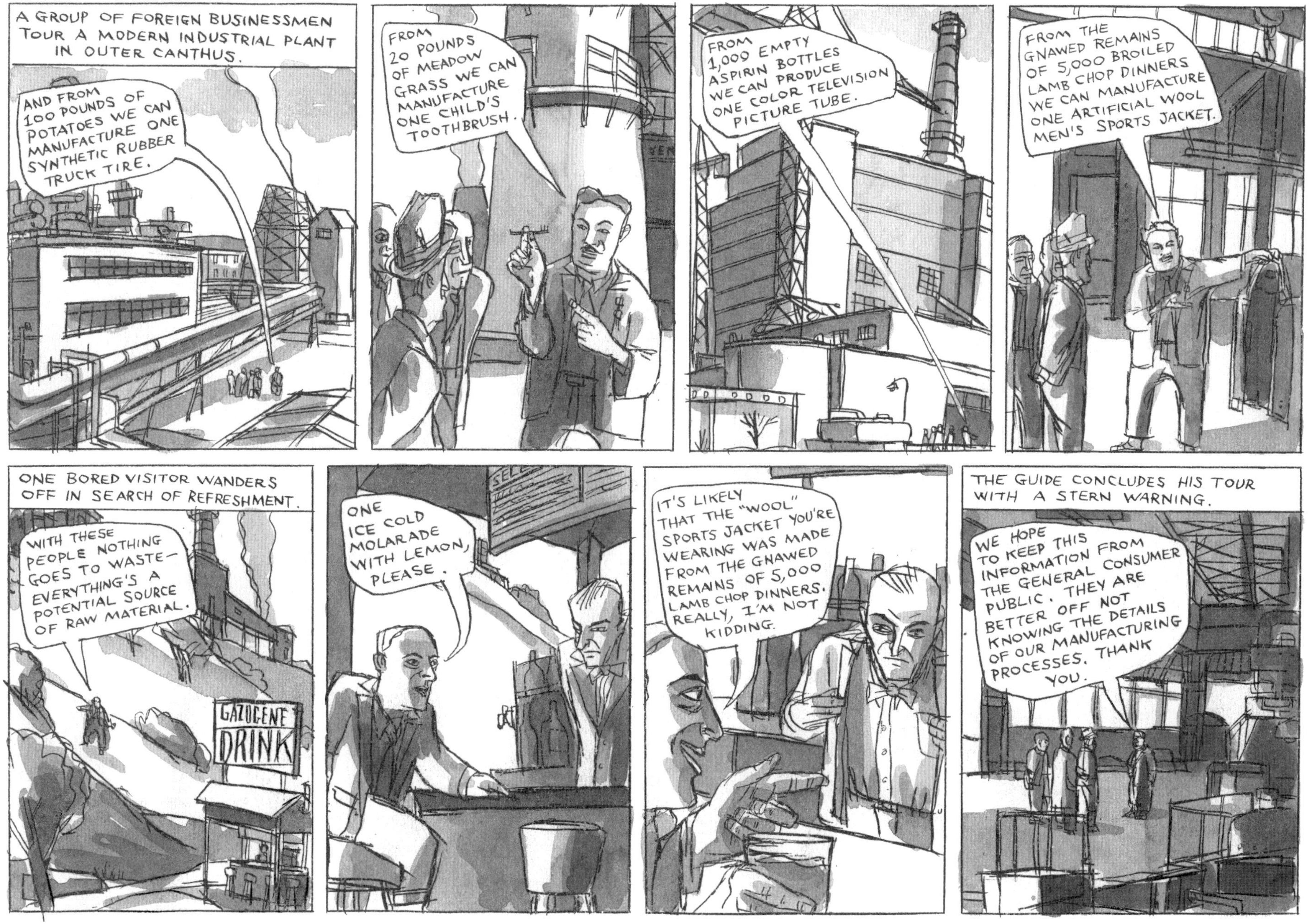
A GROUP OF FOREIGN BUSINESSMEN TOUR A MODERN INDUSTRIAL PLANT IN OUTER CANTHUS.
AND FROM 100 POUNDS OF POTATOES WE CAN MANUFACTURE ONE SYNTHETIC RUBBER TRUCK TIRE.
FROM 20 POUNDS OF MEADOW GRASS WE CAN MANUFACTURE ONE CHILD'S TOOTHBRUSH.
FROM 1,009 EMPTY ASPIRIN BOTTLES WE CAN PRODUCE ONE COLOR TELEVISION PICTURE TUBE.
FROM THE GNAWED REMAINS OF 5,000 BROILED LAMB CHOP DINNERS WE CAN MANUFACTURE ONE ARTIFICIAL WOOL MEN'S SPORTS JACKET.
ONE BORED VISITOR WANDERS OFF IN SEARCH OF REFRESHMENT.
WITH THESE PEOPLE NOTHING GOES TO WASTE- EVERYTHING'S A POTENTIAL SOURCE OF RAW MATERIAL.
GAZOGENE
DRINK
ONE ICE COLD MOLARADE WITH LEMON, PLEASE.
IT'S LIKELY THAT THE "WOOL" SPORTS JACKET YOU'RE WEARING WAS MADE FROM THE GNAWED REMAINS OF 5,000 LAMB CHOP DINNERS. REALLY, I'M NOT KIDDING.
THE GUIDE CONCLUDES HIS TOUR WITH A STERN WARNING.
WE HOPE TO KEEP THIS INFORMATION FROM THE GENERAL CONSUMER PUBLIC. THEY ARE BETTER OFF NOT KNOWING THE DETAILS OF OUR MANUFACTURING PROCESSES. THANK YOU.

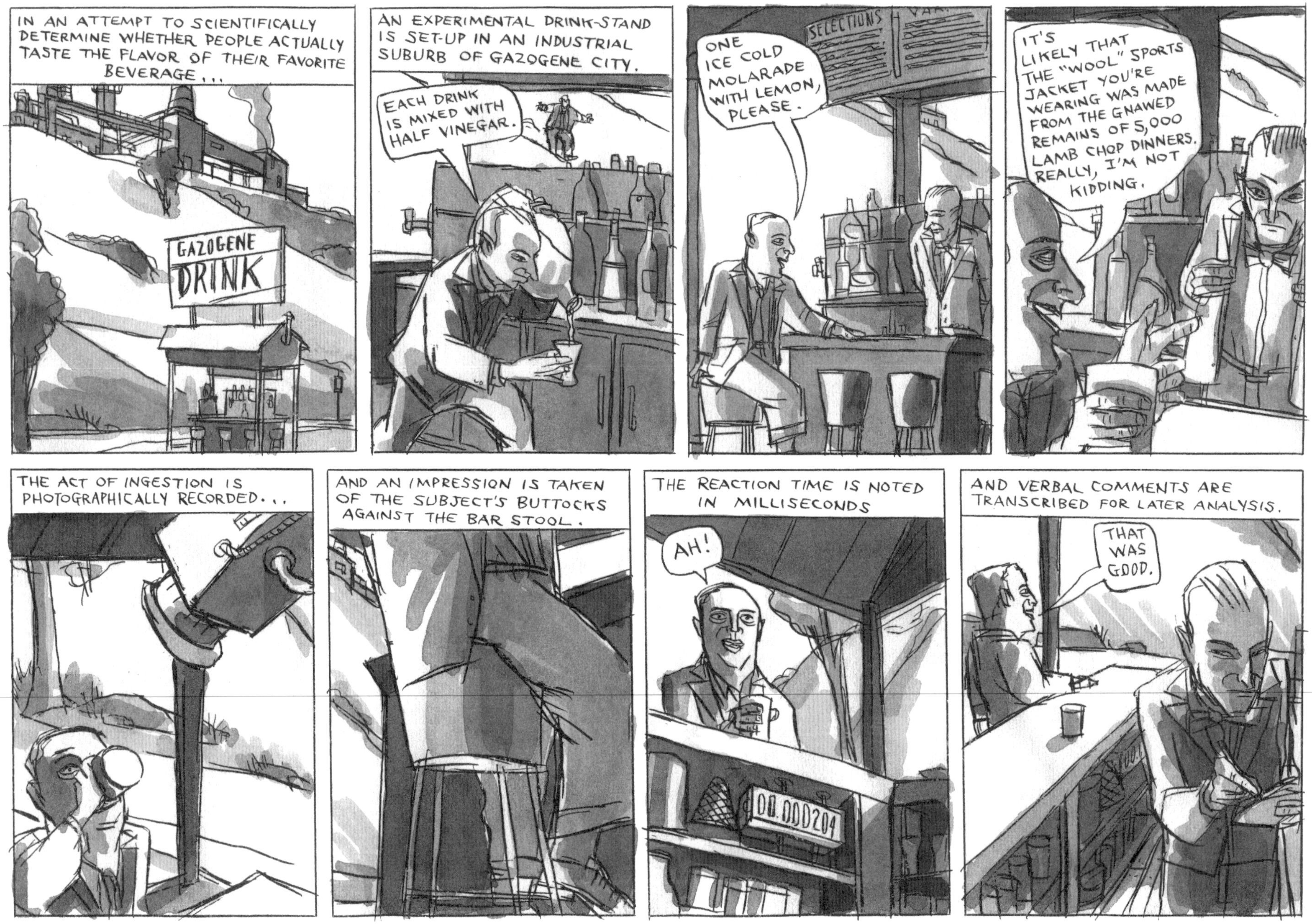
IN AN ATTEMPT TO SCIENTIFICALLY DETERMINE WHETHER PEOPLE ACTUALLY TASTE THE FLAVOR OF THEIR FAVORITE BEVERAGE...
GAZOGENE DRINK
AN EXPERIMENTAL DRINK-STAND IS SET-UP IN AN INDUSTRIAL SUBURB OF GAZOGENE CITY.
EACH DRINK IS MIXED WITH HALF VINEGAR.
SELECTIONS
ONE ICE COLD MOLARADE WITH LEMON, PLEASE.
IT'S LIKELY THAT THE "WOOL" SPORTS JACKET YOU'RE WEARING WAS MADE FROM THE GNAWED REMAINS OF 5,000 LAMB CHOP DINNERS. REALLY, I'M NOT KIDDING.
THE ACT OF INGESTION IS PHOTOGRAPHICALLY RECORDED...
AND AN IMPRESSION IS TAKEN OF THE SUBJECT'S BUTTOCKS AGAINST THE BAR STOOL.
THE REACTION TIME IS NOTED IN MILLISECONDS
AH!
00.000204
AND VERBAL COMMENTS ARE TRANSCRIBED FOR LATER ANALYSIS.
THAT WAS GOOD.

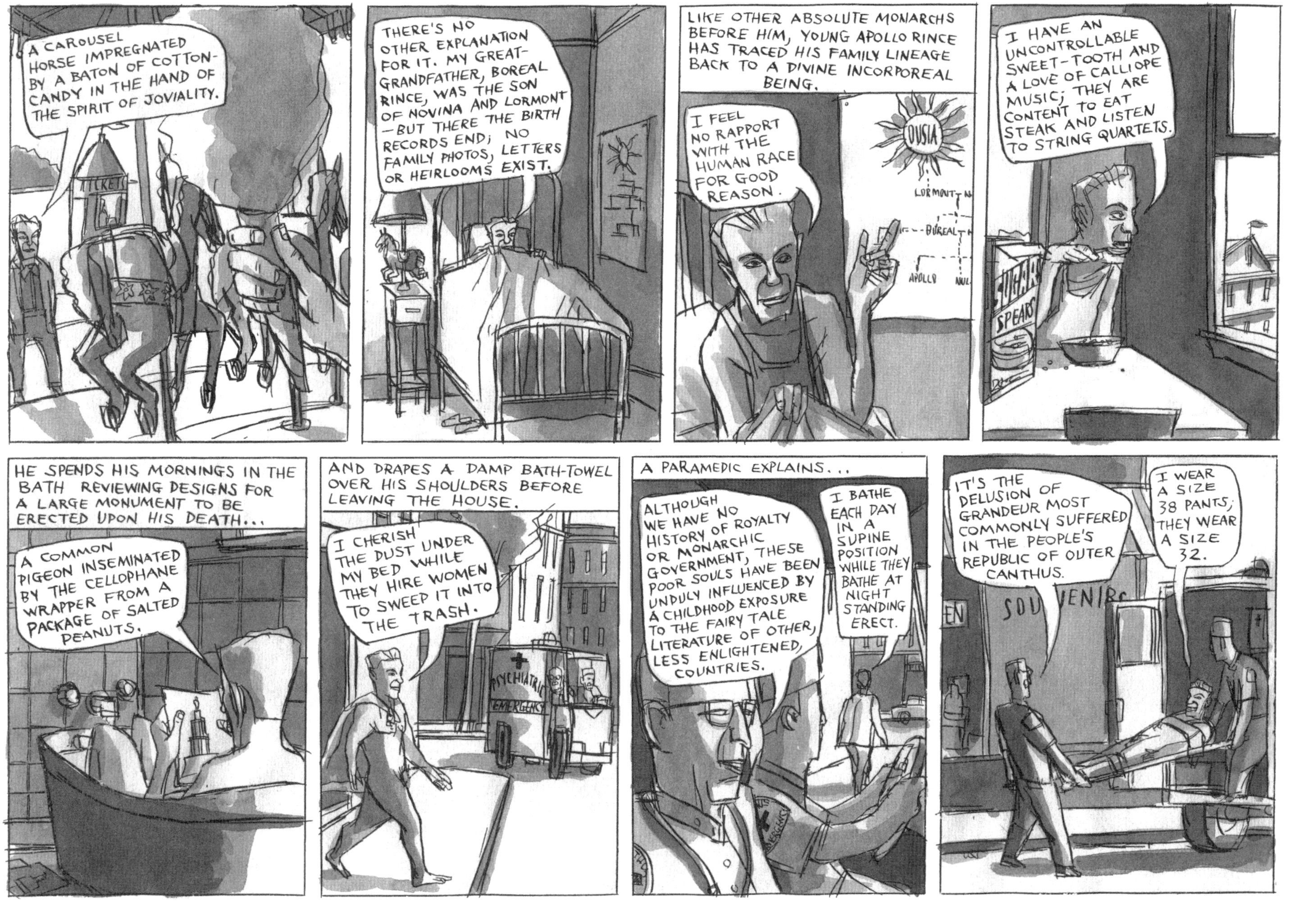
A CAROUSEL HORSE IMPREGNATED BY A BATON OF COTTON-CANDY IN THE HAND OF THE SPIRIT OF JOVIALITY.
TICKETS
THERE'S NO OTHER EXPLANATION FOR IT. MY GREAT-GRANDFATHER, BOREAL RINCE, WAS THE SON OF NOVINA AND LORMONT —BUT THERE THE BIRTH RECORDS END; NO FAMILY PHOTOS, LETTERS OR HEIRLOOMS EXIST.
LIKE OTHER ABSOLUTE MONARCHS BEFORE HIM, YOUNG APOLLO RINCE HAS TRACED HIS FAMILY LINEAGE BACK TO A DIVINE INCORPOREAL BEING.
I FEEL NO RAPPORT WITH THE HUMAN RACE FOR GOOD REASON.
OUSIA
LORMOUT
BOREAL
APOLLO
I HAVE AN UNCONTROLLABLE SWEET-TOOTH AND A LOVE OF CALLIOPE MUSIC; THEY ARE CONTENT TO EAT STEAK AND LISTEN TO STRING QUARTETS.
SUGAR SPEARS
HE SPENDS HIS MORNINGS IN THE BATH REVIEWING DESIGNS FOR A LARGE MONUMENT TO BE ERECTED UPON HIS DEATH...
A COMMON PIGEON INSEMINATED BY THE CELLOPHANE WRAPPER FROM A PACKAGE OF SALTED PEANUTS.
AND DRAPES A DAMP BATH-TOWEL OVER HIS SHOULDERS BEFORE LEAVING THE HOUSE.
I CHERISH THE DUST UNDER MY BED WHILE THEY HIRE WOMEN TO SWEEP IT INTO THE TRASH.
PSYCHIATRIC EMERGENCY
A PARAMEDIC EXPLAINS...
ALTHOUGH WE HAVE NO HISTORY OF ROYALTY OR MONARCHIC GOVERNMENT, THESE POOR SOULS HAVE BEEN UNDULY INFLUENCED BY A CHILDHOOD EXPOSURE TO THE FAIRY TALE LITERATURE OF OTHER, LESS ENLIGHTENED, COUNTRIES.
I BATHE EACH DAY IN A SUPINE POSITION WHILE THEY BATHE AT NIGHT STANDING ERECT.
IT'S THE DELUSION OF GRANDEUR MOST COMMONLY SUFFERED IN THE PEOPLE'S REPUBLIC OF OUTER CANTHUS.
I WEAR A SIZE 38 PANTS; THEY WEAR A SIZE 32.
SOUVENIRS

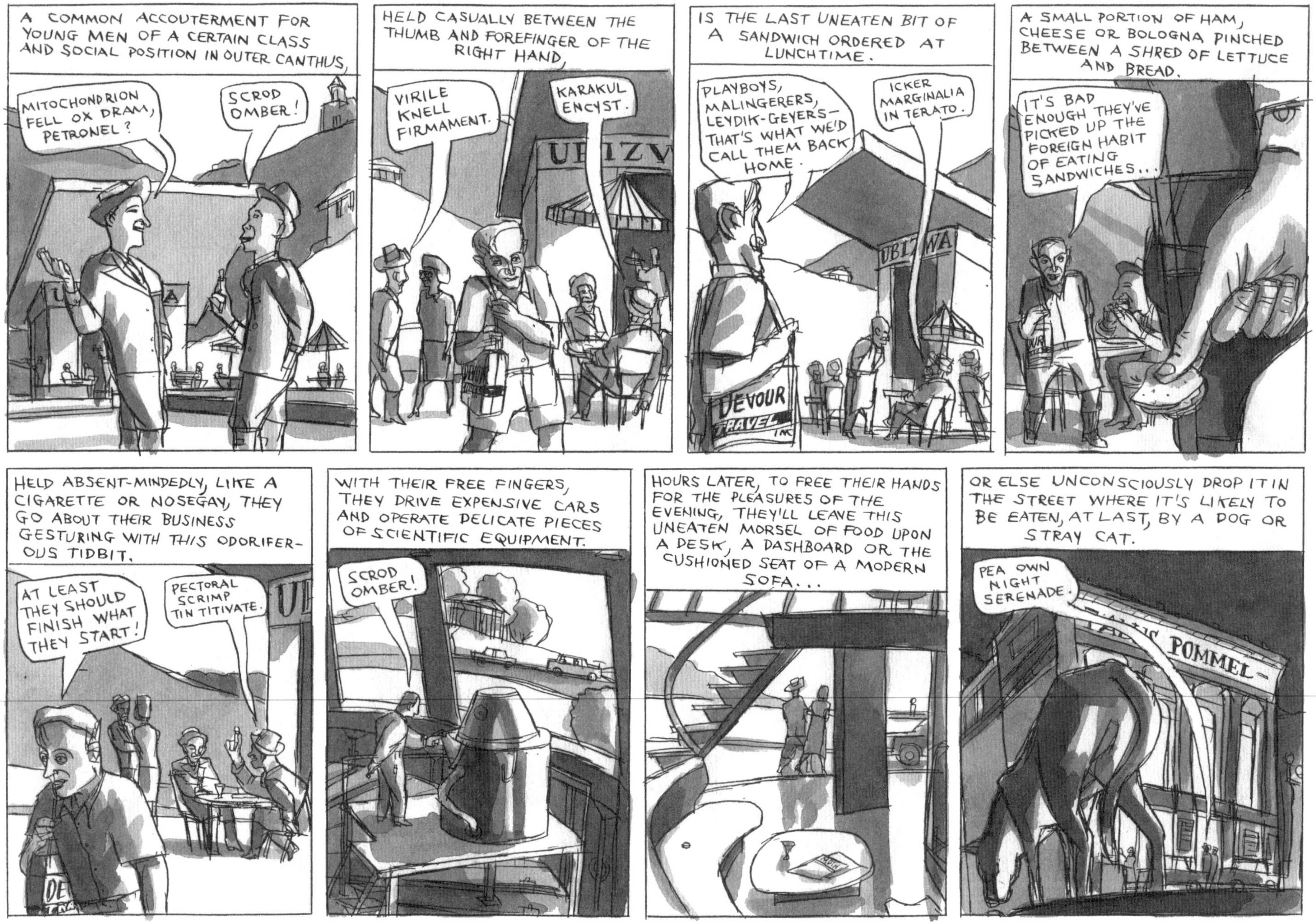
A COMMON ACCOUTERMENT FOR YOUNG MEN OF A CERTAIN CLASS AND SOCIAL POSITION IN OUTER CANTHUS,
MITOCHONDRION FELL OX DRAM, PETRONEL?
SCROD OMBER!
HELD CASUALLY BETWEEN THE THUMB AND FOREFINGER OF THE RIGHT HAND,
VIRILE KNELL FIRMAMENT.
KARAKUL ENCYST.
IS THE LAST UNEATEN BIT OF A SANDWICH ORDERED AT LUNCHTIME.
PLAYBOYS, MALINGERERS, LEYDIK-GEYERS— THAT'S WHAT WE'D CALL THEM BACK HOME.
ICKER MARGINALIA IN TERATO.
DEVOUR TRAVEL
A SMALL PORTION OF HAM, CHEESE OR BOLOGNA PINCHED BETWEEN A SHRED OF LETTUCE AND BREAD.
IT'S BAD ENOUGH THEY'VE PICKED UP THE FOREIGN HABIT OF EATING SANDWICHES...
HELD ABSENT-MINDEDLY, LIKE A CIGARETTE OR NOSEGAY, THEY GO ABOUT THEIR BUSINESS GESTURING WITH THIS ODORIFEROUS TIDBIT.
AT LEAST THEY SHOULD FINISH WHAT THEY START!
PECTORAL SCRIMP TIN TITIVATE.
WITH THEIR FREE FINGERS, THEY DRIVE EXPENSIVE CARS AND OPERATE DELICATE PIECES OF SCIENTIFIC EQUIPMENT.
SCROD OMBER!
HOURS LATER, TO FREE THEIR HANDS FOR THE PLEASURES OF THE EVENING, THEY'LL LEAVE THIS UNEATEN MORSEL OF FOOD UPON A DESK, A DASHBOARD OR THE CUSHIONED SEAT OF A MODERN SOFA...
OR ELSE UNCONSCIOUSLY DROP IT IN THE STREET WHERE IT'S LIKELY TO BE EATEN, AT LAST, BY A DOG OR STRAY CAT.
PEA OWN NIGHT SERENADE.
POMMEL

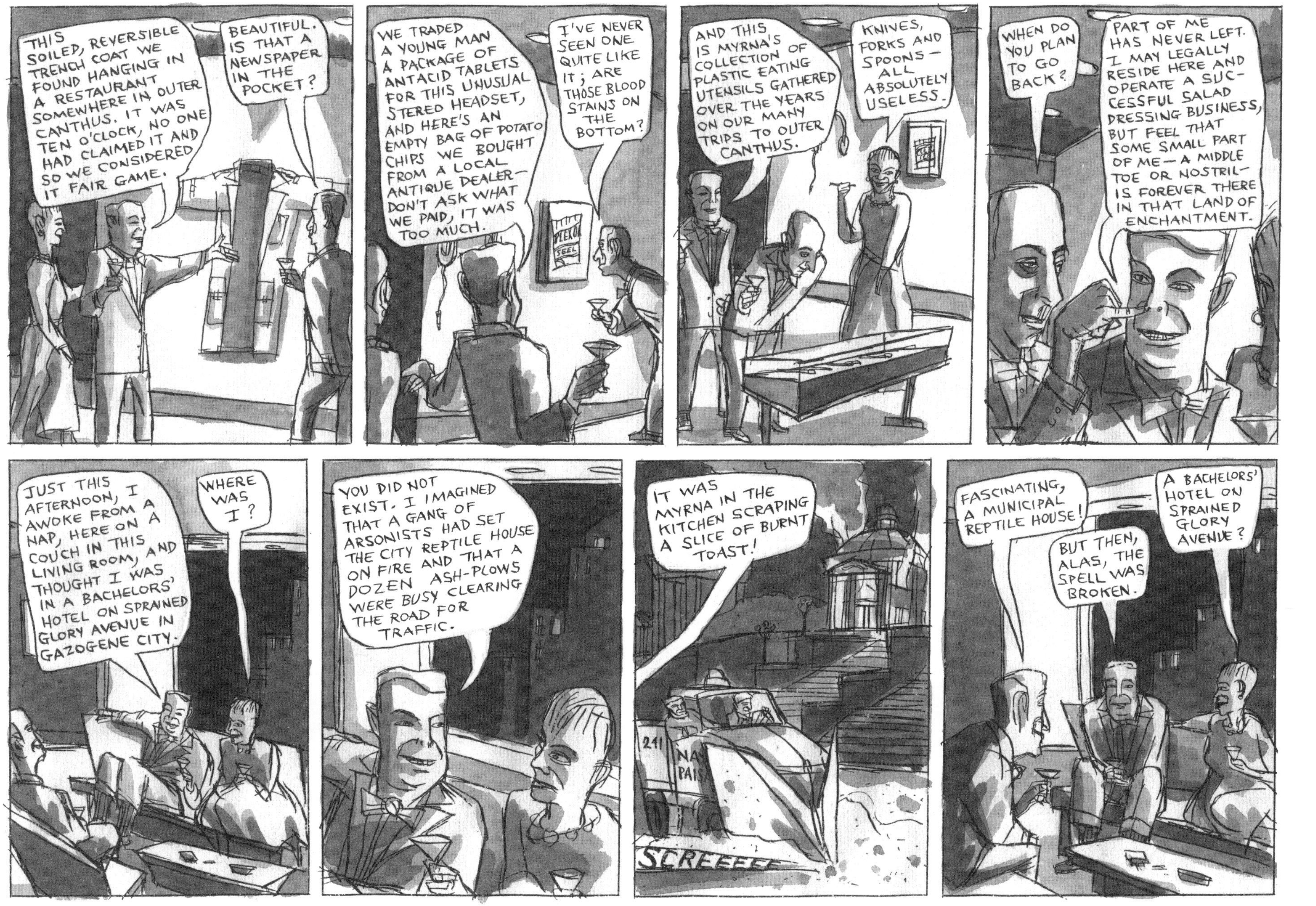
THIS SOILED, REVERSIBLE TRENCH COAT WE FOUND HANGING IN A RESTAURANT SOMEWHERE IN OUTER CANTHUS. IT WAS TEN O'CLOCK, NO ONE HAD CLAIMED IT AND SO WE CONSIDERED IT FAIR GAME.
BEAUTIFUL. IS THAT A NEWSPAPER IN THE POCKET?
WE TRADED A YOUNG MAN A PACKAGE OF ANTACID TABLETS FOR THIS UNUSUAL STEREO HEADSET, AND HERE'S AN EMPTY BAG OF POTATO CHIPS WE BOUGHT FROM A LOCAL ANTIQUE DEALER— DON'T ASK WHAT WE PAID, IT WAS TOO MUCH.
I'VE NEVER SEEN ONE QUITE LIKE IT; ARE THOSE BLOOD STAINS ON THE BOTTOM?
AND THIS IS MYRNA'S COLLECTION OF PLASTIC EATING UTENSILS GATHERED OVER THE YEARS ON OUR MANY TRIPS TO OUTER CANTHUS.
KNIVES, FORKS AND SPOONS— ALL ABSOLUTELY USELESS.
WHEN DO YOU PLAN TO GO BACK?
PART OF ME HAS NEVER LEFT. I MAY LEGALLY RESIDE HERE AND OPERATE A SUCCESSFUL SALAD DRESSING BUSINESS, BUT FEEL THAT SOME SMALL PART OF ME— A MIDDLE TOE OR NOSTRIL— IS FOREVER THERE IN THAT LAND OF ENCHANTMENT.
JUST THIS AFTERNOON, I AWOKE FROM A NAP, HERE ON A COUCH IN THIS LIVING ROOM, AND THOUGHT I WAS IN A BACHELORS' HOTEL ON SPRAINED GLORY AVENUE IN GAZOGENE CITY.
WHERE WAS I?
YOU DID NOT EXIST. I IMAGINED THAT A GANG OF ARSONISTS HAD SET THE CITY REPTILE HOUSE ON FIRE AND THAT A DOZEN ASH-PLOWS WERE BUSY CLEARING THE ROAD FOR TRAFFIC.
IT WAS MYRNA IN THE KITCHEN SCRAPING A SLICE OF BURNT TOAST!
241
SCREEEEEE
FASCINATING, A MUNICIPAL REPTILE HOUSE!
A BACHELORS' HOTEL ON SPRAINED GLORY AVENUE?
BUT THEN, ALAS, THE SPELL WAS BROKEN.

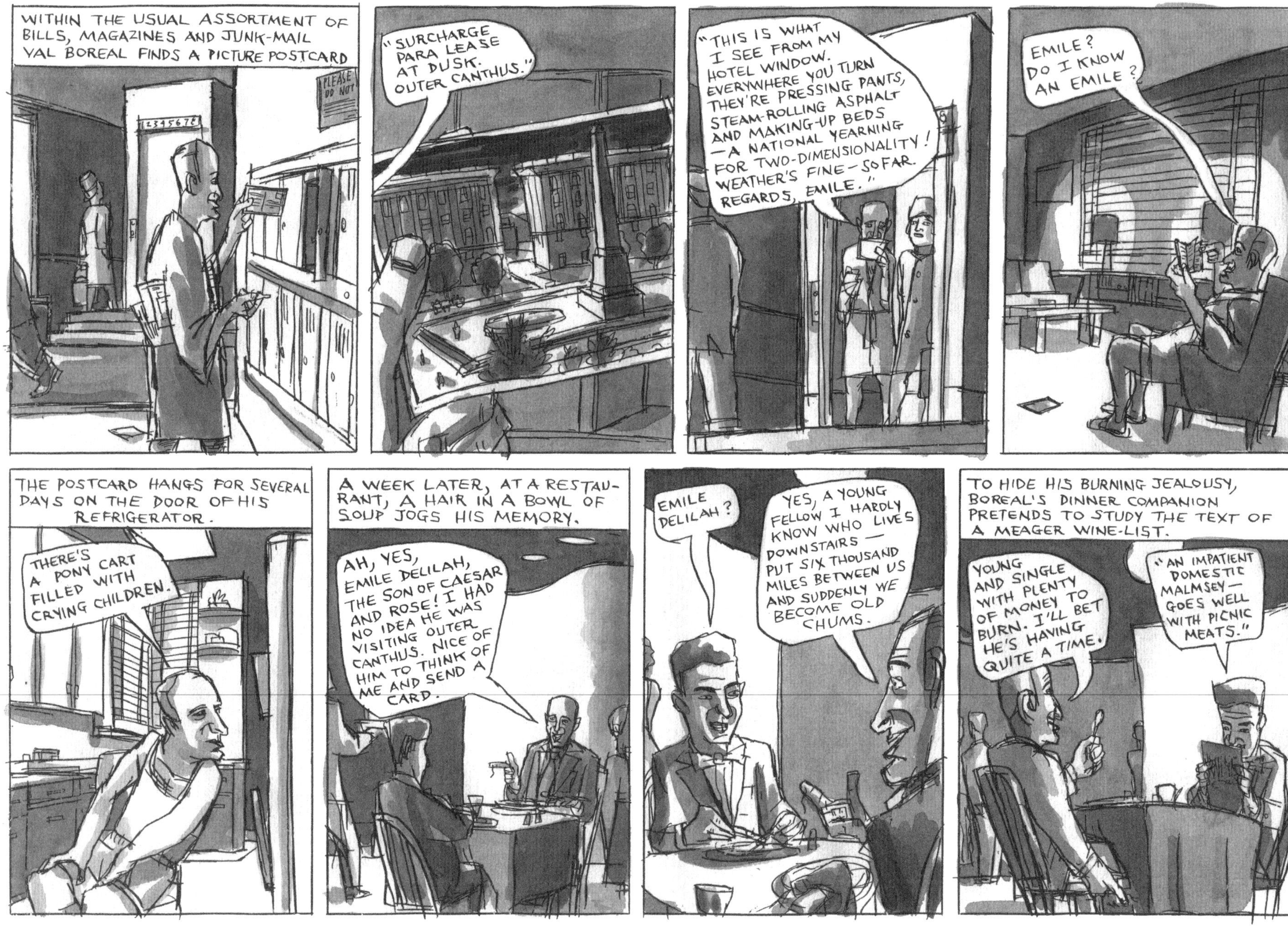
WITHIN THE USUAL ASSORTMENT OF BILLS, MAGAZINES AND JUNK-MAIL VAL BOREAL FINDS A PICTURE POSTCARD
PLEASE DO NOT
12345678
"SURCHARGE PARA LEASE AT DUSK. OUTER CANTHUS."
"THIS IS WHAT I SEE FROM MY HOTEL WINDOW. EVERYWHERE YOU TURN THEY'RE PRESSING PANTS, STEAM-ROLLING ASPHALT AND MAKING-UP BEDS —A NATIONAL YEARNING FOR TWO-DIMENSIONALITY! WEATHER'S FINE—SO FAR. REGARDS, EMILE."
EMILE? DO I KNOW AN EMILE?
THE POSTCARD HANGS FOR SEVERAL DAYS ON THE DOOR OF HIS REFRIGERATOR.
THERE'S A PONY CART FILLED WITH CRYING CHILDREN.
A WEEK LATER, AT A RESTAURANT, A HAIR IN A BOWL OF SOUP JOGS HIS MEMORY.
AH, YES, EMILE DELILAH, THE SON OF CAESAR AND ROSE! I HAD NO IDEA HE WAS VISITING OUTER CANTHUS. NICE OF HIM TO THINK OF ME AND SEND A CARD.
EMILE DELILAH?
YES, A YOUNG FELLOW I HARDLY KNOW WHO LIVES DOWNSTAIRS — PUT SIX THOUSAND MILES BETWEEN US AND SUDDENLY WE BECOME OLD CHUMS.
TO HIDE HIS BURNING JEALOUSY, BOREAL'S DINNER COMPANION PRETENDS TO STUDY THE TEXT OF A MEAGER WINE-LIST.
YOUNG AND SINGLE WITH PLENTY OF MONEY TO BURN. I'LL BET HE'S HAVING QUITE A TIME.
"AN IMPATIENT DOMESTIC MALMSEY—GOES WELL WITH PICNIC MEATS."

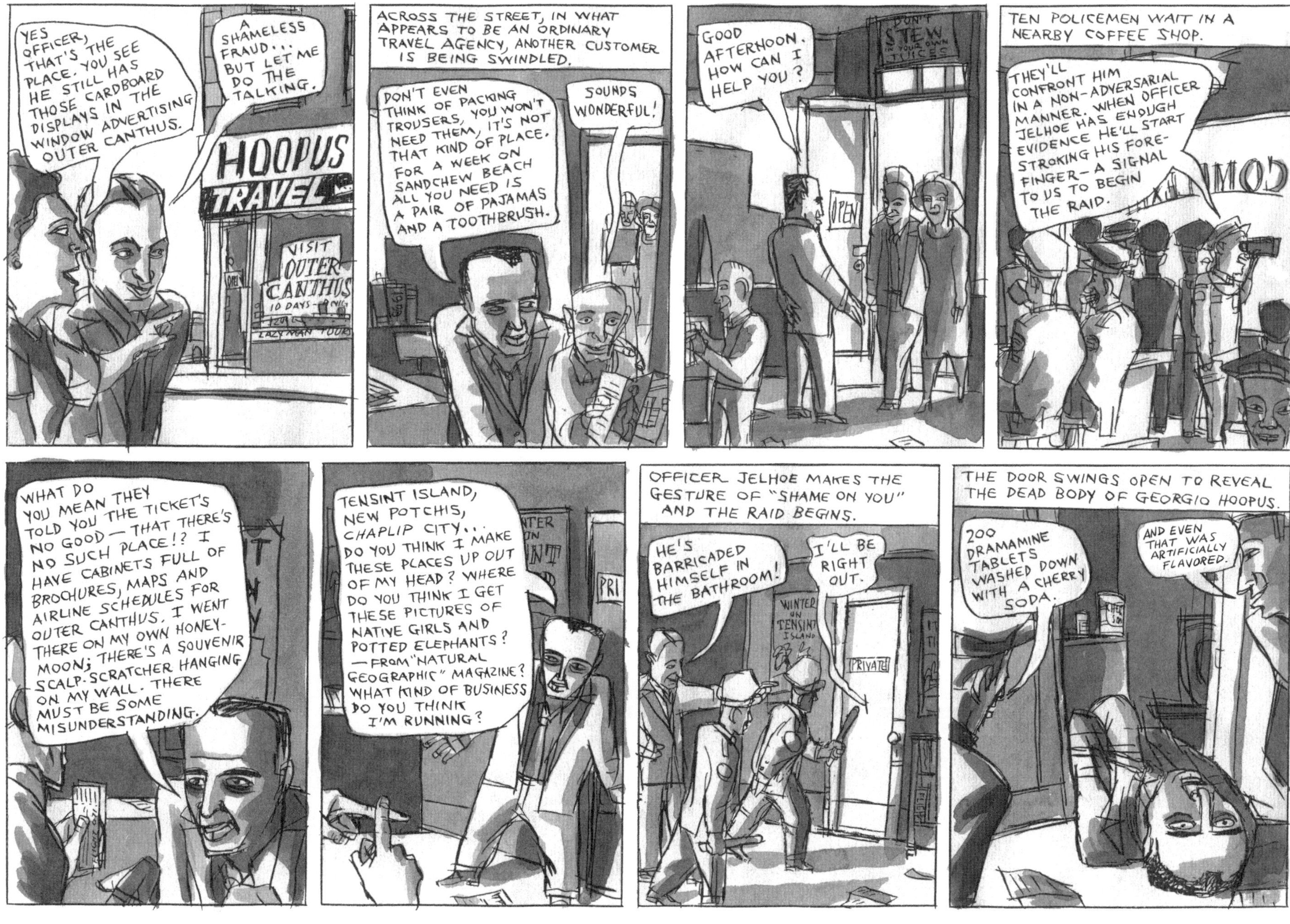
YES OFFICER, THAT'S THE PLACE. YOU SEE HE STILL HAS THOSE CARDBOARD DISPLAYS IN THE WINDOW ADVERTISING OUTER CANTHUS.
A SHAMELESS FRAUD... BUT LET ME DO THE TALKING.
HOOPUS TRAVEL
VISIT OUTER CANTHUS
10 DAYS
LAZYMAN TOURS
ACROSS THE STREET, IN WHAT APPEARS TO BE AN ORDINARY TRAVEL AGENCY, ANOTHER CUSTOMER IS BEING SWINDLED.
DON'T EVEN THINK OF PACKING TROUSERS, YOU WON'T NEED THEM, IT'S NOT THAT KIND OF PLACE. FOR A WEEK ON SANDCHEW BEACH ALL YOU NEED IS A PAIR OF PAJAMAS AND A TOOTHBRUSH.
SOUNDS WONDERFUL!
DON'T STEW IN YOUR OWN JUICES
GOOD AFTERNOON. HOW CAN I HELP YOU?
OPEN
TEN POLICEMEN WAIT IN A NEARBY COFFEE SHOP.
THEY'LL CONFRONT HIM IN A NON-ADVERSARIAL MANNER. WHEN OFFICER JELHOE HAS ENOUGH EVIDENCE HE'LL START STROKING HIS FORE-FINGER—A SIGNAL TO US TO BEGIN THE RAID.
WHAT DO YOU MEAN THEY TOLD YOU THE TICKET'S NO GOOD—THAT THERE'S NO SUCH PLACE!? I HAVE CABINETS FULL OF BROCHURES, MAPS AND AIRLINE SCHEDULES FOR OUTER CANTHUS. I WENT THERE ON MY OWN HONEY-MOON; THERE'S A SOUVENIR SCALP-SCRATCHER HANGING ON MY WALL. THERE MUST BE SOME MISUNDERSTANDING.
TENSINT ISLAND, NEW POTCHIS, CHAPLIP CITY... DO YOU THINK I MAKE THESE PLACES UP OUT OF MY HEAD? WHERE DO YOU THINK I GET THESE PICTURES OF NATIVE GIRLS AND POTTED ELEPHANTS? —FROM "NATURAL GEOGRAPHIC" MAGAZINE? WHAT KIND OF BUSINESS DO YOU THINK I'M RUNNING?
OFFICER JELHOE MAKES THE GESTURE OF "SHAME ON YOU" AND THE RAID BEGINS.
HE'S BARRICADED HIMSELF IN THE BATHROOM!
I'LL BE RIGHT OUT.
WINTER ON TENSINT ISLAND
PRIVATE
THE DOOR SWINGS OPEN TO REVEAL THE DEAD BODY OF GEORGIO HOOPUS.
200 DRAMAMINE TABLETS WASHED DOWN WITH A CHERRY SODA.
AND EVEN THAT WAS ARTIFICIALLY FLAVORED.

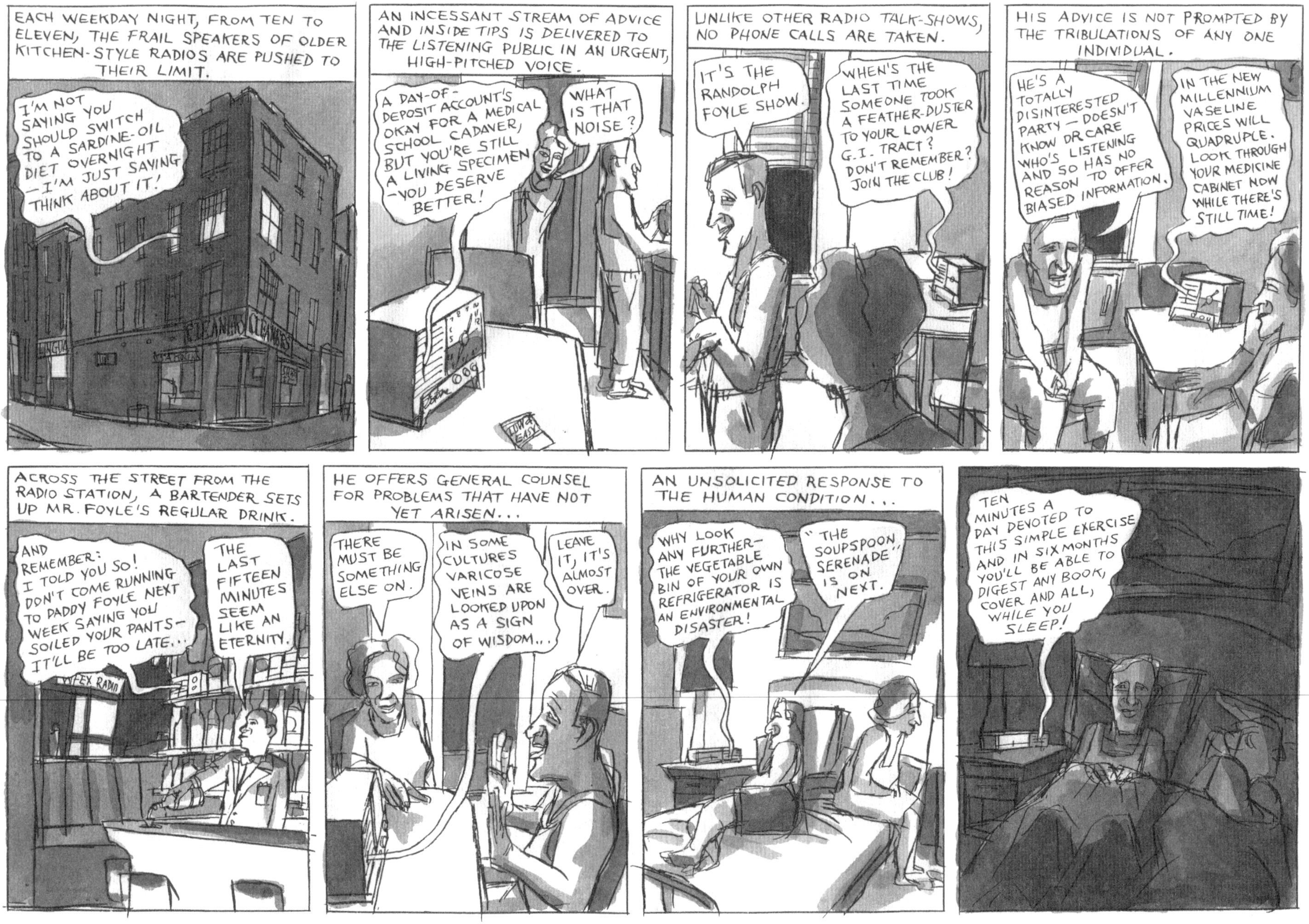
EACH WEEKDAY NIGHT, FROM TEN TO ELEVEN, THE FRAIL SPEAKERS OF OLDER KITCHEN-STYLE RADIOS ARE PUSHED TO THEIR LIMIT.
I'M NOT SAYING YOU SHOULD SWITCH TO A SARDINE-OIL DIET OVERNIGHT —I'M JUST SAYING THINK ABOUT IT!
AN INCESSANT STREAM OF ADVICE AND INSIDE TIPS IS DELIVERED TO THE LISTENING PUBLIC IN AN URGENT, HIGH-PITCHED VOICE.
A DAY-OF-DEPOSIT ACCOUNT'S OKAY FOR A MEDICAL SCHOOL CADAVER, BUT YOU'RE STILL A LIVING SPECIMEN —YOU DESERVE BETTER!
WHAT IS THAT NOISE?
UNLIKE OTHER RADIO TALK-SHOWS, NO PHONE CALLS ARE TAKEN.
IT'S THE RANDOLPH FOYLE SHOW.
WHEN'S THE LAST TIME SOMEONE TOOK A FEATHER-DUSTER TO YOUR LOWER G.I. TRACT? DON'T REMEMBER? JOIN THE CLUB!
HIS ADVICE IS NOT PROMPTED BY THE TRIBULATIONS OF ANY ONE INDIVIDUAL.
HE'S A TOTALLY DISINTERESTED PARTY — DOESN'T KNOW OR CARE WHO'S LISTENING AND SO HAS NO REASON TO OFFER BIASED INFORMATION.
IN THE NEW MILLENNIUM VASELINE PRICES WILL QUADRUPLE. LOOK THROUGH YOUR MEDICINE CABINET NOW WHILE THERE'S STILL TIME!
ACROSS THE STREET FROM THE RADIO STATION, A BARTENDER SETS UP MR. FOYLE'S REGULAR DRINK.
AND REMEMBER: I TOLD YOU SO! DON'T COME RUNNING TO DADDY FOYLE NEXT WEEK SAYING YOU SOILED YOUR PANTS— IT'LL BE TOO LATE...
THE LAST FIFTEEN MINUTES SEEM LIKE AN ETERNITY.
HE OFFERS GENERAL COUNSEL FOR PROBLEMS THAT HAVE NOT YET ARISEN...
THERE MUST BE SOMETHING ELSE ON.
IN SOME CULTURES VARICOSE VEINS ARE LOOKED UPON AS A SIGN OF WISDOM...
LEAVE IT, IT'S ALMOST OVER.
AN UNSOLICITED RESPONSE TO THE HUMAN CONDITION...
WHY LOOK ANY FURTHER— THE VEGETABLE BIN OF YOUR OWN REFRIGERATOR IS AN ENVIRONMENTAL DISASTER!
"THE SOUPSPOON SERENADE" IS ON NEXT.
TEN MINUTES A DAY DEVOTED TO THIS SIMPLE EXERCISE AND IN SIX MONTHS YOU'LL BE ABLE TO DIGEST ANY BOOK, COVER AND ALL, WHILE YOU SLEEP!

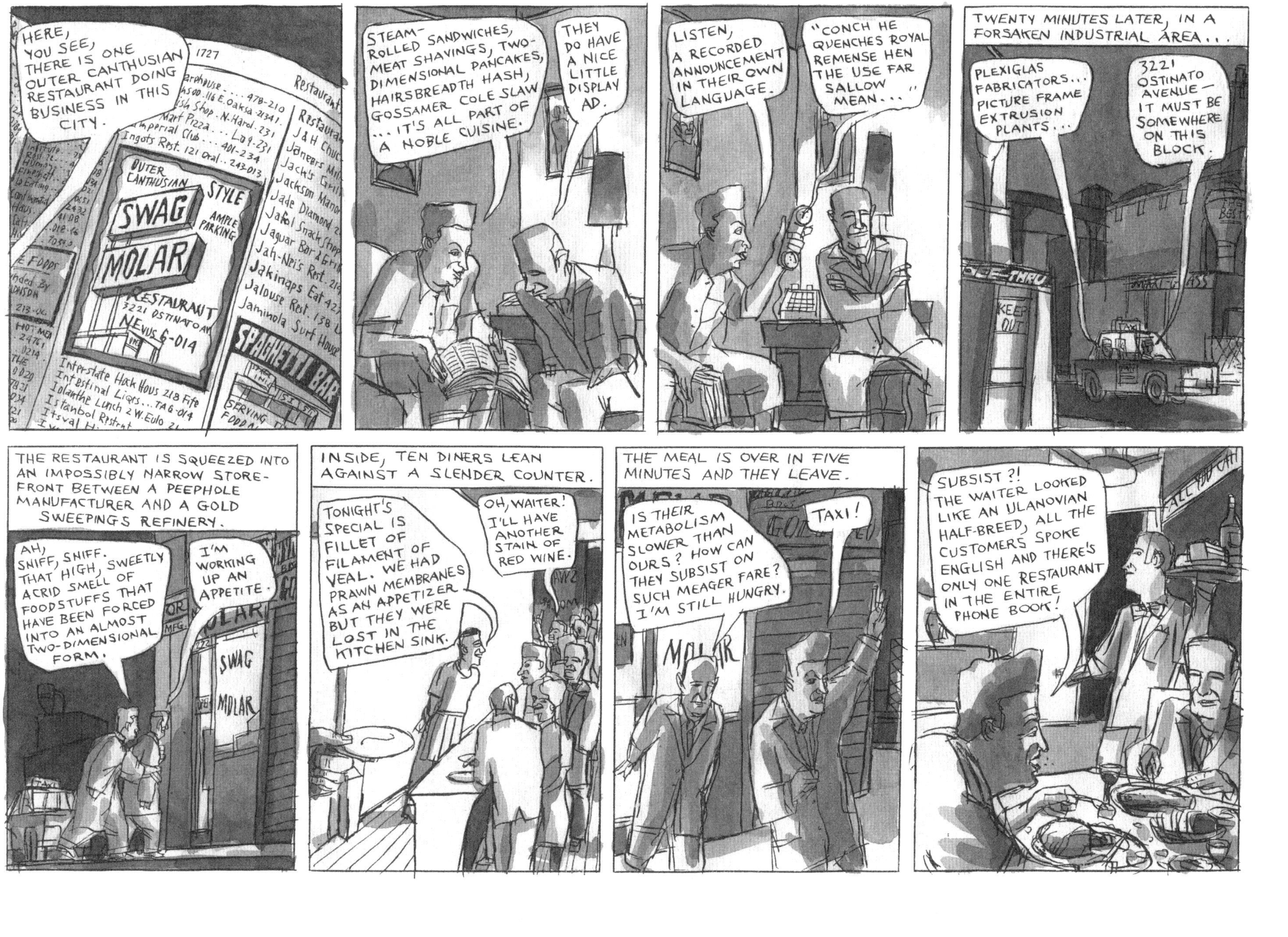
HERE, YOU SEE, THERE IS ONE OUTER CANTHUSIAN RESTAURANT DOING BUSINESS IN THIS CITY.
OUTER CANTHUSIAN STYLE
SWAG MOLAR
AMPLE PARKING
RESTAURANT 3221 OSTINATO AV NEVUS 6-014
SPAGHETTI BAR
STEAM-ROLLED SANDWICHES, TWO-MEAT SHAVINGS, TWO-DIMENSIONAL PANCAKES, HAIRSBREADTH HASH, GOSSAMER COLE SLAW ... IT'S ALL PART OF A NOBLE CUISINE.
THEY DO HAVE A NICE LITTLE DISPLAY AD.
LISTEN, A RECORDED ANNOUNCEMENT IN THEIR OWN LANGUAGE.
"CONCH HE QUENCHES ROYAL REMENSE HEN THE USE FAR SALLOW MEAN ..."
TWENTY MINUTES LATER, IN A FORSAKEN INDUSTRIAL AREA...
PLEXIGLAS FABRICATORS... PICTURE FRAME EXTRUSION PLANTS...
3221 OSTINATO AVENUE — IT MUST BE SOMEWHERE ON THIS BLOCK.
KEEP OUT
THE RESTAURANT IS SQUEEZED INTO AN IMPOSSIBLY NARROW STORE-FRONT BETWEEN A PEEPHOLE MANUFACTURER AND A GOLD SWEEPINGS REFINERY.
AH, SNIFF, SNIFF. THAT HIGH, SWEETLY ACRID SMELL OF FOODSTUFFS THAT HAVE BEEN FORCED INTO AN ALMOST TWO-DIMENSIONAL FORM.
I'M WORKING UP AN APPETITE.
SWAG MOLAR
INSIDE, TEN DINERS LEAN AGAINST A SLENDER COUNTER.
TONIGHT'S SPECIAL IS FILLET OF FILAMENT OF VEAL. WE HAD PRAWN MEMBRANES AS AN APPETIZER BUT THEY WERE LOST IN THE KITCHEN SINK.
OH, WAITER! I'LL HAVE ANOTHER STAIN OF RED WINE.
THE MEAL IS OVER IN FIVE MINUTES AND THEY LEAVE.
IS THEIR METABOLISM SLOWER THAN OURS? HOW CAN THEY SUBSIST ON SUCH MEAGER FARE? I'M STILL HUNGRY.
TAXI!
MOLAR
SUBSIST?! THE WAITER LOOKED LIKE AN ULANOVIAN HALF-BREED, ALL THE CUSTOMERS SPOKE ENGLISH AND THERE'S ONLY ONE RESTAURANT IN THE ENTIRE PHONE BOOK!

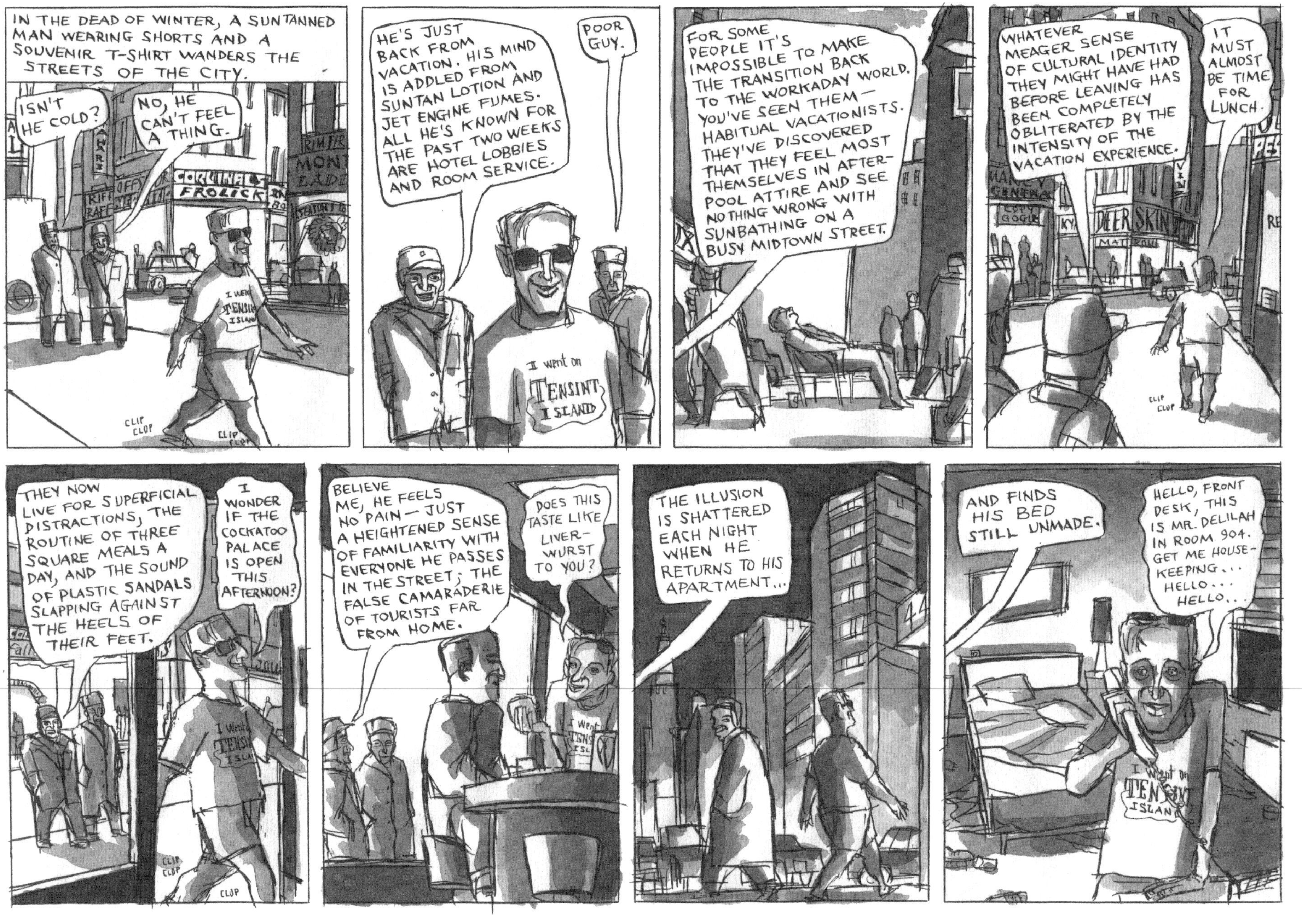
IN THE DEAD OF WINTER, A SUNTANNED MAN WEARING SHORTS AND A SOUVENIR T-SHIRT WANDERS THE STREETS OF THE CITY.
ISN'T HE COLD?
NO, HE CAN'T FEEL A THING.
FROLICK
CLIP CLOP
CLIP CLOP
HE'S JUST BACK FROM VACATION. HIS MIND IS ADDLED FROM SUNTAN LOTION AND JET ENGINE FUMES. ALL HE'S KNOWN FOR THE PAST TWO WEEKS ARE HOTEL LOBBIES AND ROOM SERVICE.
POOR GUY.
I went on TENSINT ISLAND
FOR SOME PEOPLE IT'S IMPOSSIBLE TO MAKE THE TRANSITION BACK TO THE WORKADAY WORLD. YOU'VE SEEN THEM— HABITUAL VACATIONISTS. THEY'VE DISCOVERED THAT THEY FEEL MOST THEMSELVES IN AFTER-POOL ATTIRE AND SEE NOTHING WRONG WITH SUNBATHING ON A BUSY MIDTOWN STREET.
WHATEVER MEAGER SENSE OF CULTURAL IDENTITY THEY MIGHT HAVE HAD BEFORE LEAVING HAS BEEN COMPLETELY OBLITERATED BY THE INTENSITY OF THE VACATION EXPERIENCE.
IT MUST ALMOST BE TIME FOR LUNCH.
DEER SKIN
CLIP CLOP
THEY NOW LIVE FOR SUPERFICIAL DISTRACTIONS, THE ROUTINE OF THREE SQUARE MEALS A DAY, AND THE SOUND OF PLASTIC SANDALS SLAPPING AGAINST THE HEELS OF THEIR FEET.
I WONDER IF THE COCKATOO PALACE IS OPEN THIS AFTERNOON?
CLIP CLOP
CLOP
BELIEVE ME, HE FEELS NO PAIN— JUST A HEIGHTENED SENSE OF FAMILIARITY WITH EVERYONE HE PASSES IN THE STREET; THE FALSE CAMARADERIE OF TOURISTS FAR FROM HOME.
DOES THIS TASTE LIKE LIVER-WURST TO YOU?
THE ILLUSION IS SHATTERED EACH NIGHT WHEN HE RETURNS TO HIS APARTMENT...
AND FINDS HIS BED STILL UNMADE.
HELLO, FRONT DESK, THIS IS MR. DELILAH IN ROOM 904. GET ME HOUSE-KEEPING... HELLO... HELLO...

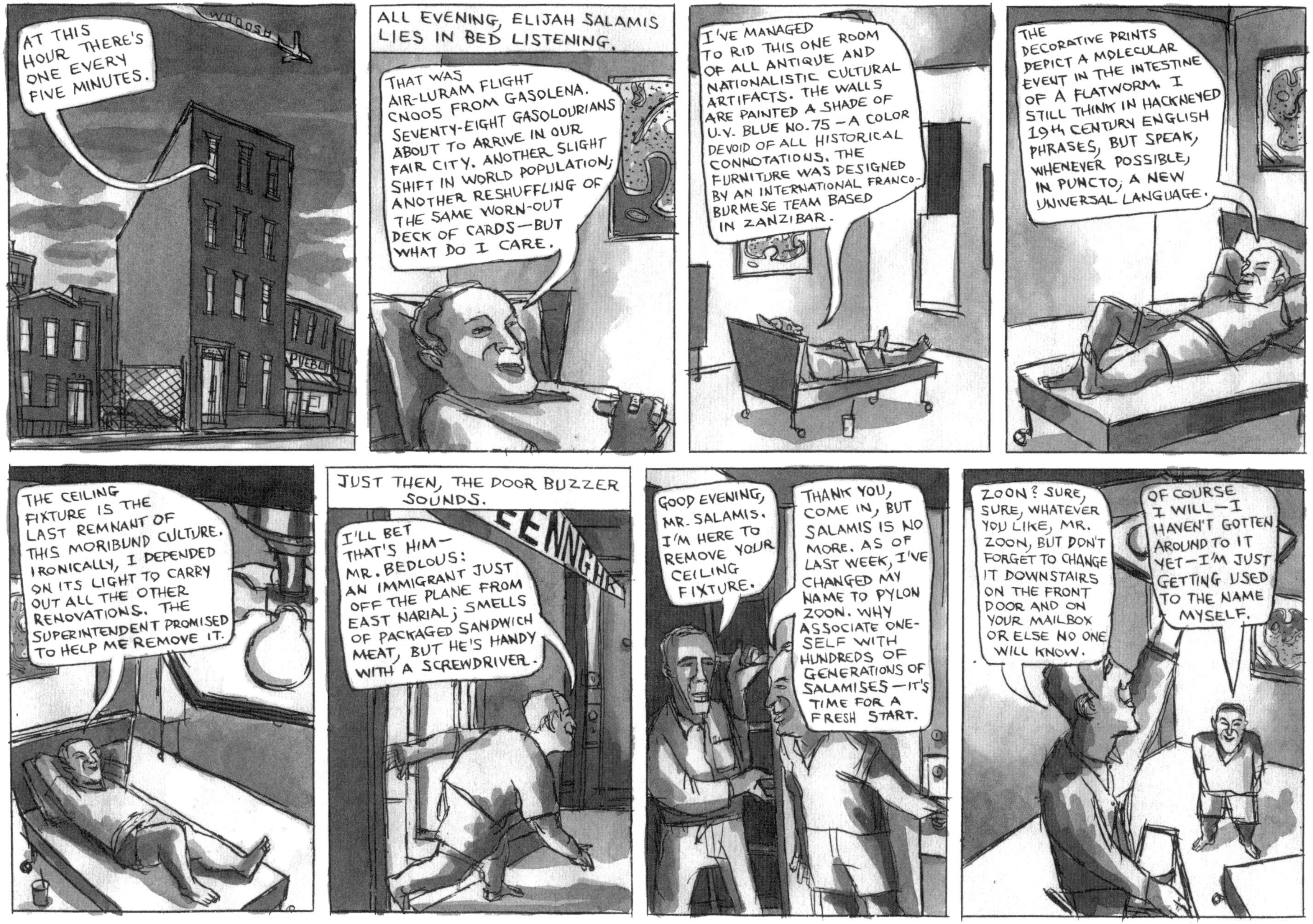
WOOOSH
AT THIS HOUR THERE'S ONE EVERY FIVE MINUTES.
PUEBLO
ALL EVENING, ELIJAH SALAMIS LIES IN BED LISTENING.
THAT WAS AIR-LURAM FLIGHT CN005 FROM GASOLENA. SEVENTY-EIGHT GASOLOURIANS ABOUT TO ARRIVE IN OUR FAIR CITY. ANOTHER SLIGHT SHIFT IN WORLD POPULATION; ANOTHER RESHUFFLING OF THE SAME WORN-OUT DECK OF CARDS—BUT WHAT DO I CARE.
I'VE MANAGED TO RID THIS ONE ROOM OF ALL ANTIQUE AND NATIONALISTIC CULTURAL ARTIFACTS. THE WALLS ARE PAINTED A SHADE OF U.V. BLUE NO. 75—A COLOR DEVOID OF ALL HISTORICAL CONNOTATIONS. THE FURNITURE WAS DESIGNED BY AN INTERNATIONAL FRANCO-BURMESE TEAM BASED IN ZANZIBAR.
THE DECORATIVE PRINTS DEPICT A MOLECULAR EVENT IN THE INTESTINE OF A FLATWORM. I STILL THINK IN HACKNEYED 19th CENTURY ENGLISH PHRASES, BUT SPEAK, WHENEVER POSSIBLE, IN PUNCTO; A NEW UNIVERSAL LANGUAGE.
THE CEILING FIXTURE IS THE LAST REMNANT OF THIS MORIBUND CULTURE. IRONICALLY, I DEPENDED ON ITS LIGHT TO CARRY OUT ALL THE OTHER RENOVATIONS. THE SUPERINTENDENT PROMISED TO HELP ME REMOVE IT.
JUST THEN, THE DOOR BUZZER SOUNDS.
EENNGH
I'LL BET THAT'S HIM—MR. BEDLOUS: AN IMMIGRANT JUST OFF THE PLANE FROM EAST NARIAL; SMELLS OF PACKAGED SANDWICH MEAT, BUT HE'S HANDY WITH A SCREWDRIVER.
GOOD EVENING, MR. SALAMIS. I'M HERE TO REMOVE YOUR CEILING FIXTURE.
THANK YOU, COME IN, BUT SALAMIS IS NO MORE. AS OF LAST WEEK, I'VE CHANGED MY NAME TO PYLON ZOON. WHY ASSOCIATE ONESELF WITH HUNDREDS OF GENERATIONS OF SALAMISES—IT'S TIME FOR A FRESH START.
ZOON? SURE, SURE, WHATEVER YOU LIKE, MR. ZOON, BUT DON'T FORGET TO CHANGE IT DOWNSTAIRS ON THE FRONT DOOR AND ON YOUR MAILBOX OR ELSE NO ONE WILL KNOW.
OF COURSE I WILL—I HAVEN'T GOTTEN AROUND TO IT YET—I'M JUST GETTING USED TO THE NAME MYSELF.

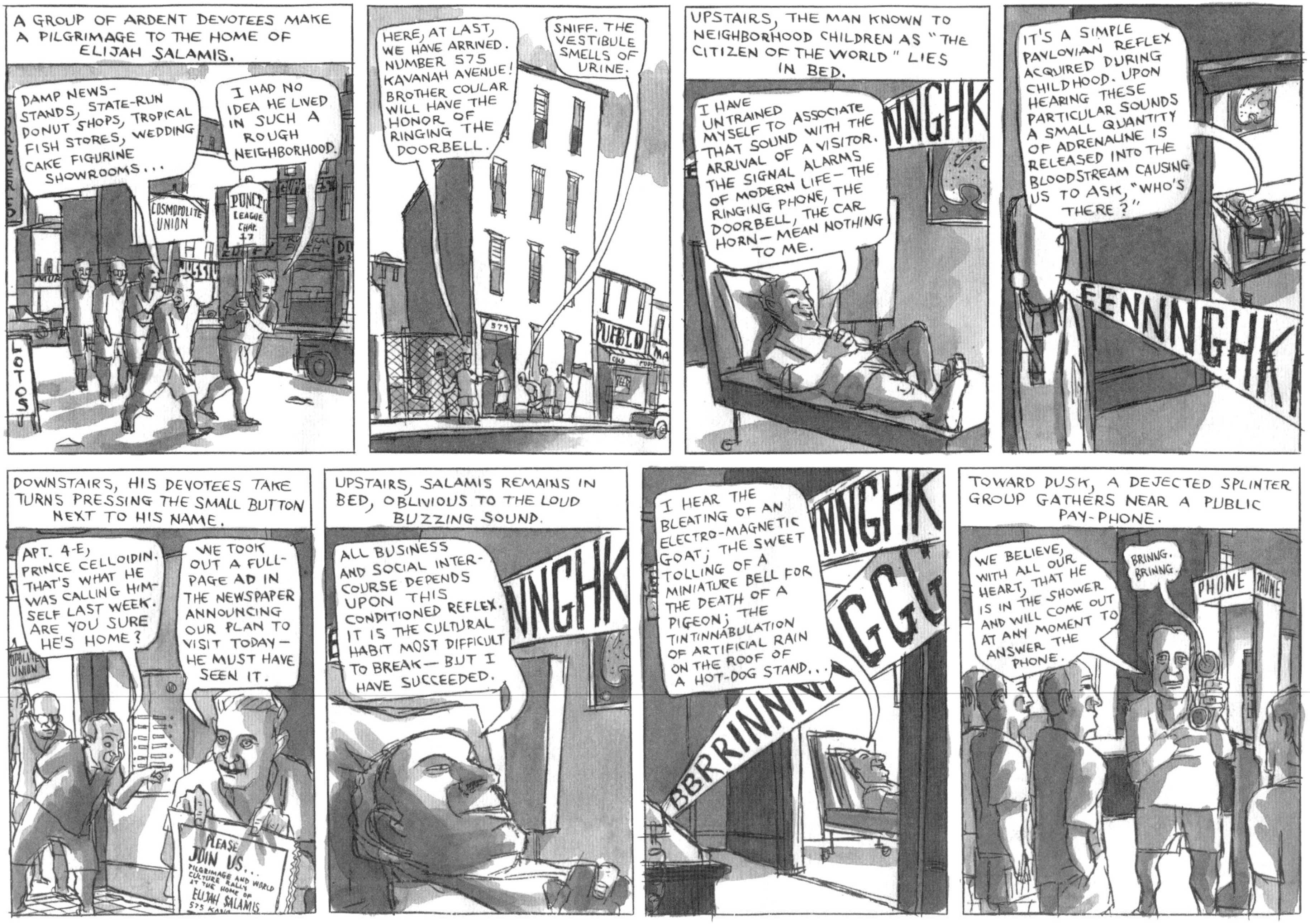
A GROUP OF ARDENT DEVOTEES MAKE A PILGRIMAGE TO THE HOME OF ELIJAH SALAMIS.
DAMP NEWS-STANDS, STATE-RUN DONUT SHOPS, TROPICAL FISH STORES, WEDDING CAKE FIGURINE SHOWROOMS...
I HAD NO IDEA HE LIVED IN SUCH A ROUGH NEIGHBORHOOD.
COSMOPOLITE UNION
PUNCT LEAGUE CHAP. 17
LOTOS
HERE, AT LAST, WE HAVE ARRIVED. NUMBER 575 KAVANAH AVENUE! BROTHER COULAR WILL HAVE THE HONOR OF RINGING THE DOORBELL.
SNIFF. THE VESTIBULE SMELLS OF URINE.
575
PUEBLO
UPSTAIRS, THE MAN KNOWN TO NEIGHBORHOOD CHILDREN AS "THE CITIZEN OF THE WORLD" LIES IN BED.
I HAVE UNTRAINED MYSELF TO ASSOCIATE THAT SOUND WITH THE ARRIVAL OF A VISITOR. THE SIGNAL ALARMS OF MODERN LIFE— THE RINGING PHONE, THE DOORBELL, THE CAR HORN— MEAN NOTHING TO ME.
NNGHK
IT'S A SIMPLE PAVLOVIAN REFLEX ACQUIRED DURING CHILDHOOD. UPON HEARING THESE PARTICULAR SOUNDS A SMALL QUANTITY OF ADRENALINE IS RELEASED INTO THE BLOODSTREAM CAUSING US TO ASK, "WHO'S THERE?"
EENNNGHK
DOWNSTAIRS, HIS DEVOTEES TAKE TURNS PRESSING THE SMALL BUTTON NEXT TO HIS NAME.
APT. 4-E, PRINCE CELLOIDIN. THAT'S WHAT HE WAS CALLING HIMSELF LAST WEEK. ARE YOU SURE HE'S HOME?
WE TOOK OUT A FULL-PAGE AD IN THE NEWSPAPER ANNOUNCING OUR PLAN TO VISIT TODAY— HE MUST HAVE SEEN IT.
PLEASE JOIN US... PILGRIMAGE AND WORLD CULTURE RALLY AT THE HOME OF ELIJAH SALAMIS
UPSTAIRS, SALAMIS REMAINS IN BED, OBLIVIOUS TO THE LOUD BUZZING SOUND.
ALL BUSINESS AND SOCIAL INTER-COURSE DEPENDS UPON THIS CONDITIONED REFLEX. IT IS THE CULTURAL HABIT MOST DIFFICULT TO BREAK— BUT I HAVE SUCCEEDED.
NNGHK
I HEAR THE BLEATING OF AN ELECTRO-MAGNETIC GOAT; THE SWEET TOLLING OF A MINIATURE BELL FOR THE DEATH OF A PIGEON; THE TINTINNABULATION OF ARTIFICIAL RAIN ON THE ROOF OF A HOT-DOG STAND...
NNGHK
GGG
BBRRINNNN
TOWARD DUSK, A DEJECTED SPLINTER GROUP GATHERS NEAR A PUBLIC PAY-PHONE.
WE BELIEVE, WITH ALL OUR HEART, THAT HE IS IN THE SHOWER AND WILL COME OUT AT ANY MOMENT TO ANSWER THE PHONE.
BRINNG. BRINNG.
PHONE
PHONE

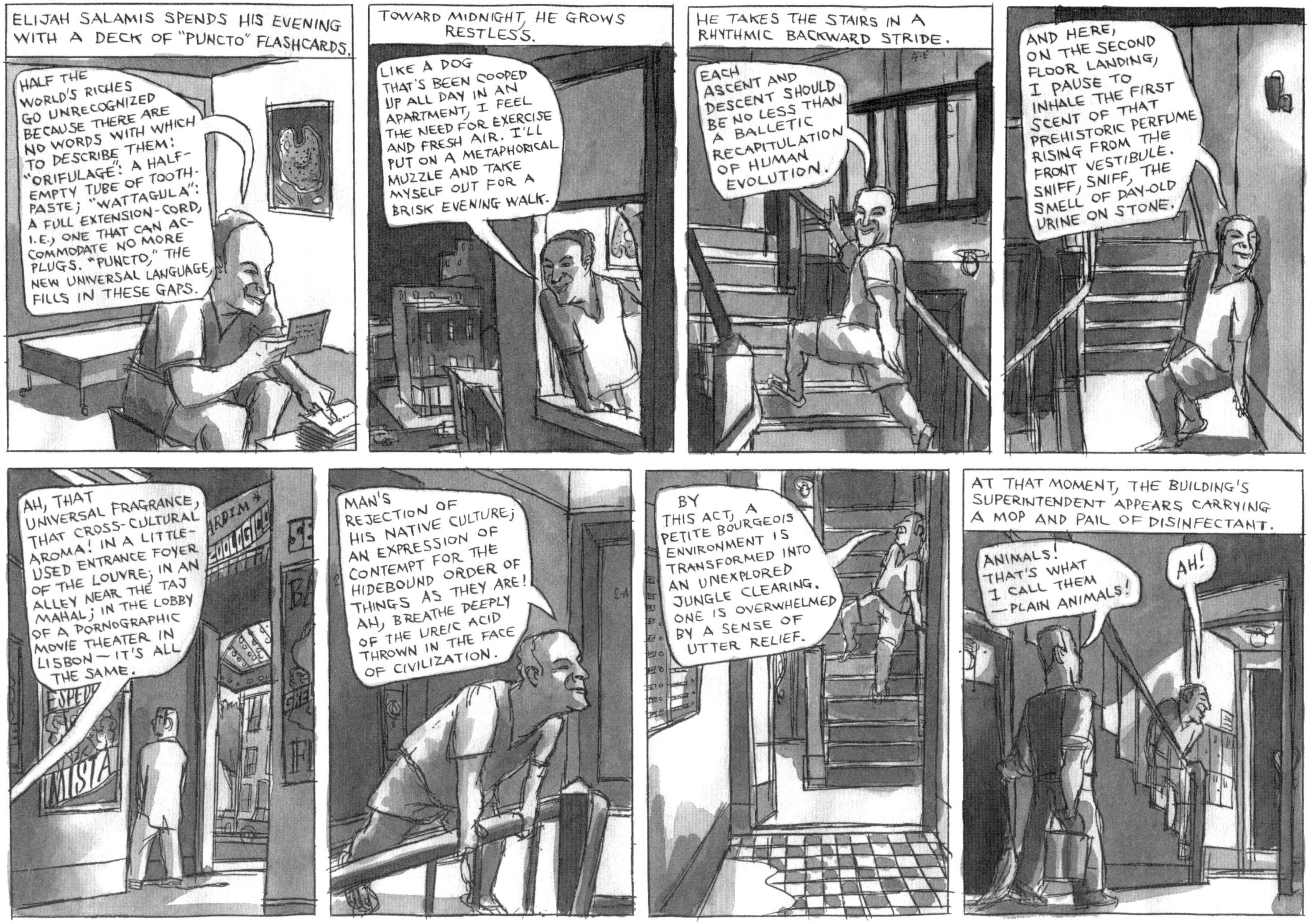
ELIJAH SALAMIS SPENDS HIS EVENING WITH A DECK OF "PUNCTO" FLASHCARDS.
HALF THE WORLD'S RICHES GO UNRECOGNIZED BECAUSE THERE ARE NO WORDS WITH WHICH TO DESCRIBE THEM: "ORIFULAGE": A HALF-EMPTY TUBE OF TOOTH-PASTE; "WATTAGULA": A FULL EXTENSION-CORD, I.E., ONE THAT CAN AC-COMMODATE NO MORE PLUGS. "PUNCTO," THE NEW UNIVERSAL LANGUAGE, FILLS IN THESE GAPS.
TOWARD MIDNIGHT, HE GROWS RESTLESS.
LIKE A DOG THAT'S BEEN COOPED UP ALL DAY IN AN APARTMENT, I FEEL THE NEED FOR EXERCISE AND FRESH AIR. I'LL PUT ON A METAPHORICAL MUZZLE AND TAKE MYSELF OUT FOR A BRISK EVENING WALK.
HE TAKES THE STAIRS IN A RHYTHMIC BACKWARD STRIDE.
EACH ASCENT AND DESCENT SHOULD BE NO LESS THAN A BALLETIC RECAPITULATION OF HUMAN EVOLUTION.
AND HERE, ON THE SECOND FLOOR LANDING, I PAUSE TO INHALE THE FIRST SCENT OF THAT PREHISTORIC PERFUME RISING FROM THE FRONT VESTIBULE. SNIFF, SNIFF, THE SMELL OF DAY-OLD URINE ON STONE.
AH, THAT UNIVERSAL FRAGRANCE, THAT CROSS-CULTURAL AROMA! IN A LITTLE-USED ENTRANCE FOYER OF THE LOUVRE; IN AN ALLEY NEAR THE TAJ MAHAL; IN THE LOBBY OF A PORNOGRAPHIC MOVIE THEATER IN LISBON—IT'S ALL THE SAME.
MAN'S REJECTION OF HIS NATIVE CULTURE; AN EXPRESSION OF CONTEMPT FOR THE HIDEBOUND ORDER OF THINGS AS THEY ARE! AH, BREATHE DEEPLY OF THE URIC ACID THROWN IN THE FACE OF CIVILIZATION.
BY THIS ACT, A PETITE BOURGEOIS ENVIRONMENT IS TRANSFORMED INTO AN UNEXPLORED JUNGLE CLEARING. ONE IS OVERWHELMED BY A SENSE OF UTTER RELIEF.
AT THAT MOMENT, THE BUILDING'S SUPERINTENDENT APPEARS CARRYING A MOP AND PAIL OF DISINFECTANT.
ANIMALS! THAT'S WHAT I CALL THEM—PLAIN ANIMALS!
AH!

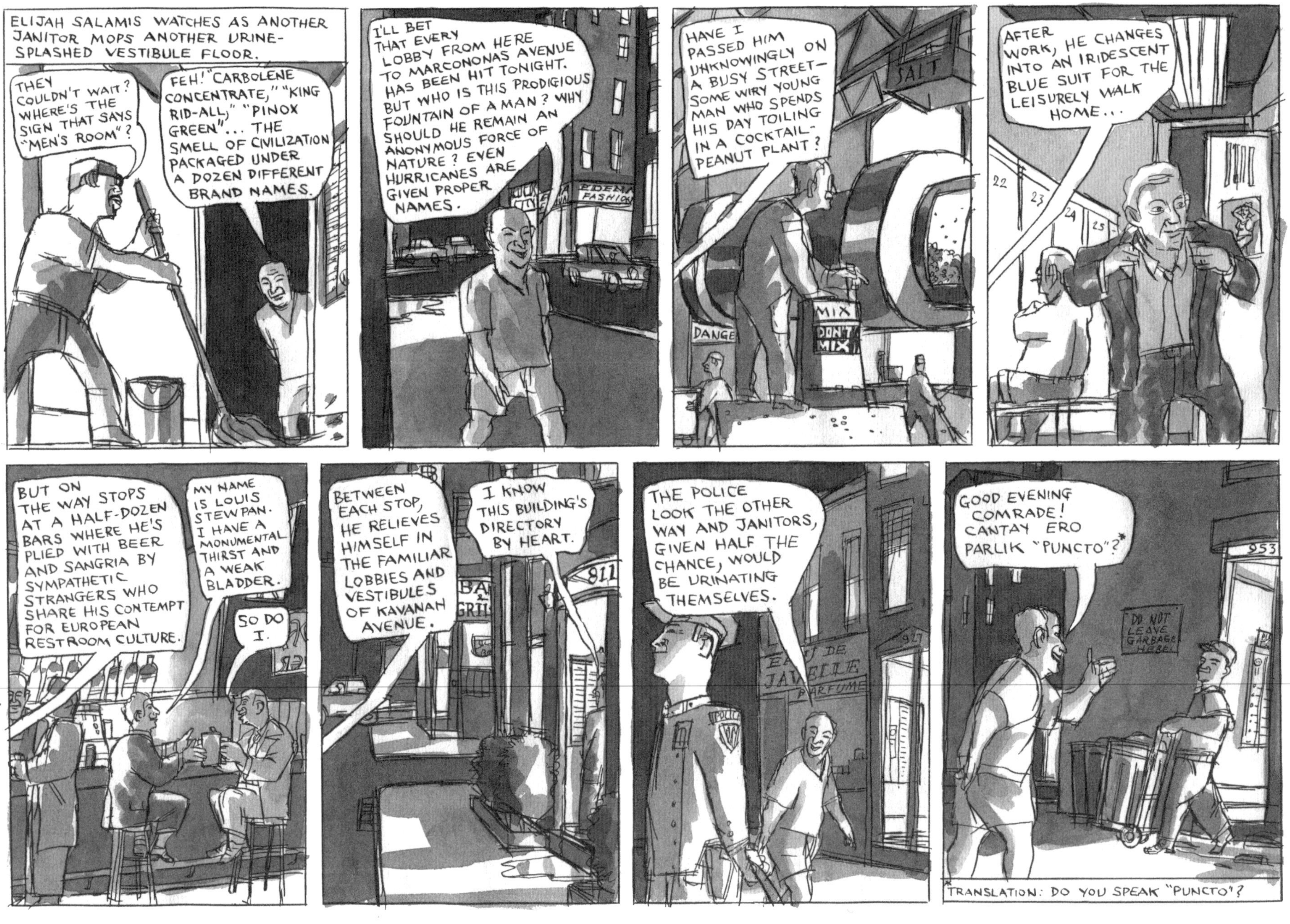
ELIJAH SALAMIS WATCHES AS ANOTHER JANITOR MOPS ANOTHER URINE-SPLASHED VESTIBULE FLOOR.
THEY COULDN'T WAIT? WHERE'S THE SIGN THAT SAYS "MEN'S ROOM"?
FEH! "CARBOLENE CONCENTRATE," "KING RID-ALL," "PINOX GREEN"... THE SMELL OF CIVILIZATION PACKAGED UNDER A DOZEN DIFFERENT BRAND NAMES.
I'LL BET THAT EVERY LOBBY FROM HERE TO MARCONONAS AVENUE HAS BEEN HIT TONIGHT. BUT WHO IS THIS PRODIGIOUS FOUNTAIN OF A MAN? WHY SHOULD HE REMAIN AN ANONYMOUS FORCE OF NATURE? EVEN HURRICANES ARE GIVEN PROPER NAMES.
HAVE I PASSED HIM UNKNOWINGLY ON A BUSY STREET— SOME WIRY YOUNG MAN WHO SPENDS HIS DAY TOILING IN A COCKTAIL-PEANUT PLANT?
SALT
MIX
DON'T MIX
AFTER WORK, HE CHANGES INTO AN IRIDESCENT BLUE SUIT FOR THE LEISURELY WALK HOME...
BUT ON THE WAY STOPS AT A HALF-DOZEN BARS WHERE HE'S PLIED WITH BEER AND SANGRIA BY SYMPATHETIC STRANGERS WHO SHARE HIS CONTEMPT FOR EUROPEAN RESTROOM CULTURE.
MY NAME IS LOUIS STEWPAN. I HAVE A MONUMENTAL THIRST AND A WEAK BLADDER.
SO DO I.
BETWEEN EACH STOP, HE RELIEVES HIMSELF IN THE FAMILIAR LOBBIES AND VESTIBULES OF KAVANAH AVENUE.
I KNOW THIS BUILDING'S DIRECTORY BY HEART.
811
THE POLICE LOOK THE OTHER WAY AND JANITORS, GIVEN HALF THE CHANCE, WOULD BE URINATING THEMSELVES.
927
JAVELLE
PARFUME
GOOD EVENING COMRADE! CANTAY ERO PARLIK "PUNCTO"?*
953
DO NOT LEAVE GARBAGE HERE!
*TRANSLATION: DO YOU SPEAK "PUNCTO"?

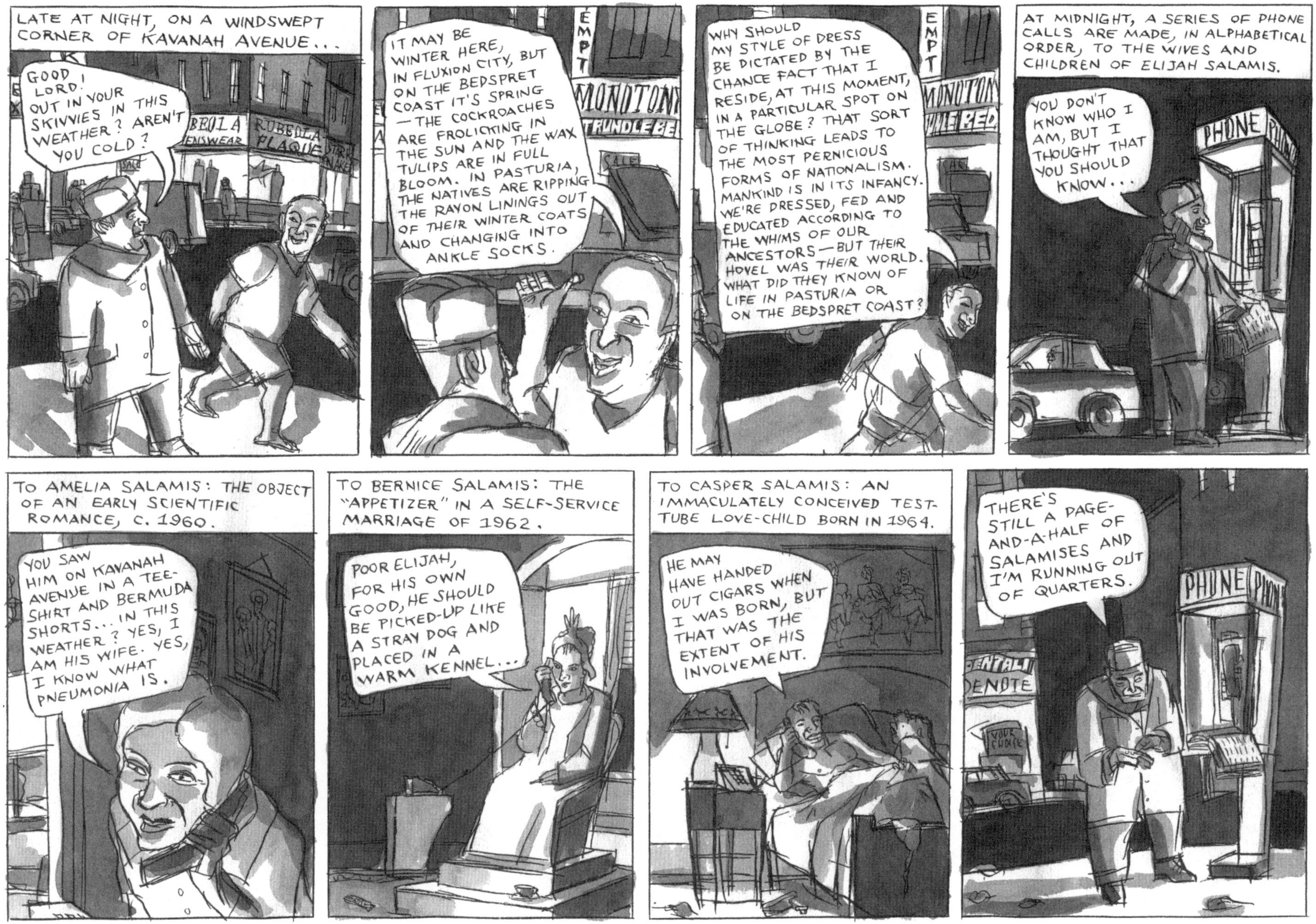
LATE AT NIGHT, ON A WINDSWEPT CORNER OF KAVANAH AVENUE...
GOOD LORD! OUT IN YOUR SKIVVIES IN THIS WEATHER? AREN'T YOU COLD?
IT MAY BE WINTER HERE, BUT IN FLUXION CITY, ON THE BEDSPRET COAST IT'S SPRING—THE COCKROACHES ARE FROLICKING IN THE SUN AND THE WAX TULIPS ARE IN FULL BLOOM. IN PASTURIA, THE NATIVES ARE RIPPING THE RAYON LININGS OUT OF THEIR WINTER COATS AND CHANGING INTO ANKLE SOCKS.
WHY SHOULD MY STYLE OF DRESS BE DICTATED BY THE CHANCE FACT THAT I RESIDE, AT THIS MOMENT, IN A PARTICULAR SPOT ON THE GLOBE? THAT SORT OF THINKING LEADS TO THE MOST PERNICIOUS FORMS OF NATIONALISM. MANKIND IS IN ITS INFANCY. WE'RE DRESSED, FED AND EDUCATED ACCORDING TO THE WHIMS OF OUR ANCESTORS—BUT THEIR HOVEL WAS THEIR WORLD. WHAT DID THEY KNOW OF LIFE IN PASTURIA OR ON THE BEDSPRET COAST?
AT MIDNIGHT, A SERIES OF PHONE CALLS ARE MADE, IN ALPHABETICAL ORDER, TO THE WIVES AND CHILDREN OF ELIJAH SALAMIS.
YOU DON'T KNOW WHO I AM, BUT I THOUGHT THAT YOU SHOULD KNOW...
PHONE
TO AMELIA SALAMIS: THE OBJECT OF AN EARLY SCIENTIFIC ROMANCE, C. 1960.
YOU SAW HIM ON KAVANAH AVENUE IN A TEE-SHIRT AND BERMUDA SHORTS... IN THIS WEATHER? YES, I AM HIS WIFE. YES, I KNOW WHAT PNEUMONIA IS.
TO BERNICE SALAMIS: THE "APPETIZER" IN A SELF-SERVICE MARRIAGE OF 1962.
POOR ELIJAH, FOR HIS OWN GOOD, HE SHOULD BE PICKED-UP LIKE A STRAY DOG AND PLACED IN A WARM KENNEL...
TO CASPER SALAMIS: AN IMMACULATELY CONCEIVED TEST-TUBE LOVE-CHILD BORN IN 1964.
HE MAY HAVE HANDED OUT CIGARS WHEN I WAS BORN, BUT THAT WAS THE EXTENT OF HIS INVOLVEMENT.
THERE'S STILL A PAGE-AND-A-HALF OF SALAMISES AND I'M RUNNING OUT OF QUARTERS.
PHONE

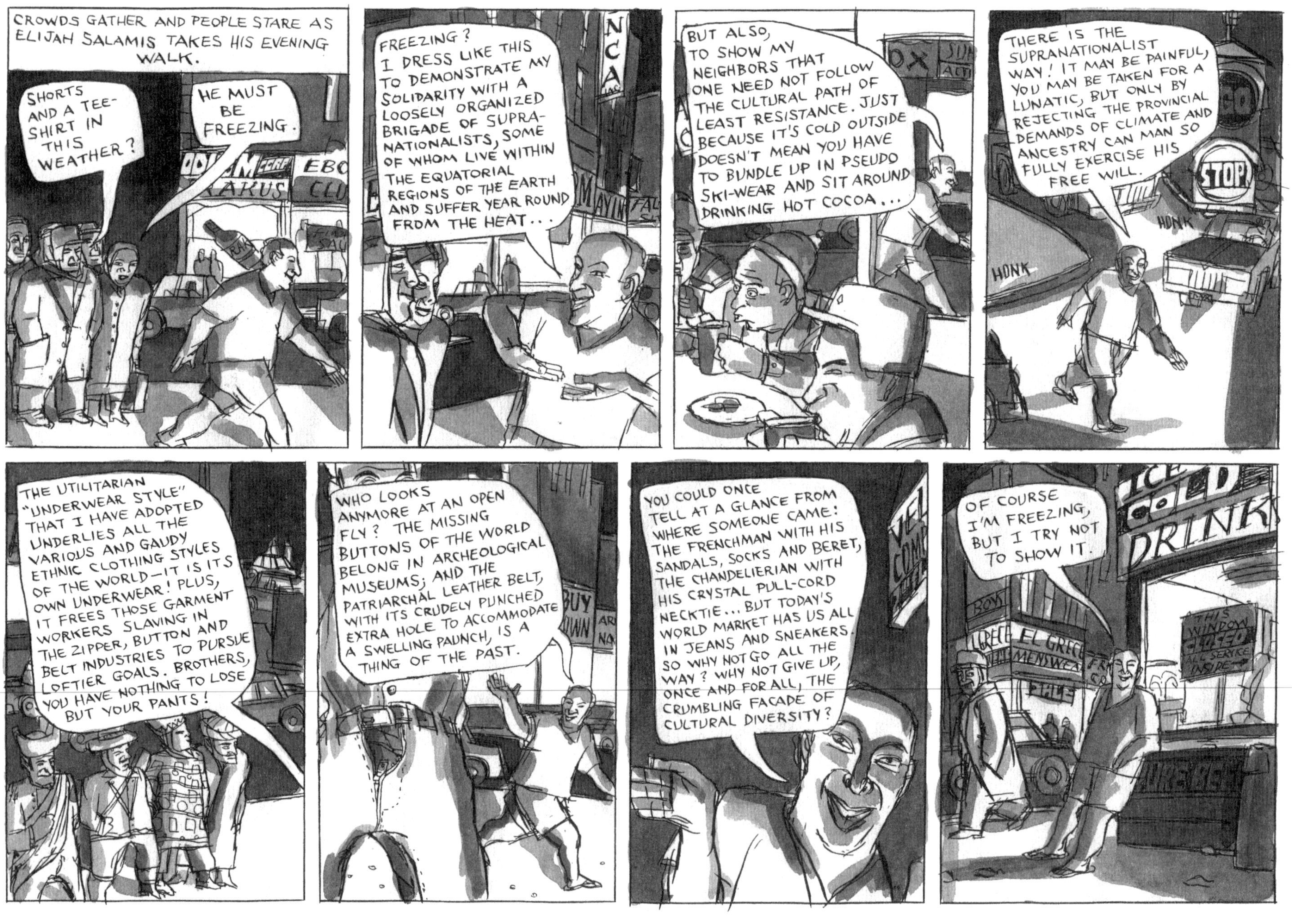
CROWDS GATHER AND PEOPLE STARE AS ELIJAH SALAMIS TAKES HIS EVENING WALK.
SHORTS AND A TEE-SHIRT IN THIS WEATHER?
HE MUST BE FREEZING.
FREEZING? I DRESS LIKE THIS TO DEMONSTRATE MY SOLIDARITY WITH A LOOSELY ORGANIZED BRIGADE OF SUPRA-NATIONALISTS, SOME OF WHOM LIVE WITHIN THE EQUATORIAL REGIONS OF THE EARTH AND SUFFER YEAR ROUND FROM THE HEAT...
BUT ALSO, TO SHOW MY NEIGHBORS THAT ONE NEED NOT FOLLOW THE CULTURAL PATH OF LEAST RESISTANCE. JUST BECAUSE IT'S COLD OUTSIDE DOESN'T MEAN YOU HAVE TO BUNDLE UP IN PSEUDO SKI-WEAR AND SIT AROUND DRINKING HOT COCOA...
THERE IS THE SUPRANATIONALIST WAY! IT MAY BE PAINFUL, YOU MAY BE TAKEN FOR A LUNATIC, BUT ONLY BY REJECTING THE PROVINCIAL DEMANDS OF CLIMATE AND ANCESTRY CAN MAN SO FULLY EXERCISE HIS FREE WILL.
STOP
HONK
HONK
THE UTILITARIAN "UNDERWEAR STYLE" THAT I HAVE ADOPTED UNDERLIES ALL THE VARIOUS AND GAUDY ETHNIC CLOTHING STYLES OF THE WORLD—IT IS ITS OWN UNDERWEAR! PLUS, IT FREES THOSE GARMENT WORKERS SLAVING IN THE ZIPPER, BUTTON AND BELT INDUSTRIES TO PURSUE LOFTIER GOALS. BROTHERS, YOU HAVE NOTHING TO LOSE BUT YOUR PANTS!
WHO LOOKS ANYMORE AT AN OPEN FLY? THE MISSING BUTTONS OF THE WORLD BELONG IN ARCHEOLOGICAL MUSEUMS; AND THE PATRIARCHAL LEATHER BELT, WITH ITS CRUDELY PUNCHED EXTRA HOLE TO ACCOMMODATE A SWELLING PAUNCH, IS A THING OF THE PAST.
YOU COULD ONCE TELL AT A GLANCE FROM WHERE SOMEONE CAME: THE FRENCHMAN WITH HIS SANDALS, SOCKS AND BERET, THE CHANDELIERIAN WITH HIS CRYSTAL PULL-CORD NECKTIE... BUT TODAY'S WORLD MARKET HAS US ALL IN JEANS AND SNEAKERS. SO WHY NOT GO ALL THE WAY? WHY NOT GIVE UP, ONCE AND FOR ALL, THE CRUMBLING FACADE OF CULTURAL DIVERSITY?
OF COURSE I'M FREEZING, BUT I TRY NOT TO SHOW IT.
ICE COLD DRINK
EL GRECO MENSWEAR

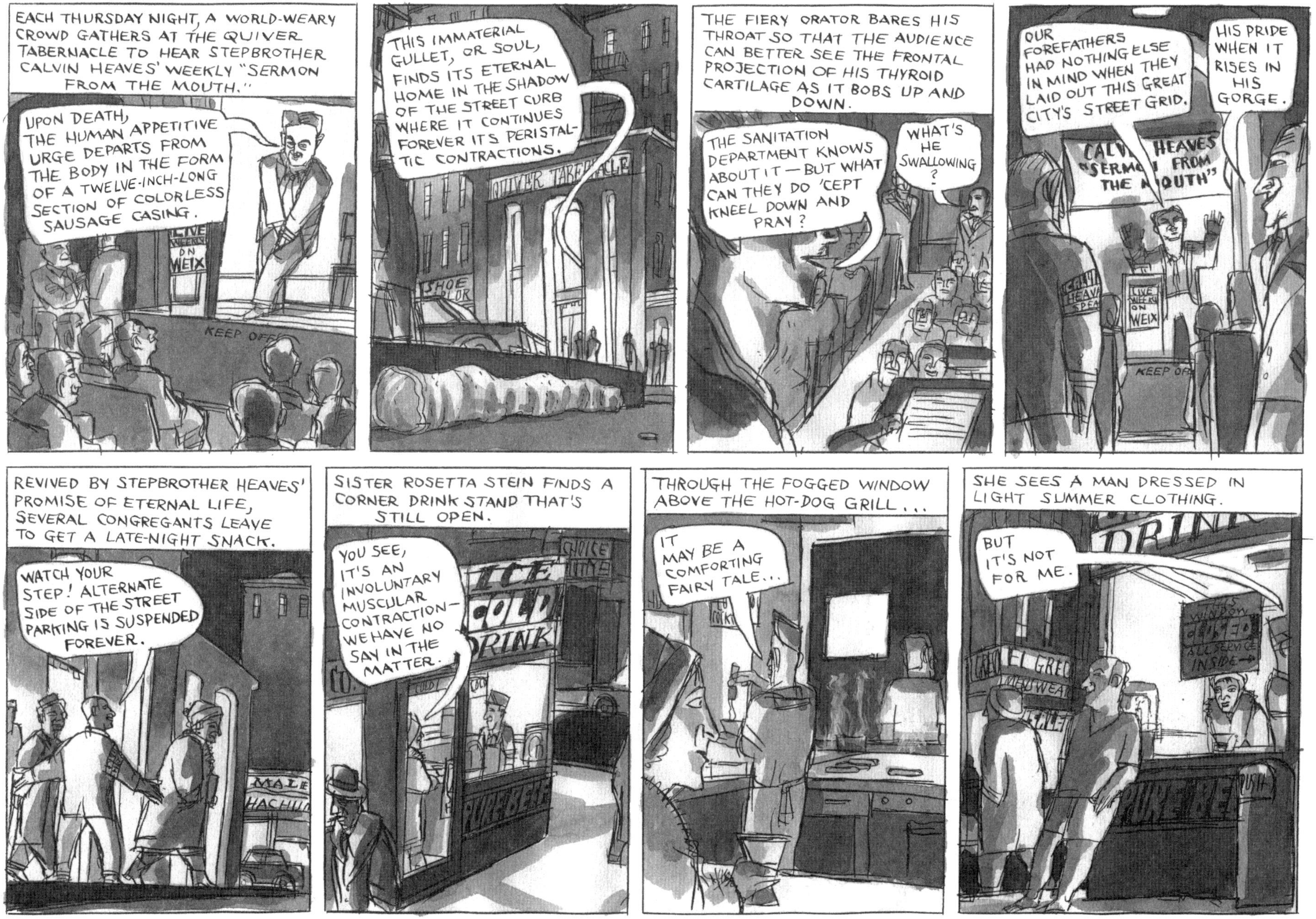
EACH THURSDAY NIGHT, A WORLD-WEARY CROWD GATHERS AT THE QUIVER TABERNACLE TO HEAR STEPBROTHER CALVIN HEAVES' WEEKLY "SERMON FROM THE MOUTH."
UPON DEATH, THE HUMAN APPETITIVE URGE DEPARTS FROM THE BODY IN THE FORM OF A TWELVE-INCH-LONG SECTION OF COLORLESS SAUSAGE CASING.
WEIX
KEEP OFF
THIS IMMATERIAL GULLET, OR SOUL, FINDS ITS ETERNAL HOME IN THE SHADOW OF THE STREET CURB WHERE IT CONTINUES FOREVER ITS PERISTALTIC CONTRACTIONS.
THE FIERY ORATOR BARES HIS THROAT SO THAT THE AUDIENCE CAN BETTER SEE THE FRONTAL PROJECTION OF HIS THYROID CARTILAGE AS IT BOBS UP AND DOWN.
THE SANITATION DEPARTMENT KNOWS ABOUT IT — BUT WHAT CAN THEY DO 'CEPT KNEEL DOWN AND PRAY?
WHAT'S HE SWALLOWING?
OUR FOREFATHERS HAD NOTHING ELSE IN MIND WHEN THEY LAID OUT THIS GREAT CITY'S STREET GRID.
HIS PRIDE WHEN IT RISES IN HIS GORGE.
WEIX
REVIVED BY STEPBROTHER HEAVES' PROMISE OF ETERNAL LIFE, SEVERAL CONGREGANTS LEAVE TO GET A LATE-NIGHT SNACK.
WATCH YOUR STEP! ALTERNATE SIDE OF THE STREET PARKING IS SUSPENDED FOREVER.
SISTER ROSETTA STEIN FINDS A CORNER DRINK STAND THAT'S STILL OPEN.
YOU SEE, IT'S AN INVOLUNTARY MUSCULAR CONTRACTION— WE HAVE NO SAY IN THE MATTER.
DRINK
THROUGH THE FOGGED WINDOW ABOVE THE HOT-DOG GRILL...
IT MAY BE A COMFORTING FAIRY TALE...
SHE SEES A MAN DRESSED IN LIGHT SUMMER CLOTHING.
BUT IT'S NOT FOR ME.
ALL SERVICE INSIDE →

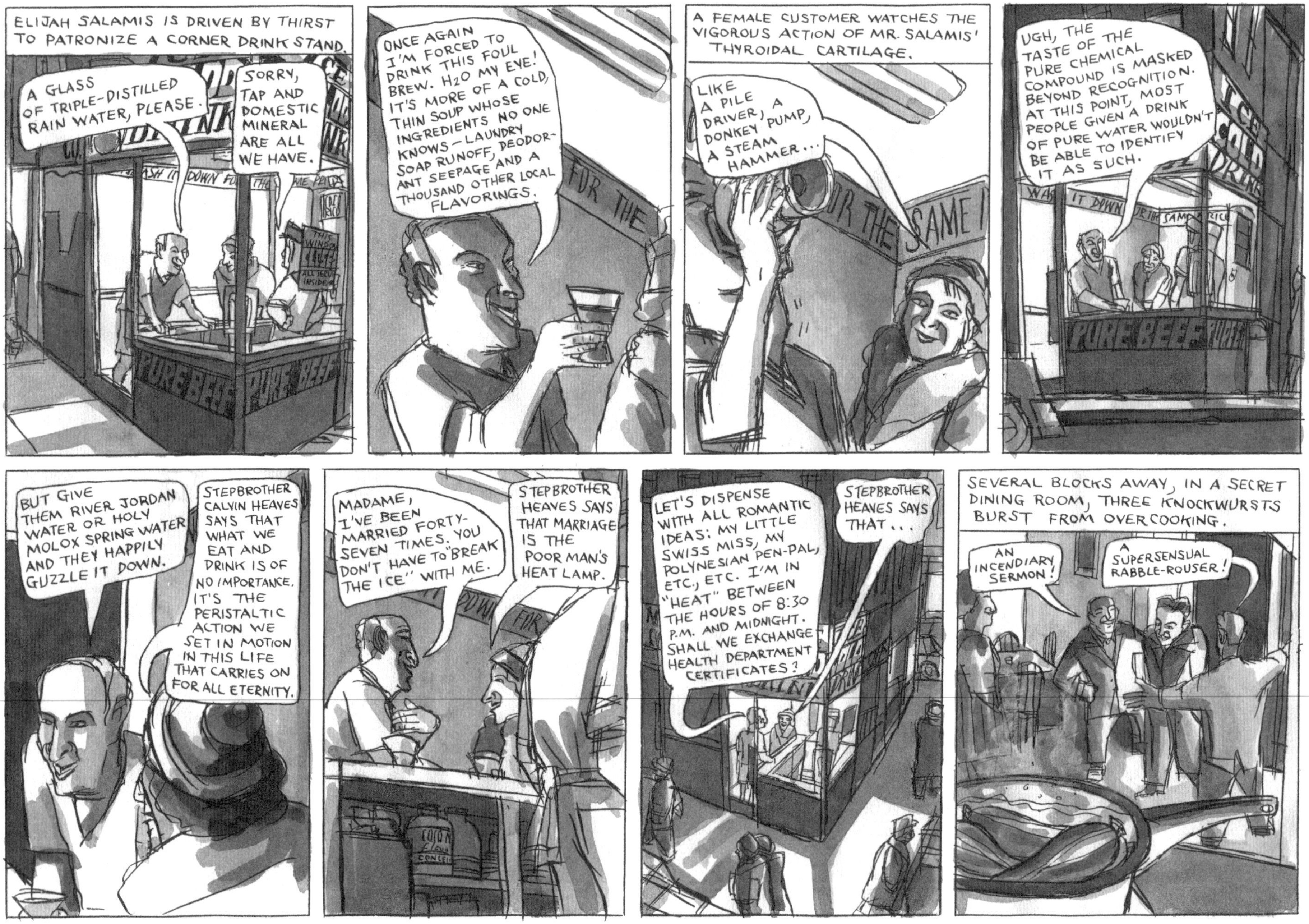
ELIJAH SALAMIS IS DRIVEN BY THIRST TO PATRONIZE A CORNER DRINK STAND.
A GLASS OF TRIPLE-DISTILLED RAIN WATER, PLEASE.
SORRY, TAP AND DOMESTIC MINERAL ARE ALL WE HAVE.
PURE BEEF PURE BEEF
ONCE AGAIN I'M FORCED TO DRINK THIS FOUL BREW. H_2O MY EYE! IT'S MORE OF A COLD, THIN SOUP WHOSE INGREDIENTS NO ONE KNOWS—LAUNDRY SOAP RUNOFF, DEODORANT SEEPAGE AND A THOUSAND OTHER LOCAL FLAVORINGS.
FOR THE
A FEMALE CUSTOMER WATCHES THE VIGOROUS ACTION OF MR. SALAMIS' THYROIDAL CARTILAGE.
LIKE A PILE DRIVER, A DONKEY PUMP, A STEAM HAMMER...
FOR THE SAME
UGH, THE TASTE OF THE PURE CHEMICAL COMPOUND IS MASKED BEYOND RECOGNITION. AT THIS POINT, MOST PEOPLE GIVEN A DRINK OF PURE WATER WOULDN'T BE ABLE TO IDENTIFY IT AS SUCH.
PURE BEEF
BUT GIVE THEM RIVER JORDAN WATER OR HOLY MOLOX SPRING WATER AND THEY HAPPILY GUZZLE IT DOWN.
STEPBROTHER CALVIN HEAVES SAYS THAT WHAT WE EAT AND DRINK IS OF NO IMPORTANCE. IT'S THE PERISTALTIC ACTION WE SET IN MOTION IN THIS LIFE THAT CARRIES ON FOR ALL ETERNITY.
MADAME, I'VE BEEN MARRIED FORTY-SEVEN TIMES. YOU DON'T HAVE TO "BREAK THE ICE" WITH ME.
STEPBROTHER HEAVES SAYS THAT MARRIAGE IS THE POOR MAN'S HEAT LAMP.
LET'S DISPENSE WITH ALL ROMANTIC IDEAS: MY LITTLE SWISS MISS, MY POLYNESIAN PEN-PAL, ETC., ETC. I'M IN "HEAT" BETWEEN THE HOURS OF 8:30 P.M. AND MIDNIGHT. SHALL WE EXCHANGE HEALTH DEPARTMENT CERTIFICATES?
STEPBROTHER HEAVES SAYS THAT...
SEVERAL BLOCKS AWAY, IN A SECRET DINING ROOM, THREE KNOCKWURSTS BURST FROM OVERCOOKING.
AN INCENDIARY SERMON!
A SUPERSENSUAL RABBLE-ROUSER!

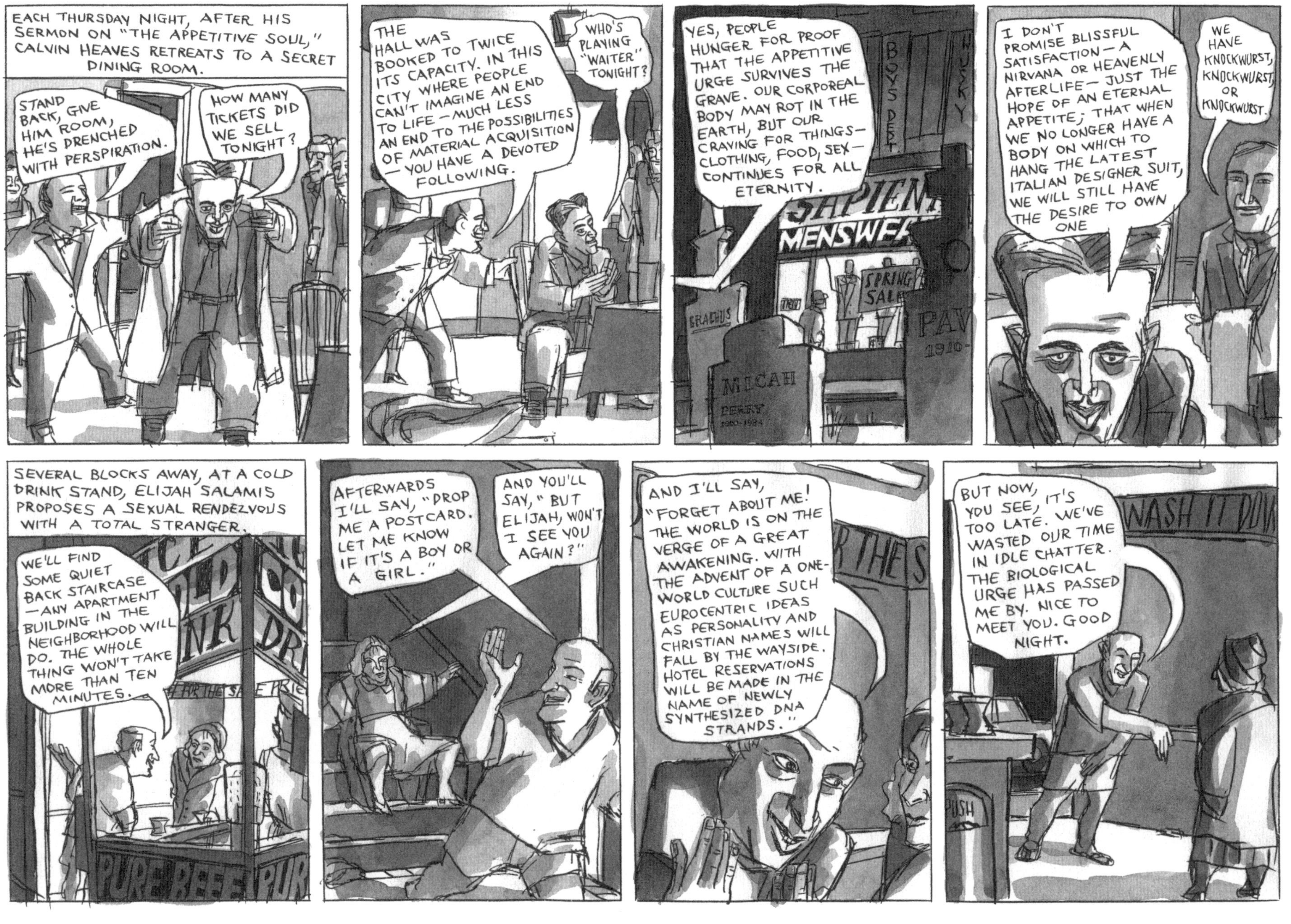
EACH THURSDAY NIGHT, AFTER HIS SERMON ON "THE APPETITIVE SOUL," CALVIN HEAVES RETREATS TO A SECRET DINING ROOM.
STAND BACK, GIVE HIM ROOM, HE'S DRENCHED WITH PERSPIRATION.
HOW MANY TICKETS DID WE SELL TONIGHT?
THE HALL WAS BOOKED TO TWICE ITS CAPACITY. IN THIS CITY WHERE PEOPLE CAN'T IMAGINE AN END TO LIFE—MUCH LESS AN END TO THE POSSIBILITIES OF MATERIAL ACQUISITION —YOU HAVE A DEVOTED FOLLOWING.
WHO'S PLAYING "WAITER" TONIGHT?
YES, PEOPLE HUNGER FOR PROOF THAT THE APPETITIVE URGE SURVIVES THE GRAVE. OUR CORPOREAL BODY MAY ROT IN THE EARTH, BUT OUR CRAVING FOR THINGS—CLOTHING, FOOD, SEX—CONTINUES FOR ALL ETERNITY.
BOYS DEPT.
HUSKY
MENSWEA
SPRING SAL
MICAH
I DON'T PROMISE BLISSFUL SATISFACTION—A NIRVANA OR HEAVENLY AFTERLIFE—JUST THE HOPE OF AN ETERNAL APPETITE; THAT WHEN WE NO LONGER HAVE A BODY ON WHICH TO HANG THE LATEST ITALIAN DESIGNER SUIT, WE WILL STILL HAVE THE DESIRE TO OWN ONE
WE HAVE KNOCKWURST, KNOCKWURST, OR KNOCKWURST.
SEVERAL BLOCKS AWAY, AT A COLD DRINK STAND, ELIJAH SALAMIS PROPOSES A SEXUAL RENDEZVOUS WITH A TOTAL STRANGER.
WE'LL FIND SOME QUIET BACK STAIRCASE —ANY APARTMENT BUILDING IN THE NEIGHBORHOOD WILL DO. THE WHOLE THING WON'T TAKE MORE THAN TEN MINUTES.
PURE BEEF
AFTERWARDS I'LL SAY, "DROP ME A POSTCARD. LET ME KNOW IF IT'S A BOY OR A GIRL."
AND YOU'LL SAY, "BUT ELIJAH, WON'T I SEE YOU AGAIN?"
AND I'LL SAY, "FORGET ABOUT ME! THE WORLD IS ON THE VERGE OF A GREAT AWAKENING. WITH THE ADVENT OF A ONE-WORLD CULTURE SUCH EUROCENTRIC IDEAS AS PERSONALITY AND CHRISTIAN NAMES WILL FALL BY THE WAYSIDE. HOTEL RESERVATIONS WILL BE MADE IN THE NAME OF NEWLY SYNTHESIZED DNA STRANDS."
BUT NOW, YOU SEE, IT'S TOO LATE. WE'VE WASTED OUR TIME IN IDLE CHATTER. THE BIOLOGICAL URGE HAS PASSED ME BY. NICE TO MEET YOU. GOOD NIGHT.
WASH IT DOW
PUSH

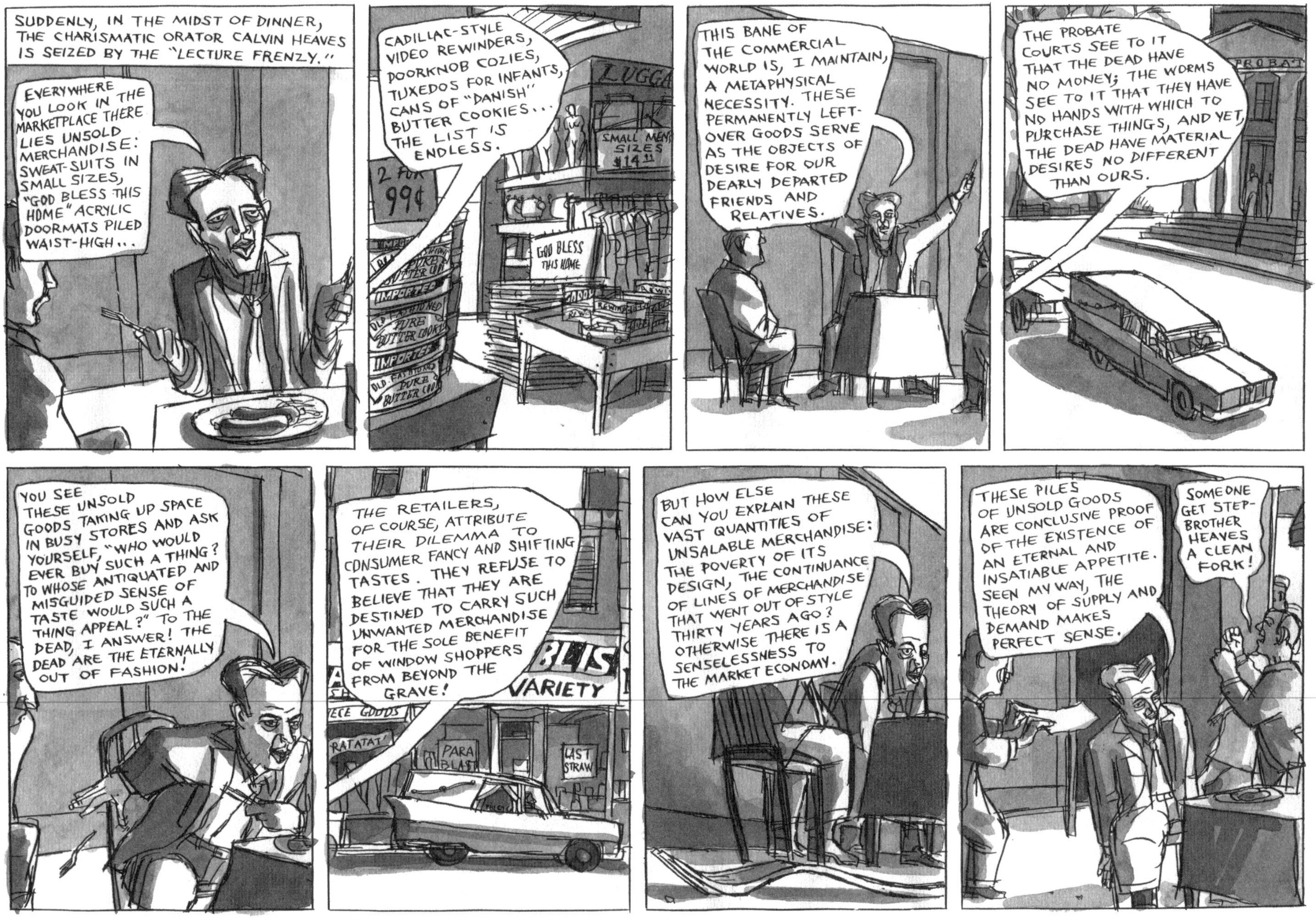

SUDDENLY, IN THE MIDST OF DINNER, THE CHARISMATIC ORATOR CALVIN HEAVES IS SEIZED BY THE "LECTURE FRENZY."
EVERYWHERE YOU LOOK IN THE MARKETPLACE THERE LIES UNSOLD MERCHANDISE: SWEAT-SUITS IN SMALL SIZES, "GOD BLESS THIS HOME" ACRYLIC DOORMATS PILED WAIST-HIGH...
CADILLAC-STYLE VIDEO REWINDERS, DOORKNOB COZIES, TUXEDOS FOR INFANTS, CANS OF "DANISH" BUTTER COOKIES... THE LIST IS ENDLESS.
2 FOR 99¢
SMALL MEN'S SIZES
GOD BLESS THIS HOME
THIS BANE OF THE COMMERCIAL WORLD IS, I MAINTAIN, A METAPHYSICAL NECESSITY. THESE PERMANENTLY LEFT-OVER GOODS SERVE AS THE OBJECTS OF DESIRE FOR OUR DEARLY DEPARTED FRIENDS AND RELATIVES.
THE PROBATE COURTS SEE TO IT THAT THE DEAD HAVE NO MONEY; THE WORMS SEE TO IT THAT THEY HAVE NO HANDS WITH WHICH TO PURCHASE THINGS, AND YET, THE DEAD HAVE MATERIAL DESIRES NO DIFFERENT THAN OURS.
YOU SEE THESE UNSOLD GOODS TAKING UP SPACE IN BUSY STORES AND ASK YOURSELF, "WHO WOULD EVER BUY SUCH A THING? TO WHOSE ANTIQUATED AND MISGUIDED SENSE OF TASTE WOULD SUCH A THING APPEAL?" TO THE DEAD, I ANSWER! THE DEAD ARE THE ETERNALLY OUT OF FASHION!
THE RETAILERS, OF COURSE, ATTRIBUTE THEIR DILEMMA TO CONSUMER FANCY AND SHIFTING TASTES. THEY REFUSE TO BELIEVE THAT THEY ARE DESTINED TO CARRY SUCH UNWANTED MERCHANDISE FOR THE SOLE BENEFIT OF WINDOW SHOPPERS FROM BEYOND THE GRAVE!
VARIETY
LAST STRAW
BUT HOW ELSE CAN YOU EXPLAIN THESE VAST QUANTITIES OF UNSALABLE MERCHANDISE: THE POVERTY OF ITS DESIGN, THE CONTINUANCE OF LINES OF MERCHANDISE THAT WENT OUT OF STYLE THIRTY YEARS AGO? OTHERWISE THERE IS A SENSELESSNESS TO THE MARKET ECONOMY.
THESE PILES OF UNSOLD GOODS ARE CONCLUSIVE PROOF OF THE EXISTENCE OF AN ETERNAL AND INSATIABLE APPETITE. SEEN MY WAY, THE THEORY OF SUPPLY AND DEMAND MAKES PERFECT SENSE.
SOMEONE GET STEP-BROTHER HEAVES A CLEAN FORK!

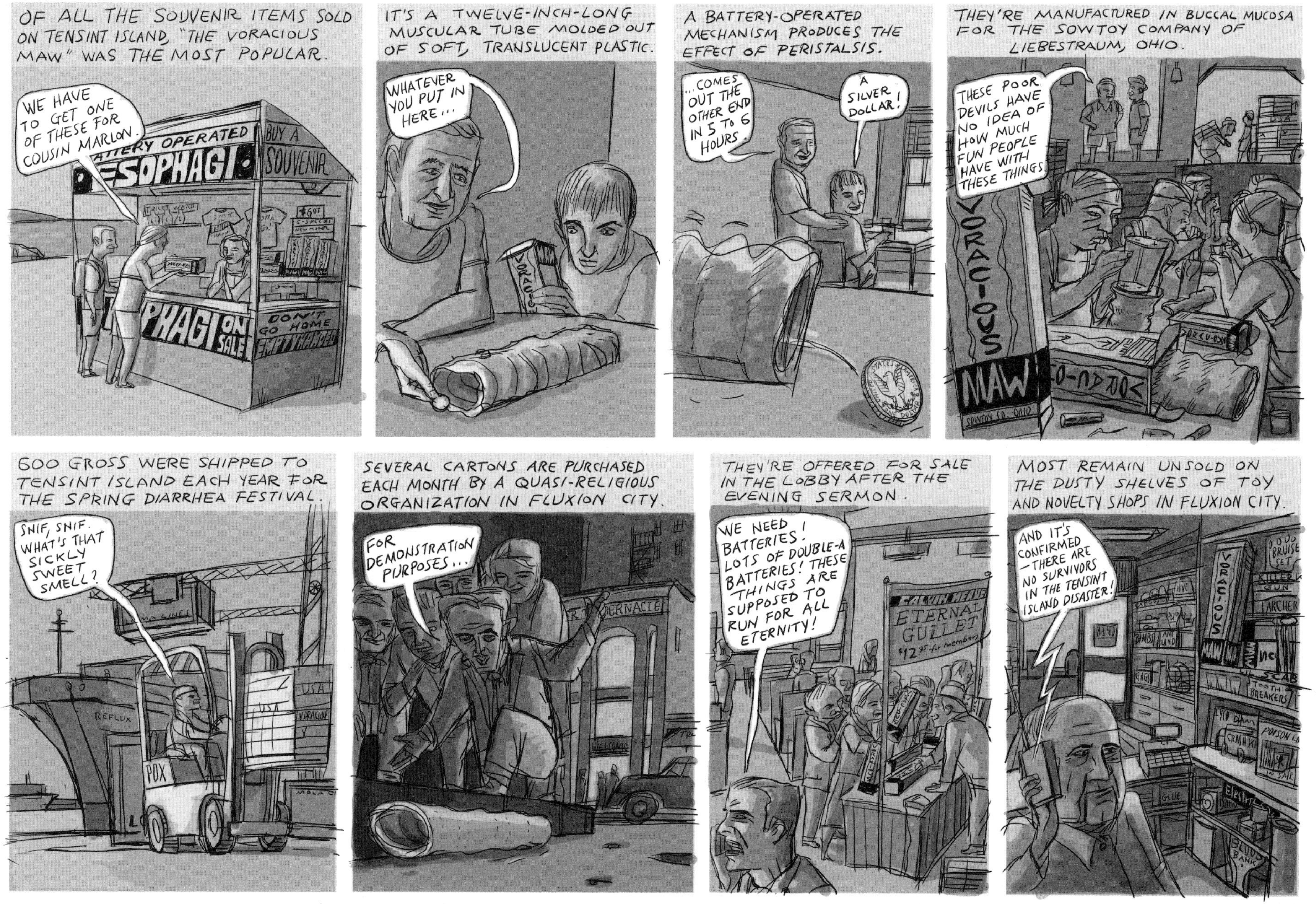
OF ALL THE SOUVENIR ITEMS SOLD ON TENSINT ISLAND, "THE VORACIOUS MAW" WAS THE MOST POPULAR.
WE HAVE TO GET ONE OF THESE FOR COUSIN MARLON.
BUY A SOUVENIR
ON SALE
DON'T GO HOME EMPTY-HANDED
IT'S A TWELVE-INCH-LONG MUSCULAR TUBE MOLDED OUT OF SOFT, TRANSLUCENT PLASTIC.
WHATEVER YOU PUT IN HERE...
A BATTERY-OPERATED MECHANISM PRODUCES THE EFFECT OF PERISTALSIS.
...COMES OUT THE OTHER END IN 5 TO 6 HOURS.
A SILVER DOLLAR!
THEY'RE MANUFACTURED IN BUCCAL MUCOSA FOR THE SOWTOY COMPANY OF LIEBESTRAUM, OHIO.
THESE POOR DEVILS HAVE NO IDEA OF HOW MUCH FUN PEOPLE HAVE WITH THESE THINGS.
VORACIOUS MAW
SOWTOY CO. OHIO
600 GROSS WERE SHIPPED TO TENSINT ISLAND EACH YEAR FOR THE SPRING DIARRHEA FESTIVAL.
SNIF, SNIF. WHAT'S THAT SICKLY SWEET SMELL?
REFLUX
PDX
USA
SEVERAL CARTONS ARE PURCHASED EACH MONTH BY A QUASI-RELIGIOUS ORGANIZATION IN FLUXION CITY.
FOR DEMONSTRATION PURPOSES...
THEY'RE OFFERED FOR SALE IN THE LOBBY AFTER THE EVENING SERMON.
WE NEED BATTERIES! LOTS OF DOUBLE-A BATTERIES! THESE THINGS ARE SUPPOSED TO RUN FOR ALL ETERNITY!
ETERNAL GULLET $12.95 for members
MOST REMAIN UNSOLD ON THE DUSTY SHELVES OF TOY AND NOVELTY SHOPS IN FLUXION CITY.
AND IT'S CONFIRMED —THERE ARE NO SURVIVORS IN THE TENSINT ISLAND DISASTER!
VORACIOUS
MAW
TOOTH BREAKERS
GLUE

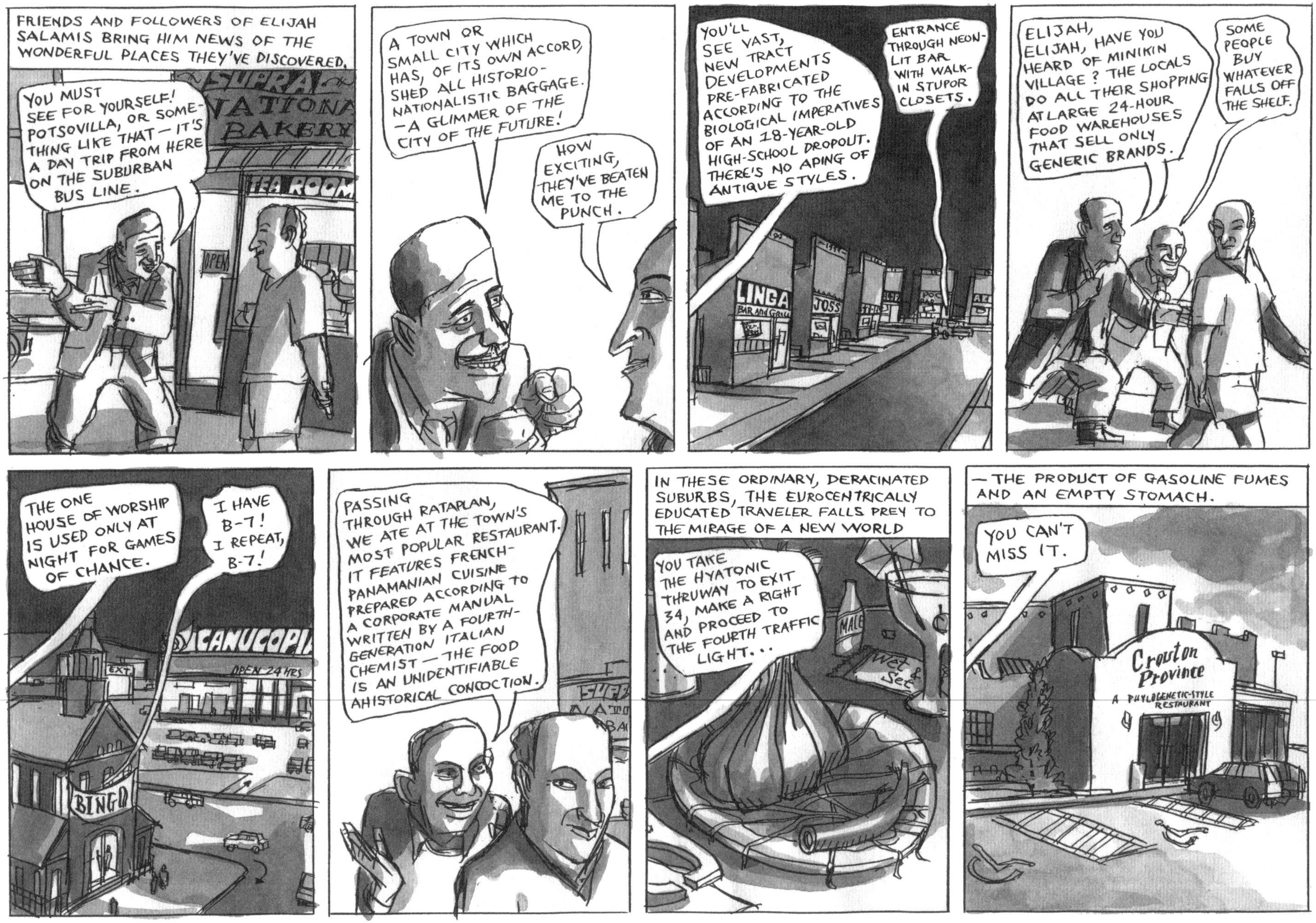
FRIENDS AND FOLLOWERS OF ELIJAH SALAMIS BRING HIM NEWS OF THE WONDERFUL PLACES THEY'VE DISCOVERED.
YOU MUST SEE FOR YOURSELF! POTSOVILLA, OR SOME-THING LIKE THAT— IT'S A DAY TRIP FROM HERE ON THE SUBURBAN BUS LINE.
BAKERY
OPEN
A TOWN OR SMALL CITY WHICH HAS, OF ITS OWN ACCORD, SHED ALL HISTORIO-NATIONALISTIC BAGGAGE. —A GLIMMER OF THE CITY OF THE FUTURE!
HOW EXCITING, THEY'VE BEATEN ME TO THE PUNCH.
YOU'LL SEE VAST, NEW TRACT DEVELOPMENTS PRE-FABRICATED ACCORDING TO THE BIOLOGICAL IMPERATIVES OF AN 18-YEAR-OLD HIGH-SCHOOL DROPOUT. THERE'S NO APING OF ANTIQUE STYLES.
ENTRANCE THROUGH NEON-LIT BAR WITH WALK-IN STUPOR CLOSETS.
LINGA
BAR AND GRILL
JOSS
ELIJAH, ELIJAH, HAVE YOU HEARD OF MINIKIN VILLAGE? THE LOCALS DO ALL THEIR SHOPPING AT LARGE 24-HOUR FOOD WAREHOUSES THAT SELL ONLY GENERIC BRANDS.
SOME PEOPLE BUY WHATEVER FALLS OFF THE SHELF.
THE ONE HOUSE OF WORSHIP IS USED ONLY AT NIGHT FOR GAMES OF CHANCE.
I HAVE B-7! I REPEAT, B-7!
OPEN 24 HRS
BINGO
PASSING THROUGH RATAPLAN, WE ATE AT THE TOWN'S MOST POPULAR RESTAURANT. IT FEATURES FRENCH-PANAMANIAN CUISINE PREPARED ACCORDING TO A CORPORATE MANUAL WRITTEN BY A FOURTH-GENERATION ITALIAN CHEMIST— THE FOOD IS AN UNIDENTIFIABLE AHISTORICAL CONCOCTION.
IN THESE ORDINARY, DERACINATED SUBURBS, THE EUROCENTRICALLY EDUCATED TRAVELER FALLS PREY TO THE MIRAGE OF A NEW WORLD
YOU TAKE THE HYATONIC THRUWAY TO EXIT 34, MAKE A RIGHT AND PROCEED TO THE FOURTH TRAFFIC LIGHT...
Wet & Set
—THE PRODUCT OF GASOLINE FUMES AND AN EMPTY STOMACH.
YOU CAN'T MISS IT.
Crouton Province
A PHYLOGENETIC-STYLE RESTAURANT

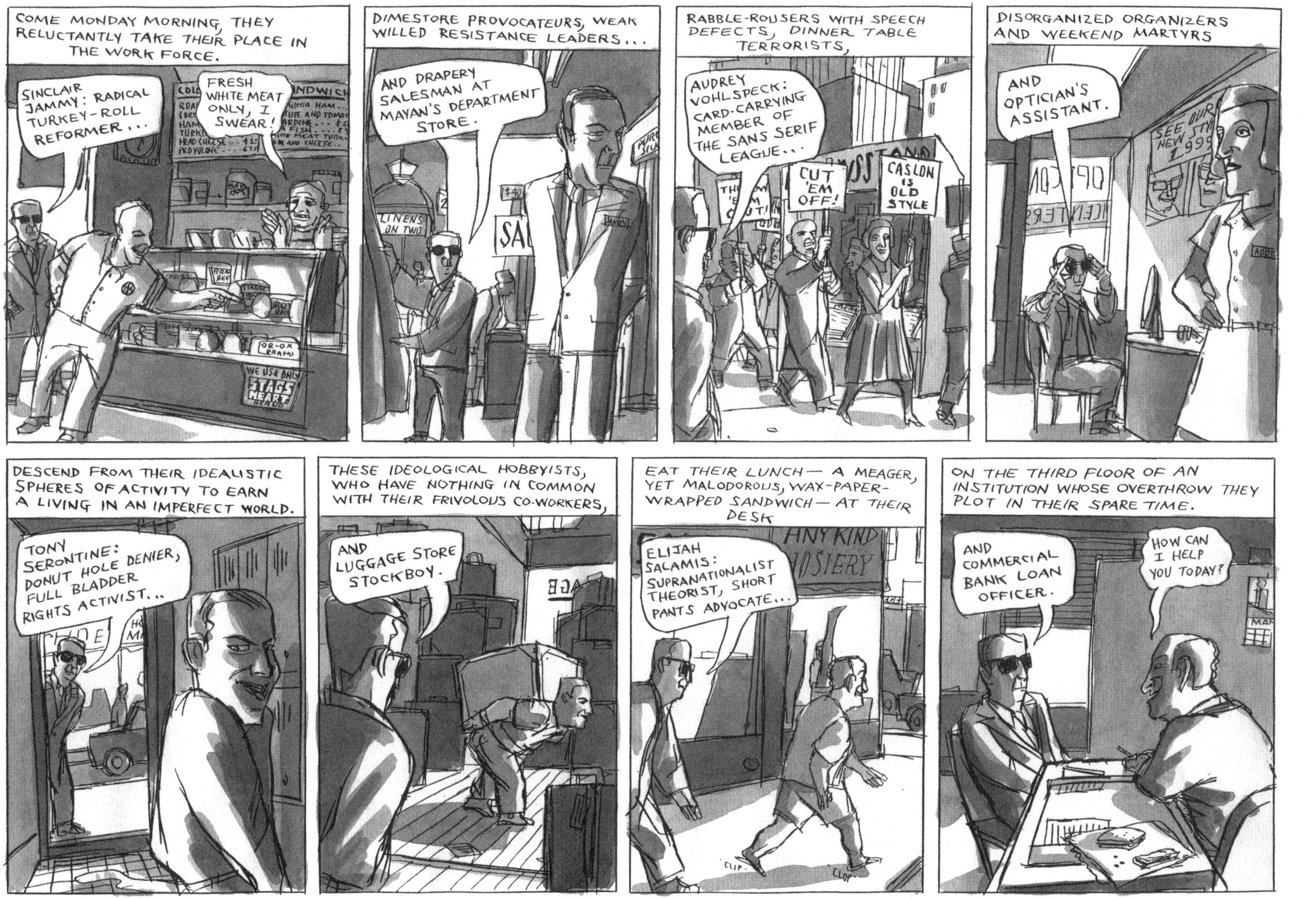
COME MONDAY MORNING, THEY RELUCTANTLY TAKE THEIR PLACE IN THE WORK FORCE.
SINCLAIR JAMMY: RADICAL TURKEY-ROLL REFORMER...
FRESH WHITE MEAT ONLY, I SWEAR!
WE USE ONLY STAGS HEART BRAND
DIMESTORE PROVOCATEURS, WEAK WILLED RESISTANCE LEADERS...
AND DRAPERY SALESMAN AT MAYAN'S DEPARTMENT STORE.
LINENS ON TWO
RABBLE-ROUSERS WITH SPEECH DEFECTS, DINNER TABLE TERRORISTS,
AUDREY VOHLSPECK: CARD-CARRYING MEMBER OF THE SANS SERIF LEAGUE...
CUT 'EM OFF!
CASLON IS OLD STYLE
DISORGANIZED ORGANIZERS AND WEEKEND MARTYRS
AND OPTICIAN'S ASSISTANT.
DESCEND FROM THEIR IDEALISTIC SPHERES OF ACTIVITY TO EARN A LIVING IN AN IMPERFECT WORLD.
TONY SERONTINE: DONUT HOLE DENIER, FULL BLADDER RIGHTS ACTIVIST...
THESE IDEOLOGICAL HOBBYISTS, WHO HAVE NOTHING IN COMMON WITH THEIR FRIVOLOUS CO-WORKERS,
AND LUGGAGE STORE STOCKBOY.
EAT THEIR LUNCH— A MEAGER, YET MALODOROUS, WAX-PAPER-WRAPPED SANDWICH— AT THEIR DESK
ANY KIND HOSIERY
ELIJAH SALAMIS: SUPRANATIONALIST THEORIST, SHORT PANTS ADVOCATE...
CLIP.
CLOP
ON THE THIRD FLOOR OF AN INSTITUTION WHOSE OVERTHROW THEY PLOT IN THEIR SPARE TIME.
AND COMMERCIAL BANK LOAN OFFICER.
HOW CAN I HELP YOU TODAY?

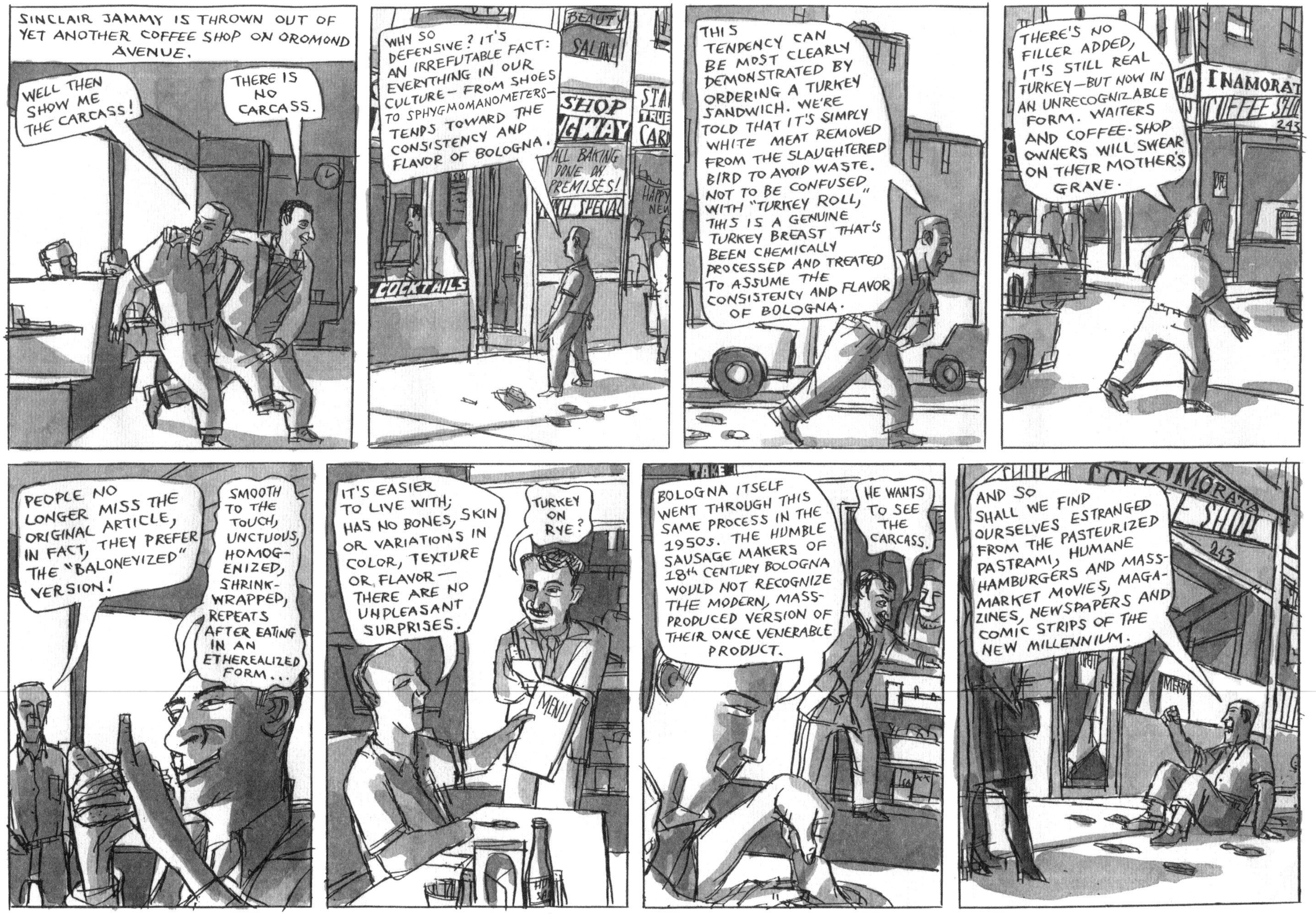
SINCLAIR JAMMY IS THROWN OUT OF YET ANOTHER COFFEE SHOP ON OROMOND AVENUE.
WELL THEN SHOW ME THE CARCASS!
THERE IS NO CARCASS.
WHY SO DEFENSIVE? IT'S AN IRREFUTABLE FACT: EVERYTHING IN OUR CULTURE— FROM SHOES TO SPHYGMOMANOMETERS— TENDS TOWARD THE CONSISTENCY AND FLAVOR OF BOLOGNA.
BEAUTY
SALON
ALL BAKING DONE ON PREMISES!
COCKTAILS
THIS TENDENCY CAN BE MOST CLEARLY DEMONSTRATED BY ORDERING A TURKEY SANDWICH. WE'RE TOLD THAT IT'S SIMPLY WHITE MEAT REMOVED FROM THE SLAUGHTERED BIRD TO AVOID WASTE. NOT TO BE CONFUSED WITH "TURKEY ROLL," THIS IS A GENUINE TURKEY BREAST THAT'S BEEN CHEMICALLY PROCESSED AND TREATED TO ASSUME THE CONSISTENCY AND FLAVOR OF BOLOGNA.
THERE'S NO FILLER ADDED, IT'S STILL REAL TURKEY—BUT NOW IN AN UNRECOGNIZABLE FORM. WAITERS AND COFFEE-SHOP OWNERS WILL SWEAR ON THEIR MOTHER'S GRAVE.
INAMORAT
243
PEOPLE NO LONGER MISS THE ORIGINAL ARTICLE, IN FACT, THEY PREFER THE "BALONEYIZED" VERSION!
SMOOTH TO THE TOUCH, UNCTUOUS, HOMOGENIZED, SHRINK-WRAPPED, REPEATS AFTER EATING IN AN ETHEREALIZED FORM...
IT'S EASIER TO LIVE WITH; HAS NO BONES, SKIN OR VARIATIONS IN COLOR, TEXTURE OR FLAVOR— THERE ARE NO UNPLEASANT SURPRISES.
TURKEY ON RYE?
MENU
BOLOGNA ITSELF WENT THROUGH THIS SAME PROCESS IN THE 1950s. THE HUMBLE SAUSAGE MAKERS OF 18th CENTURY BOLOGNA WOULD NOT RECOGNIZE THE MODERN, MASS-PRODUCED VERSION OF THEIR ONCE VENERABLE PRODUCT.
HE WANTS TO SEE THE CARCASS.
AND SO SHALL WE FIND OURSELVES ESTRANGED FROM THE PASTEURIZED PASTRAMI, HUMANE HAMBURGERS AND MASS-MARKET MOVIES, MAGAZINES, NEWSPAPERS AND COMIC STRIPS OF THE NEW MILLENNIUM.
243

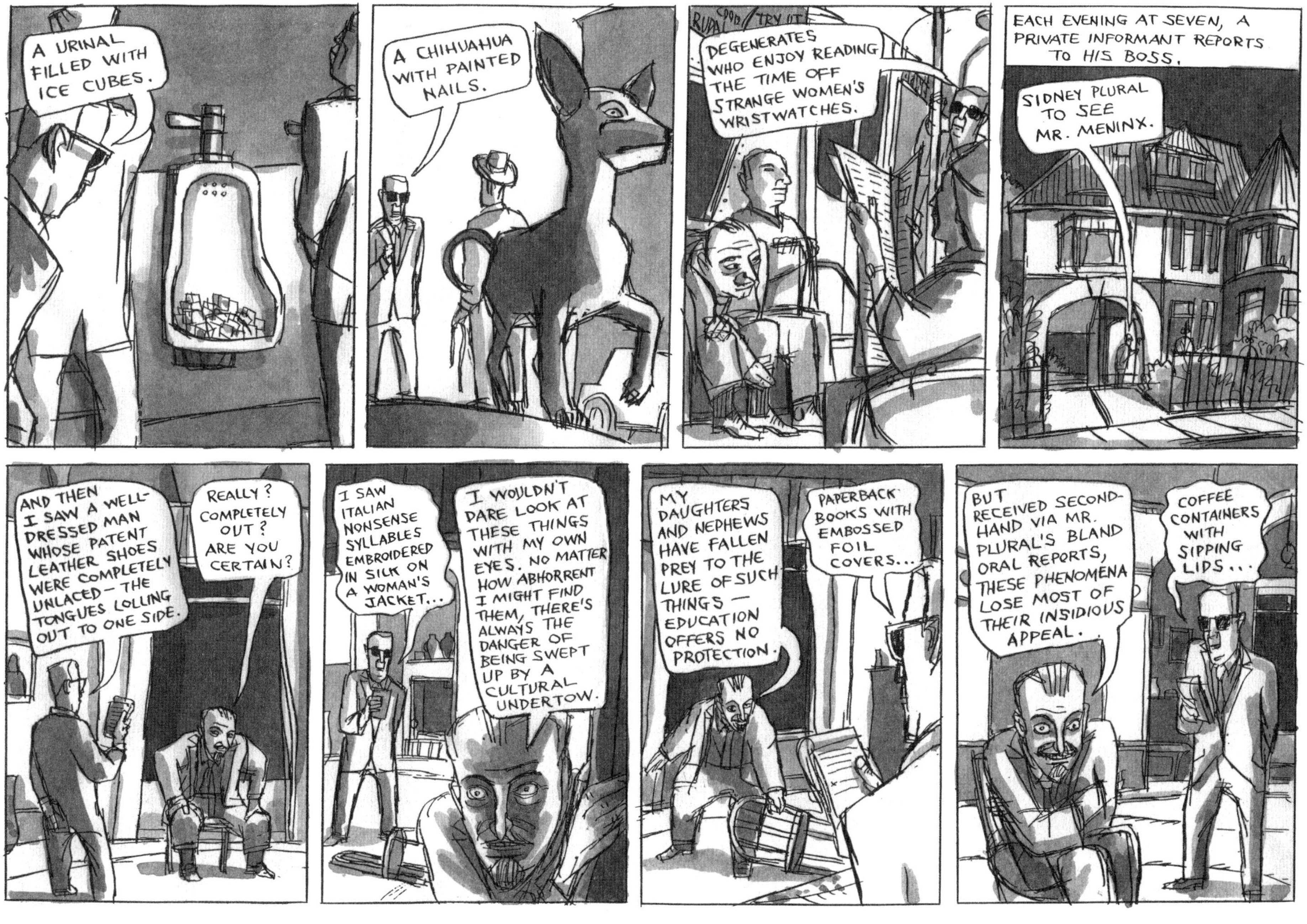
A URINAL FILLED WITH ICE CUBES.
A CHIHUAHUA WITH PAINTED NAILS.
DEGENERATES WHO ENJOY READING THE TIME OFF STRANGE WOMEN'S WRISTWATCHES.
EACH EVENING AT SEVEN, A PRIVATE INFORMANT REPORTS TO HIS BOSS.
SIDNEY PLURAL TO SEE MR. MENINX.
AND THEN I SAW A WELL-DRESSED MAN WHOSE PATENT LEATHER SHOES WERE COMPLETELY UNLACED— THE TONGUES LOLLING OUT TO ONE SIDE.
REALLY? COMPLETELY OUT? ARE YOU CERTAIN?
I SAW ITALIAN NONSENSE SYLLABLES EMBROIDERED IN SILK ON A WOMAN'S JACKET...
I WOULDN'T DARE LOOK AT THESE THINGS WITH MY OWN EYES. NO MATTER HOW ABHORRENT I MIGHT FIND THEM, THERE'S ALWAYS THE DANGER OF BEING SWEPT UP BY A CULTURAL UNDERTOW.
MY DAUGHTERS AND NEPHEWS HAVE FALLEN PREY TO THE LURE OF SUCH THINGS — EDUCATION OFFERS NO PROTECTION.
PAPERBACK BOOKS WITH EMBOSSED FOIL COVERS...
BUT RECEIVED SECOND-HAND VIA MR. PLURAL'S BLAND ORAL REPORTS, THESE PHENOMENA LOSE MOST OF THEIR INSIDIOUS APPEAL.
COFFEE CONTAINERS WITH SIPPING LIDS...

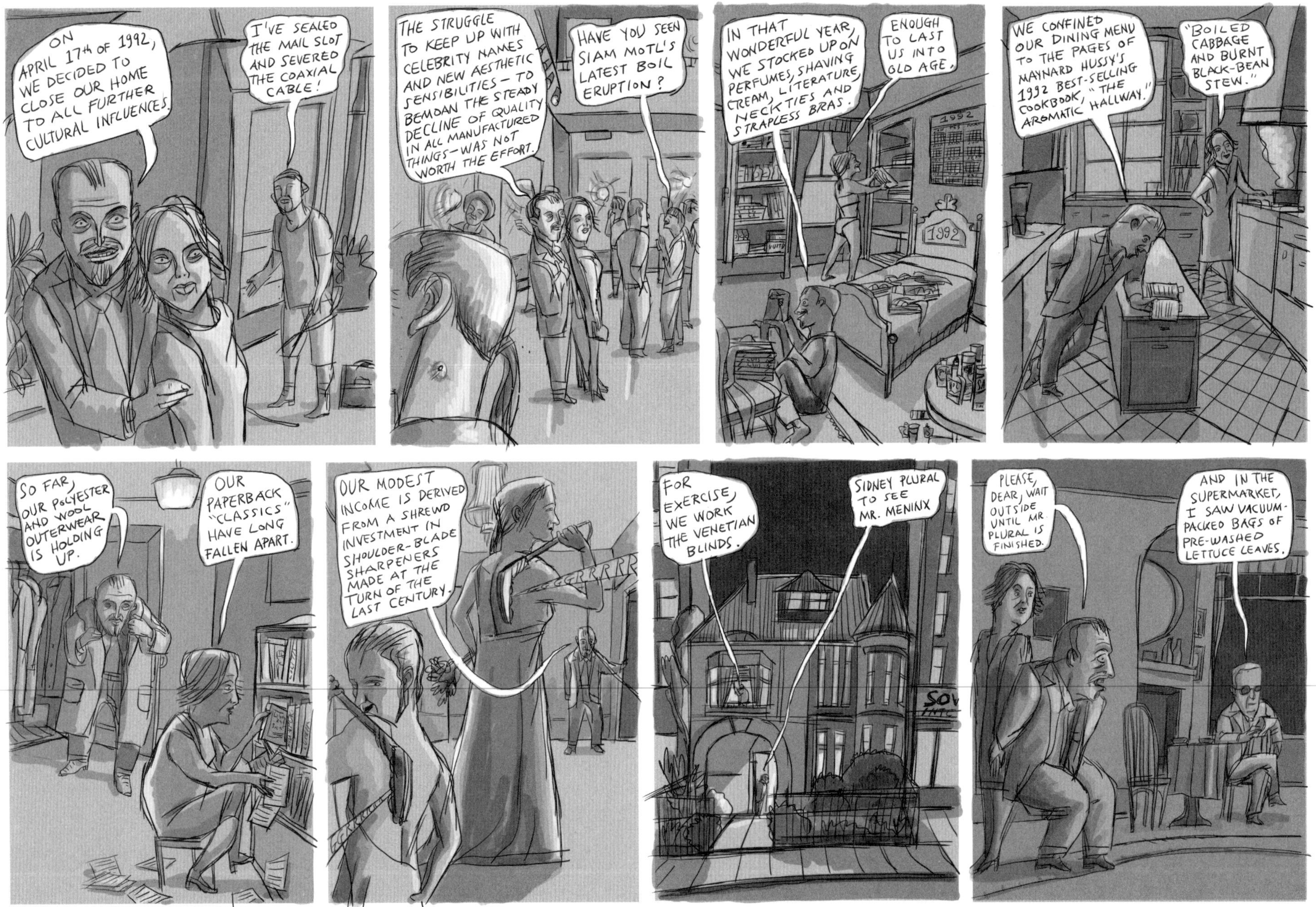
ON APRIL 17th OF 1992, WE DECIDED TO CLOSE OUR HOME TO ALL FURTHER CULTURAL INFLUENCES.
I'VE SEALED THE MAIL SLOT AND SEVERED THE COAXIAL CABLE!
THE STRUGGLE TO KEEP UP WITH CELEBRITY NAMES AND NEW AESTHETIC SENSIBILITIES—TO BEMOAN THE STEADY DECLINE OF QUALITY IN ALL MANUFACTURED THINGS—WAS NOT WORTH THE EFFORT.
HAVE YOU SEEN SIAM MOTL'S LATEST BOIL ERUPTION?
IN THAT WONDERFUL YEAR, WE STOCKED UP ON PERFUMES, SHAVING CREAM, LITERATURE, NECKTIES AND STRAPLESS BRAS.
ENOUGH TO LAST US INTO OLD AGE.
1992
1992
WE CONFINED OUR DINING MENU TO THE PAGES OF MAYNARD HUSSY'S 1992 BEST-SELLING COOKBOOK, "THE AROMATIC HALLWAY."
"BOILED CABBAGE AND BURNT BLACK-BEAN STEW."
SO FAR, OUR POLYESTER AND WOOL OUTERWEAR IS HOLDING UP.
OUR PAPERBACK "CLASSICS" HAVE LONG FALLEN APART.
OUR MODEST INCOME IS DERIVED FROM A SHREWD INVESTMENT IN SHOULDER-BLADE SHARPENERS MADE AT THE TURN OF THE LAST CENTURY.
FOR EXERCISE, WE WORK THE VENETIAN BLINDS.
SIDNEY PLURAL TO SEE MR. MENINX
PLEASE, DEAR, WAIT OUTSIDE UNTIL MR. PLURAL IS FINISHED.
AND IN THE SUPERMARKET, I SAW VACUUM-PACKED BAGS OF PRE-WASHED LETTUCE LEAVES.

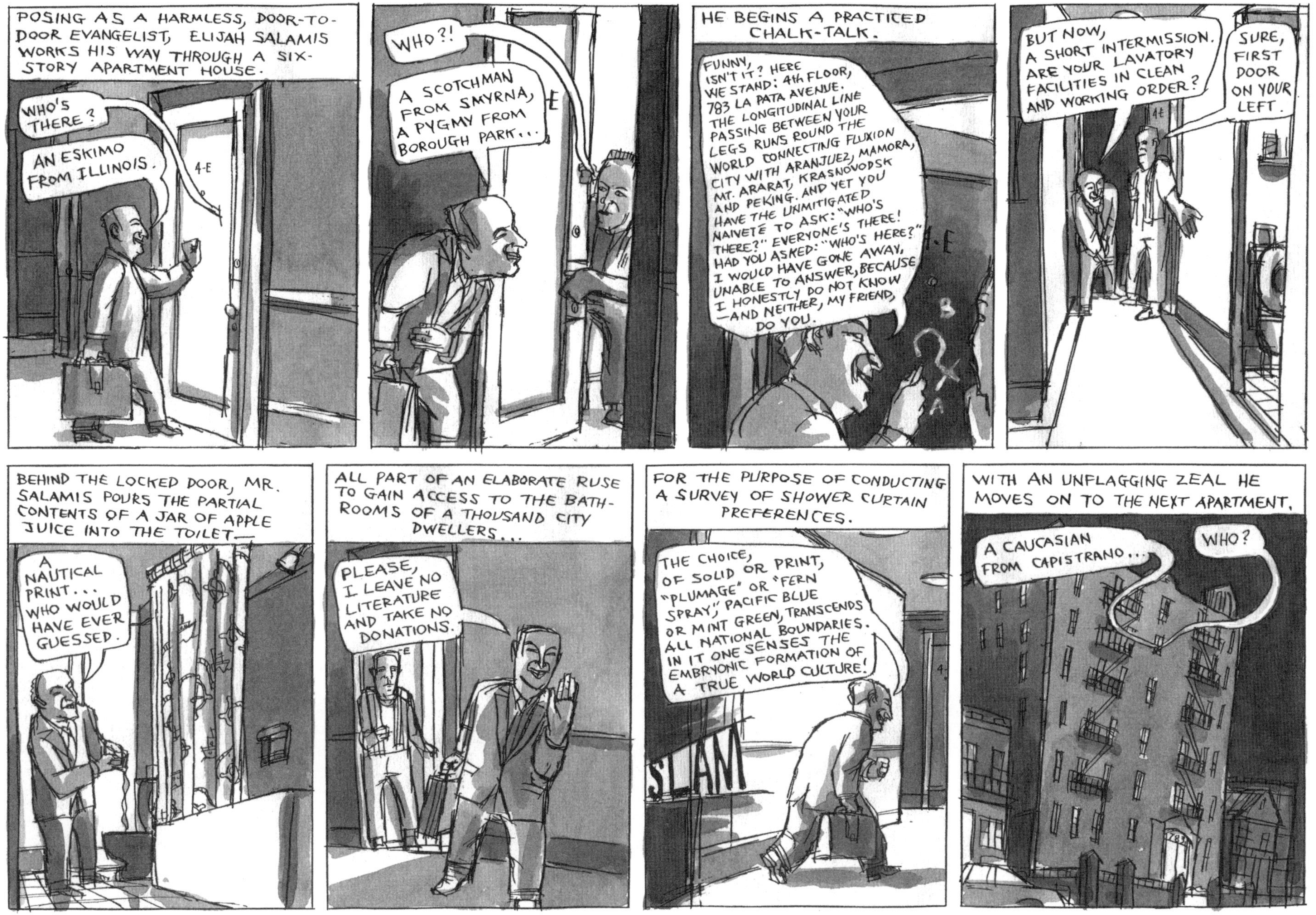
POSING AS A HARMLESS, DOOR-TO-DOOR EVANGELIST, ELIJAH SALAMIS WORKS HIS WAY THROUGH A SIX-STORY APARTMENT HOUSE.
WHO'S THERE?
AN ESKIMO FROM ILLINOIS.
4-E
WHO?!
A SCOTCHMAN FROM SMYRNA, A PYGMY FROM BOROUGH PARK...
HE BEGINS A PRACTICED CHALK-TALK.
FUNNY, ISN'T IT? HERE WE STAND: 4th FLOOR, 783 LA PATA AVENUE. THE LONGITUDINAL LINE PASSING BETWEEN YOUR LEGS RUNS ROUND THE WORLD CONNECTING FLUXION CITY WITH ARANJUEZ, MAMORA, MT. ARARAT, KRASNOVODSK AND PEKING. AND YET YOU HAVE THE UNMITIGATED NAIVETÉ TO ASK: "WHO'S THERE?" EVERYONE'S THERE! HAD YOU ASKED: "WHO'S HERE?" I WOULD HAVE GONE AWAY, UNABLE TO ANSWER, BECAUSE I HONESTLY DO NOT KNOW —AND NEITHER, MY FRIEND, DO YOU.
BUT NOW, A SHORT INTERMISSION. ARE YOUR LAVATORY FACILITIES IN CLEAN AND WORKING ORDER?
SURE, FIRST DOOR ON YOUR LEFT.
BEHIND THE LOCKED DOOR, MR. SALAMIS POURS THE PARTIAL CONTENTS OF A JAR OF APPLE JUICE INTO THE TOILET—
A NAUTICAL PRINT... WHO WOULD HAVE EVER GUESSED.
ALL PART OF AN ELABORATE RUSE TO GAIN ACCESS TO THE BATHROOMS OF A THOUSAND CITY DWELLERS...
PLEASE, I LEAVE NO LITERATURE AND TAKE NO DONATIONS.
FOR THE PURPOSE OF CONDUCTING A SURVEY OF SHOWER CURTAIN PREFERENCES.
THE CHOICE, OF SOLID OR PRINT, "PLUMAGE" OR "FERN SPRAY," PACIFIC BLUE OR MINT GREEN, TRANSCENDS ALL NATIONAL BOUNDARIES. IN IT ONE SENSES THE EMBRYONIC FORMATION OF A TRUE WORLD CULTURE!
SLAM
WITH AN UNFLAGGING ZEAL HE MOVES ON TO THE NEXT APARTMENT.
A CAUCASIAN FROM CAPISTRANO...
WHO?
783

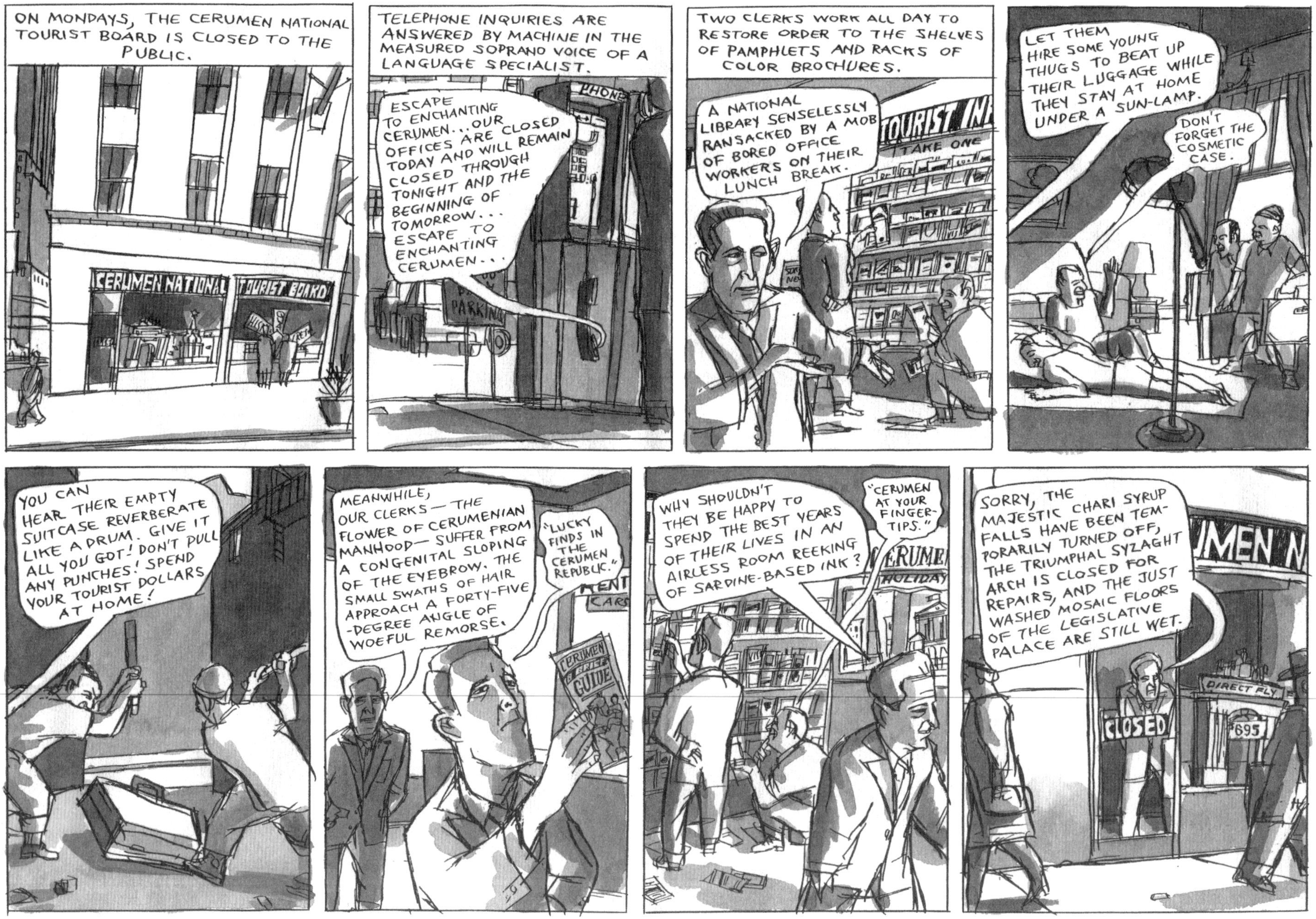
ON MONDAYS, THE CERUMEN NATIONAL TOURIST BOARD IS CLOSED TO THE PUBLIC.
CERUMEN NATIONAL TOURIST BOARD
TELEPHONE INQUIRIES ARE ANSWERED BY MACHINE IN THE MEASURED SOPRANO VOICE OF A LANGUAGE SPECIALIST.
PHONE
ESCAPE TO ENCHANTING CERUMEN... OUR OFFICES ARE CLOSED TODAY AND WILL REMAIN CLOSED THROUGH TONIGHT AND THE BEGINNING OF TOMORROW... ESCAPE TO ENCHANTING CERUMEN...
PARKING
TWO CLERKS WORK ALL DAY TO RESTORE ORDER TO THE SHELVES OF PAMPHLETS AND RACKS OF COLOR BROCHURES.
A NATIONAL LIBRARY SENSELESSLY RANSACKED BY A MOB OF BORED OFFICE WORKERS ON THEIR LUNCH BREAK.
TAKE ONE
LET THEM HIRE SOME YOUNG THUGS TO BEAT UP THEIR LUGGAGE WHILE THEY STAY AT HOME UNDER A SUN-LAMP.
DON'T FORGET THE COSMETIC CASE.
YOU CAN HEAR THEIR EMPTY SUITCASE REVERBERATE LIKE A DRUM. GIVE IT ALL YOU GOT! DON'T PULL ANY PUNCHES! SPEND YOUR TOURIST DOLLARS AT HOME!
MEANWHILE, OUR CLERKS—THE FLOWER OF CERUMENIAN MANHOOD—SUFFER FROM A CONGENITAL SLOPING OF THE EYEBROW. THE SMALL SWATHS OF HAIR APPROACH A FORTY-FIVE-DEGREE ANGLE OF WOEFUL REMORSE.
"LUCKY FINDS IN THE CERUMEN REPUBLIC."
CERUMEN A BRIEF GUIDE
CARS
WHY SHOULDN'T THEY BE HAPPY TO SPEND THE BEST YEARS OF THEIR LIVES IN AN AIRLESS ROOM REEKING OF SARDINE-BASED INK?
"CERUMEN AT YOUR FINGER-TIPS."
HOLIDAY
SORRY, THE MAJESTIC CHARI SYRUP FALLS HAVE BEEN TEMPORARILY TURNED OFF, THE TRIUMPHAL SYZAGHT ARCH IS CLOSED FOR REPAIRS, AND THE JUST WASHED MOSAIC FLOORS OF THE LEGISLATIVE PALACE ARE STILL WET.
CLOSED
DIRECT FLY
$695

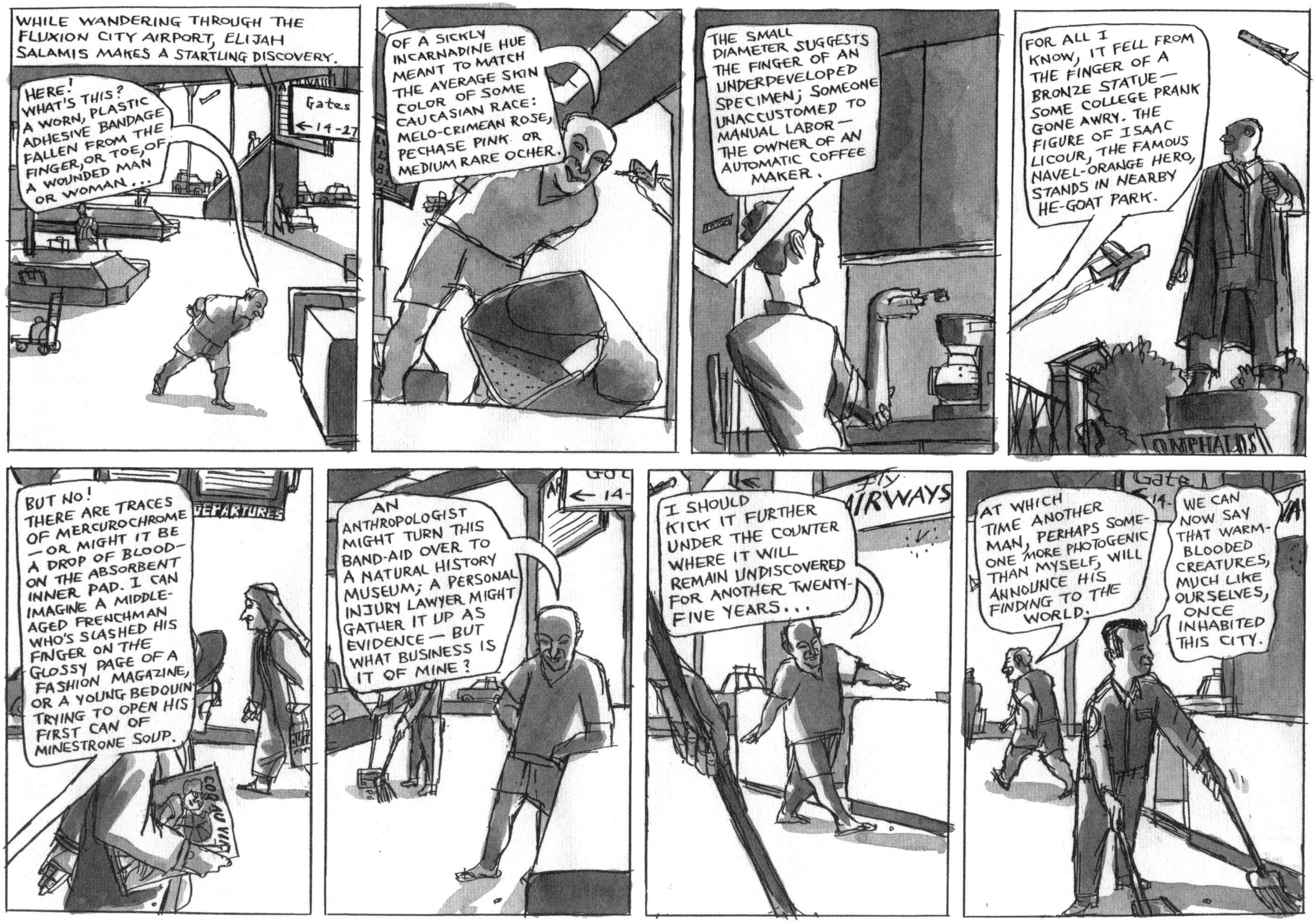
WHILE WANDERING THROUGH THE FLUXION CITY AIRPORT, ELIJAH SALAMIS MAKES A STARTLING DISCOVERY.
HERE! WHAT'S THIS? A WORN, PLASTIC ADHESIVE BANDAGE FALLEN FROM THE FINGER, OR TOE, OF A WOUNDED MAN OR WOMAN...
Gates ←14-27
OF A SICKLY INCARNADINE HUE MEANT TO MATCH THE AVERAGE SKIN COLOR OF SOME CAUCASIAN RACE: MELO-CRIMEAN ROSE, PECHASE PINK OR MEDIUM RARE OCHER.
THE SMALL DIAMETER SUGGESTS THE FINGER OF AN UNDERDEVELOPED SPECIMEN; SOMEONE UNACCUSTOMED TO MANUAL LABOR— THE OWNER OF AN AUTOMATIC COFFEE MAKER.
FOR ALL I KNOW, IT FELL FROM THE FINGER OF A BRONZE STATUE— SOME COLLEGE PRANK GONE AWRY. THE FIGURE OF ISAAC LICOUR, THE FAMOUS NAVEL-ORANGE HERO, STANDS IN NEARBY HE-GOAT PARK.
OMPHALOS
DEPARTURES
BUT NO! THERE ARE TRACES OF MERCUROCHROME —OR MIGHT IT BE A DROP OF BLOOD— ON THE ABSORBENT INNER PAD. I CAN IMAGINE A MIDDLE-AGED FRENCHMAN WHO'S SLASHED HIS FINGER ON THE GLOSSY PAGE OF A FASHION MAGAZINE, OR A YOUNG BEDOUIN TRYING TO OPEN HIS FIRST CAN OF MINESTRONE SOUP.
AN ANTHROPOLOGIST MIGHT TURN THIS BAND-AID OVER TO A NATURAL HISTORY MUSEUM; A PERSONAL INJURY LAWYER MIGHT GATHER IT UP AS EVIDENCE— BUT WHAT BUSINESS IS IT OF MINE?
AIRWAYS
I SHOULD KICK IT FURTHER UNDER THE COUNTER WHERE IT WILL REMAIN UNDISCOVERED FOR ANOTHER TWENTY-FIVE YEARS...
AT WHICH TIME ANOTHER MAN, PERHAPS SOMEONE MORE PHOTOGENIC THAN MYSELF, WILL ANNOUNCE HIS FINDING TO THE WORLD.
WE CAN NOW SAY THAT WARM-BLOODED CREATURES, MUCH LIKE OURSELVES, ONCE INHABITED THIS CITY.

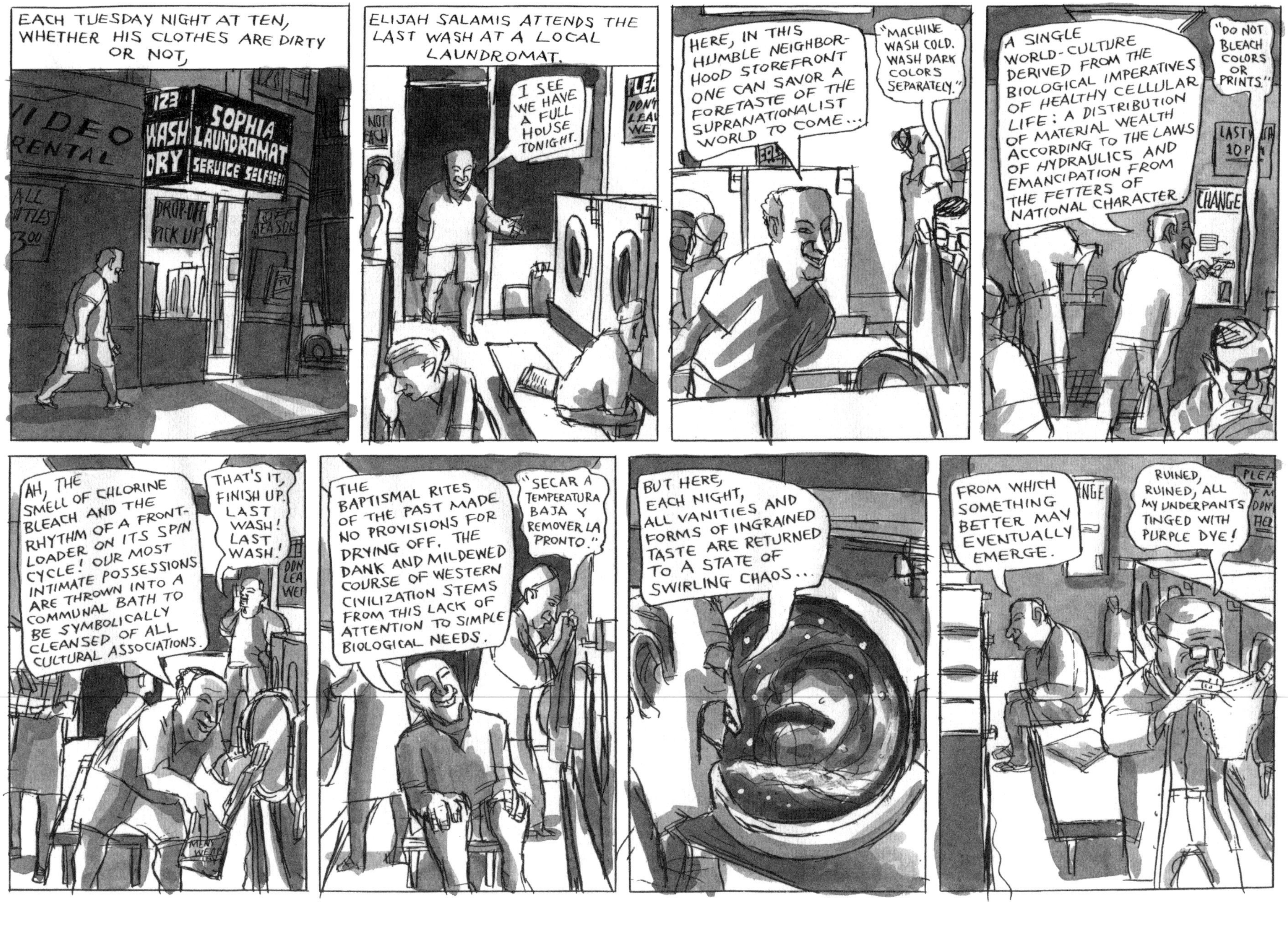
EACH TUESDAY NIGHT AT TEN, WHETHER HIS CLOTHES ARE DIRTY OR NOT,
SOPHIA LAUNDROMAT
ELIJAH SALAMIS ATTENDS THE LAST WASH AT A LOCAL LAUNDROMAT.
I SEE WE HAVE A FULL HOUSE TONIGHT.
HERE, IN THIS HUMBLE NEIGHBOR-HOOD STOREFRONT ONE CAN SAVOR A FORETASTE OF THE SUPRANATIONALIST WORLD TO COME...
"MACHINE WASH COLD. WASH DARK COLORS SEPARATELY."
A SINGLE WORLD-CULTURE DERIVED FROM THE BIOLOGICAL IMPERATIVES OF HEALTHY CELLULAR LIFE: A DISTRIBUTION OF MATERIAL WEALTH ACCORDING TO THE LAWS OF HYDRAULICS AND EMANCIPATION FROM THE FETTERS OF NATIONAL CHARACTER
"DO NOT BLEACH COLORS OR PRINTS."
CHANGE
AH, THE SMELL OF CHLORINE BLEACH AND THE RHYTHM OF A FRONT-LOADER ON ITS SPIN CYCLE! OUR MOST INTIMATE POSSESSIONS ARE THROWN INTO A COMMUNAL BATH TO BE SYMBOLICALLY CLEANSED OF ALL CULTURAL ASSOCIATIONS.
THAT'S IT, FINISH UP. LAST WASH! LAST WASH!
THE BAPTISMAL RITES OF THE PAST MADE NO PROVISIONS FOR DRYING OFF. THE DANK AND MILDEWED COURSE OF WESTERN CIVILIZATION STEMS FROM THIS LACK OF ATTENTION TO SIMPLE BIOLOGICAL NEEDS.
"SECAR A TEMPERATURA BAJA Y REMOVER LA PRONTO."
BUT HERE, EACH NIGHT, ALL VANITIES AND FORMS OF INGRAINED TASTE ARE RETURNED TO A STATE OF SWIRLING CHAOS...
FROM WHICH SOMETHING BETTER MAY EVENTUALLY EMERGE.
RUINED, RUINED, ALL MY UNDERPANTS TINGED WITH PURPLE DYE!

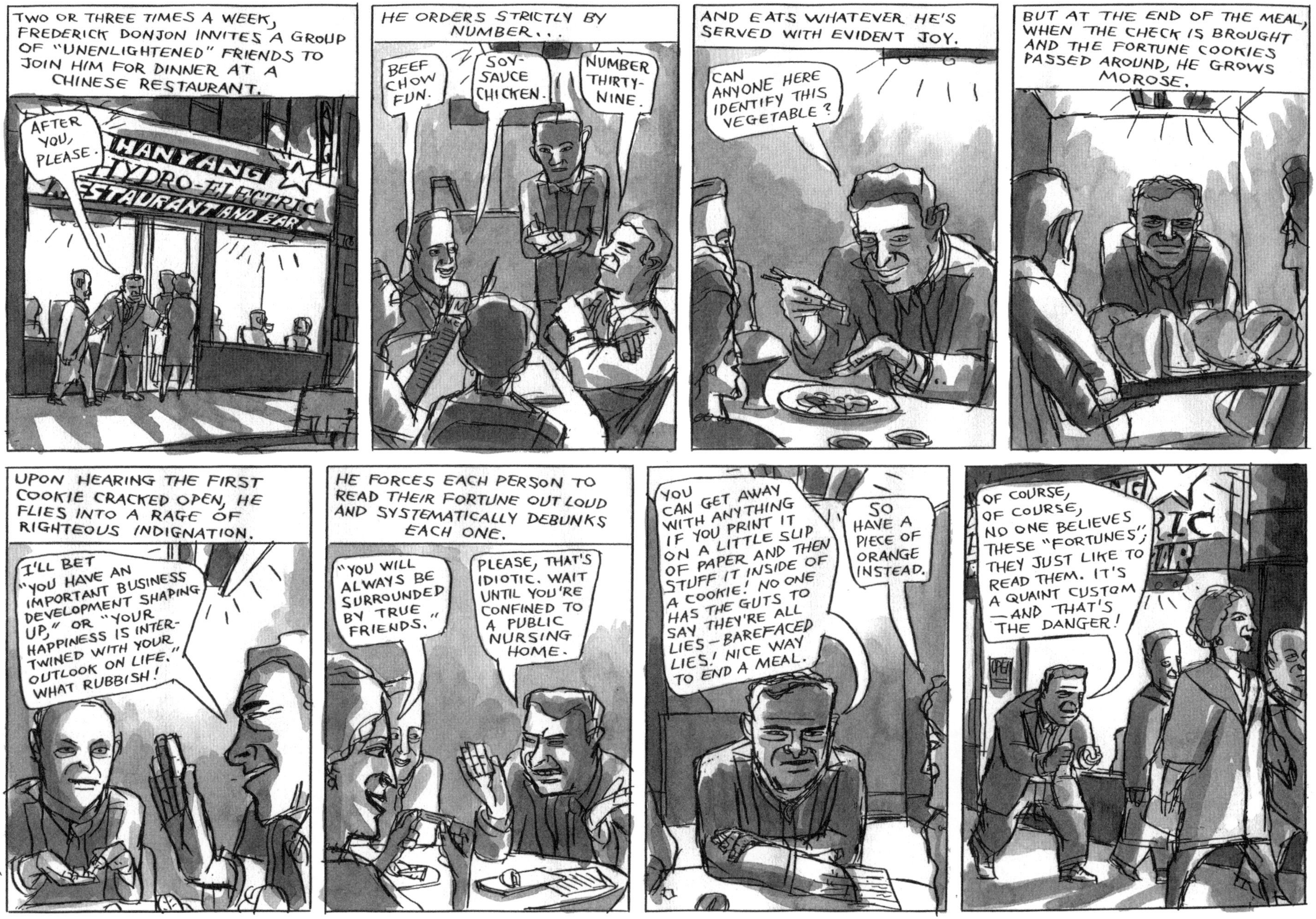

TWO OR THREE TIMES A WEEK, FREDERICK DONJON INVITES A GROUP OF "UNENLIGHTENED" FRIENDS TO JOIN HIM FOR DINNER AT A CHINESE RESTAURANT.
AFTER YOU, PLEASE.
HANYANG
HYDRO-ELECTRIC
ESTAURANT AND BAR
HE ORDERS STRICTLY BY NUMBER...
BEEF CHOW FUN.
SOY-SAUCE CHICKEN.
NUMBER THIRTY-NINE.
AND EATS WHATEVER HE'S SERVED WITH EVIDENT JOY.
CAN ANYONE HERE IDENTIFY THIS VEGETABLE?
BUT AT THE END OF THE MEAL, WHEN THE CHECK IS BROUGHT AND THE FORTUNE COOKIES PASSED AROUND, HE GROWS MOROSE.
UPON HEARING THE FIRST COOKIE CRACKED OPEN, HE FLIES INTO A RAGE OF RIGHTEOUS INDIGNATION.
I'LL BET "YOU HAVE AN IMPORTANT BUSINESS DEVELOPMENT SHAPING UP," OR "YOUR HAPPINESS IS INTERTWINED WITH YOUR OUTLOOK ON LIFE." WHAT RUBBISH!
HE FORCES EACH PERSON TO READ THEIR FORTUNE OUT LOUD AND SYSTEMATICALLY DEBUNKS EACH ONE.
"YOU WILL ALWAYS BE SURROUNDED BY TRUE FRIENDS."
PLEASE, THAT'S IDIOTIC. WAIT UNTIL YOU'RE CONFINED TO A PUBLIC NURSING HOME.
YOU CAN GET AWAY WITH ANYTHING IF YOU PRINT IT ON A LITTLE SLIP OF PAPER AND THEN STUFF IT INSIDE OF A COOKIE! NO ONE HAS THE GUTS TO SAY THEY'RE ALL LIES—BAREFACED LIES! NICE WAY TO END A MEAL.
SO HAVE A PIECE OF ORANGE INSTEAD.
OF COURSE, OF COURSE, NO ONE BELIEVES THESE "FORTUNES"; THEY JUST LIKE TO READ THEM. IT'S A QUAINT CUSTOM—AND THAT'S THE DANGER!

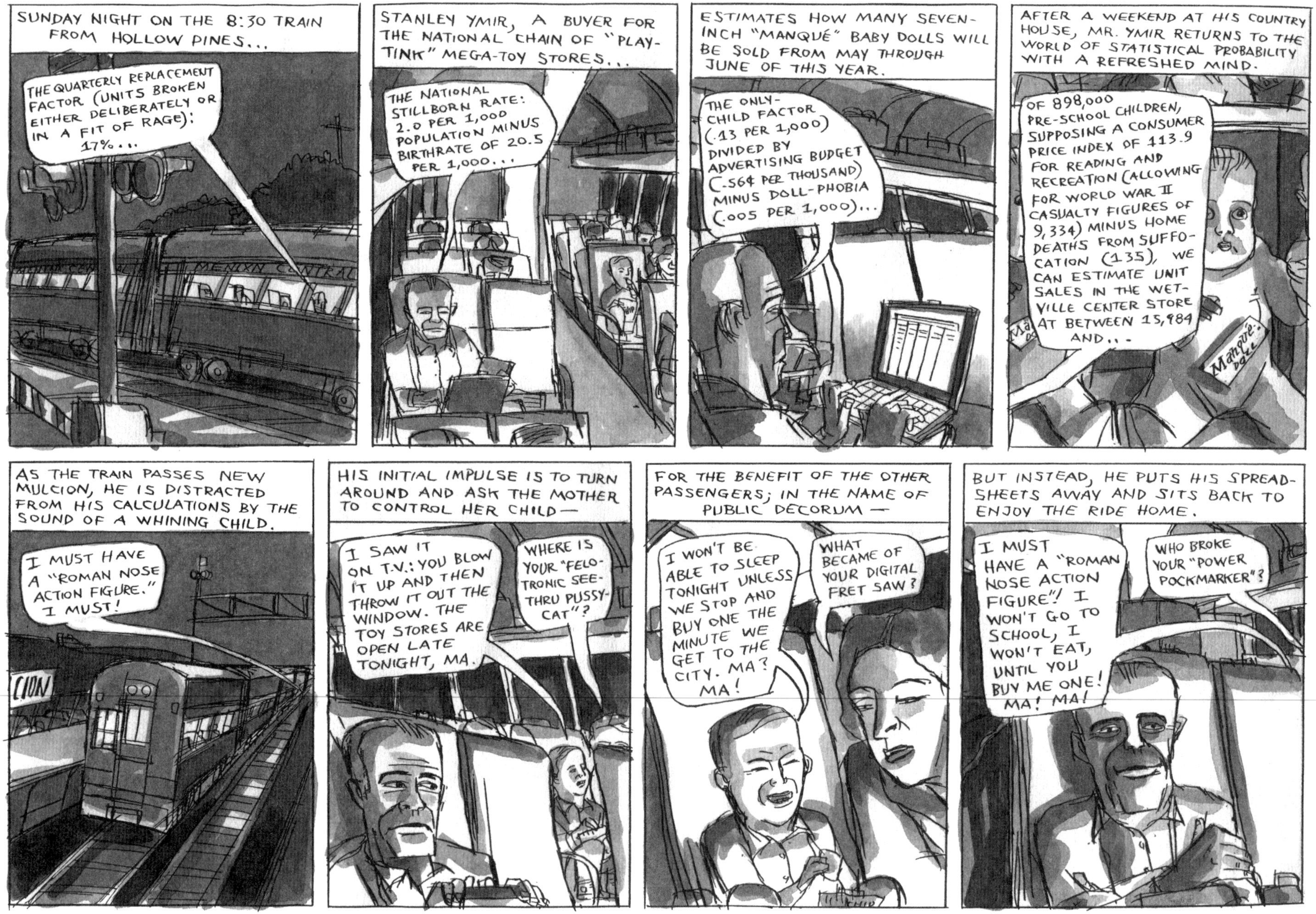
SUNDAY NIGHT ON THE 8:30 TRAIN FROM HOLLOW PINES...
THE QUARTERLY REPLACEMENT FACTOR (UNITS BROKEN EITHER DELIBERATELY OR IN A FIT OF RAGE): 17%...
STANLEY YMIR, A BUYER FOR THE NATIONAL CHAIN OF "PLAY-TINK" MEGA-TOY STORES...
THE NATIONAL STILLBORN RATE: 2.0 PER 1,000 POPULATION MINUS BIRTHRATE OF 20.5 PER 1,000...
ESTIMATES HOW MANY SEVEN-INCH "MANQUÉ" BABY DOLLS WILL BE SOLD FROM MAY THROUGH JUNE OF THIS YEAR.
THE ONLY-CHILD FACTOR (.13 PER 1,000) DIVIDED BY ADVERTISING BUDGET (.56¢ PER THOUSAND) MINUS DOLL-PHOBIA (.005 PER 1,000)...
AFTER A WEEKEND AT HIS COUNTRY HOUSE, MR. YMIR RETURNS TO THE WORLD OF STATISTICAL PROBABILITY WITH A REFRESHED MIND.
OF 898,000 PRE-SCHOOL CHILDREN, SUPPOSING A CONSUMER PRICE INDEX OF 113.9 FOR READING AND RECREATION (ALLOWING FOR WORLD WAR II CASUALTY FIGURES OF 9,334) MINUS HOME DEATHS FROM SUFFOCATION (135), WE CAN ESTIMATE UNIT SALES IN THE WETVILLE CENTER STORE AT BETWEEN 15,984 AND...
Manqué DOLL
AS THE TRAIN PASSES NEW MULCION, HE IS DISTRACTED FROM HIS CALCULATIONS BY THE SOUND OF A WHINING CHILD.
I MUST HAVE A "ROMAN NOSE ACTION FIGURE." I MUST!
CION
HIS INITIAL IMPULSE IS TO TURN AROUND AND ASK THE MOTHER TO CONTROL HER CHILD—
I SAW IT ON T.V.: YOU BLOW IT UP AND THEN THROW IT OUT THE WINDOW. THE TOY STORES ARE OPEN LATE TONIGHT, MA.
WHERE IS YOUR "FELOTRONIC SEE-THRU PUSSYCAT"?
FOR THE BENEFIT OF THE OTHER PASSENGERS; IN THE NAME OF PUBLIC DECORUM—
I WON'T BE ABLE TO SLEEP TONIGHT UNLESS WE STOP AND BUY ONE THE MINUTE WE GET TO THE CITY. MA? MA!
WHAT BECAME OF YOUR DIGITAL FRET SAW?
BUT INSTEAD, HE PUTS HIS SPREADSHEETS AWAY AND SITS BACK TO ENJOY THE RIDE HOME.
I MUST HAVE A "ROMAN NOSE ACTION FIGURE"! I WON'T GO TO SCHOOL, I WON'T EAT, UNTIL YOU BUY ME ONE! MA! MA!
WHO BROKE YOUR "POWER POCKMARKER"?

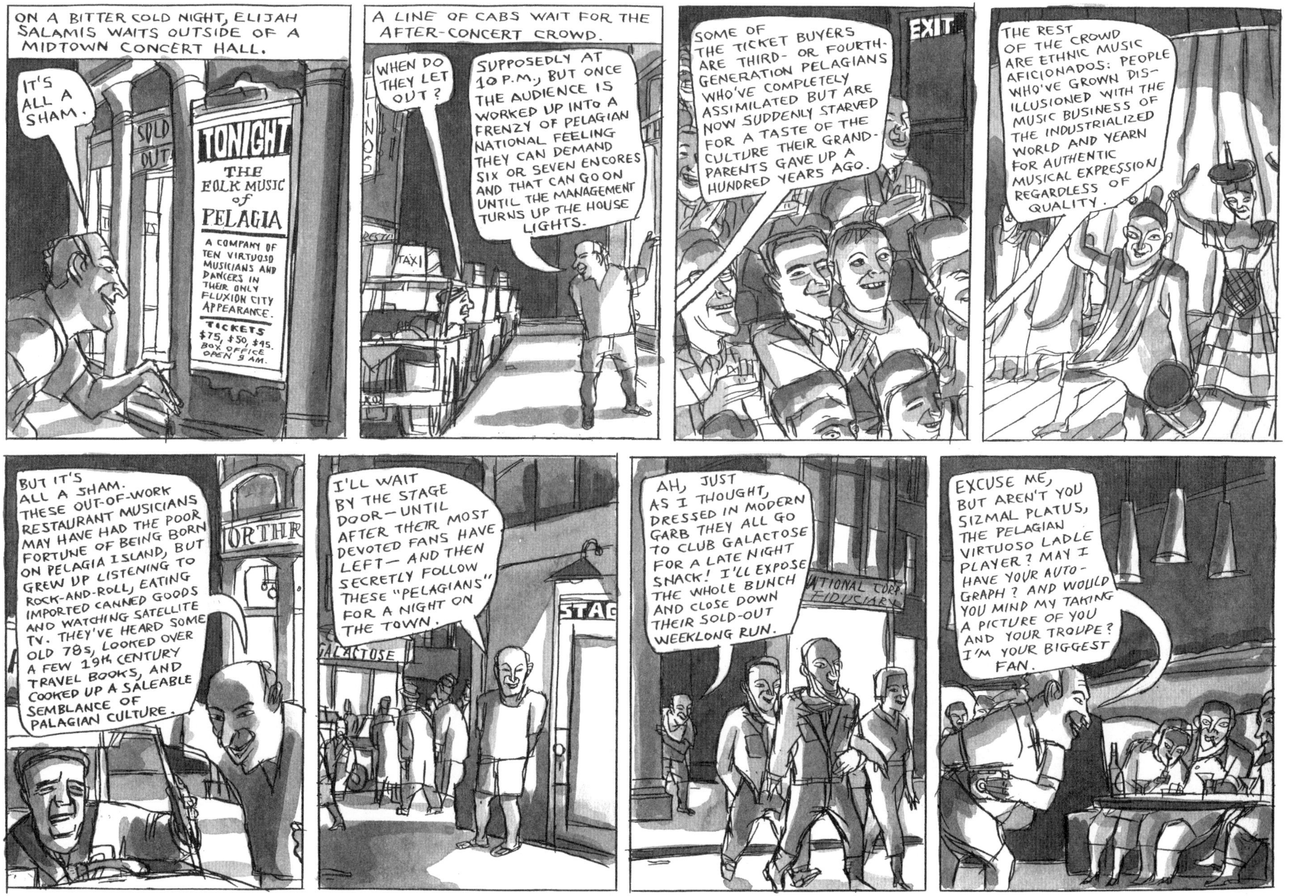
ON A BITTER COLD NIGHT, ELIJAH SALAMIS WAITS OUTSIDE OF A MIDTOWN CONCERT HALL.
IT'S ALL A SHAM.
SOLD OUT
TONIGHT
THE FOLK MUSIC of PELAGIA
A COMPANY OF TEN VIRTUOSO MUSICIANS AND DANCERS IN THEIR ONLY FLUXION CITY APPEARANCE.
TICKETS $75, $50, $45.
BOX OFFICE OPEN 9 AM.
A LINE OF CABS WAIT FOR THE AFTER-CONCERT CROWD.
WHEN DO THEY LET OUT?
SUPPOSEDLY AT 10 P.M., BUT ONCE THE AUDIENCE IS WORKED UP INTO A FRENZY OF PELAGIAN NATIONAL FEELING THEY CAN DEMAND SIX OR SEVEN ENCORES AND THAT CAN GO ON UNTIL THE MANAGEMENT TURNS UP THE HOUSE LIGHTS.
TAXI
EXIT
SOME OF THE TICKET BUYERS ARE THIRD- OR FOURTH-GENERATION PELAGIANS WHO'VE COMPLETELY ASSIMILATED BUT ARE NOW SUDDENLY STARVED FOR A TASTE OF THE CULTURE THEIR GRAND-PARENTS GAVE UP A HUNDRED YEARS AGO.
THE REST OF THE CROWD ARE ETHNIC MUSIC AFICIONADOS: PEOPLE WHO'VE GROWN DIS-ILLUSIONED WITH THE MUSIC BUSINESS OF THE INDUSTRIALIZED WORLD AND YEARN FOR AUTHENTIC MUSICAL EXPRESSION REGARDLESS OF QUALITY.
BUT IT'S ALL A SHAM. THESE OUT-OF-WORK RESTAURANT MUSICIANS MAY HAVE HAD THE POOR FORTUNE OF BEING BORN ON PELAGIA ISLAND, BUT GREW UP LISTENING TO ROCK-AND-ROLL, EATING IMPORTED CANNED GOODS AND WATCHING SATELLITE TV. THEY'VE HEARD SOME OLD 78s, LOOKED OVER A FEW 19th CENTURY TRAVEL BOOKS, AND COOKED UP A SALEABLE SEMBLANCE OF PALAGIAN CULTURE.
I'LL WAIT BY THE STAGE DOOR—UNTIL AFTER THEIR MOST DEVOTED FANS HAVE LEFT—AND THEN SECRETLY FOLLOW THESE "PELAGIANS" FOR A NIGHT ON THE TOWN.
GALACTOSE
AH, JUST AS I THOUGHT, DRESSED IN MODERN GARB THEY ALL GO TO CLUB GALACTOSE FOR A LATE NIGHT SNACK! I'LL EXPOSE THE WHOLE BUNCH AND CLOSE DOWN THEIR SOLD-OUT WEEKLONG RUN.
EXCUSE ME, BUT AREN'T YOU SIZMAL PLATUS, THE PELAGIAN VIRTUOSO LADLE PLAYER? MAY I HAVE YOUR AUTO-GRAPH? AND WOULD YOU MIND MY TAKING A PICTURE OF YOU AND YOUR TROUPE? I'M YOUR BIGGEST FAN.

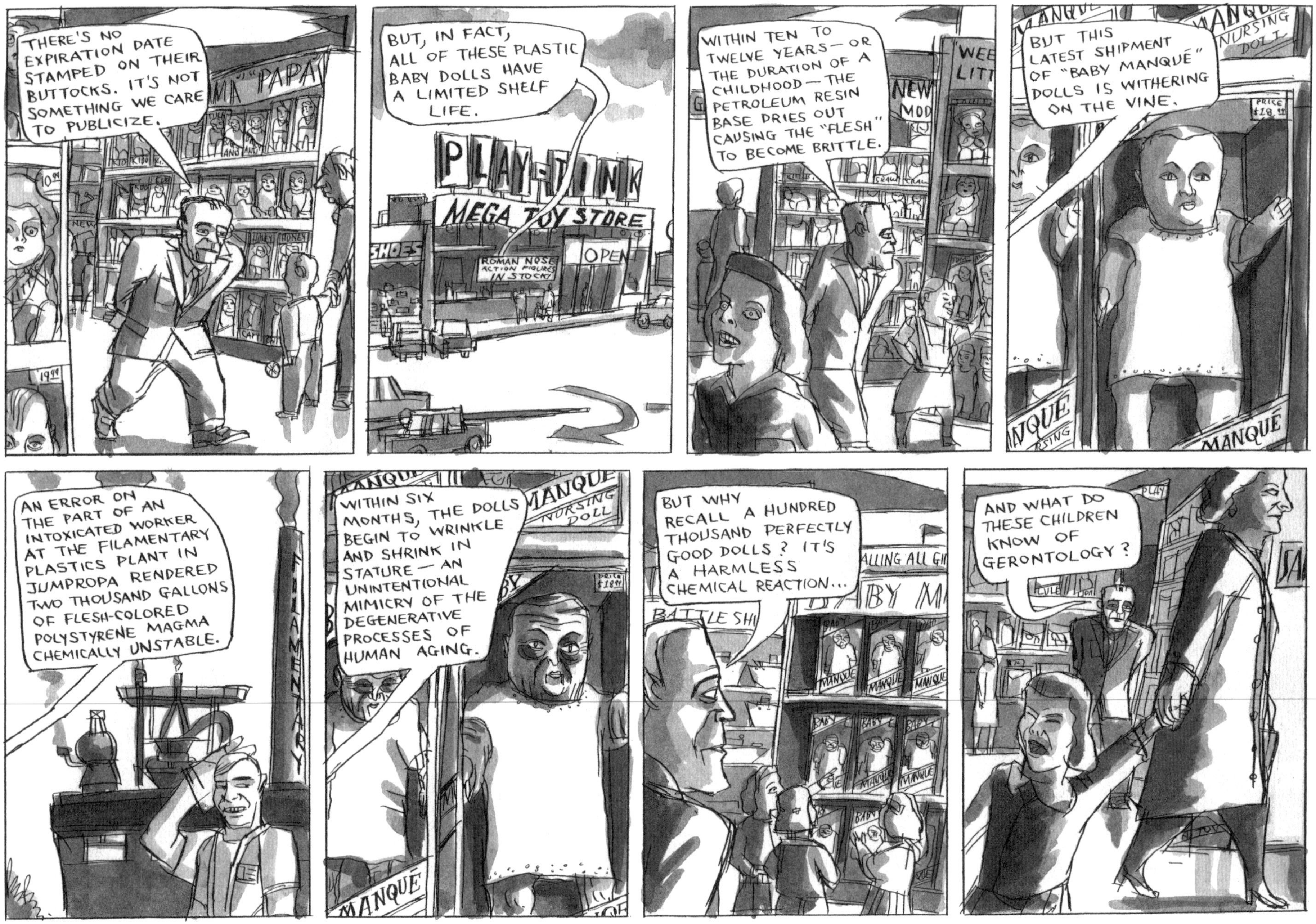
THERE'S NO EXPIRATION DATE STAMPED ON THEIR BUTTOCKS. IT'S NOT SOMETHING WE CARE TO PUBLICIZE.
BUT, IN FACT, ALL OF THESE PLASTIC BABY DOLLS HAVE A LIMITED SHELF LIFE.
PLAY-TINK
MEGA TOY STORE
SHOES
ROMAN NOSE ACTION FIGURES IN STOCK!
OPEN
WITHIN TEN TO TWELVE YEARS—OR THE DURATION OF A CHILDHOOD—THE PETROLEUM RESIN BASE DRIES OUT CAUSING THE "FLESH" TO BECOME BRITTLE.
BUT THIS LATEST SHIPMENT OF "BABY MANQUÉ" DOLLS IS WITHERING ON THE VINE.
MANQUÉ
AN ERROR ON THE PART OF AN INTOXICATED WORKER AT THE FILAMENTARY PLASTICS PLANT IN JUMPROPA RENDERED TWO THOUSAND GALLONS OF FLESH-COLORED POLYSTYRENE MAGMA CHEMICALLY UNSTABLE.
FILAMENTARY
MANQUE
NURSING DOLL
WITHIN SIX MONTHS, THE DOLLS BEGIN TO WRINKLE AND SHRINK IN STATURE—AN UNINTENTIONAL MIMICRY OF THE DEGENERATIVE PROCESSES OF HUMAN AGING.
MANQUÉ
BUT WHY RECALL A HUNDRED THOUSAND PERFECTLY GOOD DOLLS? IT'S A HARMLESS CHEMICAL REACTION...
AND WHAT DO THESE CHILDREN KNOW OF GERONTOLOGY?

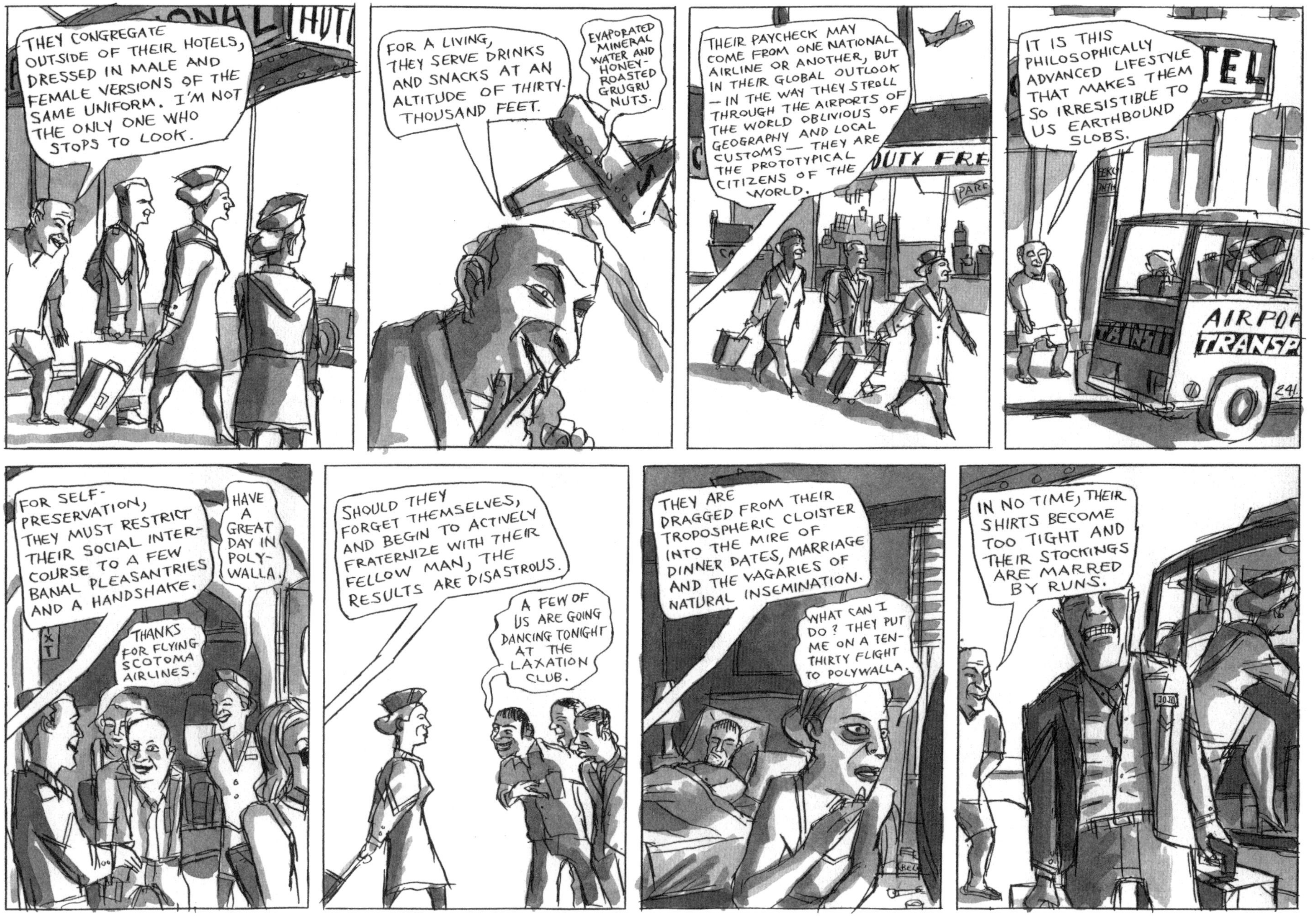
THEY CONGREGATE OUTSIDE OF THEIR HOTELS, DRESSED IN MALE AND FEMALE VERSIONS OF THE SAME UNIFORM. I'M NOT THE ONLY ONE WHO STOPS TO LOOK.
FOR A LIVING, THEY SERVE DRINKS AND SNACKS AT AN ALTITUDE OF THIRTY-THOUSAND FEET.
EVAPORATED MINERAL WATER AND HONEY-ROASTED GRUGRU NUTS.
THEIR PAYCHECK MAY COME FROM ONE NATIONAL AIRLINE OR ANOTHER, BUT IN THEIR GLOBAL OUTLOOK — IN THE WAY THEY STROLL THROUGH THE AIRPORTS OF THE WORLD OBLIVIOUS OF GEOGRAPHY AND LOCAL CUSTOMS — THEY ARE THE PROTOTYPICAL CITIZENS OF THE WORLD.
DUTY FRE
GIFT
IT IS THIS PHILOSOPHICALLY ADVANCED LIFESTYLE THAT MAKES THEM SO IRRESISTIBLE TO US EARTHBOUND SLOBS.
TEL
AIRPO
TRANSP
241
FOR SELF-PRESERVATION, THEY MUST RESTRICT THEIR SOCIAL INTER-COURSE TO A FEW BANAL PLEASANTRIES AND A HANDSHAKE.
HAVE A GREAT DAY IN POLY-WALLA.
THANKS FOR FLYING SCOTOMA AIRLINES.
SHOULD THEY FORGET THEMSELVES, AND BEGIN TO ACTIVELY FRATERNIZE WITH THEIR FELLOW MAN, THE RESULTS ARE DISASTROUS.
A FEW OF US ARE GOING DANCING TONIGHT AT THE LAXATION CLUB.
THEY ARE DRAGGED FROM THEIR TROPOSPHERIC CLOISTER INTO THE MIRE OF DINNER DATES, MARRIAGE AND THE VAGARIES OF NATURAL INSEMINATION.
WHAT CAN I DO? THEY PUT ME ON A TEN-THIRTY FLIGHT TO POLYWALLA.
IN NO TIME, THEIR SHIRTS BECOME TOO TIGHT AND THEIR STOCKINGS ARE MARRED BY RUNS.

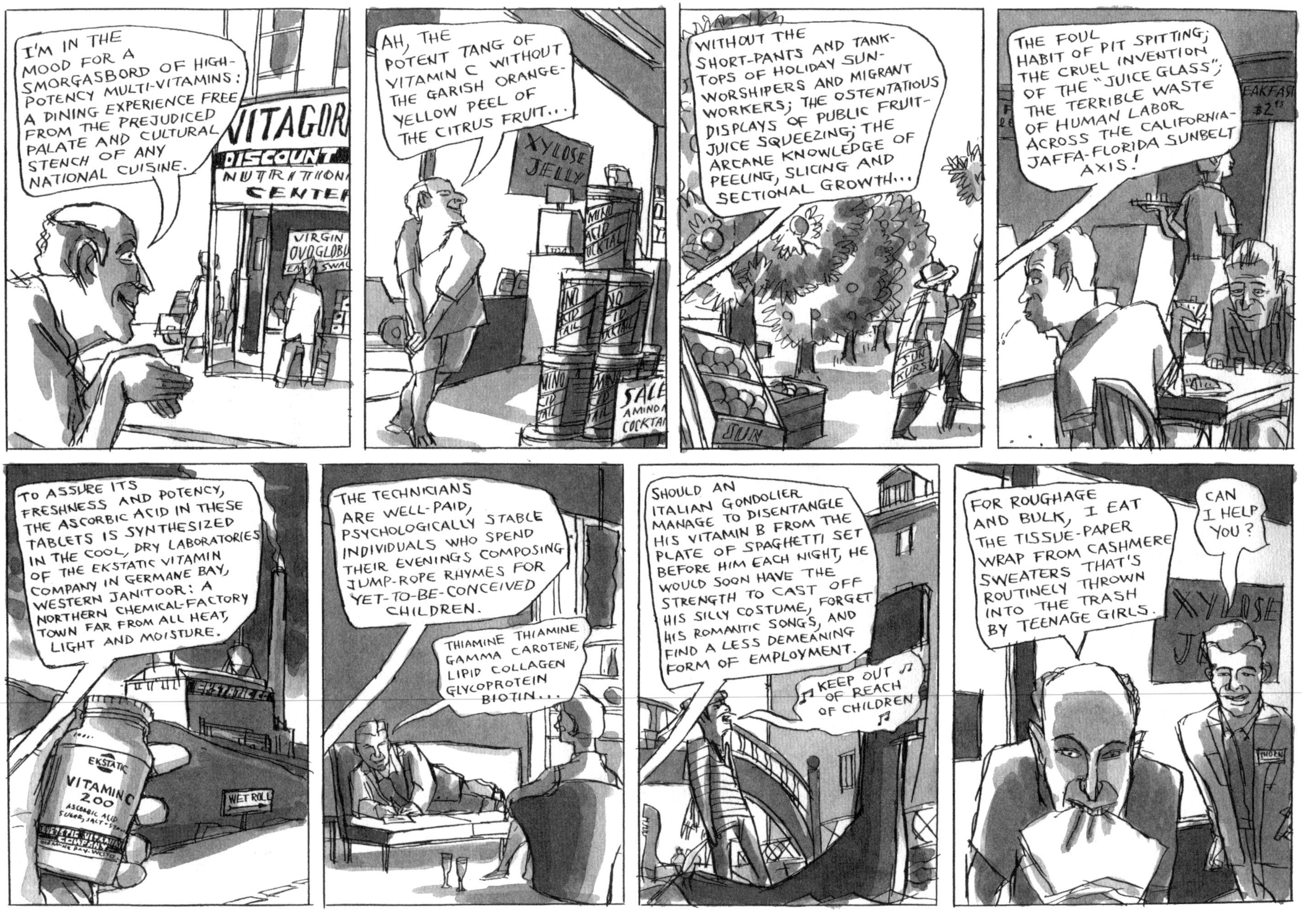
I'M IN THE MOOD FOR A SMORGASBORD OF HIGH-POTENCY MULTI-VITAMINS: A DINING EXPERIENCE FREE FROM THE PREJUDICED PALATE AND CULTURAL STENCH OF ANY NATIONAL CUISINE.
DISCOUNT
CENTER
VIRGIN
AH, THE POTENT TANG OF VITAMIN C WITHOUT THE GARISH ORANGE-YELLOW PEEL OF THE CITRUS FRUIT...
XYLOSE JELLY
SALE
WITHOUT THE SHORT-PANTS AND TANK-TOPS OF HOLIDAY SUN-WORSHIPERS AND MIGRANT WORKERS; THE OSTENTATIOUS DISPLAYS OF PUBLIC FRUIT-JUICE SQUEEZING; THE ARCANE KNOWLEDGE OF PEELING, SLICING AND SECTIONAL GROWTH...
SUN
THE FOUL HABIT OF PIT SPITTING; THE CRUEL INVENTION OF THE "JUICE GLASS"; THE TERRIBLE WASTE OF HUMAN LABOR ACROSS THE CALIFORNIA-JAFFA-FLORIDA SUNBELT AXIS!
TO ASSURE ITS FRESHNESS AND POTENCY, THE ASCORBIC ACID IN THESE TABLETS IS SYNTHESIZED IN THE COOL, DRY LABORATORIES OF THE EKSTATIC VITAMIN COMPANY IN GERMANE BAY, WESTERN JANITOOR: A NORTHERN CHEMICAL-FACTORY TOWN FAR FROM ALL HEAT, LIGHT AND MOISTURE.
EKSTATIC
VITAMIN C 200
ASCORBIC ACID
WET ROLL
THE TECHNICIANS ARE WELL-PAID, PSYCHOLOGICALLY STABLE INDIVIDUALS WHO SPEND THEIR EVENINGS COMPOSING JUMP-ROPE RHYMES FOR YET-TO-BE-CONCEIVED CHILDREN.
THIAMINE THIAMINE GAMMA CAROTENE, LIPID COLLAGEN GLYCOPROTEIN BIOTIN...
SHOULD AN ITALIAN GONDOLIER MANAGE TO DISENTANGLE HIS VITAMIN B FROM THE PLATE OF SPAGHETTI SET BEFORE HIM EACH NIGHT, HE WOULD SOON HAVE THE STRENGTH TO CAST OFF HIS SILLY COSTUME, FORGET HIS ROMANTIC SONGS, AND FIND A LESS DEMEANING FORM OF EMPLOYMENT.
♫ KEEP OUT ♫ OF REACH OF CHILDREN ♫
FOR ROUGHAGE AND BULK, I EAT THE TISSUE-PAPER WRAP FROM CASHMERE SWEATERS THAT'S ROUTINELY THROWN INTO THE TRASH BY TEENAGE GIRLS.
CAN I HELP YOU?

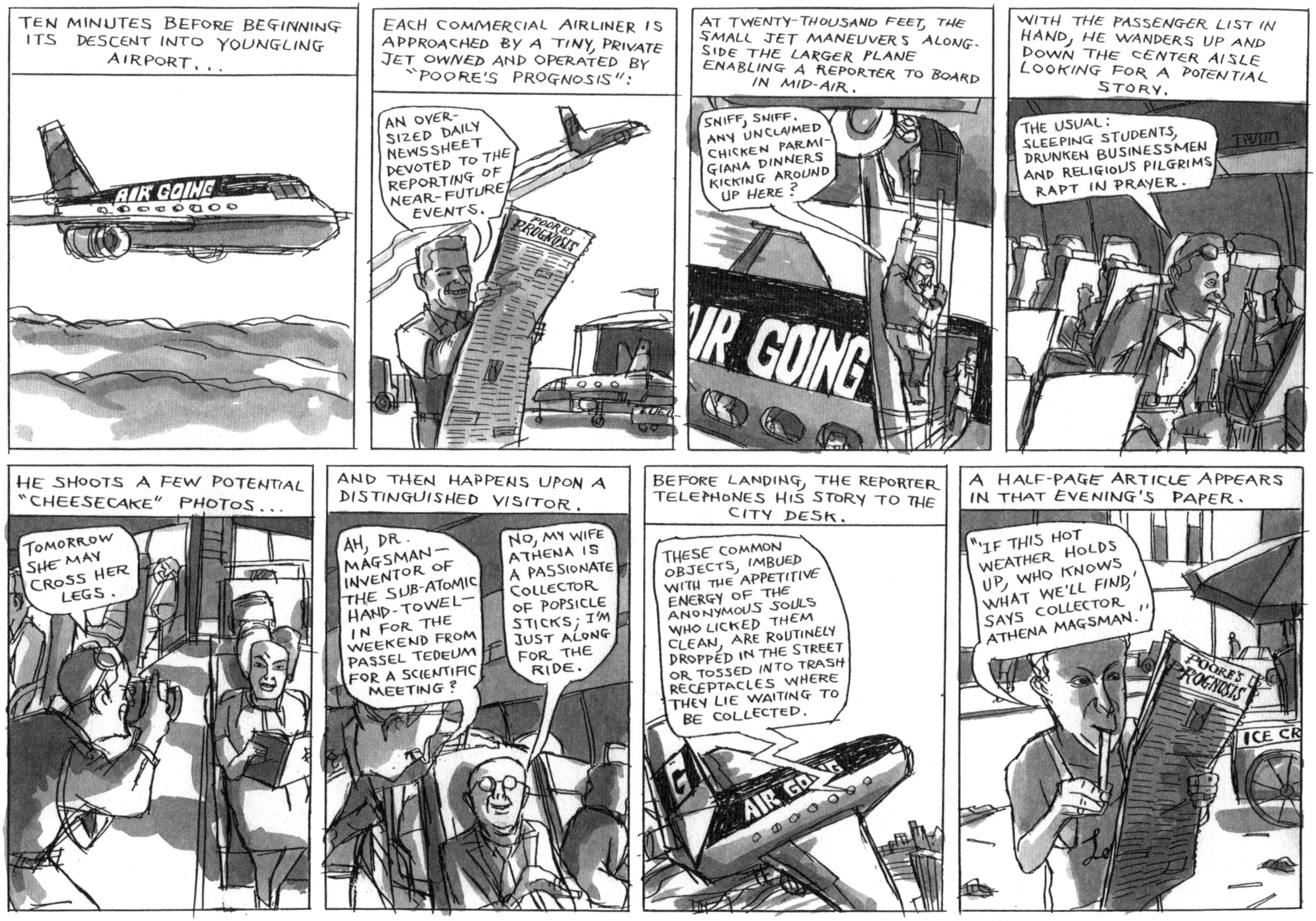
TEN MINUTES BEFORE BEGINNING ITS DESCENT INTO YOUNGLING AIRPORT...
AIR GOING
EACH COMMERCIAL AIRLINER IS APPROACHED BY A TINY, PRIVATE JET OWNED AND OPERATED BY "POORE'S PROGNOSIS":
AN OVER-SIZED DAILY NEWSSHEET DEVOTED TO THE REPORTING OF NEAR-FUTURE EVENTS.
POORE'S PROGNOSIS
AT TWENTY-THOUSAND FEET, THE SMALL JET MANEUVERS ALONG-SIDE THE LARGER PLANE ENABLING A REPORTER TO BOARD IN MID-AIR.
SNIFF, SNIFF. ANY UNCLAIMED CHICKEN PARMI-GIANA DINNERS KICKING AROUND UP HERE?
IR GOING
WITH THE PASSENGER LIST IN HAND, HE WANDERS UP AND DOWN THE CENTER AISLE LOOKING FOR A POTENTIAL STORY.
THE USUAL: SLEEPING STUDENTS, DRUNKEN BUSINESSMEN AND RELIGIOUS PILGRIMS RAPT IN PRAYER.
HE SHOOTS A FEW POTENTIAL "CHEESECAKE" PHOTOS...
TOMORROW SHE MAY CROSS HER LEGS.
AND THEN HAPPENS UPON A DISTINGUISHED VISITOR.
AH, DR. MAGSMAN—INVENTOR OF THE SUB-ATOMIC HAND-TOWEL—IN FOR THE WEEKEND FROM PASSEL TEDEUM FOR A SCIENTIFIC MEETING?
NO, MY WIFE ATHENA IS A PASSIONATE COLLECTOR OF POPSICLE STICKS; I'M JUST ALONG FOR THE RIDE.
BEFORE LANDING, THE REPORTER TELEPHONES HIS STORY TO THE CITY DESK.
THESE COMMON OBJECTS, IMBUED WITH THE APPETITIVE ENERGY OF THE ANONYMOUS SOULS WHO LICKED THEM CLEAN, ARE ROUTINELY DROPPED IN THE STREET OR TOSSED INTO TRASH RECEPTACLES WHERE THEY LIE WAITING TO BE COLLECTED.
AIR GOING
A HALF-PAGE ARTICLE APPEARS IN THAT EVENING'S PAPER.
"'IF THIS HOT WEATHER HOLDS UP, WHO KNOWS WHAT WE'LL FIND,' SAYS COLLECTOR ATHENA MAGSMAN."
POORE'S PROGNOSIS
ICE CR

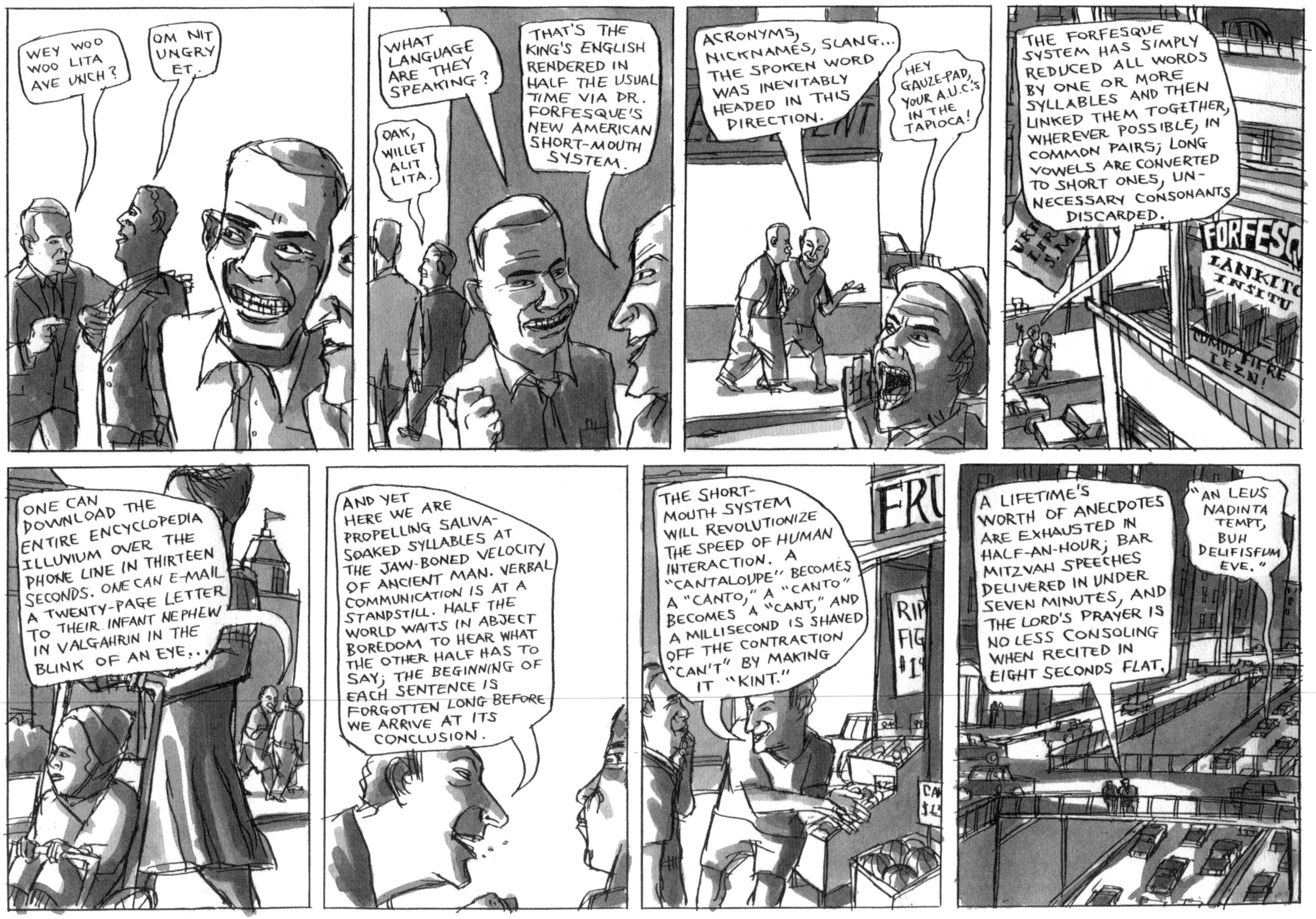
WEY WOO WOO LITA AVE UNCH?
OM NIT UNGRY ET.
WHAT LANGUAGE ARE THEY SPEAKING?
THAT'S THE KING'S ENGLISH RENDERED IN HALF THE USUAL TIME VIA DR. FORFESQUE'S NEW AMERICAN SHORT-MOUTH SYSTEM.
OAK, WILLET ALIT LITA.
ACRONYMS, NICKNAMES, SLANG... THE SPOKEN WORD WAS INEVITABLY HEADED IN THIS DIRECTION.
HEY GAUZE-PAD, YOUR A.U.C.'S IN THE TAPIOCA!
THE FORFESQUE SYSTEM HAS SIMPLY REDUCED ALL WORDS BY ONE OR MORE SYLLABLES AND THEN LINKED THEM TOGETHER, WHEREVER POSSIBLE, IN COMMON PAIRS; LONG VOWELS ARE CONVERTED TO SHORT ONES, UNNECESSARY CONSONANTS DISCARDED.
FORFESQ
LANKITO INSITU
COMUP FIFRE LEZN!
ONE CAN DOWNLOAD THE ENTIRE ENCYCLOPEDIA ILLUVIUM OVER THE PHONE LINE IN THIRTEEN SECONDS. ONE CAN E-MAIL A TWENTY-PAGE LETTER TO THEIR INFANT NEPHEW IN VALGAHRIN IN THE BLINK OF AN EYE...
AND YET HERE WE ARE PROPELLING SALIVA-SOAKED SYLLABLES AT THE JAW-BONED VELOCITY OF ANCIENT MAN. VERBAL COMMUNICATION IS AT A STANDSTILL. HALF THE WORLD WAITS IN ABJECT BOREDOM TO HEAR WHAT THE OTHER HALF HAS TO SAY; THE BEGINNING OF EACH SENTENCE IS FORGOTTEN LONG BEFORE WE ARRIVE AT ITS CONCLUSION.
THE SHORT-MOUTH SYSTEM WILL REVOLUTIONIZE THE SPEED OF HUMAN INTERACTION. A "CANTALOUPE" BECOMES A "CANTO," A "CANTO" BECOMES A "CANT," AND A MILLISECOND IS SHAVED OFF THE CONTRACTION "CAN'T" BY MAKING IT "KINT."
FRU
A LIFETIME'S WORTH OF ANECDOTES ARE EXHAUSTED IN HALF-AN-HOUR; BAR MITZVAH SPEECHES DELIVERED IN UNDER SEVEN MINUTES, AND THE LORD'S PRAYER IS NO LESS CONSOLING WHEN RECITED IN EIGHT SECONDS FLAT.
"AN LEUS NADINTA TEMPT, BUH DELIFISFUM EVE."

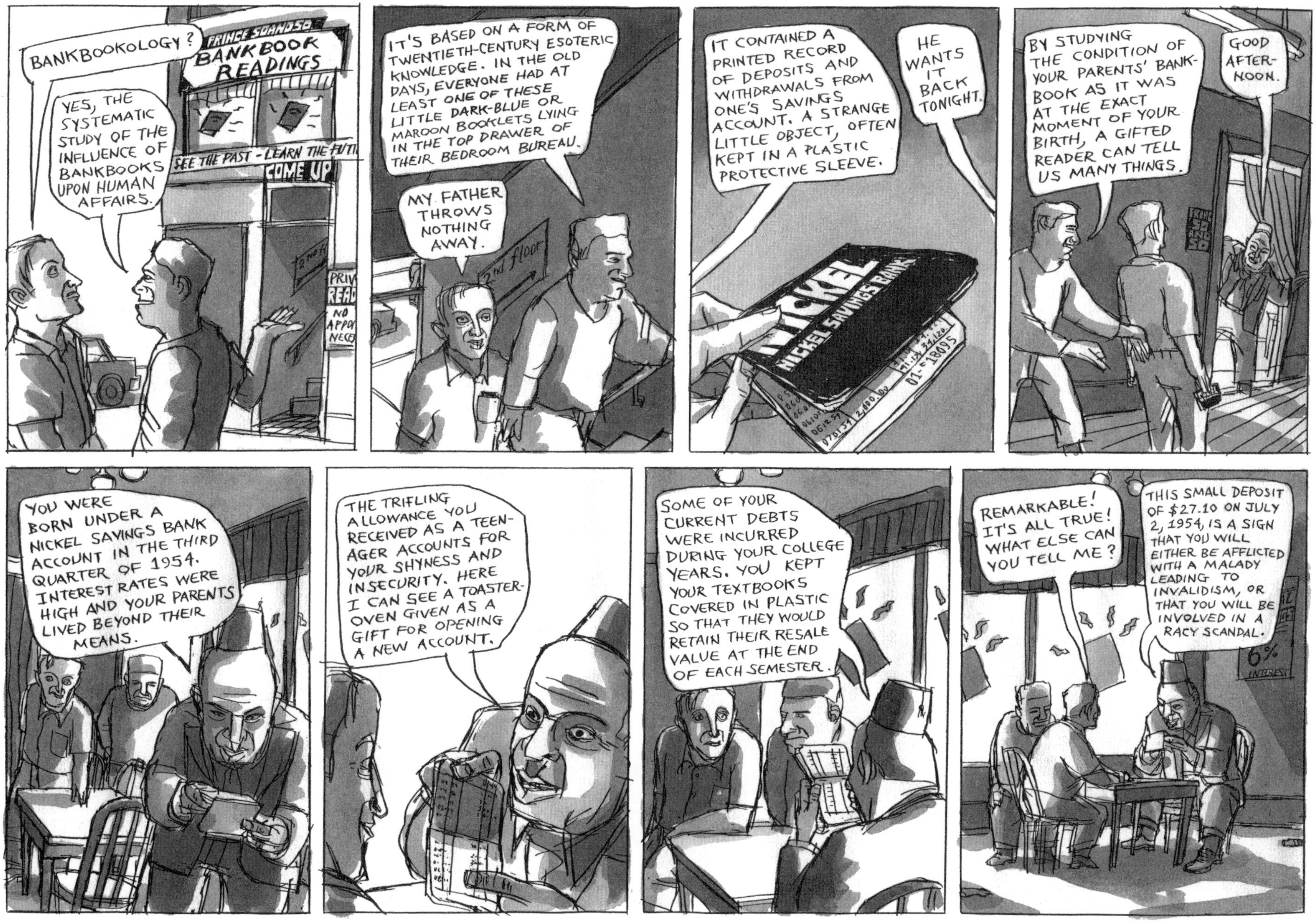
BANKBOOKOLOGY?
PRINCE SOANDSO BANKBOOK READINGS
YES, THE SYSTEMATIC STUDY OF THE INFLUENCE OF BANKBOOKS UPON HUMAN AFFAIRS.
SEE THE PAST - LEARN THE FUTU
COME UP
IT'S BASED ON A FORM OF TWENTIETH-CENTURY ESOTERIC KNOWLEDGE. IN THE OLD DAYS, EVERYONE HAD AT LEAST ONE OF THESE LITTLE DARK-BLUE OR MAROON BOOKLETS LYING IN THE TOP DRAWER OF THEIR BEDROOM BUREAU.
MY FATHER THROWS NOTHING AWAY.
2nd floor
IT CONTAINED A PRINTED RECORD OF DEPOSITS AND WITHDRAWALS FROM ONE'S SAVINGS ACCOUNT. A STRANGE LITTLE OBJECT, OFTEN KEPT IN A PLASTIC PROTECTIVE SLEEVE.
HE WANTS IT BACK TONIGHT.
NICKEL
NICKEL SAVINGS BANK
BY STUDYING THE CONDITION OF YOUR PARENTS' BANKBOOK AS IT WAS AT THE EXACT MOMENT OF YOUR BIRTH, A GIFTED READER CAN TELL US MANY THINGS.
GOOD AFTERNOON.
YOU WERE BORN UNDER A NICKEL SAVINGS BANK ACCOUNT IN THE THIRD QUARTER OF 1954. INTEREST RATES WERE HIGH AND YOUR PARENTS LIVED BEYOND THEIR MEANS.
THE TRIFLING ALLOWANCE YOU RECEIVED AS A TEENAGER ACCOUNTS FOR YOUR SHYNESS AND INSECURITY. HERE I CAN SEE A TOASTER-OVEN GIVEN AS A GIFT FOR OPENING A NEW ACCOUNT.
SOME OF YOUR CURRENT DEBTS WERE INCURRED DURING YOUR COLLEGE YEARS. YOU KEPT YOUR TEXTBOOKS COVERED IN PLASTIC SO THAT THEY WOULD RETAIN THEIR RESALE VALUE AT THE END OF EACH SEMESTER.
REMARKABLE! IT'S ALL TRUE! WHAT ELSE CAN YOU TELL ME?
THIS SMALL DEPOSIT OF $27.10 ON JULY 2, 1954, IS A SIGN THAT YOU WILL EITHER BE AFFLICTED WITH A MALADY LEADING TO INVALIDISM, OR THAT YOU WILL BE INVOLVED IN A RACY SCANDAL.
6% INTEREST

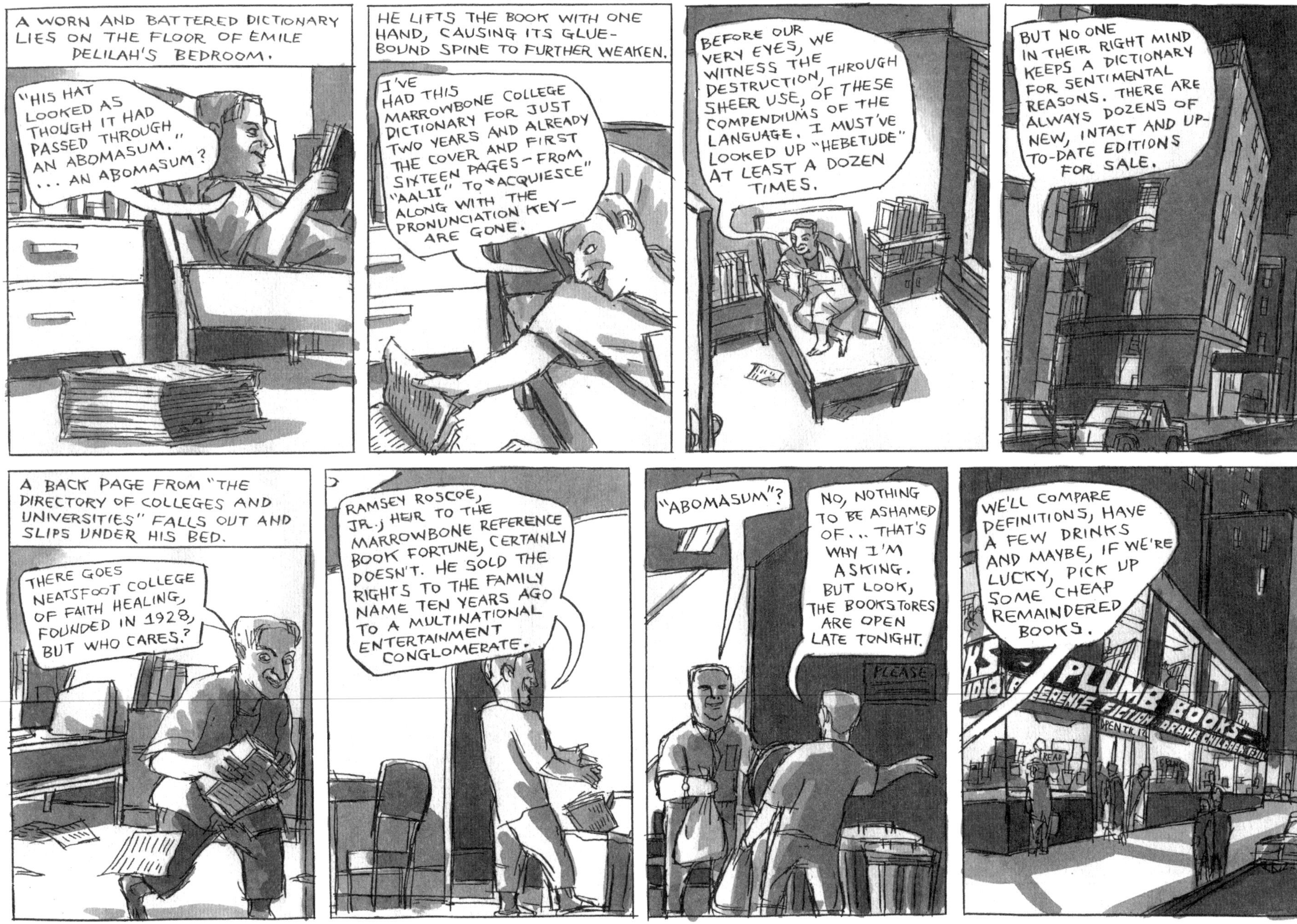
A WORN AND BATTERED DICTIONARY LIES ON THE FLOOR OF EMILE DELILAH'S BEDROOM.
"HIS HAT LOOKED AS THOUGH IT HAD PASSED THROUGH AN ABOMASUM." ... AN ABOMASUM?
HE LIFTS THE BOOK WITH ONE HAND, CAUSING ITS GLUE-BOUND SPINE TO FURTHER WEAKEN.
I'VE HAD THIS MARROWBONE COLLEGE DICTIONARY FOR JUST TWO YEARS AND ALREADY THE COVER AND FIRST SIXTEEN PAGES—FROM "AALII" TO "ACQUIESCE" ALONG WITH THE PRONUNCIATION KEY—ARE GONE.
BEFORE OUR VERY EYES, WE WITNESS THE DESTRUCTION, THROUGH SHEER USE, OF THESE COMPENDIUMS OF THE LANGUAGE. I MUST'VE LOOKED UP "HEBETUDE" AT LEAST A DOZEN TIMES.
BUT NO ONE IN THEIR RIGHT MIND KEEPS A DICTIONARY FOR SENTIMENTAL REASONS. THERE ARE ALWAYS DOZENS OF NEW, INTACT AND UP-TO-DATE EDITIONS FOR SALE.
A BACK PAGE FROM "THE DIRECTORY OF COLLEGES AND UNIVERSITIES" FALLS OUT AND SLIPS UNDER HIS BED.
THERE GOES NEATSFOOT COLLEGE OF FAITH HEALING, FOUNDED IN 1928, BUT WHO CARES?
RAMSEY ROSCOE, JR.; HEIR TO THE MARROWBONE REFERENCE BOOK FORTUNE, CERTAINLY DOESN'T. HE SOLD THE RIGHTS TO THE FAMILY NAME TEN YEARS AGO TO A MULTINATIONAL ENTERTAINMENT CONGLOMERATE.
"ABOMASUM"?
NO, NOTHING TO BE ASHAMED OF... THAT'S WHY I'M ASKING. BUT LOOK, THE BOOKSTORES ARE OPEN LATE TONIGHT.
PLEASE
WE'LL COMPARE DEFINITIONS, HAVE A FEW DRINKS AND MAYBE, IF WE'RE LUCKY, PICK UP SOME CHEAP REMAINDERED BOOKS.
PLUMB BOOKS
FICTION
DRAMA

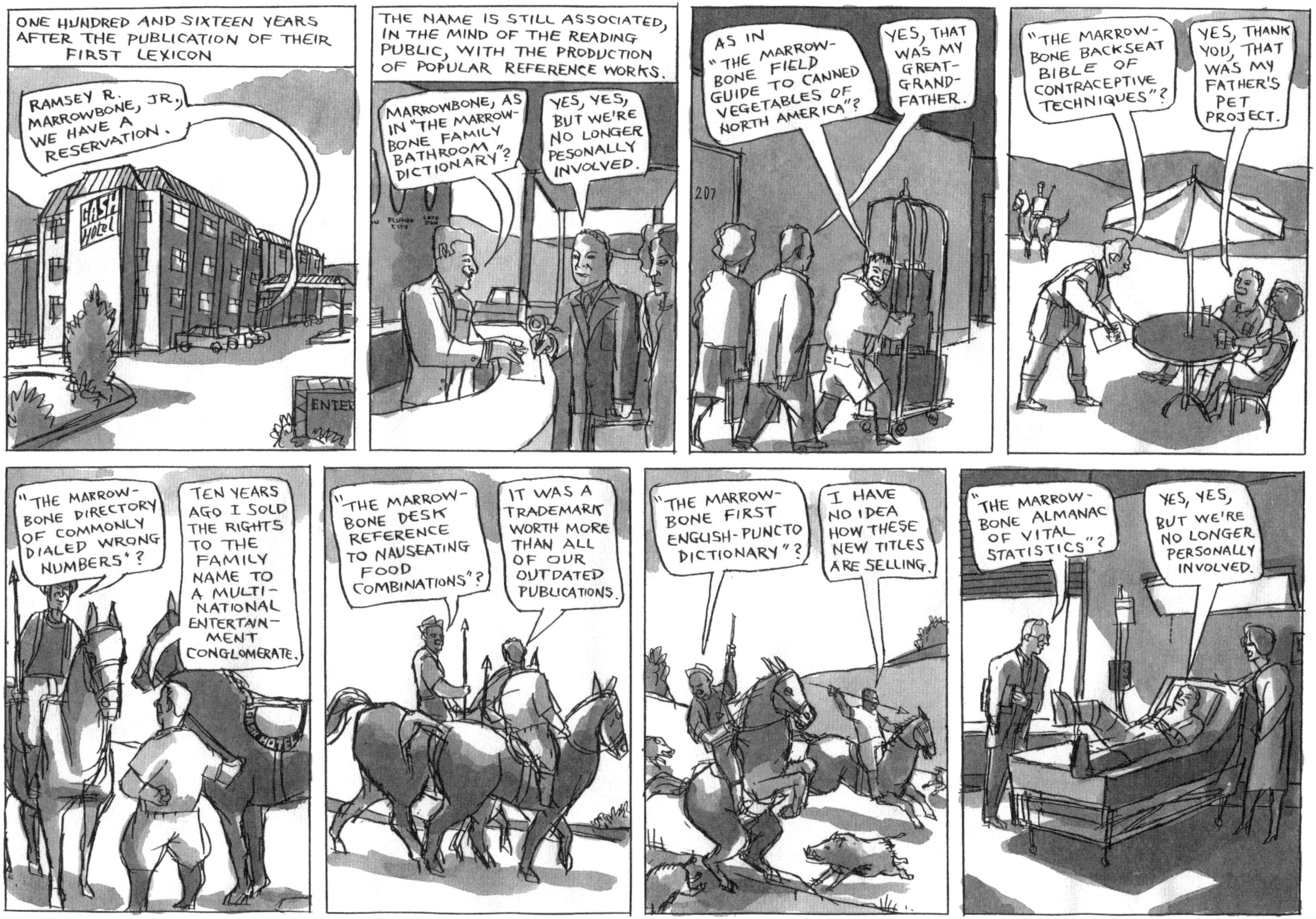
ONE HUNDRED AND SIXTEEN YEARS AFTER THE PUBLICATION OF THEIR FIRST LEXICON
RAMSEY R. MARROWBONE, JR., WE HAVE A RESERVATION.
GASH Hotel
ENTER
THE NAME IS STILL ASSOCIATED, IN THE MIND OF THE READING PUBLIC, WITH THE PRODUCTION OF POPULAR REFERENCE WORKS.
MARROWBONE, AS IN "THE MARROWBONE FAMILY BATHROOM DICTIONARY"?
YES, YES, BUT WE'RE NO LONGER PESONALLY INVOLVED.
AS IN "THE MARROWBONE FIELD GUIDE TO CANNED VEGETABLES OF NORTH AMERICA"?
YES, THAT WAS MY GREAT-GRANDFATHER.
207
"THE MARROWBONE BACKSEAT BIBLE OF CONTRACEPTIVE TECHNIQUES"?
YES, THANK YOU, THAT WAS MY FATHER'S PET PROJECT.
"THE MARROWBONE DIRECTORY OF COMMONLY DIALED WRONG NUMBERS"?
TEN YEARS AGO I SOLD THE RIGHTS TO THE FAMILY NAME TO A MULTINATIONAL ENTERTAINMENT CONGLOMERATE.
"THE MARROWBONE DESK REFERENCE TO NAUSEATING FOOD COMBINATIONS"?
IT WAS A TRADEMARK WORTH MORE THAN ALL OF OUR OUTDATED PUBLICATIONS.
"THE MARROWBONE FIRST ENGLISH-PUNCTO DICTIONARY"?
I HAVE NO IDEA HOW THESE NEW TITLES ARE SELLING.
"THE MARROWBONE ALMANAC OF VITAL STATISTICS"?
YES, YES, BUT WE'RE NO LONGER PERSONALLY INVOLVED.

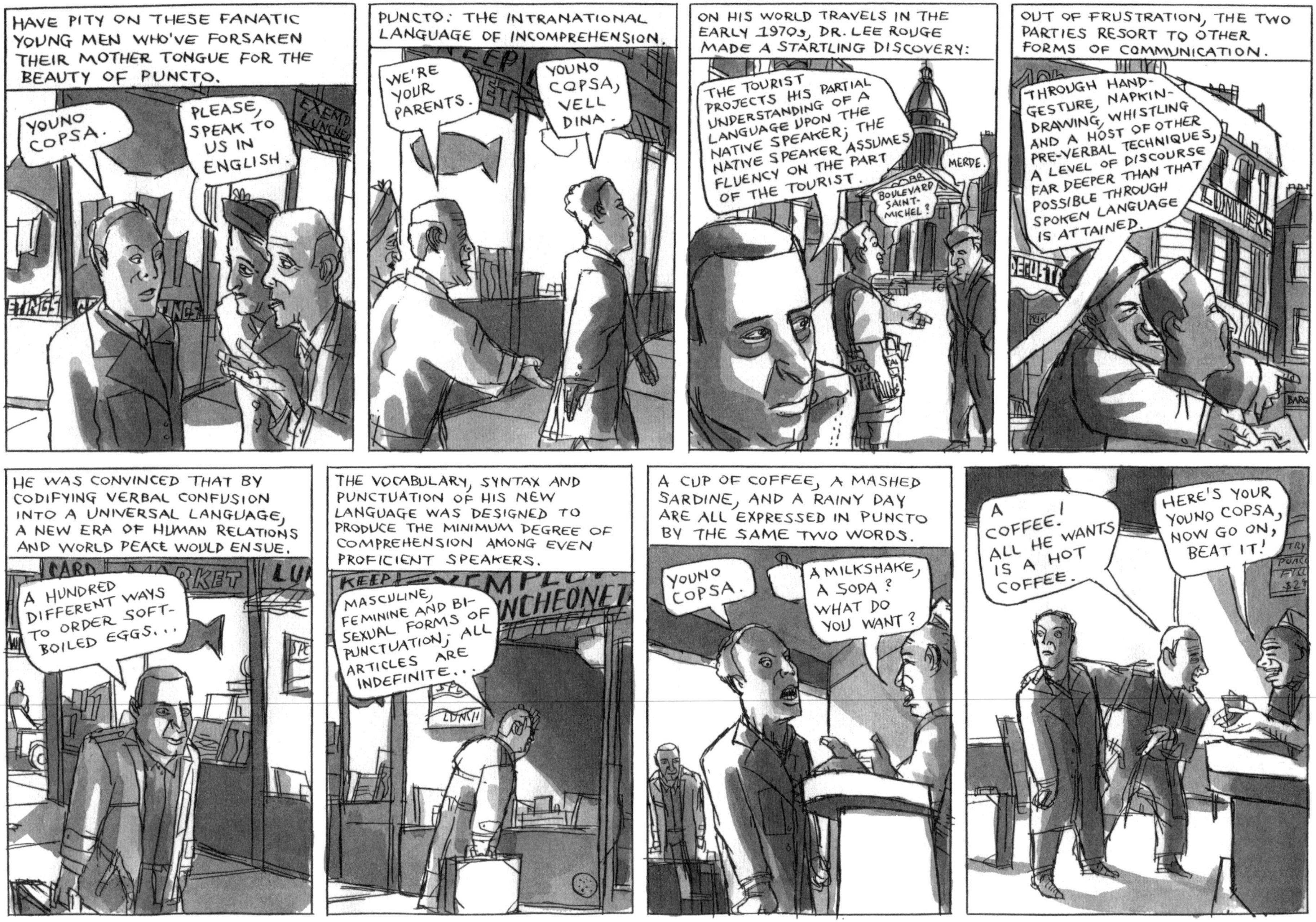
HAVE PITY ON THESE FANATIC YOUNG MEN WHO'VE FORSAKEN THEIR MOTHER TONGUE FOR THE BEAUTY OF PUNCTO.
YOUNO COPSA.
PLEASE, SPEAK TO US IN ENGLISH.
PUNCTO: THE INTRANATIONAL LANGUAGE OF INCOMPREHENSION.
WE'RE YOUR PARENTS.
YOUNO COPSA, VELL DINA.
ON HIS WORLD TRAVELS IN THE EARLY 1970s, DR. LEE ROUGE MADE A STARTLING DISCOVERY:
THE TOURIST PROJECTS HIS PARTIAL UNDERSTANDING OF A LANGUAGE UPON THE NATIVE SPEAKER; THE NATIVE SPEAKER ASSUMES FLUENCY ON THE PART OF THE TOURIST.
BOULEVARD SAINT-MICHEL?
MERDE.
OUT OF FRUSTRATION, THE TWO PARTIES RESORT TO OTHER FORMS OF COMMUNICATION.
THROUGH HAND-GESTURE, NAPKIN-DRAWING, WHISTLING AND A HOST OF OTHER PRE-VERBAL TECHNIQUES, A LEVEL OF DISCOURSE FAR DEEPER THAN THAT POSSIBLE THROUGH SPOKEN LANGUAGE IS ATTAINED.
HE WAS CONVINCED THAT BY CODIFYING VERBAL CONFUSION INTO A UNIVERSAL LANGUAGE, A NEW ERA OF HUMAN RELATIONS AND WORLD PEACE WOULD ENSUE.
A HUNDRED DIFFERENT WAYS TO ORDER SOFT-BOILED EGGS...
THE VOCABULARY, SYNTAX AND PUNCTUATION OF HIS NEW LANGUAGE WAS DESIGNED TO PRODUCE THE MINIMUM DEGREE OF COMPREHENSION AMONG EVEN PROFICIENT SPEAKERS.
MASCULINE, FEMININE AND BI-SEXUAL FORMS OF PUNCTUATION; ALL ARTICLES ARE INDEFINITE...
A CUP OF COFFEE, A MASHED SARDINE, AND A RAINY DAY ARE ALL EXPRESSED IN PUNCTO BY THE SAME TWO WORDS.
YOUNO COPSA.
A MILKSHAKE, A SODA? WHAT DO YOU WANT?
A COFFEE! ALL HE WANTS IS A HOT COFFEE.
HERE'S YOUR YOUNO COPSA, NOW GO ON, BEAT IT!

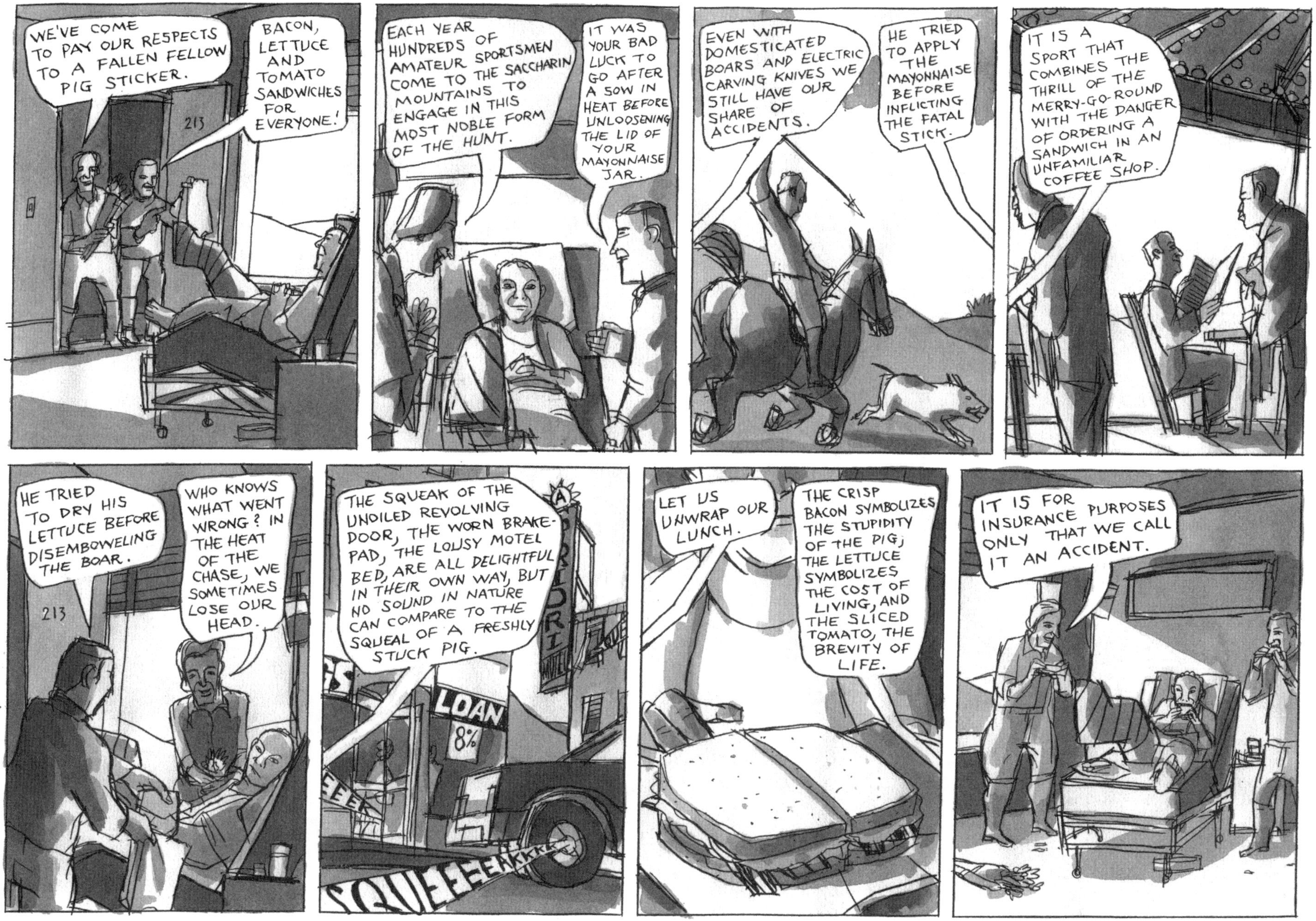

WE'VE COME TO PAY OUR RESPECTS TO A FALLEN FELLOW PIG STICKER.
BACON, LETTUCE AND TOMATO SANDWICHES FOR EVERYONE!
213
EACH YEAR HUNDREDS OF AMATEUR SPORTSMEN COME TO THE SACCHARIN MOUNTAINS TO ENGAGE IN THIS MOST NOBLE FORM OF THE HUNT.
IT WAS YOUR BAD LUCK TO GO AFTER A SOW IN HEAT BEFORE UNLOOSENING THE LID OF YOUR MAYONNAISE JAR.
EVEN WITH DOMESTICATED BOARS AND ELECTRIC CARVING KNIVES WE STILL HAVE OUR SHARE OF ACCIDENTS.
HE TRIED TO APPLY THE MAYONNAISE BEFORE INFLICTING THE FATAL STICK.
IT IS A SPORT THAT COMBINES THE THRILL OF THE MERRY-GO-ROUND WITH THE DANGER OF ORDERING A SANDWICH IN AN UNFAMILIAR COFFEE SHOP.
HE TRIED TO DRY HIS LETTUCE BEFORE DISEMBOWELING THE BOAR.
WHO KNOWS WHAT WENT WRONG? IN THE HEAT OF THE CHASE, WE SOMETIMES LOSE OUR HEAD.
213
THE SQUEAK OF THE UNOILED REVOLVING DOOR, THE WORN BRAKE-PAD, THE LOUSY MOTEL BED, ARE ALL DELIGHTFUL IN THEIR OWN WAY, BUT NO SOUND IN NATURE CAN COMPARE TO THE SQUEAL OF A FRESHLY STUCK PIG.
LOAN
8%
SQUEEEEEAKKKK
LET US UNWRAP OUR LUNCH.
THE CRISP BACON SYMBOLIZES THE STUPIDITY OF THE PIG; THE LETTUCE SYMBOLIZES THE COST OF LIVING, AND THE SLICED TOMATO, THE BREVITY OF LIFE.
IT IS FOR INSURANCE PURPOSES ONLY THAT WE CALL IT AN ACCIDENT.

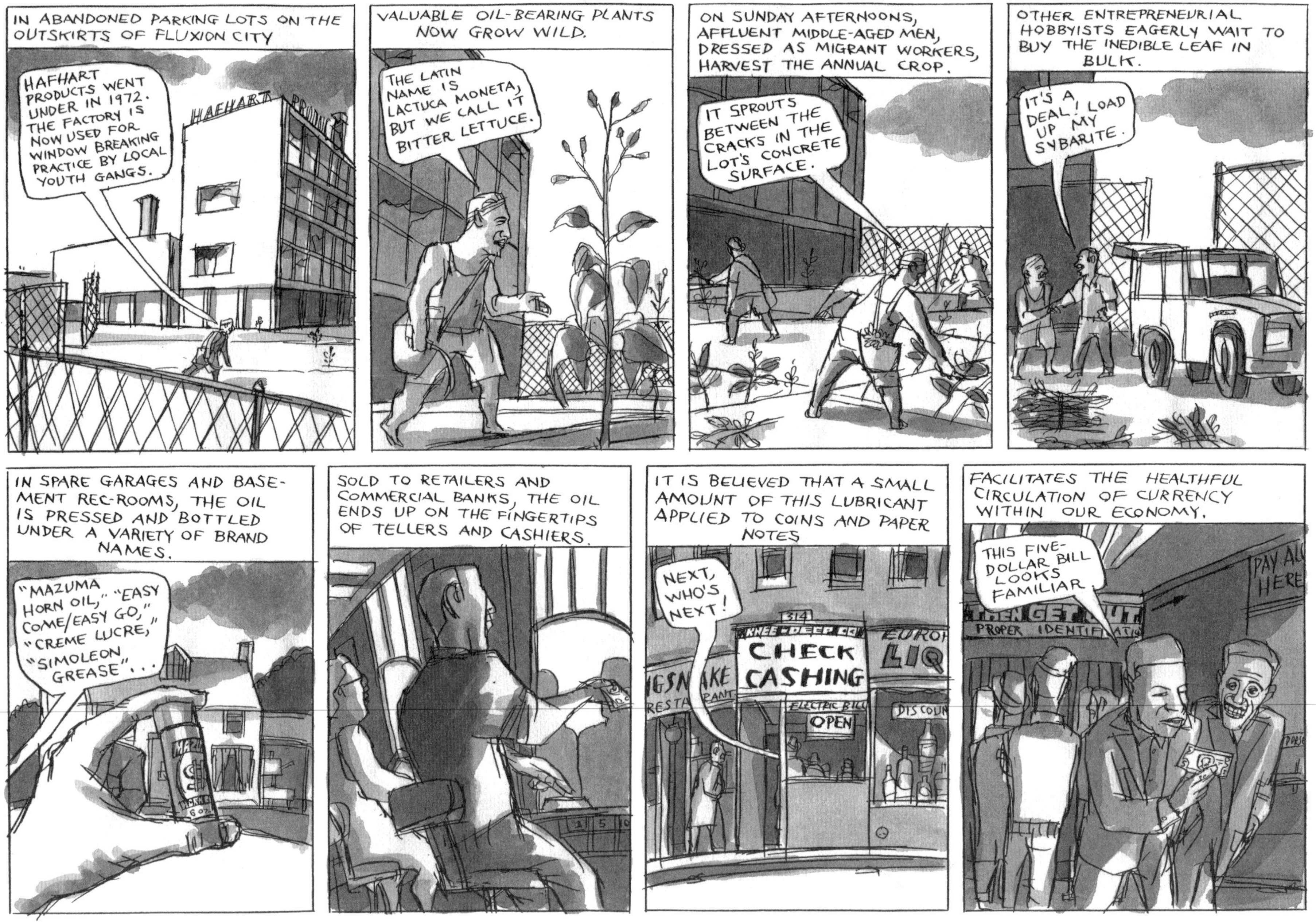
IN ABANDONED PARKING LOTS ON THE OUTSKIRTS OF FLUXION CITY
HAFHART PRODUCTS WENT UNDER IN 1972. THE FACTORY IS NOW USED FOR WINDOW BREAKING PRACTICE BY LOCAL YOUTH GANGS.
VALUABLE OIL-BEARING PLANTS NOW GROW WILD.
THE LATIN NAME IS LACTUCA MONETA, BUT WE CALL IT BITTER LETTUCE.
ON SUNDAY AFTERNOONS, AFFLUENT MIDDLE-AGED MEN, DRESSED AS MIGRANT WORKERS, HARVEST THE ANNUAL CROP.
IT SPROUTS BETWEEN THE CRACKS IN THE LOT'S CONCRETE SURFACE.
OTHER ENTREPRENEURIAL HOBBYISTS EAGERLY WAIT TO BUY THE INEDIBLE LEAF IN BULK.
IT'S A DEAL! LOAD UP MY SYBARITE.
IN SPARE GARAGES AND BASEMENT REC-ROOMS, THE OIL IS PRESSED AND BOTTLED UNDER A VARIETY OF BRAND NAMES.
"MAZUMA HORN OIL," "EASY COME/EASY GO," "CREME LUCRE," "SIMOLEON GREASE"...
SOLD TO RETAILERS AND COMMERCIAL BANKS, THE OIL ENDS UP ON THE FINGERTIPS OF TELLERS AND CASHIERS.
IT IS BELIEVED THAT A SMALL AMOUNT OF THIS LUBRICANT APPLIED TO COINS AND PAPER NOTES
NEXT, WHO'S NEXT!
314
CHECK CASHING
OPEN
FACILITATES THE HEALTHFUL CIRCULATION OF CURRENCY WITHIN OUR ECONOMY.
THIS FIVE-DOLLAR BILL LOOKS FAMILIAR.

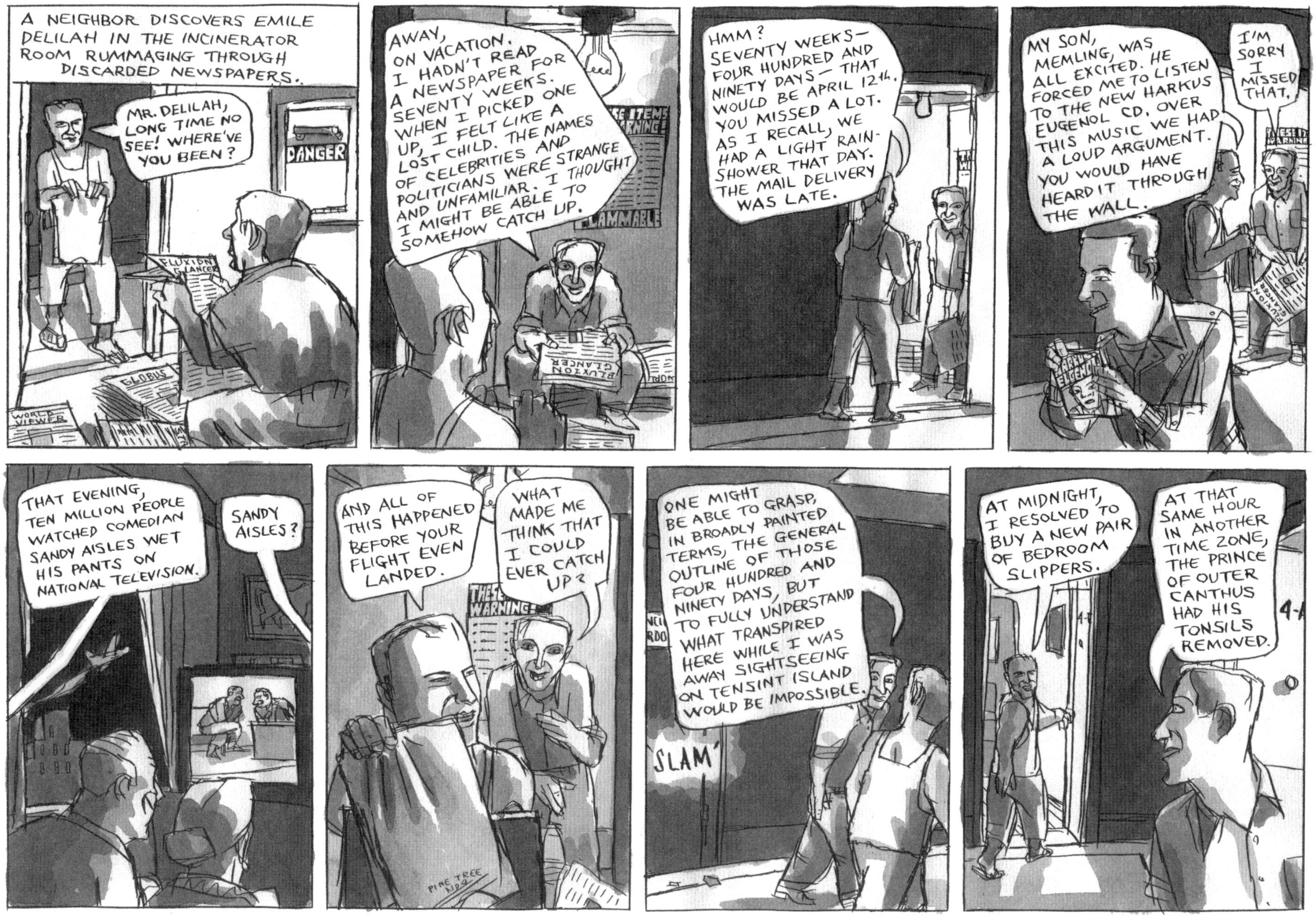
A NEIGHBOR DISCOVERS EMILE DELILAH IN THE INCINERATOR ROOM RUMMAGING THROUGH DISCARDED NEWSPAPERS.
MR. DELILAH, LONG TIME NO SEE! WHERE'VE YOU BEEN?
DANGER
FLUXION GLANCER
GLOBUS
WORLD VIEWER
AWAY, ON VACATION. I HADN'T READ A NEWSPAPER FOR SEVENTY WEEKS. WHEN I PICKED ONE UP, I FELT LIKE A LOST CHILD. THE NAMES OF CELEBRITIES AND POLITICIANS WERE STRANGE AND UNFAMILIAR. I THOUGHT I MIGHT BE ABLE TO SOMEHOW CATCH UP.
FLAMMABLE
HMM? SEVENTY WEEKS— FOUR HUNDRED AND NINETY DAYS— THAT WOULD BE APRIL 12th. YOU MISSED A LOT. AS I RECALL, WE HAD A LIGHT RAIN-SHOWER THAT DAY. THE MAIL DELIVERY WAS LATE.
MY SON, MEMLING, WAS ALL EXCITED. HE FORCED ME TO LISTEN TO THE NEW HARKUS EUGENOL CD, OVER THIS MUSIC WE HAD A LOUD ARGUMENT. YOU WOULD HAVE HEARD IT THROUGH THE WALL.
I'M SORRY I MISSED THAT.
THAT EVENING, TEN MILLION PEOPLE WATCHED COMEDIAN SANDY AISLES WET HIS PANTS ON NATIONAL TELEVISION.
SANDY AISLES?
AND ALL OF THIS HAPPENED BEFORE YOUR FLIGHT EVEN LANDED.
WHAT MADE ME THINK THAT I COULD EVER CATCH UP?
WARNING
PINE TREE No.4
ONE MIGHT BE ABLE TO GRASP, IN BROADLY PAINTED TERMS, THE GENERAL OUTLINE OF THOSE FOUR HUNDRED AND NINETY DAYS, BUT TO FULLY UNDERSTAND WHAT TRANSPIRED HERE WHILE I WAS AWAY SIGHTSEEING ON TENSINT ISLAND WOULD BE IMPOSSIBLE.
SLAM'
AT MIDNIGHT, I RESOLVED TO BUY A NEW PAIR OF BEDROOM SLIPPERS.
AT THAT SAME HOUR IN ANOTHER TIME ZONE, THE PRINCE OF OUTER CANTHUS HAD HIS TONSILS REMOVED.
4-A

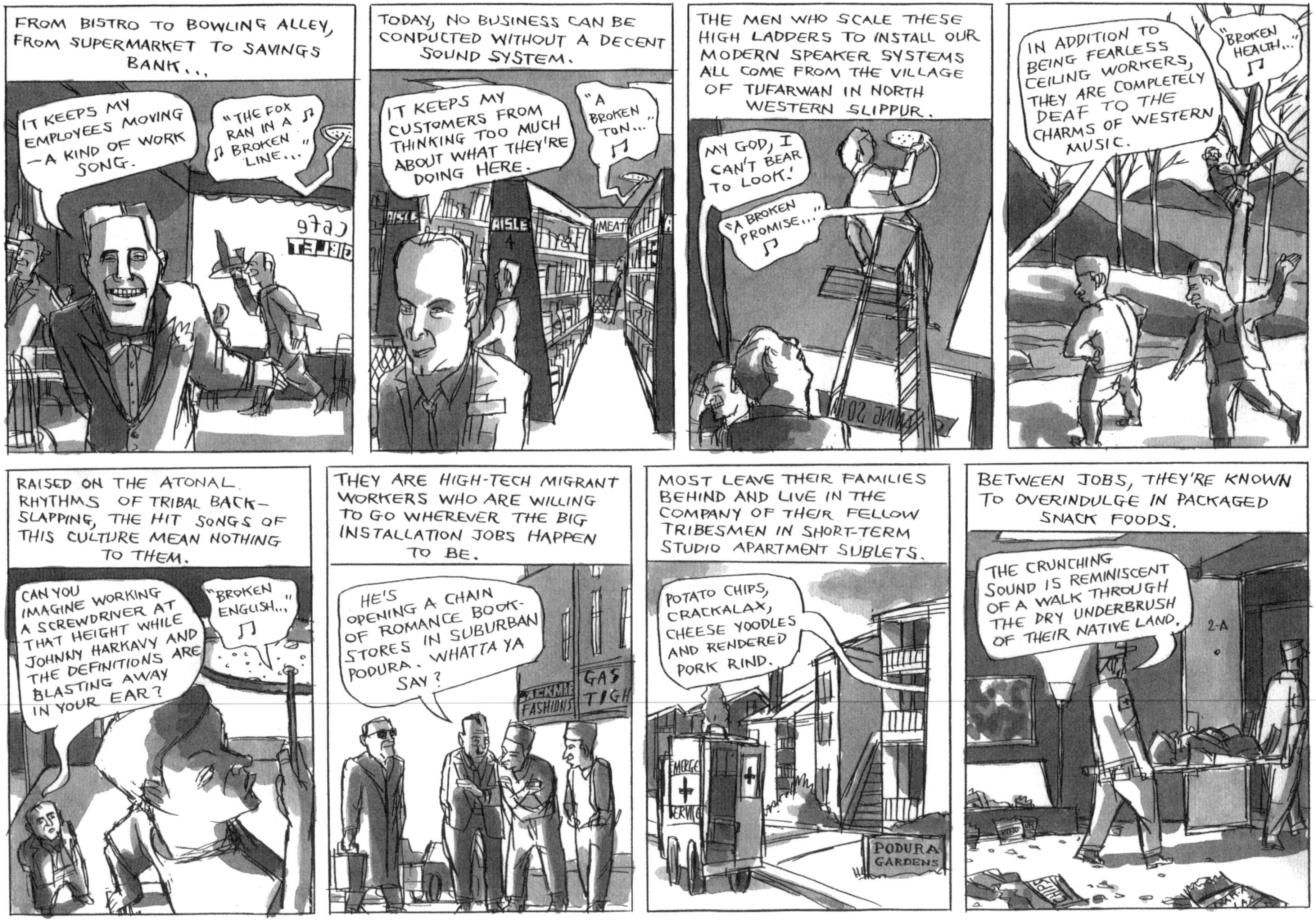
FROM BISTRO TO BOWLING ALLEY, FROM SUPERMARKET TO SAVINGS BANK...
IT KEEPS MY EMPLOYEES MOVING —A KIND OF WORK SONG.
"THE FOX RAN IN A ♫ BROKEN LINE..." ♫
CAFE
TODAY, NO BUSINESS CAN BE CONDUCTED WITHOUT A DECENT SOUND SYSTEM.
IT KEEPS MY CUSTOMERS FROM THINKING TOO MUCH ABOUT WHAT THEY'RE DOING HERE.
"A BROKEN TON..." ♫
AISLE 4
MEAT
THE MEN WHO SCALE THESE HIGH LADDERS TO INSTALL OUR MODERN SPEAKER SYSTEMS ALL COME FROM THE VILLAGE OF TUFARWAN IN NORTH WESTERN SLIPPUR.
MY GOD, I CAN'T BEAR TO LOOK!
"A BROKEN PROMISE..." ♫
IN ADDITION TO BEING FEARLESS CEILING WORKERS, THEY ARE COMPLETELY DEAF TO THE CHARMS OF WESTERN MUSIC.
"BROKEN HEALTH..." ♫
RAISED ON THE ATONAL RHYTHMS OF TRIBAL BACK-SLAPPING, THE HIT SONGS OF THIS CULTURE MEAN NOTHING TO THEM.
CAN YOU IMAGINE WORKING A SCREWDRIVER AT THAT HEIGHT WHILE JOHNNY HARKAVY AND THE DEFINITIONS ARE BLASTING AWAY IN YOUR EAR?
"BROKEN ENGLISH..." ♫
THEY ARE HIGH-TECH MIGRANT WORKERS WHO ARE WILLING TO GO WHEREVER THE BIG INSTALLATION JOBS HAPPEN TO BE.
HE'S OPENING A CHAIN OF ROMANCE BOOK-STORES IN SUBURBAN PODURA. WHATTA YA SAY?
FASHIONS
GAS
MOST LEAVE THEIR FAMILIES BEHIND AND LIVE IN THE COMPANY OF THEIR FELLOW TRIBESMEN IN SHORT-TERM STUDIO APARTMENT SUBLETS.
POTATO CHIPS, CRACKALAX, CHEESE YOODLES AND RENDERED PORK RIND.
PODURA GARDENS
BETWEEN JOBS, THEY'RE KNOWN TO OVERINDULGE IN PACKAGED SNACK FOODS.
THE CRUNCHING SOUND IS REMINISCENT OF A WALK THROUGH THE DRY UNDERBRUSH OF THEIR NATIVE LAND.
2-A

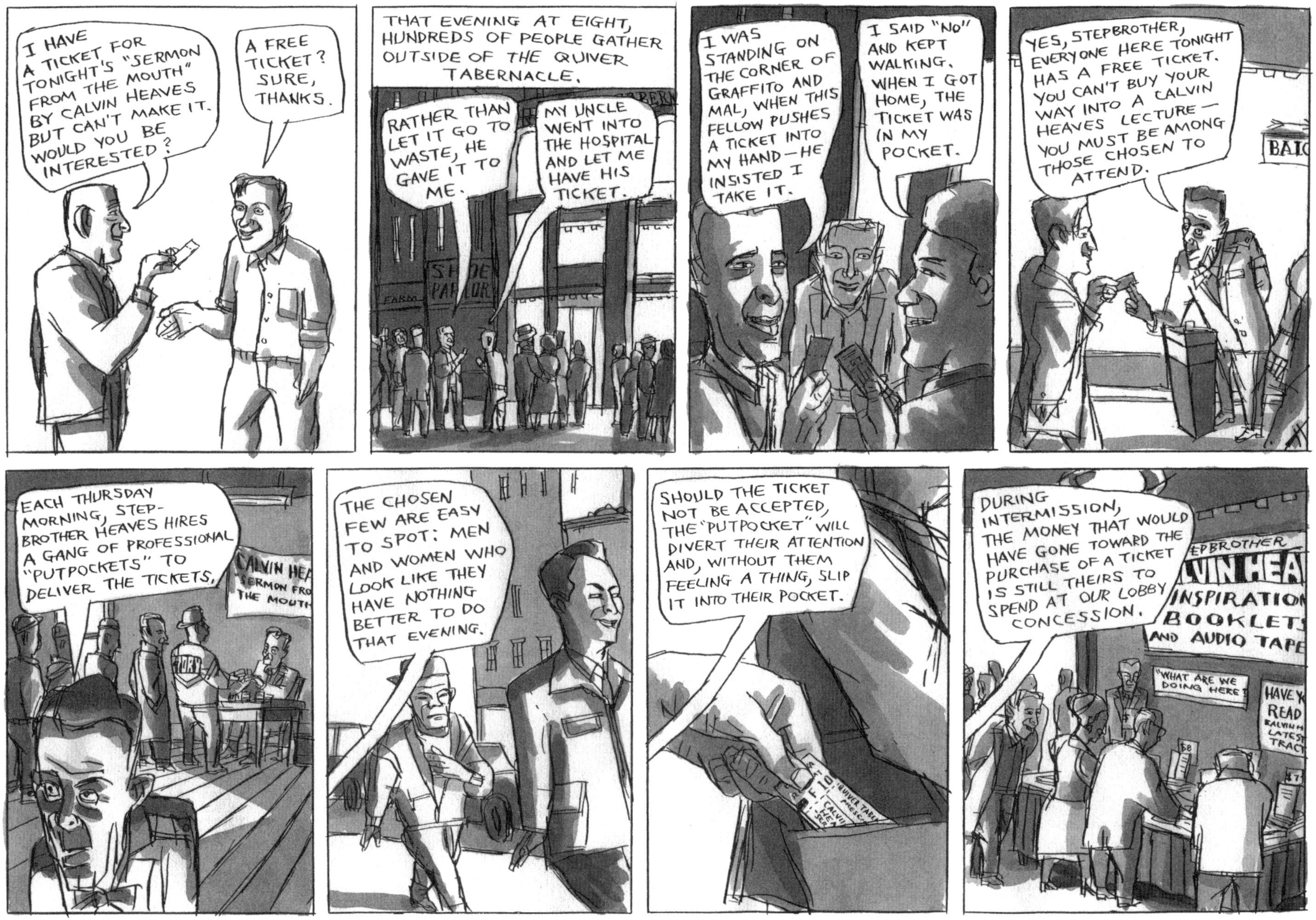
I HAVE A TICKET FOR TONIGHT'S "SERMON FROM THE MOUTH" BY CALVIN HEAVES BUT CAN'T MAKE IT. WOULD YOU BE INTERESTED?
A FREE TICKET? SURE, THANKS.
THAT EVENING AT EIGHT, HUNDREDS OF PEOPLE GATHER OUTSIDE OF THE QUIVER TABERNACLE.
RATHER THAN LET IT GO TO WASTE, HE GAVE IT TO ME.
MY UNCLE WENT INTO THE HOSPITAL AND LET ME HAVE HIS TICKET.
SHOE PARLOR
I WAS STANDING ON THE CORNER OF GRAFFITO AND MAL, WHEN THIS FELLOW PUSHES A TICKET INTO MY HAND—HE INSISTED I TAKE IT.
I SAID "NO" AND KEPT WALKING. WHEN I GOT HOME, THE TICKET WAS IN MY POCKET.
YES, STEPBROTHER, EVERYONE HERE TONIGHT HAS A FREE TICKET. YOU CAN'T BUY YOUR WAY INTO A CALVIN HEAVES LECTURE—YOU MUST BE AMONG THOSE CHOSEN TO ATTEND.
EACH THURSDAY MORNING, STEP-BROTHER HEAVES HIRES A GANG OF PROFESSIONAL "PUTPOCKETS" TO DELIVER THE TICKETS.
SERMON FRO THE MOUTH
THE CHOSEN FEW ARE EASY TO SPOT: MEN AND WOMEN WHO LOOK LIKE THEY HAVE NOTHING BETTER TO DO THAT EVENING.
SHOULD THE TICKET NOT BE ACCEPTED, THE "PUTPOCKET" WILL DIVERT THEIR ATTENTION AND, WITHOUT THEM FEELING A THING, SLIP IT INTO THEIR POCKET.
DURING INTERMISSION, THE MONEY THAT WOULD HAVE GONE TOWARD THE PURCHASE OF A TICKET IS STILL THEIRS TO SPEND AT OUR LOBBY CONCESSION.
INSPIRATION BOOKLETS AND AUDIO TAPE
"WHAT ARE WE DOING HERE?"

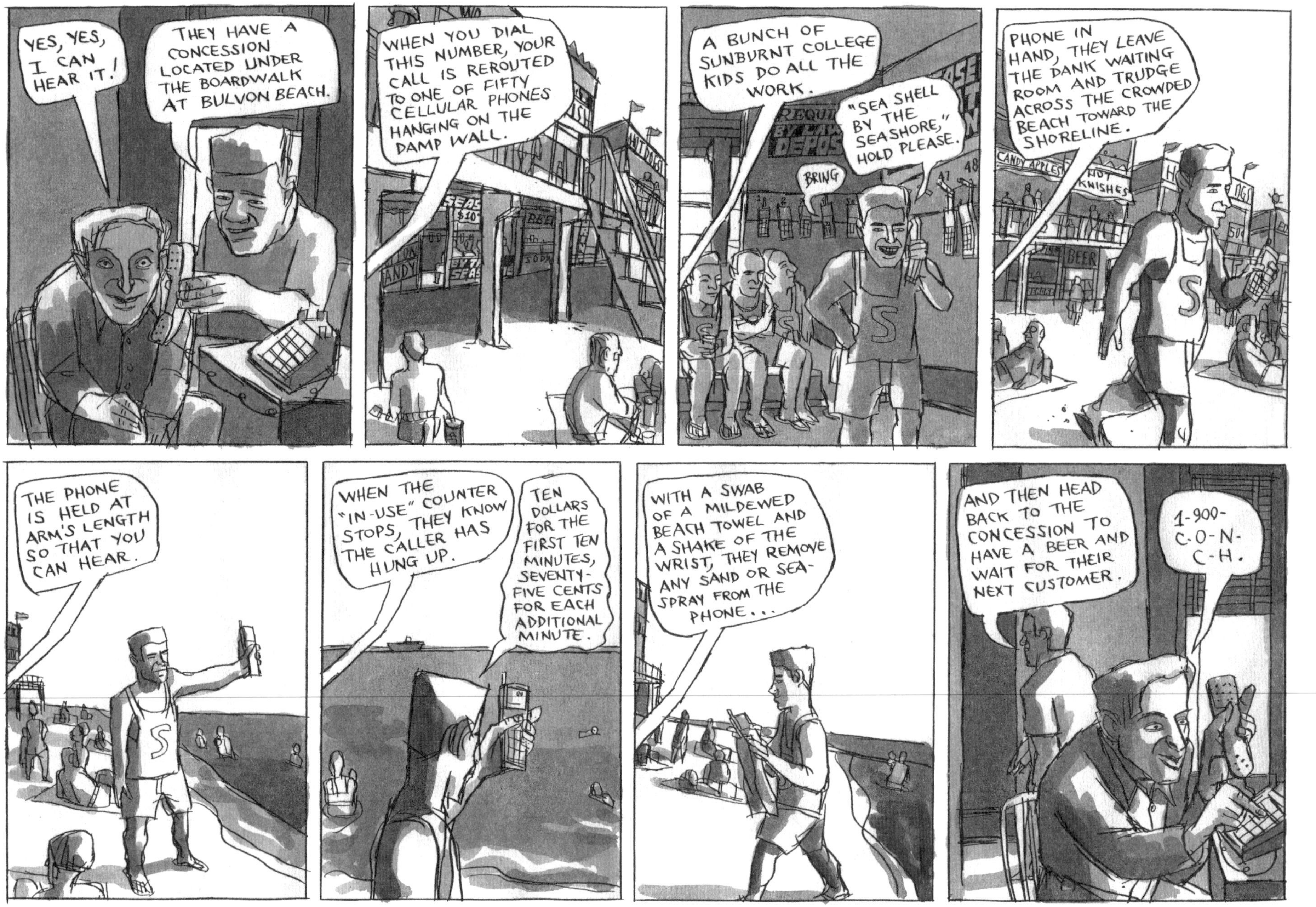
YES, YES, I CAN HEAR IT!
THEY HAVE A CONCESSION LOCATED UNDER THE BOARDWALK AT BULVON BEACH.
WHEN YOU DIAL THIS NUMBER, YOUR CALL IS REROUTED TO ONE OF FIFTY CELLULAR PHONES HANGING ON THE DAMP WALL.
A BUNCH OF SUNBURNT COLLEGE KIDS DO ALL THE WORK.
BRING
"SEA SHELL BY THE SEASHORE," HOLD PLEASE.
PHONE IN HAND, THEY LEAVE THE DANK WAITING ROOM AND TRUDGE ACROSS THE CROWDED BEACH TOWARD THE SHORELINE.
CANDY APPLES
HOT KNISHES
BEER
THE PHONE IS HELD AT ARM'S LENGTH SO THAT YOU CAN HEAR.
WHEN THE "IN-USE" COUNTER STOPS, THEY KNOW THE CALLER HAS HUNG UP.
TEN DOLLARS FOR THE FIRST TEN MINUTES, SEVENTY-FIVE CENTS FOR EACH ADDITIONAL MINUTE.
WITH A SWAB OF A MILDEWED BEACH TOWEL AND A SHAKE OF THE WRIST, THEY REMOVE ANY SAND OR SEA-SPRAY FROM THE PHONE...
AND THEN HEAD BACK TO THE CONCESSION TO HAVE A BEER AND WAIT FOR THEIR NEXT CUSTOMER.
1-900-C-O-N-C-H.

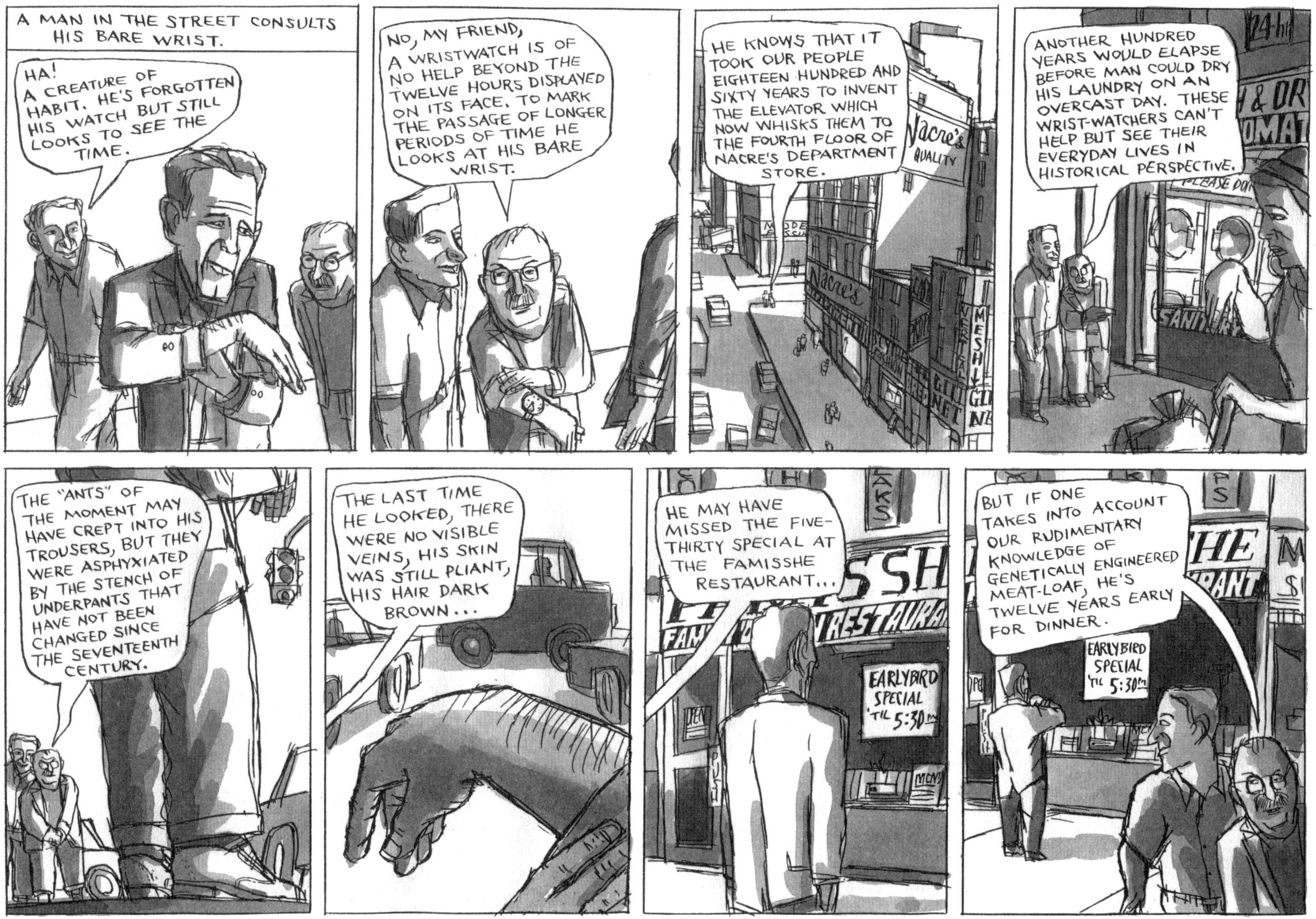
A MAN IN THE STREET CONSULTS HIS BARE WRIST.
HA! A CREATURE OF HABIT. HE'S FORGOTTEN HIS WATCH BUT STILL LOOKS TO SEE THE TIME.
NO, MY FRIEND, A WRISTWATCH IS OF NO HELP BEYOND THE TWELVE HOURS DISPLAYED ON ITS FACE. TO MARK THE PASSAGE OF LONGER PERIODS OF TIME HE LOOKS AT HIS BARE WRIST.
HE KNOWS THAT IT TOOK OUR PEOPLE EIGHTEEN HUNDRED AND SIXTY YEARS TO INVENT THE ELEVATOR WHICH NOW WHISKS THEM TO THE FOURTH FLOOR OF NACRE'S DEPARTMENT STORE.
Nacre's
QUALITY
ANOTHER HUNDRED YEARS WOULD ELAPSE BEFORE MAN COULD DRY HIS LAUNDRY ON AN OVERCAST DAY. THESE WRIST-WATCHERS CAN'T HELP BUT SEE THEIR EVERYDAY LIVES IN HISTORICAL PERSPECTIVE.
24 hr
THE "ANTS" OF THE MOMENT MAY HAVE CREPT INTO HIS TROUSERS, BUT THEY WERE ASPHYXIATED BY THE STENCH OF UNDERPANTS THAT HAVE NOT BEEN CHANGED SINCE THE SEVENTEENTH CENTURY.
THE LAST TIME HE LOOKED, THERE WERE NO VISIBLE VEINS, HIS SKIN WAS STILL PLIANT, HIS HAIR DARK BROWN...
HE MAY HAVE MISSED THE FIVE-THIRTY SPECIAL AT THE FAMISSHE RESTAURANT...
RESTAURANT
EARLYBIRD SPECIAL 'TIL 5:30PM
PUSH
BUT IF ONE TAKES INTO ACCOUNT OUR RUDIMENTARY KNOWLEDGE OF GENETICALLY ENGINEERED MEAT-LOAF, HE'S TWELVE YEARS EARLY FOR DINNER.
EARLYBIRD SPECIAL 'TIL 5:30PM

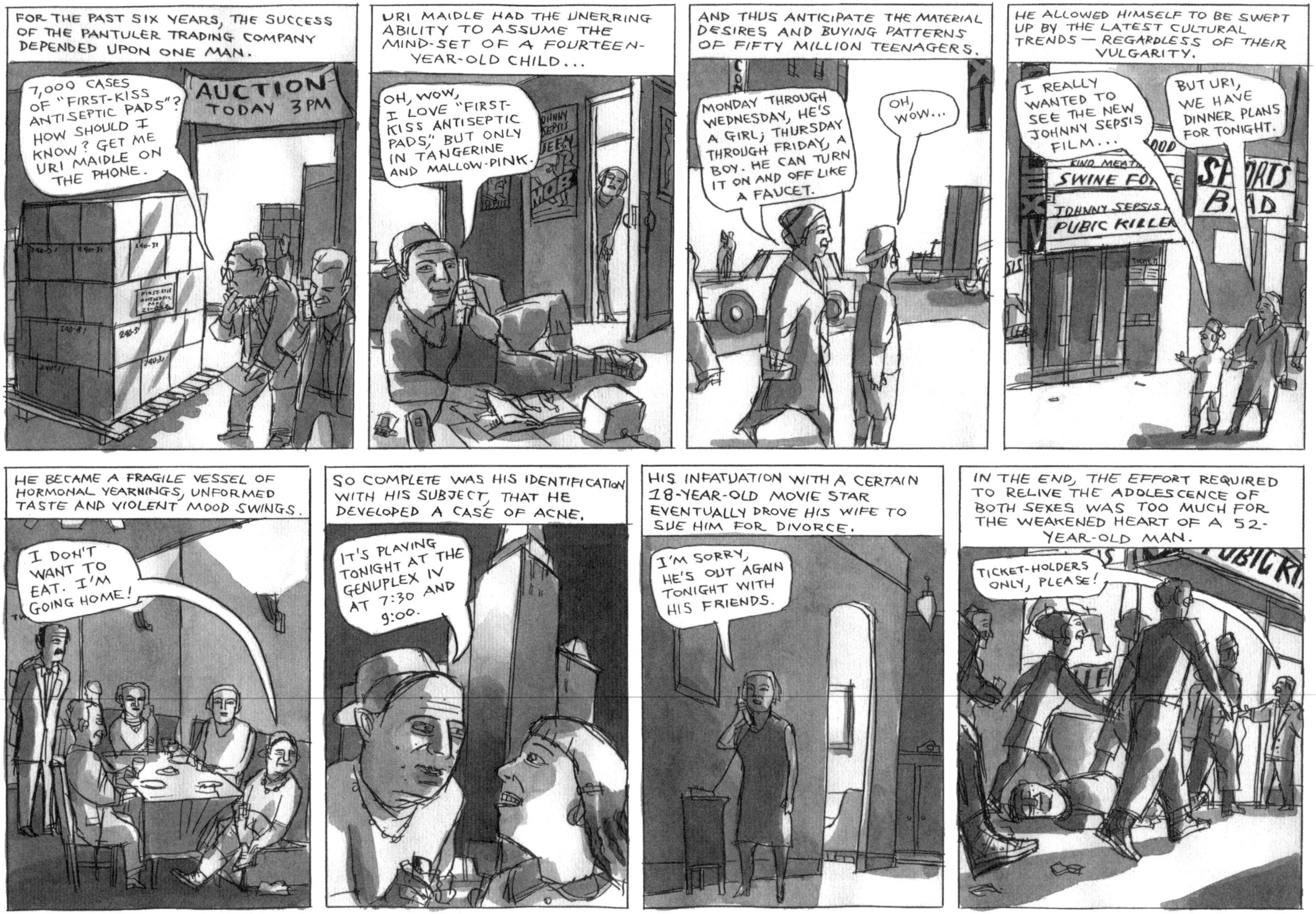
FOR THE PAST SIX YEARS, THE SUCCESS OF THE PANTULER TRADING COMPANY DEPENDED UPON ONE MAN.
AUCTION TODAY 3PM
7,000 CASES OF "FIRST-KISS ANTISEPTIC PADS"? HOW SHOULD I KNOW? GET ME URI MAIDLE ON THE PHONE.
URI MAIDLE HAD THE UNERRING ABILITY TO ASSUME THE MIND-SET OF A FOURTEEN-YEAR-OLD CHILD...
OH, WOW, I LOVE "FIRST-KISS ANTISEPTIC PADS," BUT ONLY IN TANGERINE AND MALLOW-PINK.
AND THUS ANTICIPATE THE MATERIAL DESIRES AND BUYING PATTERNS OF FIFTY MILLION TEENAGERS.
MONDAY THROUGH WEDNESDAY, HE'S A GIRL; THURSDAY THROUGH FRIDAY, A BOY. HE CAN TURN IT ON AND OFF LIKE A FAUCET.
OH, WOW...
HE ALLOWED HIMSELF TO BE SWEPT UP BY THE LATEST CULTURAL TRENDS — REGARDLESS OF THEIR VULGARITY.
I REALLY WANTED TO SEE THE NEW JOHNNY SEPSIS FILM...
BUT URI, WE HAVE DINNER PLANS FOR TONIGHT.
HE BECAME A FRAGILE VESSEL OF HORMONAL YEARNINGS, UNFORMED TASTE AND VIOLENT MOOD SWINGS.
I DON'T WANT TO EAT. I'M GOING HOME!
SO COMPLETE WAS HIS IDENTIFICATION WITH HIS SUBJECT, THAT HE DEVELOPED A CASE OF ACNE.
IT'S PLAYING TONIGHT AT THE GENUPLEX IV AT 7:30 AND 9:00.
HIS INFATUATION WITH A CERTAIN 18-YEAR-OLD MOVIE STAR EVENTUALLY DROVE HIS WIFE TO SUE HIM FOR DIVORCE.
I'M SORRY, HE'S OUT AGAIN TONIGHT WITH HIS FRIENDS.
IN THE END, THE EFFORT REQUIRED TO RELIVE THE ADOLESCENCE OF BOTH SEXES WAS TOO MUCH FOR THE WEAKENED HEART OF A 52-YEAR-OLD MAN.
TICKET-HOLDERS ONLY, PLEASE!

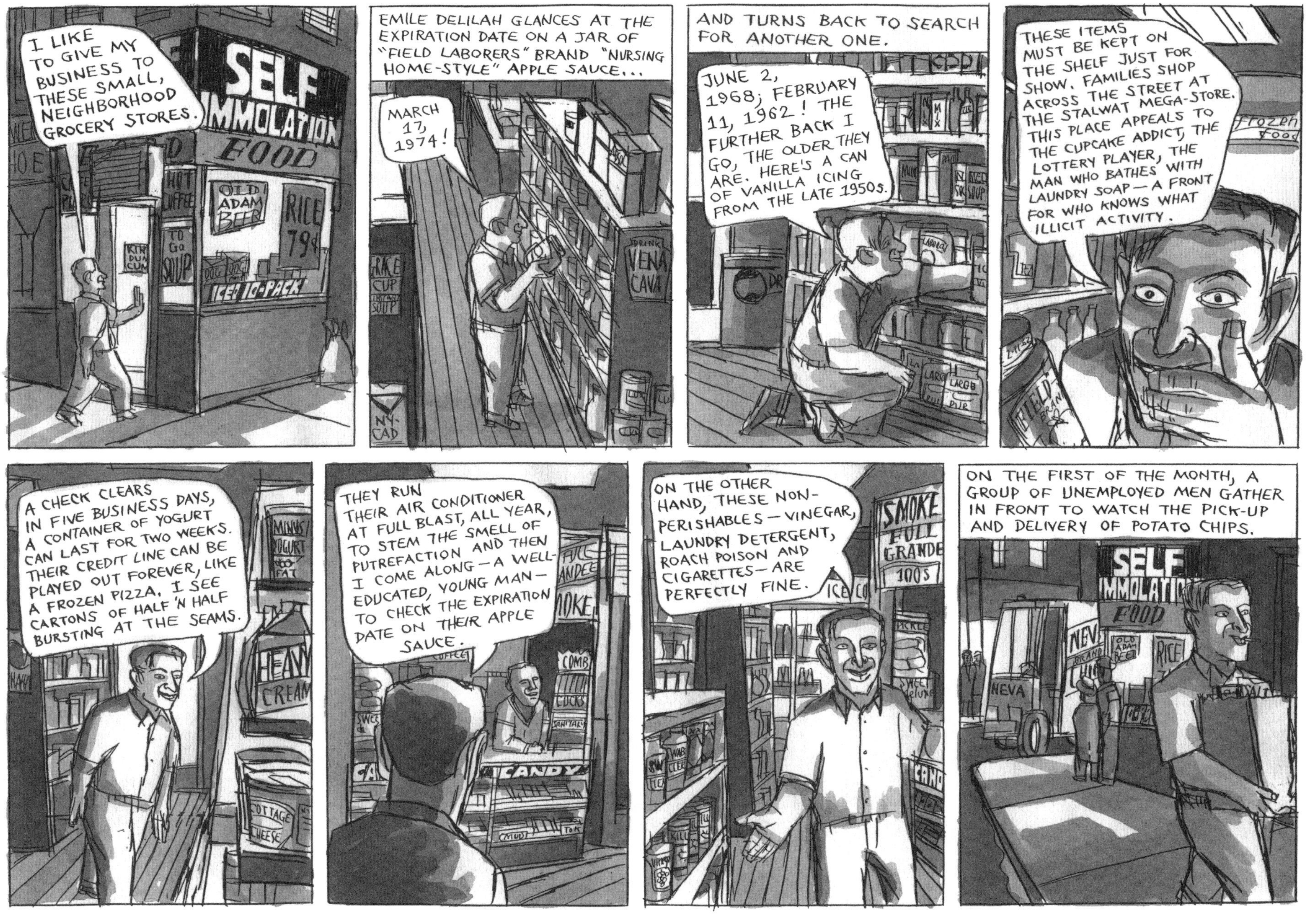
I LIKE TO GIVE MY BUSINESS TO THESE SMALL, NEIGHBORHOOD GROCERY STORES.
SELF IMMOLATION FOOD
EMILE DELILAH GLANCES AT THE EXPIRATION DATE ON A JAR OF "FIELD LABORERS" BRAND "NURSING HOME-STYLE" APPLE SAUCE...
MARCH 17, 1974!
AND TURNS BACK TO SEARCH FOR ANOTHER ONE.
JUNE 2, 1968; FEBRUARY 11, 1962! THE FURTHER BACK I GO, THE OLDER THEY ARE. HERE'S A CAN OF VANILLA ICING FROM THE LATE 1950S.
THESE ITEMS MUST BE KEPT ON THE SHELF JUST FOR SHOW. FAMILIES SHOP ACROSS THE STREET AT THE STALWAT MEGA-STORE. THIS PLACE APPEALS TO THE CUPCAKE ADDICT, THE LOTTERY PLAYER, THE MAN WHO BATHES WITH LAUNDRY SOAP—A FRONT FOR WHO KNOWS WHAT ILLICIT ACTIVITY.
A CHECK CLEARS IN FIVE BUSINESS DAYS, A CONTAINER OF YOGURT CAN LAST FOR TWO WEEKS. THEIR CREDIT LINE CAN BE PLAYED OUT FOREVER, LIKE A FROZEN PIZZA. I SEE CARTONS OF HALF 'N HALF BURSTING AT THE SEAMS.
THEY RUN THEIR AIR CONDITIONER AT FULL BLAST, ALL YEAR, TO STEM THE SMELL OF PUTREFACTION AND THEN I COME ALONG—A WELL-EDUCATED, YOUNG MAN—TO CHECK THE EXPIRATION DATE ON THEIR APPLE SAUCE.
ON THE OTHER HAND, THESE NON-PERISHABLES—VINEGAR, LAUNDRY DETERGENT, ROACH POISON AND CIGARETTES—ARE PERFECTLY FINE.
ON THE FIRST OF THE MONTH, A GROUP OF UNEMPLOYED MEN GATHER IN FRONT TO WATCH THE PICK-UP AND DELIVERY OF POTATO CHIPS.

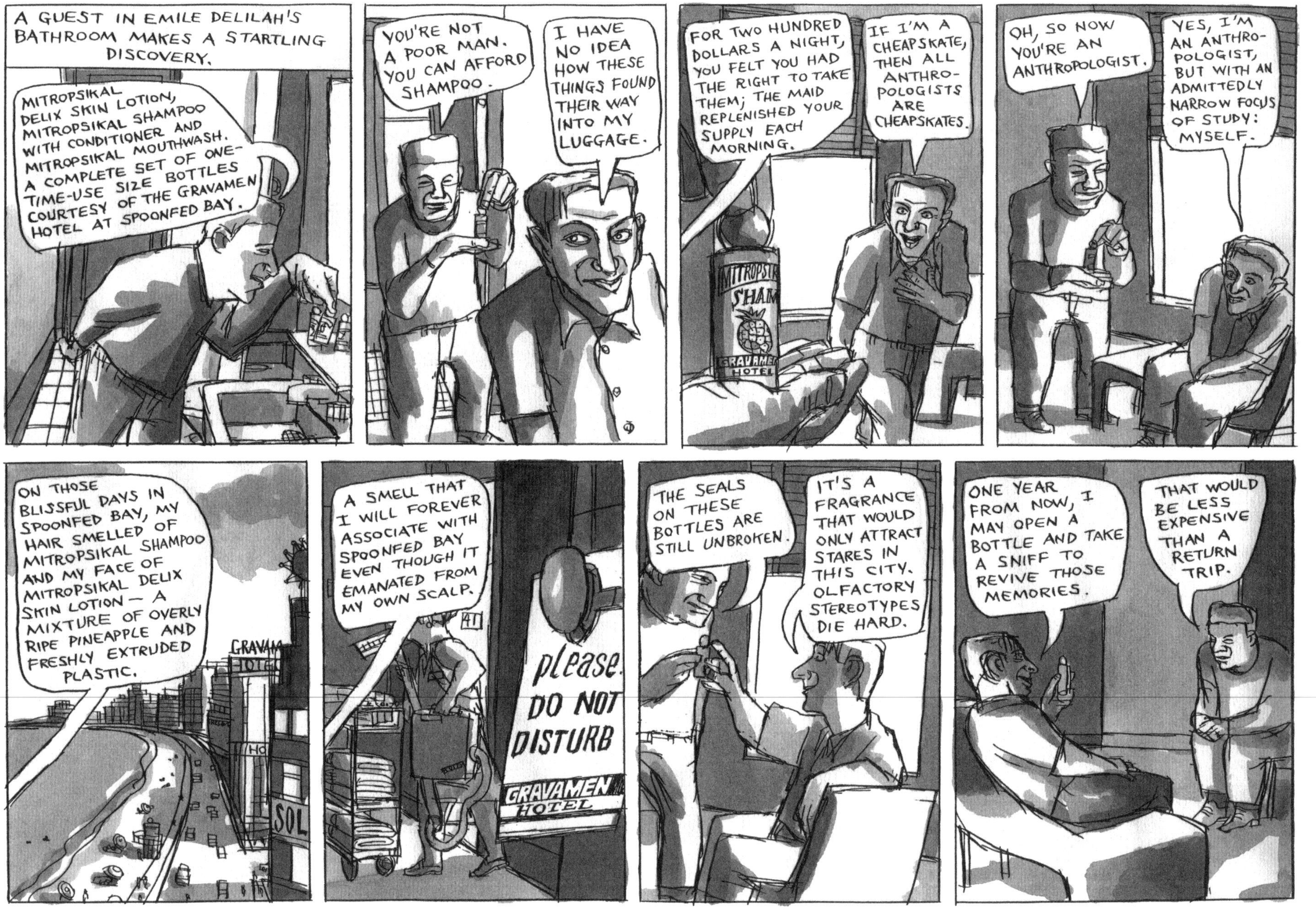
A GUEST IN EMILE DELILAH'S BATHROOM MAKES A STARTLING DISCOVERY.
MITROPSIKAL DELIX SKIN LOTION, MITROPSIKAL SHAMPOO WITH CONDITIONER AND MITROPSIKAL MOUTHWASH. A COMPLETE SET OF ONE-TIME-USE SIZE BOTTLES COURTESY OF THE GRAVAMEN HOTEL AT SPOONFED BAY.
YOU'RE NOT A POOR MAN. YOU CAN AFFORD SHAMPOO.
I HAVE NO IDEA HOW THESE THINGS FOUND THEIR WAY INTO MY LUGGAGE.
FOR TWO HUNDRED DOLLARS A NIGHT, YOU FELT YOU HAD THE RIGHT TO TAKE THEM; THE MAID REPLENISHED YOUR SUPPLY EACH MORNING.
IF I'M A CHEAPSKATE, THEN ALL ANTHROPOLOGISTS ARE CHEAPSKATES.
OH, SO NOW YOU'RE AN ANTHROPOLOGIST.
YES, I'M AN ANTHROPOLOGIST, BUT WITH AN ADMITTEDLY NARROW FOCUS OF STUDY: MYSELF.
ON THOSE BLISSFUL DAYS IN SPOONFED BAY, MY HAIR SMELLED OF MITROPSIKAL SHAMPOO AND MY FACE OF MITROPSIKAL DELIX SKIN LOTION — A MIXTURE OF OVERLY RIPE PINEAPPLE AND FRESHLY EXTRUDED PLASTIC.
A SMELL THAT I WILL FOREVER ASSOCIATE WITH SPOONFED BAY EVEN THOUGH IT EMANATED FROM MY OWN SCALP.
please. DO NOT DISTURB
GRAVAMEN HOTEL
THE SEALS ON THESE BOTTLES ARE STILL UNBROKEN.
IT'S A FRAGRANCE THAT WOULD ONLY ATTRACT STARES IN THIS CITY. OLFACTORY STEREOTYPES DIE HARD.
ONE YEAR FROM NOW, I MAY OPEN A BOTTLE AND TAKE A SNIFF TO REVIVE THOSE MEMORIES.
THAT WOULD BE LESS EXPENSIVE THAN A RETURN TRIP.

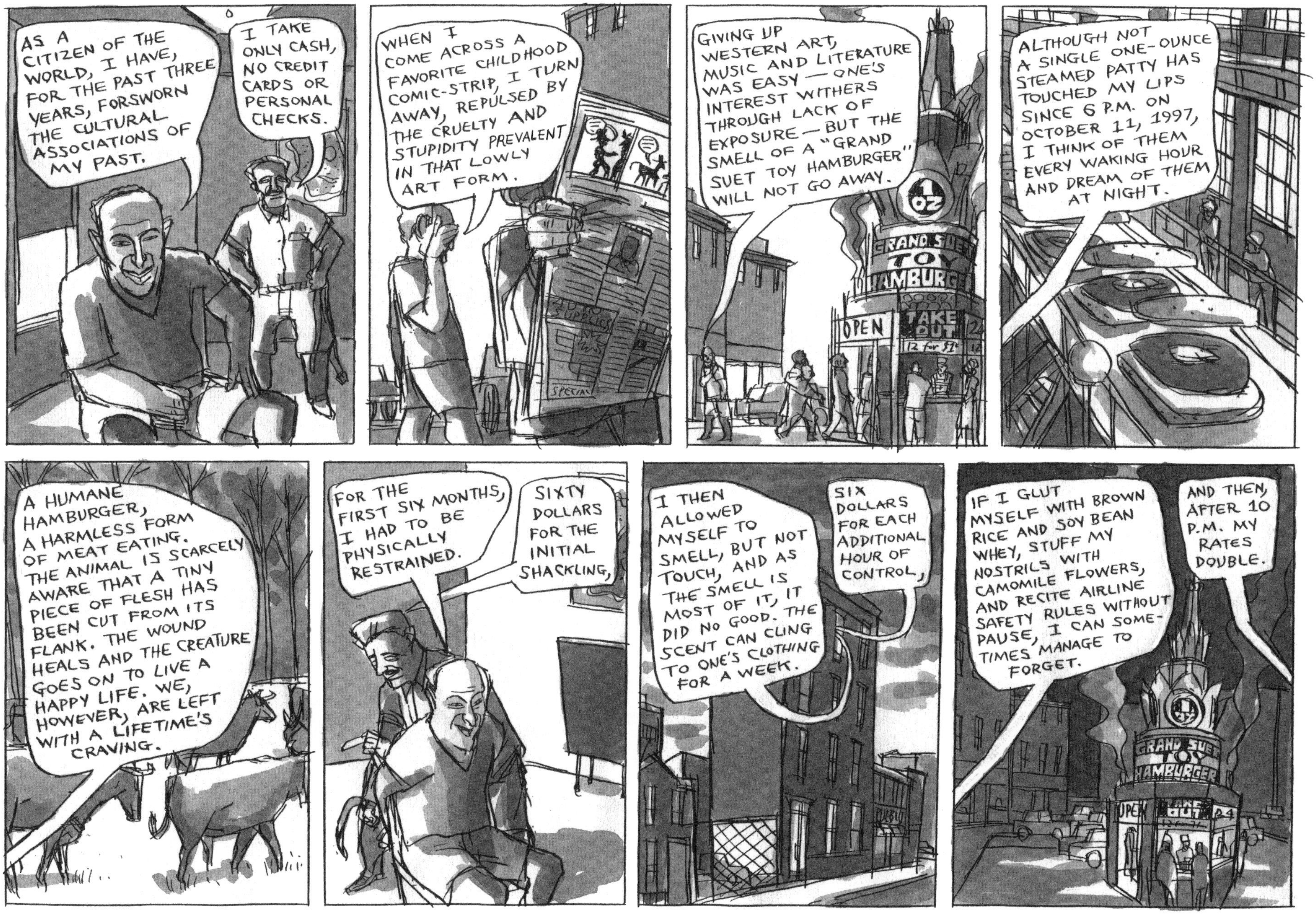
AS A CITIZEN OF THE WORLD, I HAVE, FOR THE PAST THREE YEARS, FORSWORN THE CULTURAL ASSOCIATIONS OF MY PAST.
I TAKE ONLY CASH, NO CREDIT CARDS OR PERSONAL CHECKS.
WHEN I COME ACROSS A FAVORITE CHILDHOOD COMIC-STRIP, I TURN AWAY, REPULSED BY THE CRUELTY AND STUPIDITY PREVALENT IN THAT LOWLY ART FORM.
GIVING UP WESTERN ART, MUSIC AND LITERATURE WAS EASY — ONE'S INTEREST WITHERS THROUGH LACK OF EXPOSURE — BUT THE SMELL OF A "GRAND SUET TOY HAMBURGER" WILL NOT GO AWAY.
1 OZ
GRAND SUET TOY HAMBURGER
OPEN
TAKE OUT
ALTHOUGH NOT A SINGLE ONE-OUNCE STEAMED PATTY HAS TOUCHED MY LIPS SINCE 6 P.M. ON OCTOBER 11, 1997, I THINK OF THEM EVERY WAKING HOUR AND DREAM OF THEM AT NIGHT.
A HUMANE HAMBURGER, A HARMLESS FORM OF MEAT EATING. THE ANIMAL IS SCARCELY AWARE THAT A TINY PIECE OF FLESH HAS BEEN CUT FROM ITS FLANK. THE WOUND HEALS AND THE CREATURE GOES ON TO LIVE A HAPPY LIFE. WE, HOWEVER, ARE LEFT WITH A LIFETIME'S CRAVING.
FOR THE FIRST SIX MONTHS, I HAD TO BE PHYSICALLY RESTRAINED.
SIXTY DOLLARS FOR THE INITIAL SHACKLING,
I THEN ALLOWED MYSELF TO SMELL, BUT NOT TOUCH, AND AS THE SMELL IS MOST OF IT, IT DID NO GOOD. THE SCENT CAN CLING TO ONE'S CLOTHING FOR A WEEK.
SIX DOLLARS FOR EACH ADDITIONAL HOUR OF CONTROL,
IF I GLUT MYSELF WITH BROWN RICE AND SOY BEAN WHEY, STUFF MY NOSTRILS WITH CAMOMILE FLOWERS, AND RECITE AIRLINE SAFETY RULES WITHOUT PAUSE, I CAN SOMETIMES MANAGE TO FORGET.
AND THEN, AFTER 10 P.M. MY RATES DOUBLE.
GRAND SUET TOY HAMBURGER
OPEN

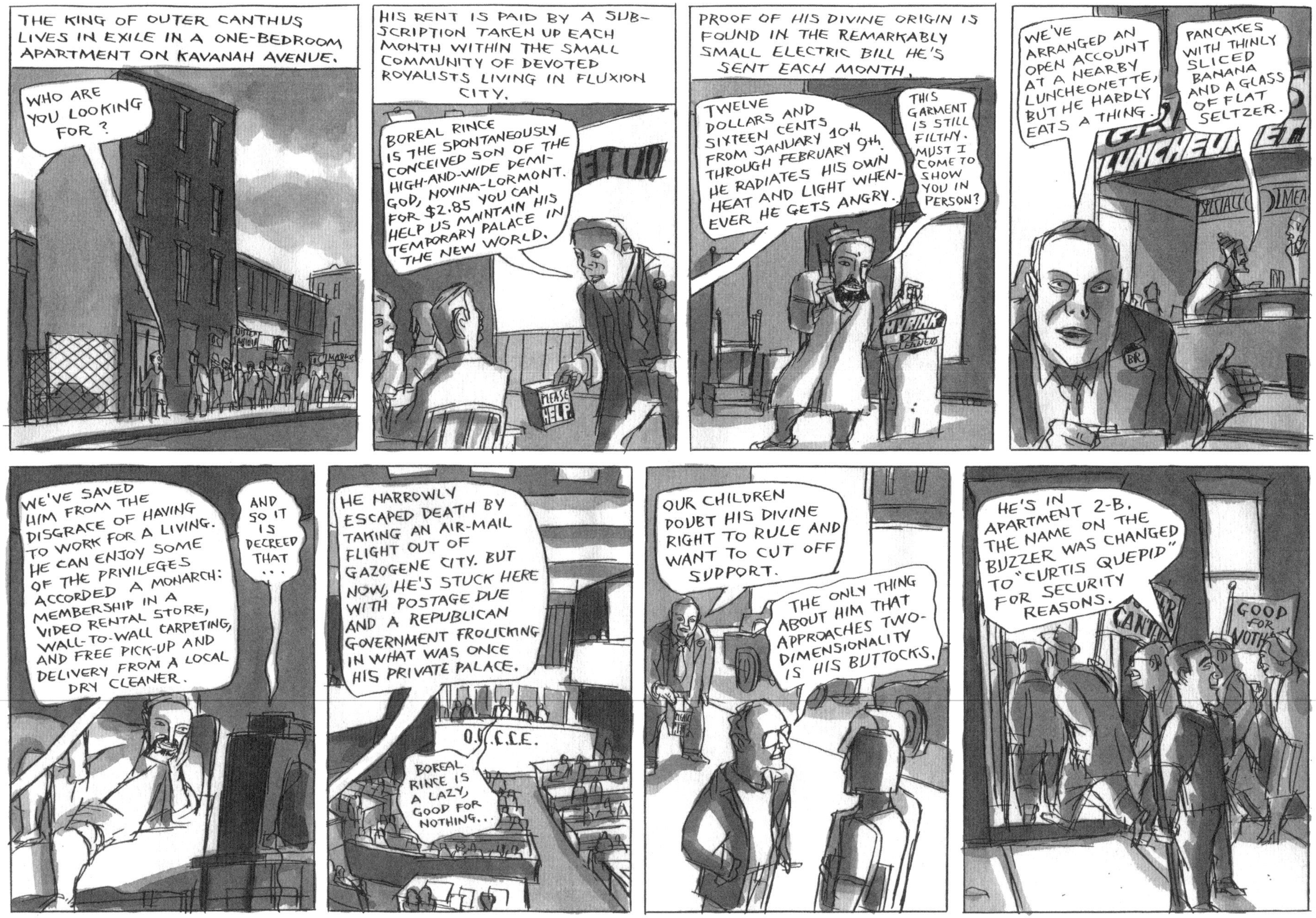
THE KING OF OUTER CANTHUS LIVES IN EXILE IN A ONE-BEDROOM APARTMENT ON KAVANAH AVENUE.
WHO ARE YOU LOOKING FOR ?
HIS RENT IS PAID BY A SUBSCRIPTION TAKEN UP EACH MONTH WITHIN THE SMALL COMMUNITY OF DEVOTED ROYALISTS LIVING IN FLUXION CITY.
BOREAL RINCE IS THE SPONTANEOUSLY CONCEIVED SON OF THE HIGH-AND-WIDE DEMI-GOD, NOVINA-LORMONT. FOR $2.85 YOU CAN HELP US MAINTAIN HIS TEMPORARY PALACE IN THE NEW WORLD.
PLEASE HELP.
PROOF OF HIS DIVINE ORIGIN IS FOUND IN THE REMARKABLY SMALL ELECTRIC BILL HE'S SENT EACH MONTH.
TWELVE DOLLARS AND SIXTEEN CENTS FROM JANUARY 10th THROUGH FEBRUARY 9th. HE RADIATES HIS OWN HEAT AND LIGHT WHENEVER HE GETS ANGRY.
THIS GARMENT IS STILL FILTHY. MUST I COME TO SHOW YOU IN PERSON?
WE'VE ARRANGED AN OPEN ACCOUNT AT A NEARBY LUNCHEONETTE, BUT HE HARDLY EATS A THING.
PANCAKES WITH THINLY SLICED BANANA AND A GLASS OF FLAT SELTZER.
WE'VE SAVED HIM FROM THE DISGRACE OF HAVING TO WORK FOR A LIVING. HE CAN ENJOY SOME OF THE PRIVILEGES ACCORDED A MONARCH: MEMBERSHIP IN A VIDEO RENTAL STORE, WALL-TO-WALL CARPETING, AND FREE PICK-UP AND DELIVERY FROM A LOCAL DRY CLEANER.
AND SO IT IS DECREED THAT . . .
HE NARROWLY ESCAPED DEATH BY TAKING AN AIR-MAIL FLIGHT OUT OF GAZOGENE CITY. BUT NOW, HE'S STUCK HERE WITH POSTAGE DUE AND A REPUBLICAN GOVERNMENT FROLICKING IN WHAT WAS ONCE HIS PRIVATE PALACE.
BOREAL RINCE IS A LAZY, GOOD FOR NOTHING...
OUR CHILDREN DOUBT HIS DIVINE RIGHT TO RULE AND WANT TO CUT OFF SUPPORT.
THE ONLY THING ABOUT HIM THAT APPROACHES TWO-DIMENSIONALITY IS HIS BUTTOCKS.
HE'S IN APARTMENT 2-B. THE NAME ON THE BUZZER WAS CHANGED TO "CURTIS QUEPID" FOR SECURITY REASONS.

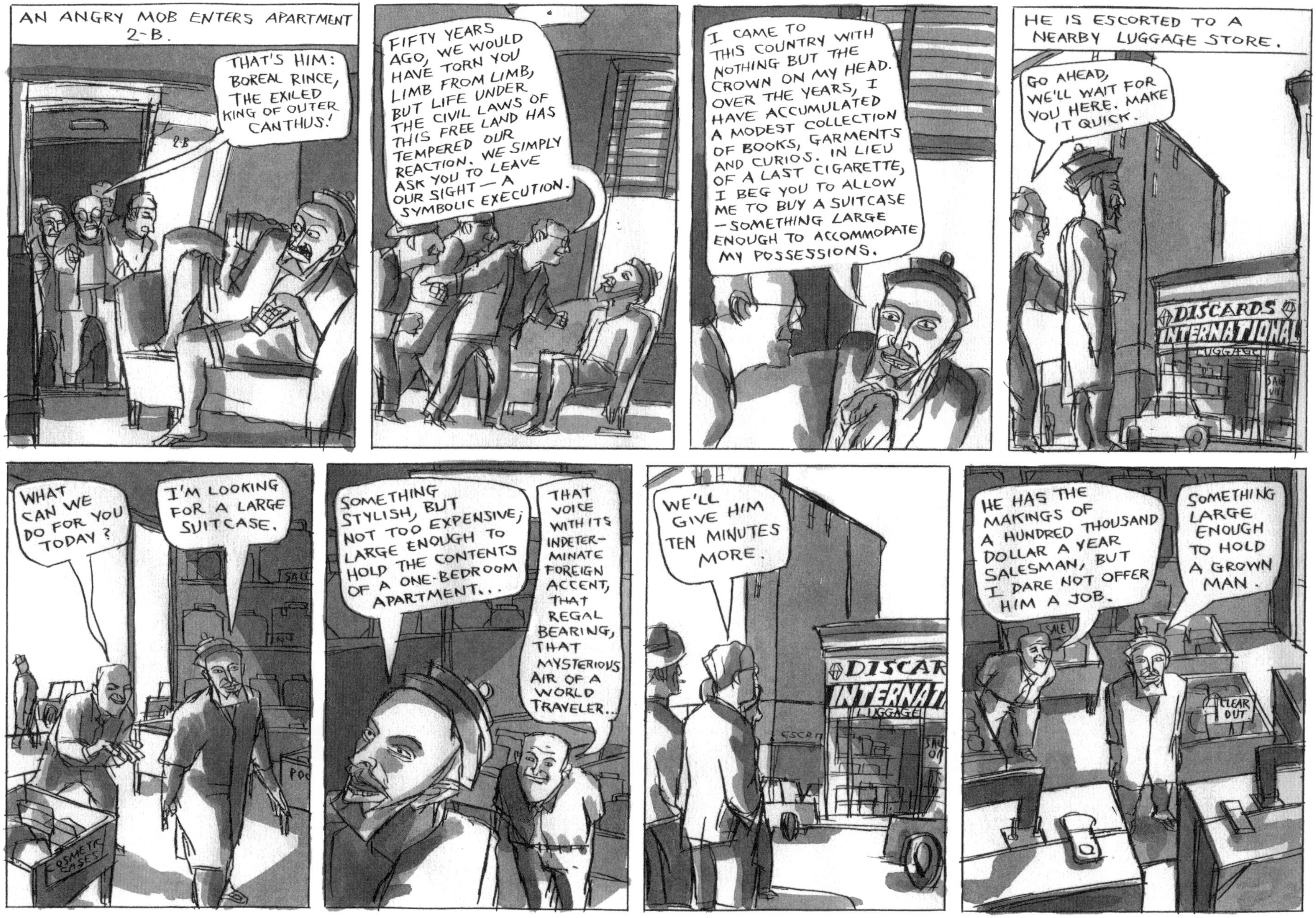

AN ANGRY MOB ENTERS APARTMENT 2-B.
THAT'S HIM: BOREAL RINCE, THE EXILED KING OF OUTER CANTHUS!
2-B
FIFTY YEARS AGO, WE WOULD HAVE TORN YOU LIMB FROM LIMB, BUT LIFE UNDER THE CIVIL LAWS OF THIS FREE LAND HAS TEMPERED OUR REACTION. WE SIMPLY ASK YOU TO LEAVE OUR SIGHT — A SYMBOLIC EXECUTION.
I CAME TO THIS COUNTRY WITH NOTHING BUT THE CROWN ON MY HEAD. OVER THE YEARS, I HAVE ACCUMULATED A MODEST COLLECTION OF BOOKS, GARMENTS AND CURIOS. IN LIEU OF A LAST CIGARETTE, I BEG YOU TO ALLOW ME TO BUY A SUITCASE — SOMETHING LARGE ENOUGH TO ACCOMMODATE MY POSSESSIONS.
HE IS ESCORTED TO A NEARBY LUGGAGE STORE.
GO AHEAD, WE'LL WAIT FOR YOU HERE. MAKE IT QUICK.
DISCARDS INTERNATIONAL
LUGGAGE
WHAT CAN WE DO FOR YOU TODAY?
I'M LOOKING FOR A LARGE SUITCASE.
COSMETIC CASES
SOMETHING STYLISH, BUT NOT TOO EXPENSIVE; LARGE ENOUGH TO HOLD THE CONTENTS OF A ONE-BEDROOM APARTMENT...
THAT VOICE WITH ITS INDETER-MINATE FOREIGN ACCENT, THAT REGAL BEARING, THAT MYSTERIOUS AIR OF A WORLD TRAVELER...
WE'LL GIVE HIM TEN MINUTES MORE.
DISCAR
INTERNATI
LUGGAGE
HE HAS THE MAKINGS OF A HUNDRED THOUSAND DOLLAR A YEAR SALESMAN, BUT I DARE NOT OFFER HIM A JOB.
SOMETHING LARGE ENOUGH TO HOLD A GROWN MAN.
SALE
CLEAR OUT

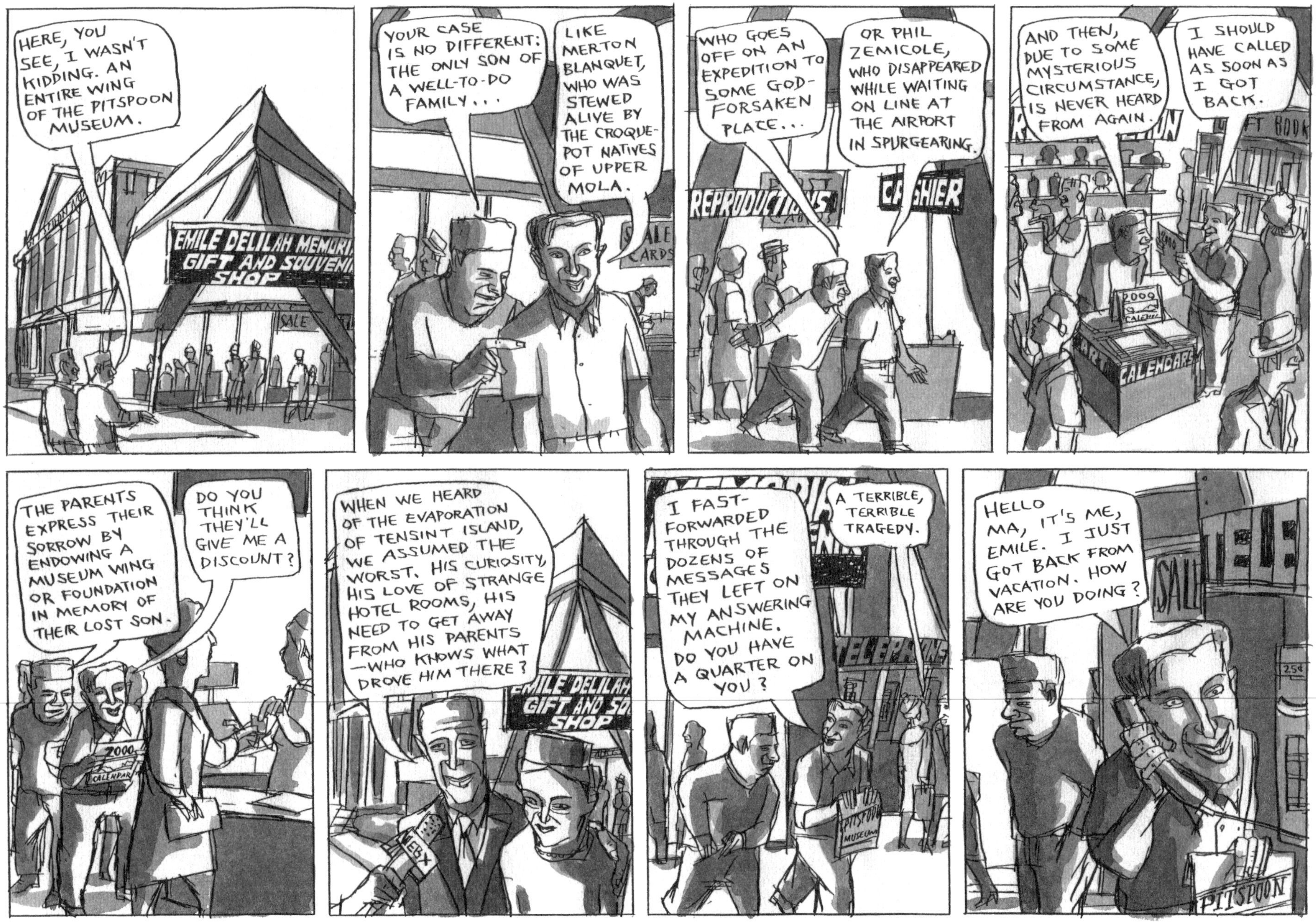
HERE, YOU SEE, I WASN'T KIDDING. AN ENTIRE WING OF THE PITSPOON MUSEUM.
YOUR CASE IS NO DIFFERENT; THE ONLY SON OF A WELL-TO-DO FAMILY...
LIKE MERTON BLANQUET, WHO WAS STEWED ALIVE BY THE CROQUEPOT NATIVES OF UPPER MOLA.
WHO GOES OFF ON AN EXPEDITION TO SOME GOD-FORSAKEN PLACE...
OR PHIL ZEMICOLE, WHO DISAPPEARED WHILE WAITING ON LINE AT THE AIRPORT IN SPURGEARING.
REPRODUCTIONS
CASHIER
AND THEN, DUE TO SOME MYSTERIOUS CIRCUMSTANCE, IS NEVER HEARD FROM AGAIN.
I SHOULD HAVE CALLED AS SOON AS I GOT BACK.
CALENDARS
THE PARENTS EXPRESS THEIR SORROW BY ENDOWING A MUSEUM WING OR FOUNDATION IN MEMORY OF THEIR LOST SON.
DO YOU THINK THEY'LL GIVE ME A DISCOUNT?
WHEN WE HEARD OF THE EVAPORATION OF TENSINT ISLAND, WE ASSUMED THE WORST. HIS CURIOSITY, HIS LOVE OF STRANGE HOTEL ROOMS, HIS NEED TO GET AWAY FROM HIS PARENTS —WHO KNOWS WHAT DROVE HIM THERE?
I FAST-FORWARDED THROUGH THE DOZENS OF MESSAGES THEY LEFT ON MY ANSWERING MACHINE. DO YOU HAVE A QUARTER ON YOU?
A TERRIBLE, TERRIBLE TRAGEDY.
HELLO MA, IT'S ME, EMILE. I JUST GOT BACK FROM VACATION. HOW ARE YOU DOING?
PITSPOON

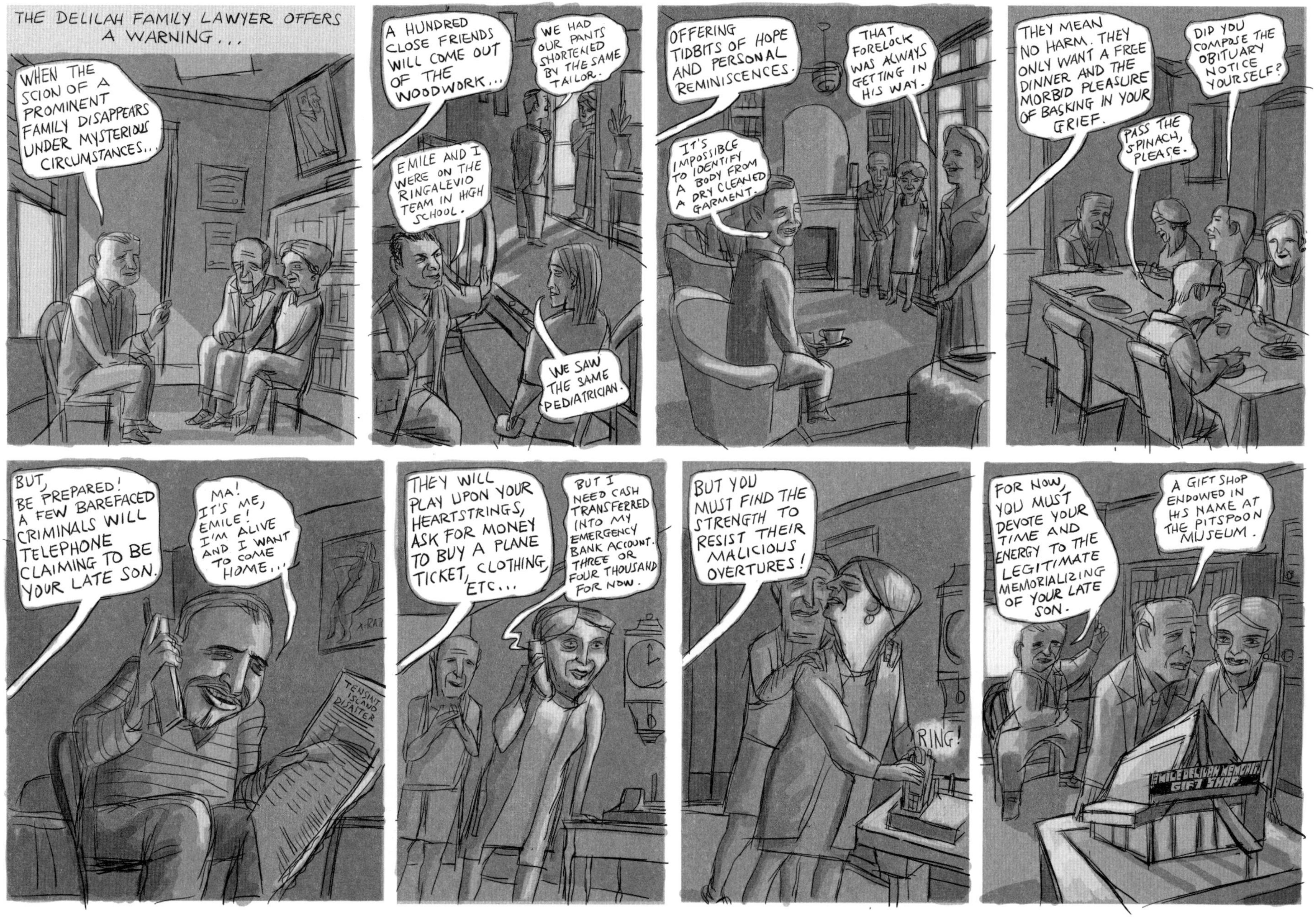
THE DELILAH FAMILY LAWYER OFFERS A WARNING...
WHEN THE SCION OF A PROMINENT FAMILY DISAPPEARS UNDER MYSTERIOUS CIRCUMSTANCES...
A HUNDRED CLOSE FRIENDS WILL COME OUT OF THE WOODWORK...
WE HAD OUR PANTS SHORTENED BY THE SAME TAILOR.
EMILE AND I WERE ON THE RINGALEVIO TEAM IN HIGH SCHOOL.
WE SAW THE SAME PEDIATRICIAN.
OFFERING TIDBITS OF HOPE AND PERSONAL REMINISCENCES.
THAT FORELOCK WAS ALWAYS GETTING IN HIS WAY.
IT'S IMPOSSIBLE TO IDENTIFY A BODY FROM A DRY CLEANED GARMENT.
THEY MEAN NO HARM. THEY ONLY WANT A FREE DINNER AND THE MORBID PLEASURE OF BASKING IN YOUR GRIEF.
DID YOU COMPOSE THE OBITUARY NOTICE YOURSELF?
PASS THE SPINACH, PLEASE.
BUT, BE PREPARED! A FEW BAREFACED CRIMINALS WILL TELEPHONE CLAIMING TO BE YOUR LATE SON.
MA! IT'S ME, EMILE! I'M ALIVE AND I WANT TO COME HOME...
THEY WILL PLAY UPON YOUR HEARTSTRINGS, ASK FOR MONEY TO BUY A PLANE TICKET, CLOTHING, ETC...
BUT I NEED CASH TRANSFERRED INTO MY EMERGENCY BANK ACCOUNT. THREE OR FOUR THOUSAND FOR NOW.
BUT YOU MUST FIND THE STRENGTH TO RESIST THEIR MALICIOUS OVERTURES!
RING!
FOR NOW, YOU MUST DEVOTE YOUR TIME AND ENERGY TO THE LEGITIMATE MEMORIALIZING OF YOUR LATE SON.
A GIFT SHOP ENDOWED IN HIS NAME AT THE PITSPOON MUSEUM.
EMILE DELILAH MEMORIAL GIFT SHOP

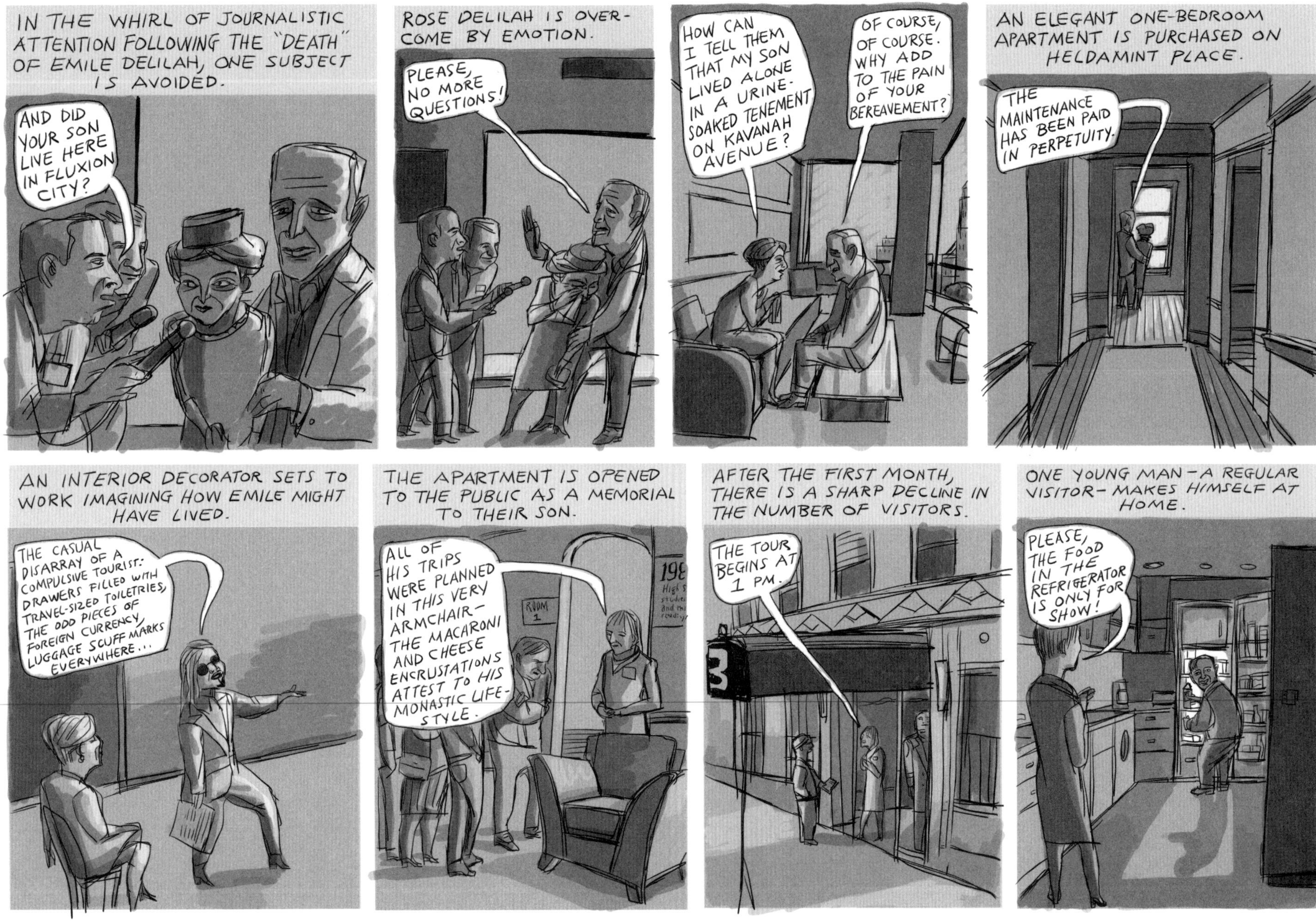

IN THE WHIRL OF JOURNALISTIC ATTENTION FOLLOWING THE "DEATH" OF EMILE DELILAH, ONE SUBJECT IS AVOIDED.
AND DID YOUR SON LIVE HERE IN FLUXION CITY?
ROSE DELILAH IS OVER-COME BY EMOTION.
PLEASE, NO MORE QUESTIONS!
HOW CAN I TELL THEM THAT MY SON LIVED ALONE IN A URINE-SOAKED TENEMENT ON KAVANAH AVENUE?
OF COURSE, OF COURSE. WHY ADD TO THE PAIN OF YOUR BEREAVEMENT?
AN ELEGANT ONE-BEDROOM APARTMENT IS PURCHASED ON HELDAMINT PLACE.
THE MAINTENANCE HAS BEEN PAID IN PERPETUITY.
AN INTERIOR DECORATOR SETS TO WORK IMAGINING HOW EMILE MIGHT HAVE LIVED.
THE CASUAL DISARRAY OF A COMPULSIVE TOURIST: DRAWERS FILLED WITH TRAVEL-SIZED TOILETRIES, THE ODD PIECES OF FOREIGN CURRENCY, LUGGAGE SCUFF MARKS EVERYWHERE...
THE APARTMENT IS OPENED TO THE PUBLIC AS A MEMORIAL TO THEIR SON.
ALL OF HIS TRIPS WERE PLANNED IN THIS VERY ARMCHAIR— THE MACARONI AND CHEESE ENCRUSTATIONS ATTEST TO HIS MONASTIC LIFE-STYLE.
ROOM 1
AFTER THE FIRST MONTH, THERE IS A SHARP DECLINE IN THE NUMBER OF VISITORS.
THE TOUR BEGINS AT 1 PM.
3
ONE YOUNG MAN— A REGULAR VISITOR— MAKES HIMSELF AT HOME.
PLEASE, THE FOOD IN THE REFRIGERATOR IS ONLY FOR SHOW!

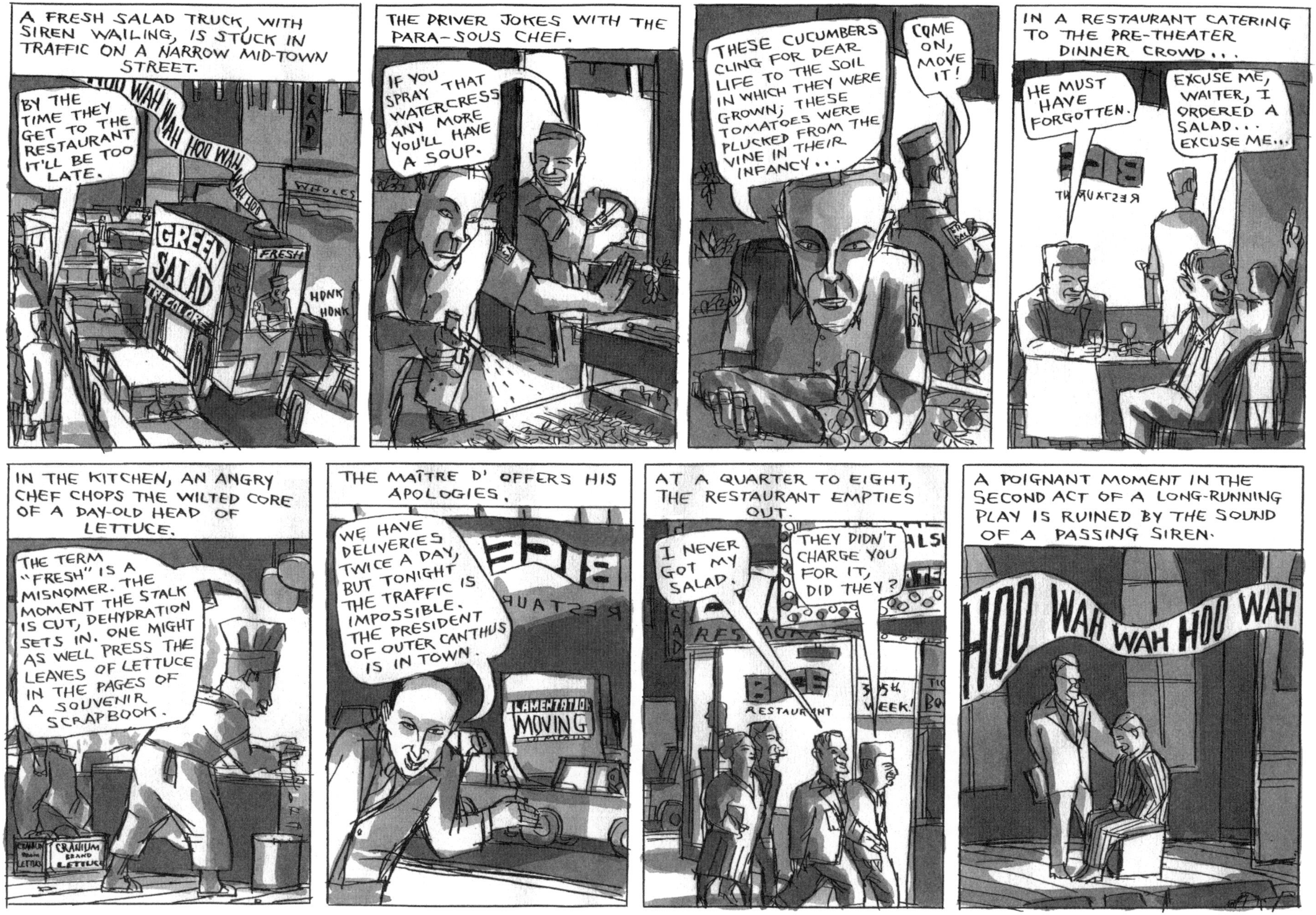
A FRESH SALAD TRUCK, WITH SIREN WAILING, IS STUCK IN TRAFFIC ON A NARROW MID-TOWN STREET.
HOO WAH WAH HOO WAH WAH HOO
BY THE TIME THEY GET TO THE RESTAURANT IT'LL BE TOO LATE.
GREEN SALAD TRE COLORE
FRESH
HONK HONK
THE DRIVER JOKES WITH THE PARA-SOUS CHEF.
IF YOU SPRAY THAT WATERCRESS ANY MORE YOU'LL HAVE A SOUP.
THESE CUCUMBERS CLING FOR DEAR LIFE TO THE SOIL IN WHICH THEY WERE GROWN; THESE TOMATOES WERE PLUCKED FROM THE VINE IN THEIR INFANCY...
COME ON, MOVE IT!
IN A RESTAURANT CATERING TO THE PRE-THEATER DINNER CROWD...
EXCUSE ME, WAITER, I ORDERED A SALAD... EXCUSE ME...
HE MUST HAVE FORGOTTEN.
IN THE KITCHEN, AN ANGRY CHEF CHOPS THE WILTED CORE OF A DAY-OLD HEAD OF LETTUCE.
THE TERM "FRESH" IS A MISNOMER. THE MOMENT THE STALK IS CUT, DEHYDRATION SETS IN. ONE MIGHT AS WELL PRESS THE LEAVES OF LETTUCE IN THE PAGES OF A SOUVENIR SCRAPBOOK.
CRANIUM BRAND LETTUCE
THE MAÎTRE D' OFFERS HIS APOLOGIES.
WE HAVE DELIVERIES TWICE A DAY, BUT TONIGHT THE TRAFFIC IS IMPOSSIBLE. THE PRESIDENT OF OUTER CANTHUS IS IN TOWN.
LAMENTATION MOVING
AT A QUARTER TO EIGHT, THE RESTAURANT EMPTIES OUT.
I NEVER GOT MY SALAD.
THEY DIDN'T CHARGE YOU FOR IT, DID THEY?
RESTAURANT
A POIGNANT MOMENT IN THE SECOND ACT OF A LONG-RUNNING PLAY IS RUINED BY THE SOUND OF A PASSING SIREN.
HOO WAH WAH HOO WAH

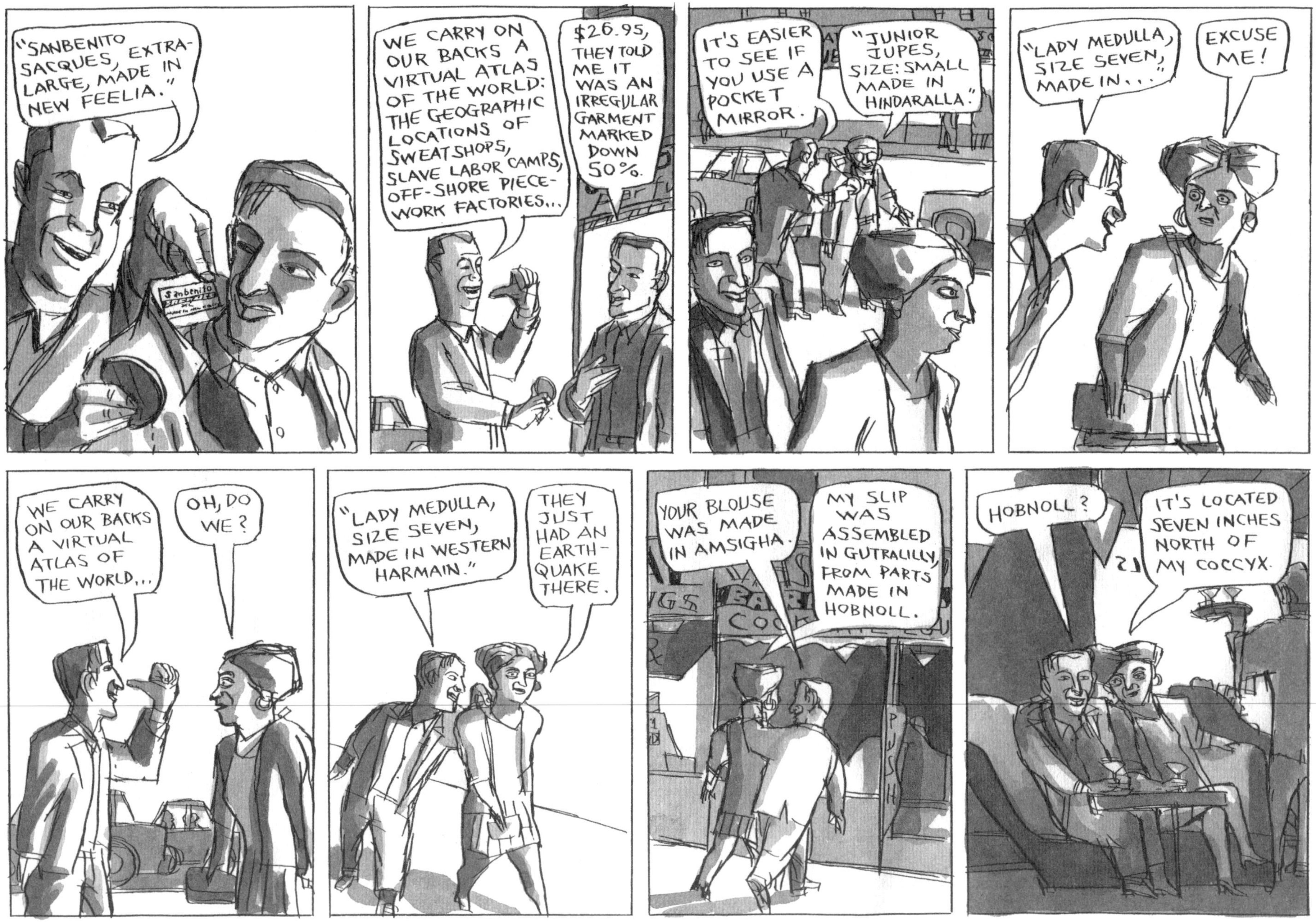
"SANBENITO SACQUES, EXTRA-LARGE, MADE IN NEW FEELIA."
WE CARRY ON OUR BACKS A VIRTUAL ATLAS OF THE WORLD: THE GEOGRAPHIC LOCATIONS OF SWEATSHOPS, SLAVE LABOR CAMPS, OFF-SHORE PIECE-WORK FACTORIES...
$26.95, THEY TOLD ME IT WAS AN IRREGULAR GARMENT MARKED DOWN 50%.
IT'S EASIER TO SEE IF YOU USE A POCKET MIRROR.
"JUNIOR JUPES, SIZE: SMALL MADE IN HINDARALLA."
"LADY MEDULLA, SIZE SEVEN, MADE IN..."
EXCUSE ME!
WE CARRY ON OUR BACKS A VIRTUAL ATLAS OF THE WORLD...
OH, DO WE?
"LADY MEDULLA, SIZE SEVEN, MADE IN WESTERN HARMAIN."
THEY JUST HAD AN EARTH-QUAKE THERE.
YOUR BLOUSE WAS MADE IN AMSIGHA.
MY SLIP WAS ASSEMBLED IN GUTRALILLY, FROM PARTS MADE IN HOBNOLL.
HOBNOLL?
IT'S LOCATED SEVEN INCHES NORTH OF MY COCCYX.

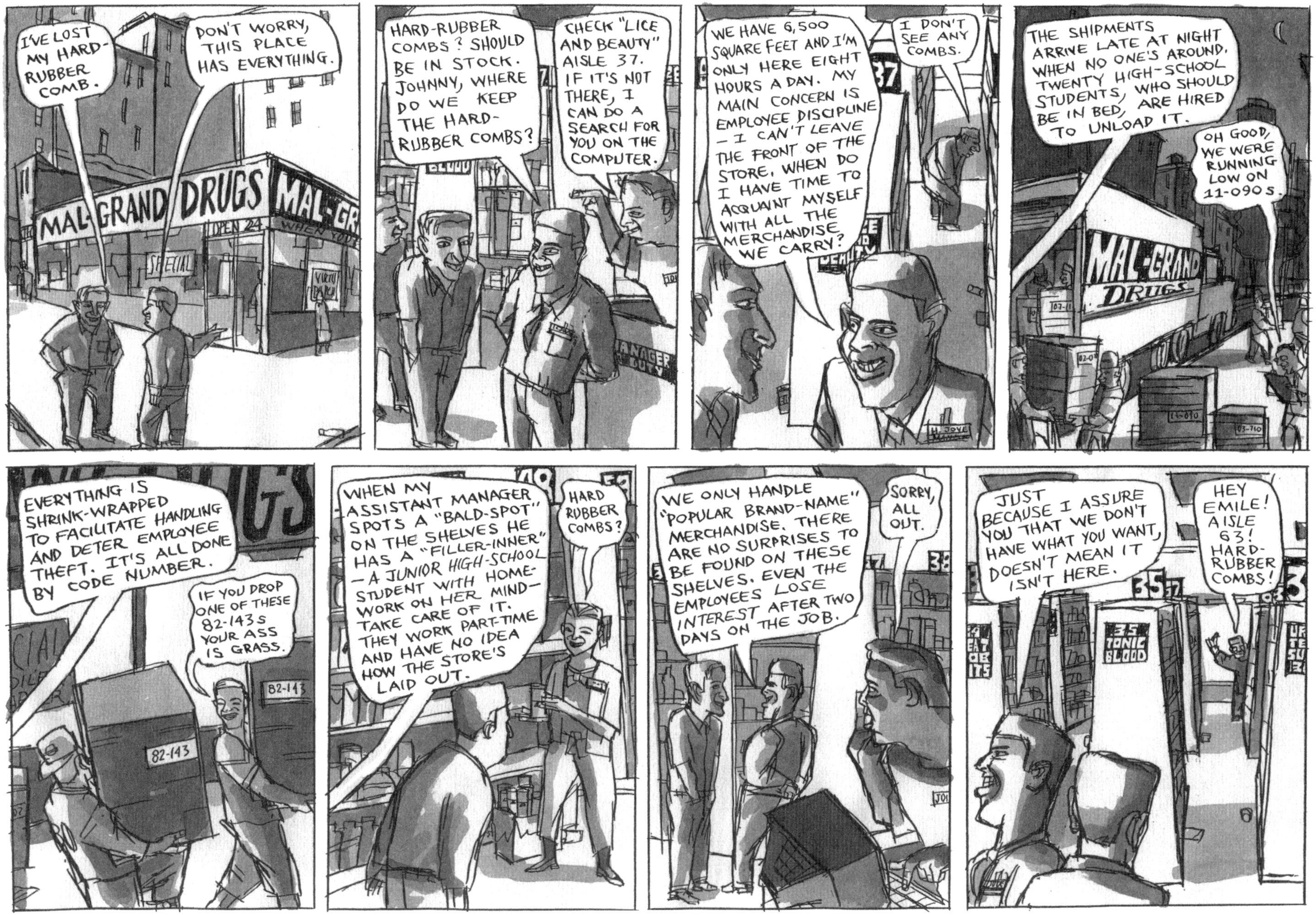
I'VE LOST MY HARD-RUBBER COMB.
DON'T WORRY, THIS PLACE HAS EVERYTHING.
MAL-GRAND DRUGS
OPEN 24
SPECIAL
HARD-RUBBER COMBS? SHOULD BE IN STOCK. JOHNNY, WHERE DO WE KEEP THE HARD-RUBBER COMBS?
CHECK "LICE AND BEAUTY" AISLE 37. IF IT'S NOT THERE, I CAN DO A SEARCH FOR YOU ON THE COMPUTER.
WE HAVE 6,500 SQUARE FEET AND I'M ONLY HERE EIGHT HOURS A DAY. MY MAIN CONCERN IS EMPLOYEE DISCIPLINE – I CAN'T LEAVE THE FRONT OF THE STORE, WHEN DO I HAVE TIME TO ACQUAINT MYSELF WITH ALL THE MERCHANDISE WE CARRY?
I DON'T SEE ANY COMBS.
THE SHIPMENTS ARRIVE LATE AT NIGHT WHEN NO ONE'S AROUND. TWENTY HIGH-SCHOOL STUDENTS, WHO SHOULD BE IN BED, ARE HIRED TO UNLOAD IT.
OH GOOD, WE WERE RUNNING LOW ON 11-090S.
MAL-GRAND DRUGS
EVERYTHING IS SHRINK-WRAPPED TO FACILITATE HANDLING AND DETER EMPLOYEE THEFT. IT'S ALL DONE BY CODE NUMBER.
IF YOU DROP ONE OF THESE 82-143S YOUR ASS IS GRASS.
82-143
WHEN MY ASSISTANT MANAGER SPOTS A "BALD-SPOT" ON THE SHELVES HE HAS A "FILLER-INNER" – A JUNIOR HIGH-SCHOOL STUDENT WITH HOME-WORK ON HER MIND – TAKE CARE OF IT. THEY WORK PART-TIME AND HAVE NO IDEA HOW THE STORE'S LAID OUT.
HARD RUBBER COMBS?
WE ONLY HANDLE "POPULAR BRAND-NAME" MERCHANDISE. THERE ARE NO SURPRISES TO BE FOUND ON THESE SHELVES. EVEN THE EMPLOYEES LOSE INTEREST AFTER TWO DAYS ON THE JOB.
SORRY, ALL OUT.
JUST BECAUSE I ASSURE YOU THAT WE DON'T HAVE WHAT YOU WANT, DOESN'T MEAN IT ISN'T HERE.
HEY EMILE! AISLE 63! HARD-RUBBER COMBS!
TONIC BLOOD

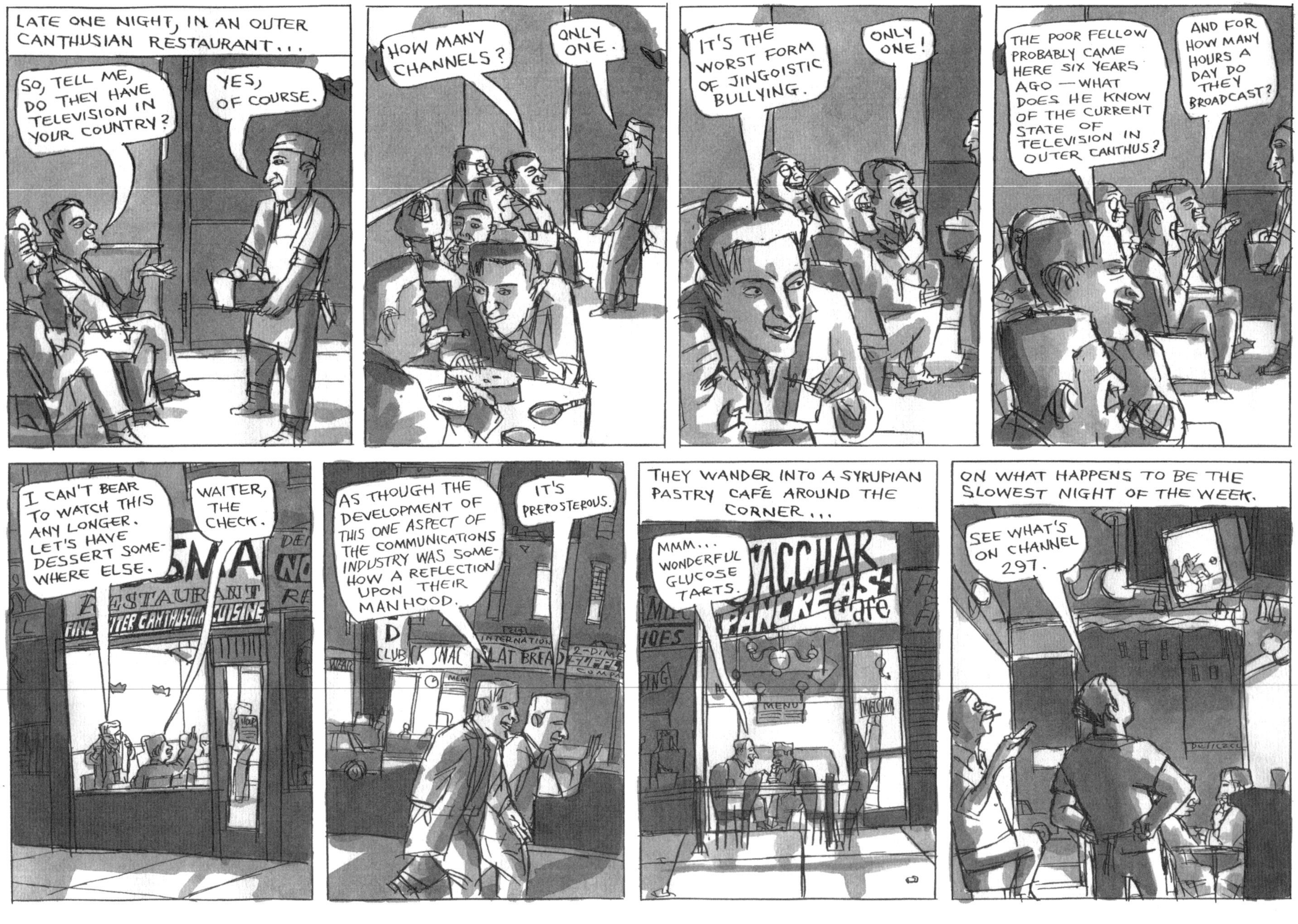
LATE ONE NIGHT, IN AN OUTER CANTHUSIAN RESTAURANT...
SO, TELL ME, DO THEY HAVE TELEVISION IN YOUR COUNTRY?
YES, OF COURSE.
HOW MANY CHANNELS?
ONLY ONE.
IT'S THE WORST FORM OF JINGOISTIC BULLYING.
ONLY ONE!
THE POOR FELLOW PROBABLY CAME HERE SIX YEARS AGO — WHAT DOES HE KNOW OF THE CURRENT STATE OF TELEVISION IN OUTER CANTHUS?
AND FOR HOW MANY HOURS A DAY DO THEY BROADCAST?
I CAN'T BEAR TO WATCH THIS ANY LONGER. LET'S HAVE DESSERT SOMEWHERE ELSE.
WAITER, THE CHECK.
AS THOUGH THE DEVELOPMENT OF THIS ONE ASPECT OF THE COMMUNICATIONS INDUSTRY WAS SOMEHOW A REFLECTION UPON THEIR MANHOOD.
IT'S PREPOSTEROUS.
THEY WANDER INTO A SYRUPIAN PASTRY CAFÉ AROUND THE CORNER...
MMM... WONDERFUL GLUCOSE TARTS.
ON WHAT HAPPENS TO BE THE SLOWEST NIGHT OF THE WEEK.
SEE WHAT'S ON CHANNEL 297.

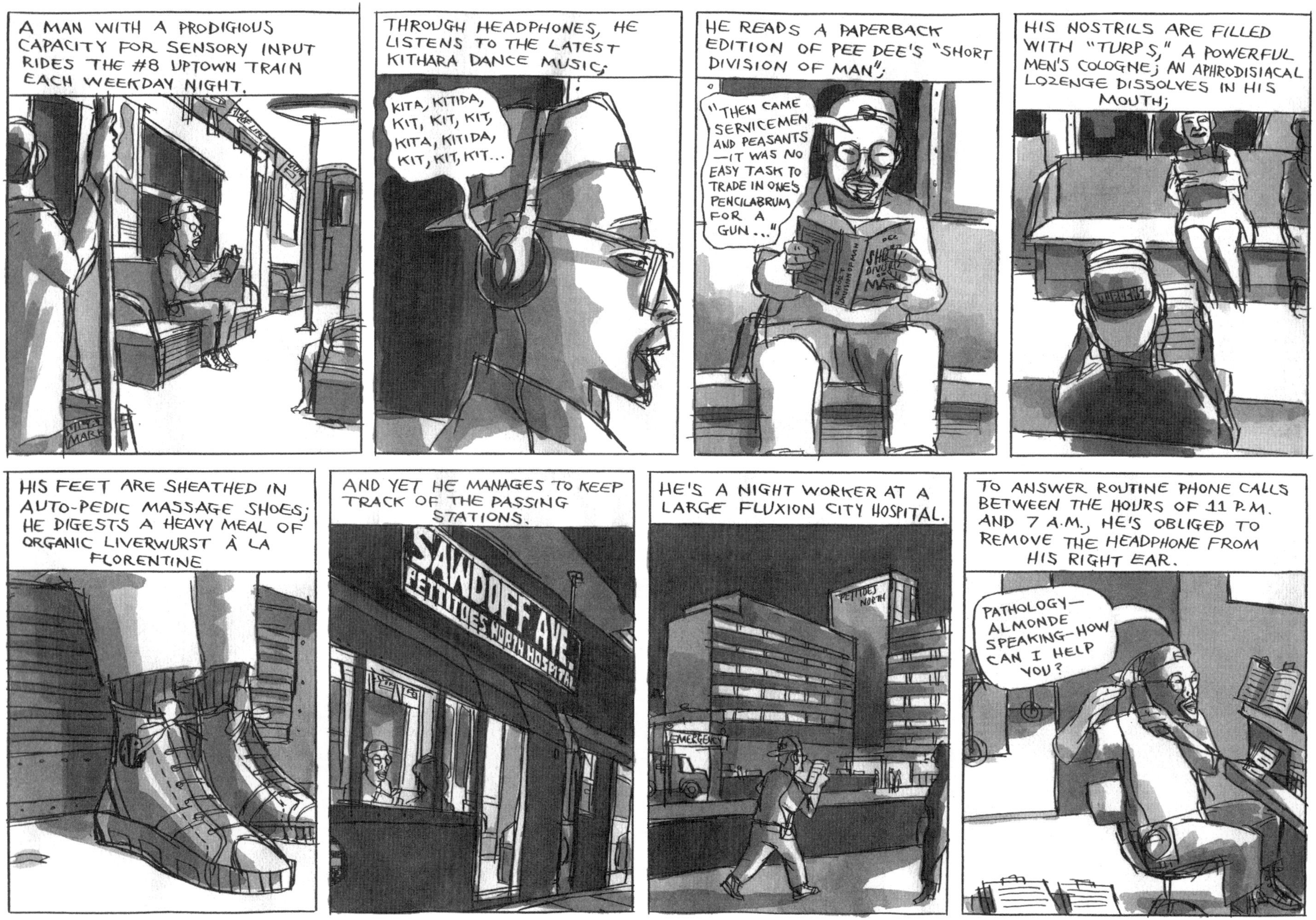
A MAN WITH A PRODIGIOUS CAPACITY FOR SENSORY INPUT RIDES THE #8 UPTOWN TRAIN EACH WEEKDAY NIGHT.
THROUGH HEADPHONES, HE LISTENS TO THE LATEST KITHARA DANCE MUSIC;
KITA, KITIDA, KIT, KIT, KIT, KITA, KITIDA, KIT, KIT, KIT...
HE READS A PAPERBACK EDITION OF PEE DEE'S "SHORT DIVISION OF MAN";
"THEN CAME SERVICEMEN AND PEASANTS —IT WAS NO EASY TASK TO TRADE IN ONE'S PENCILABRUM FOR A GUN..."
HIS NOSTRILS ARE FILLED WITH "TURPS," A POWERFUL MEN'S COLOGNE; AN APHRODISIACAL LOZENGE DISSOLVES IN HIS MOUTH;
HIS FEET ARE SHEATHED IN AUTO-PEDIC MASSAGE SHOES; HE DIGESTS A HEAVY MEAL OF ORGANIC LIVERWURST À LA FLORENTINE
AND YET HE MANAGES TO KEEP TRACK OF THE PASSING STATIONS.
SAWDOFF AVE.
PETTITOES NORTH HOSPITAL
HE'S A NIGHT WORKER AT A LARGE FLUXION CITY HOSPITAL.
PETTITOES NORTH
EMERGENCY
TO ANSWER ROUTINE PHONE CALLS BETWEEN THE HOURS OF 11 P.M. AND 7 A.M., HE'S OBLIGED TO REMOVE THE HEADPHONE FROM HIS RIGHT EAR.
PATHOLOGY— ALMONDE SPEAKING—HOW CAN I HELP YOU?

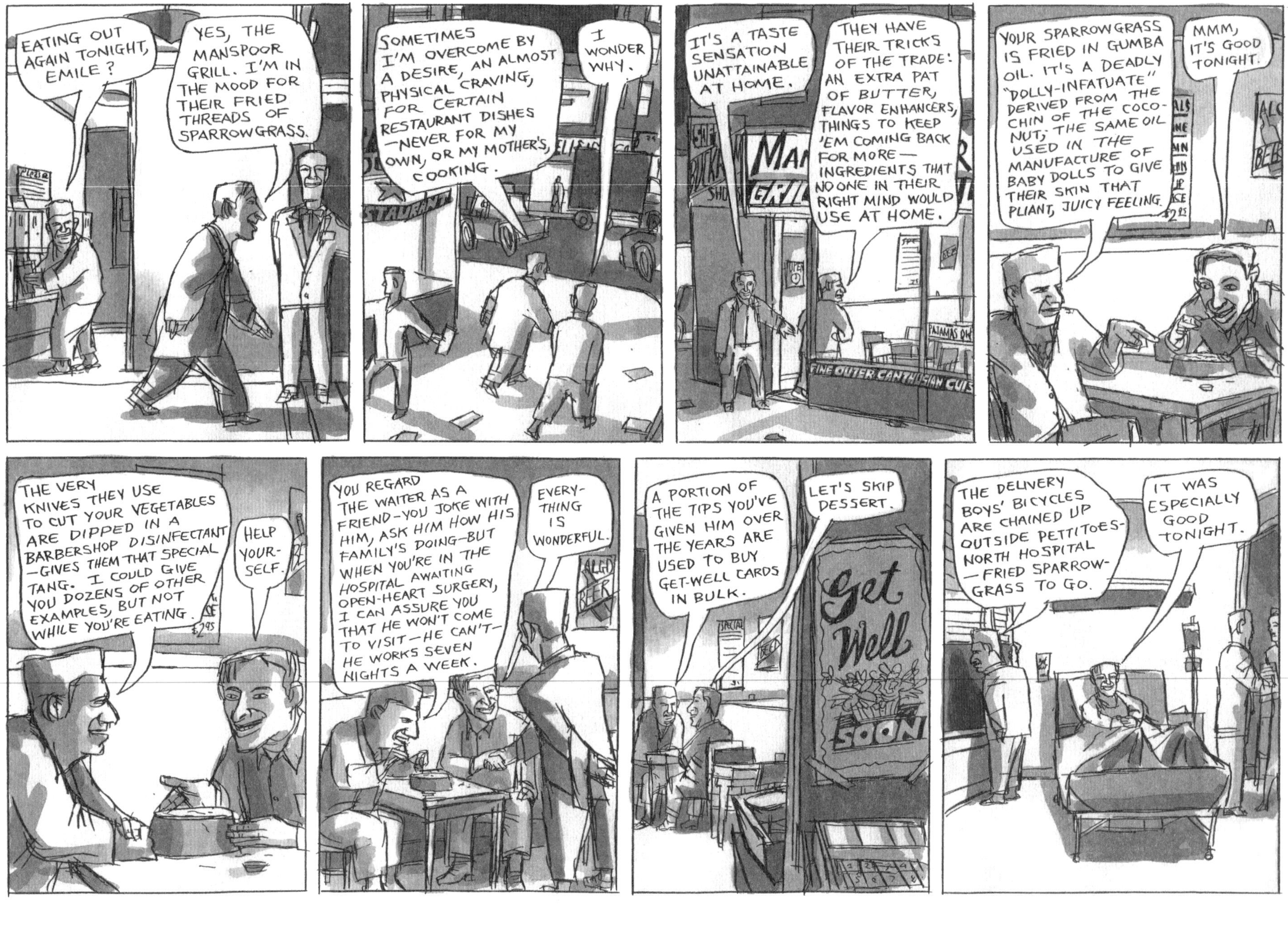
EATING OUT AGAIN TONIGHT, EMILE?
YES, THE MANSPOOR GRILL. I'M IN THE MOOD FOR THEIR FRIED THREADS OF SPARROWGRASS.
SOMETIMES I'M OVERCOME BY A DESIRE, AN ALMOST PHYSICAL CRAVING, FOR CERTAIN RESTAURANT DISHES —NEVER FOR MY OWN, OR MY MOTHER'S, COOKING.
I WONDER WHY.
IT'S A TASTE SENSATION UNATTAINABLE AT HOME.
THEY HAVE THEIR TRICKS OF THE TRADE: AN EXTRA PAT OF BUTTER, FLAVOR ENHANCERS, THINGS TO KEEP 'EM COMING BACK FOR MORE—INGREDIENTS THAT NO ONE IN THEIR RIGHT MIND WOULD USE AT HOME.
YOUR SPARROWGRASS IS FRIED IN GUMBA OIL. IT'S A DEADLY "DOLLY-INFATUATE" DERIVED FROM THE COCOCHIN OF THE COCONUT; THE SAME OIL USED IN THE MANUFACTURE OF BABY DOLLS TO GIVE THEIR SKIN THAT PLIANT, JUICY FEELING.
MMM, IT'S GOOD TONIGHT.
THE VERY KNIVES THEY USE TO CUT YOUR VEGETABLES ARE DIPPED IN A BARBERSHOP DISINFECTANT —GIVES THEM THAT SPECIAL TANG. I COULD GIVE YOU DOZENS OF OTHER EXAMPLES, BUT NOT WHILE YOU'RE EATING.
HELP YOURSELF.
YOU REGARD THE WAITER AS A FRIEND—YOU JOKE WITH HIM, ASK HIM HOW HIS FAMILY'S DOING—BUT WHEN YOU'RE IN THE HOSPITAL AWAITING OPEN-HEART SURGERY, I CAN ASSURE YOU THAT HE WON'T COME TO VISIT—HE CAN'T—HE WORKS SEVEN NIGHTS A WEEK.
EVERYTHING IS WONDERFUL.
A PORTION OF THE TIPS YOU'VE GIVEN HIM OVER THE YEARS ARE USED TO BUY GET-WELL CARDS IN BULK.
LET'S SKIP DESSERT.
Get Well SOON
THE DELIVERY BOYS' BICYCLES ARE CHAINED UP OUTSIDE PETTITOES-NORTH HOSPITAL —FRIED SPARROWGRASS TO GO.
IT WAS ESPECIALLY GOOD TONIGHT.

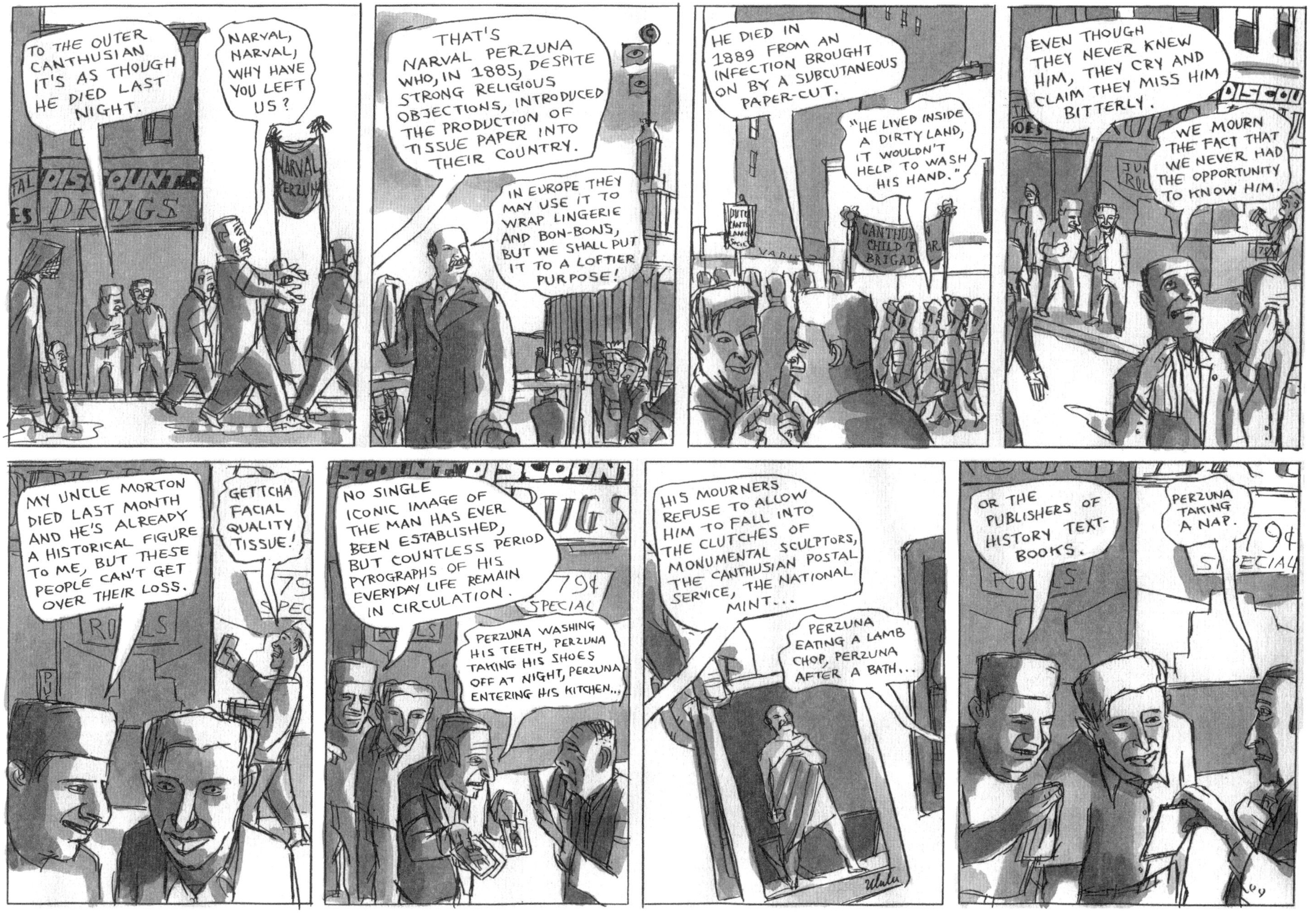

TO THE OUTER CANTHUSIAN IT'S AS THOUGH HE DIED LAST NIGHT.
NARVAL, NARVAL, WHY HAVE YOU LEFT US?
DRUGS
NARVAL PERZUNA
THAT'S NARVAL PERZUNA WHO, IN 1885, DESPITE STRONG RELIGIOUS OBJECTIONS, INTRODUCED THE PRODUCTION OF TISSUE PAPER INTO THEIR COUNTRY.
IN EUROPE THEY MAY USE IT TO WRAP LINGERIE AND BON-BONS, BUT WE SHALL PUT IT TO A LOFTIER PURPOSE!
HE DIED IN 1889 FROM AN INFECTION BROUGHT ON BY A SUBCUTANEOUS PAPER-CUT.
"HE LIVED INSIDE A DIRTY LAND, IT WOULDN'T HELP TO WASH HIS HAND."
EVEN THOUGH THEY NEVER KNEW HIM, THEY CRY AND CLAIM THEY MISS HIM BITTERLY.
WE MOURN THE FACT THAT WE NEVER HAD THE OPPORTUNITY TO KNOW HIM.
MY UNCLE MORTON DIED LAST MONTH AND HE'S ALREADY A HISTORICAL FIGURE TO ME, BUT THESE PEOPLE CAN'T GET OVER THEIR LOSS.
GETTCHA FACIAL QUALITY TISSUE!
NO SINGLE ICONIC IMAGE OF THE MAN HAS EVER BEEN ESTABLISHED, BUT COUNTLESS PERIOD PYROGRAPHS OF HIS EVERYDAY LIFE REMAIN IN CIRCULATION.
PERZUNA WASHING HIS TEETH, PERZUNA TAKING HIS SHOES OFF AT NIGHT, PERZUNA ENTERING HIS KITCHEN...
79¢ SPECIAL
HIS MOURNERS REFUSE TO ALLOW HIM TO FALL INTO THE CLUTCHES OF MONUMENTAL SCULPTORS, THE CANTHUSIAN POSTAL SERVICE, THE NATIONAL MINT...
PERZUNA EATING A LAMB CHOP, PERZUNA AFTER A BATH...
OR THE PUBLISHERS OF HISTORY TEXT-BOOKS.
PERZUNA TAKING A NAP.

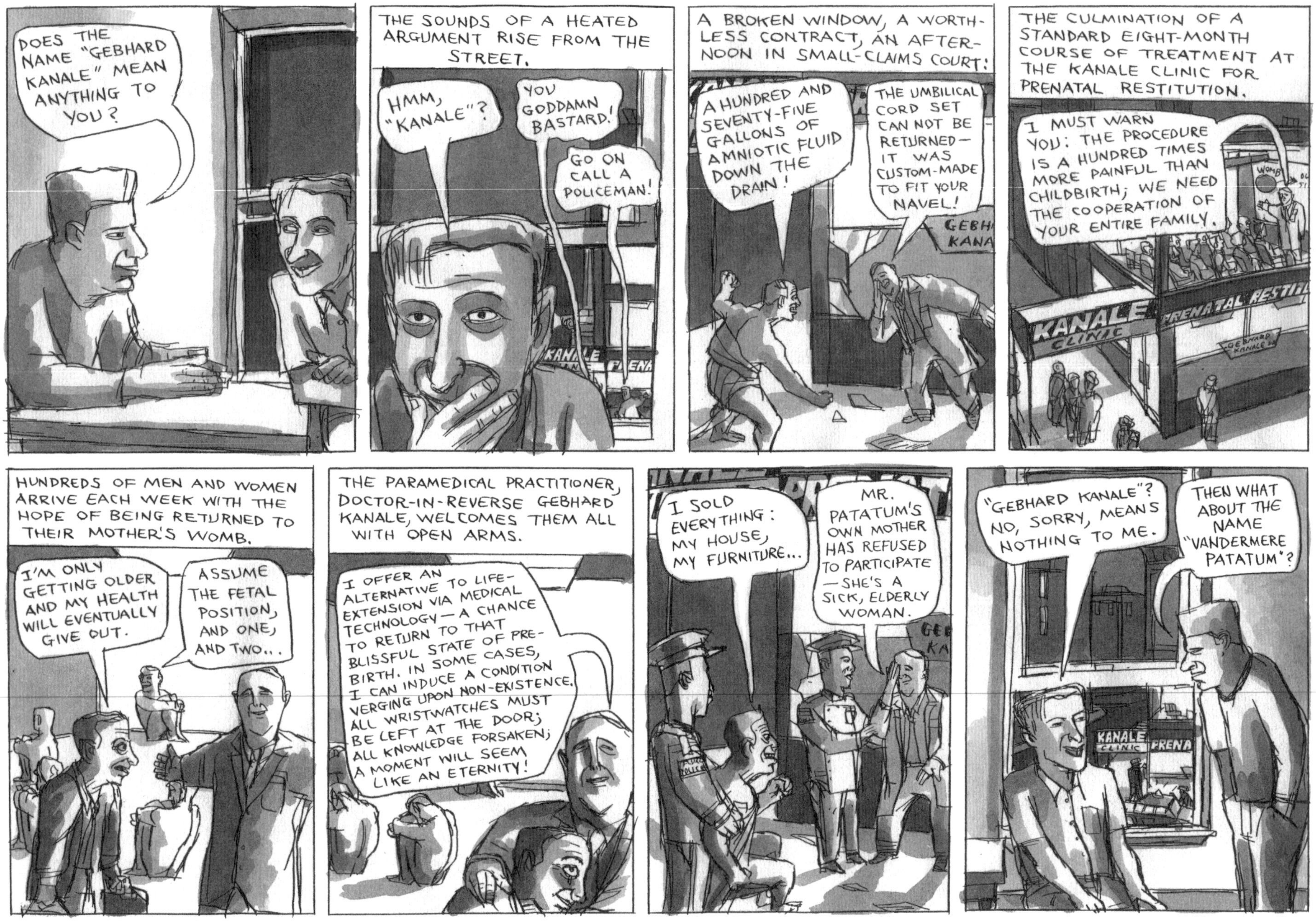
DOES THE NAME "GEBHARD KANALE" MEAN ANYTHING TO YOU?
THE SOUNDS OF A HEATED ARGUMENT RISE FROM THE STREET.
HMM, "KANALE"?
YOU GODDAMN BASTARD!
GO ON CALL A POLICEMAN!
A BROKEN WINDOW, A WORTHLESS CONTRACT, AN AFTERNOON IN SMALL-CLAIMS COURT:
A HUNDRED AND SEVENTY-FIVE GALLONS OF AMNIOTIC FLUID DOWN THE DRAIN!
THE UMBILICAL CORD SET CAN NOT BE RETURNED—IT WAS CUSTOM-MADE TO FIT YOUR NAVEL!
THE CULMINATION OF A STANDARD EIGHT-MONTH COURSE OF TREATMENT AT THE KANALE CLINIC FOR PRENATAL RESTITUTION.
I MUST WARN YOU: THE PROCEDURE IS A HUNDRED TIMES MORE PAINFUL THAN CHILDBIRTH; WE NEED THE COOPERATION OF YOUR ENTIRE FAMILY.
KANALE CLINIC
HUNDREDS OF MEN AND WOMEN ARRIVE EACH WEEK WITH THE HOPE OF BEING RETURNED TO THEIR MOTHER'S WOMB.
I'M ONLY GETTING OLDER AND MY HEALTH WILL EVENTUALLY GIVE OUT.
ASSUME THE FETAL POSITION, AND ONE, AND TWO...
THE PARAMEDICAL PRACTITIONER, DOCTOR-IN-REVERSE GEBHARD KANALE, WELCOMES THEM ALL WITH OPEN ARMS.
I OFFER AN ALTERNATIVE TO LIFE-EXTENSION VIA MEDICAL TECHNOLOGY—A CHANCE TO RETURN TO THAT BLISSFUL STATE OF PRE-BIRTH. IN SOME CASES, I CAN INDUCE A CONDITION VERGING UPON NON-EXISTENCE. WRISTWATCHES MUST ALL BE LEFT AT THE DOOR; ALL KNOWLEDGE FORSAKEN; A MOMENT WILL SEEM LIKE AN ETERNITY!
I SOLD EVERYTHING: MY HOUSE, MY FURNITURE...
MR. PATATUM'S OWN MOTHER HAS REFUSED TO PARTICIPATE—SHE'S A SICK, ELDERLY WOMAN.
"GEBHARD KANALE"? NO, SORRY, MEANS NOTHING TO ME.
THEN WHAT ABOUT THE NAME "VANDERMERE PATATUM"?
KANALE CLINIC PRENA

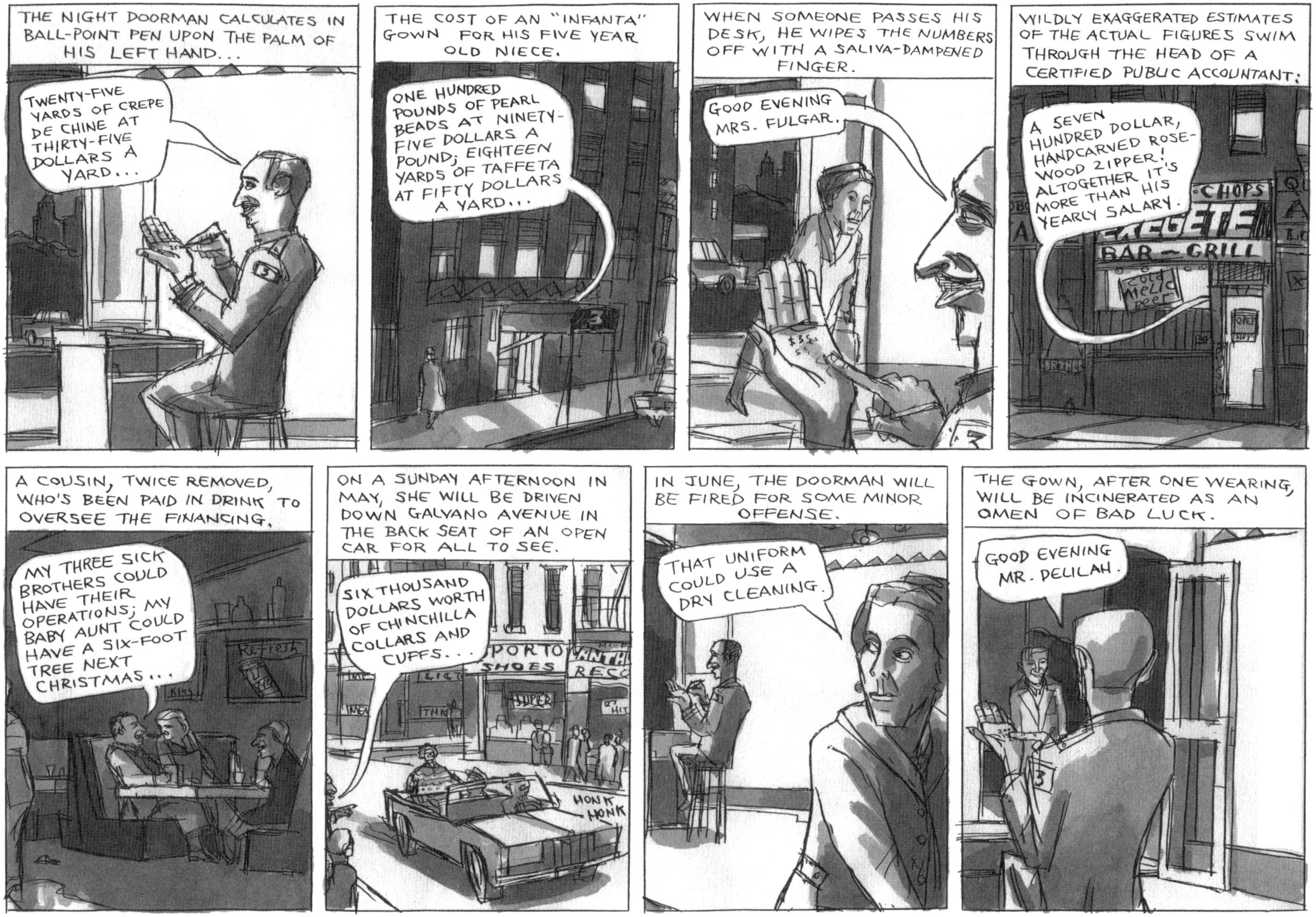
THE NIGHT DOORMAN CALCULATES IN BALL-POINT PEN UPON THE PALM OF HIS LEFT HAND...
TWENTY-FIVE YARDS OF CREPE DE CHINE AT THIRTY-FIVE DOLLARS A YARD...
THE COST OF AN "INFANTA" GOWN FOR HIS FIVE YEAR OLD NIECE.
ONE HUNDRED POUNDS OF PEARL BEADS AT NINETY-FIVE DOLLARS A POUND; EIGHTEEN YARDS OF TAFFETA AT FIFTY DOLLARS A YARD...
WHEN SOMEONE PASSES HIS DESK, HE WIPES THE NUMBERS OFF WITH A SALIVA-DAMPENED FINGER.
GOOD EVENING MRS. FULGAR.
WILDLY EXAGGERATED ESTIMATES OF THE ACTUAL FIGURES SWIM THROUGH THE HEAD OF A CERTIFIED PUBLIC ACCOUNTANT:
A SEVEN HUNDRED DOLLAR, HANDCARVED ROSE-WOOD ZIPPER! ALTOGETHER IT'S MORE THAN HIS YEARLY SALARY.
A COUSIN, TWICE REMOVED, WHO'S BEEN PAID IN DRINK TO OVERSEE THE FINANCING.
MY THREE SICK BROTHERS COULD HAVE THEIR OPERATIONS; MY BABY AUNT COULD HAVE A SIX-FOOT TREE NEXT CHRISTMAS...
ON A SUNDAY AFTERNOON IN MAY, SHE WILL BE DRIVEN DOWN GALVANO AVENUE IN THE BACK SEAT OF AN OPEN CAR FOR ALL TO SEE.
SIX THOUSAND DOLLARS WORTH OF CHINCHILLA COLLARS AND CUFFS...
HONK HONK
IN JUNE, THE DOORMAN WILL BE FIRED FOR SOME MINOR OFFENSE.
THAT UNIFORM COULD USE A DRY CLEANING.
THE GOWN, AFTER ONE WEARING, WILL BE INCINERATED AS AN OMEN OF BAD LUCK.
GOOD EVENING MR. DELILAH.

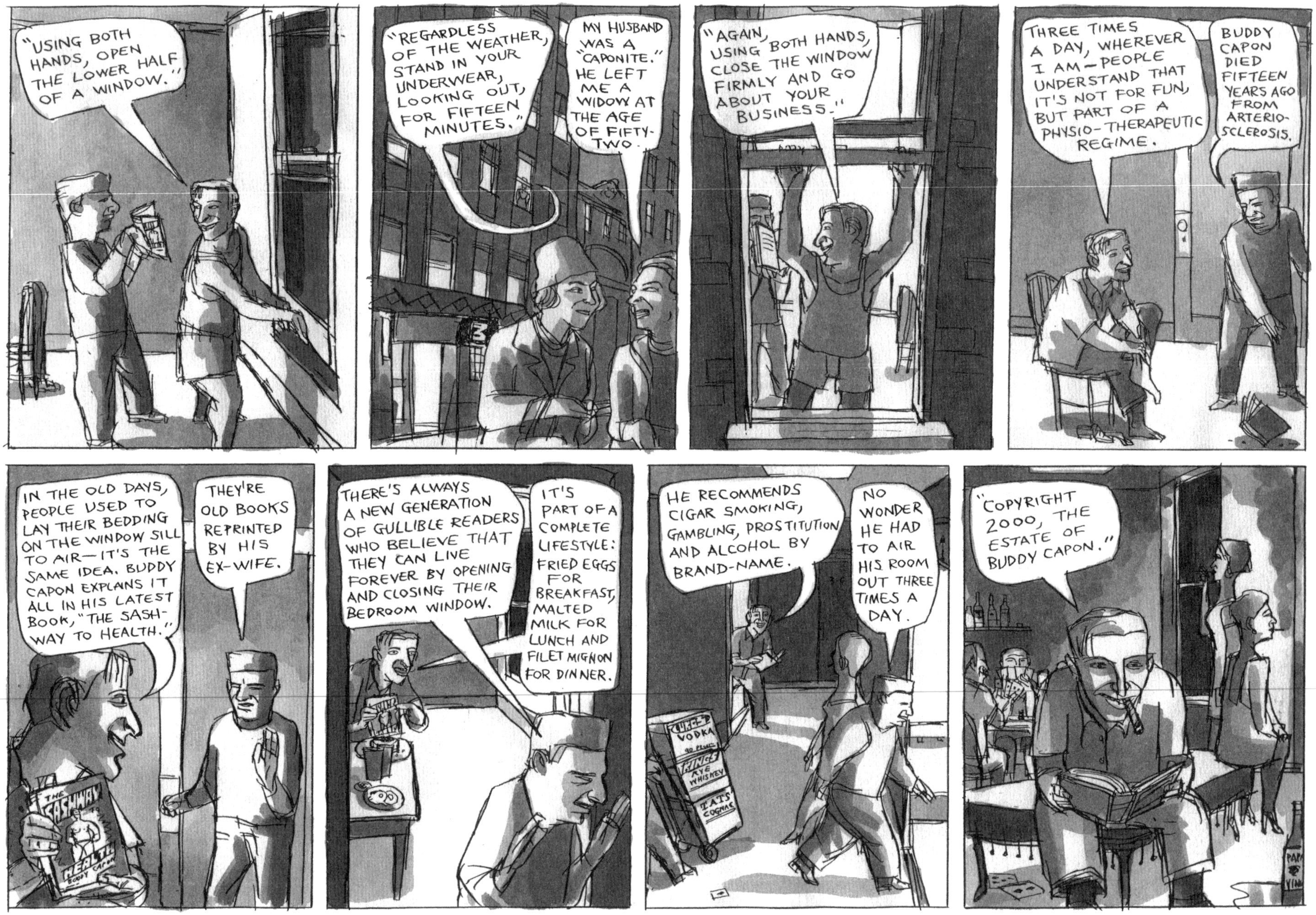
"USING BOTH HANDS, OPEN THE LOWER HALF OF A WINDOW."
"REGARDLESS OF THE WEATHER, STAND IN YOUR UNDERWEAR, LOOKING OUT, FOR FIFTEEN MINUTES."
MY HUSBAND WAS A "CAPONITE." HE LEFT ME A WIDOW AT THE AGE OF FIFTY-TWO.
"AGAIN, USING BOTH HANDS, CLOSE THE WINDOW FIRMLY AND GO ABOUT YOUR BUSINESS."
THREE TIMES A DAY, WHEREVER I AM—PEOPLE UNDERSTAND THAT IT'S NOT FOR FUN, BUT PART OF A PHYSIO-THERAPEUTIC REGIME.
BUDDY CAPON DIED FIFTEEN YEARS AGO FROM ARTERIO-SCLEROSIS.
IN THE OLD DAYS, PEOPLE USED TO LAY THEIR BEDDING ON THE WINDOW SILL TO AIR—IT'S THE SAME IDEA. BUDDY CAPON EXPLAINS IT ALL IN HIS LATEST BOOK, "THE SASH-WAY TO HEALTH."
THE SASHWAY TO HEALTH
THEY'RE OLD BOOKS REPRINTED BY HIS EX-WIFE.
THERE'S ALWAYS A NEW GENERATION OF GULLIBLE READERS WHO BELIEVE THAT THEY CAN LIVE FOREVER BY OPENING AND CLOSING THEIR BEDROOM WINDOW.
IT'S PART OF A COMPLETE LIFESTYLE: FRIED EGGS FOR BREAKFAST, MALTED MILK FOR LUNCH AND FILET MIGNON FOR DINNER.
HE RECOMMENDS CIGAR SMOKING, GAMBLING, PROSTITUTION AND ALCOHOL BY BRAND-NAME.
NO WONDER HE HAD TO AIR HIS ROOM OUT THREE TIMES A DAY.
VODKA
RYE WHISKEY
COGNAC
"COPYRIGHT 2000, THE ESTATE OF BUDDY CAPON."

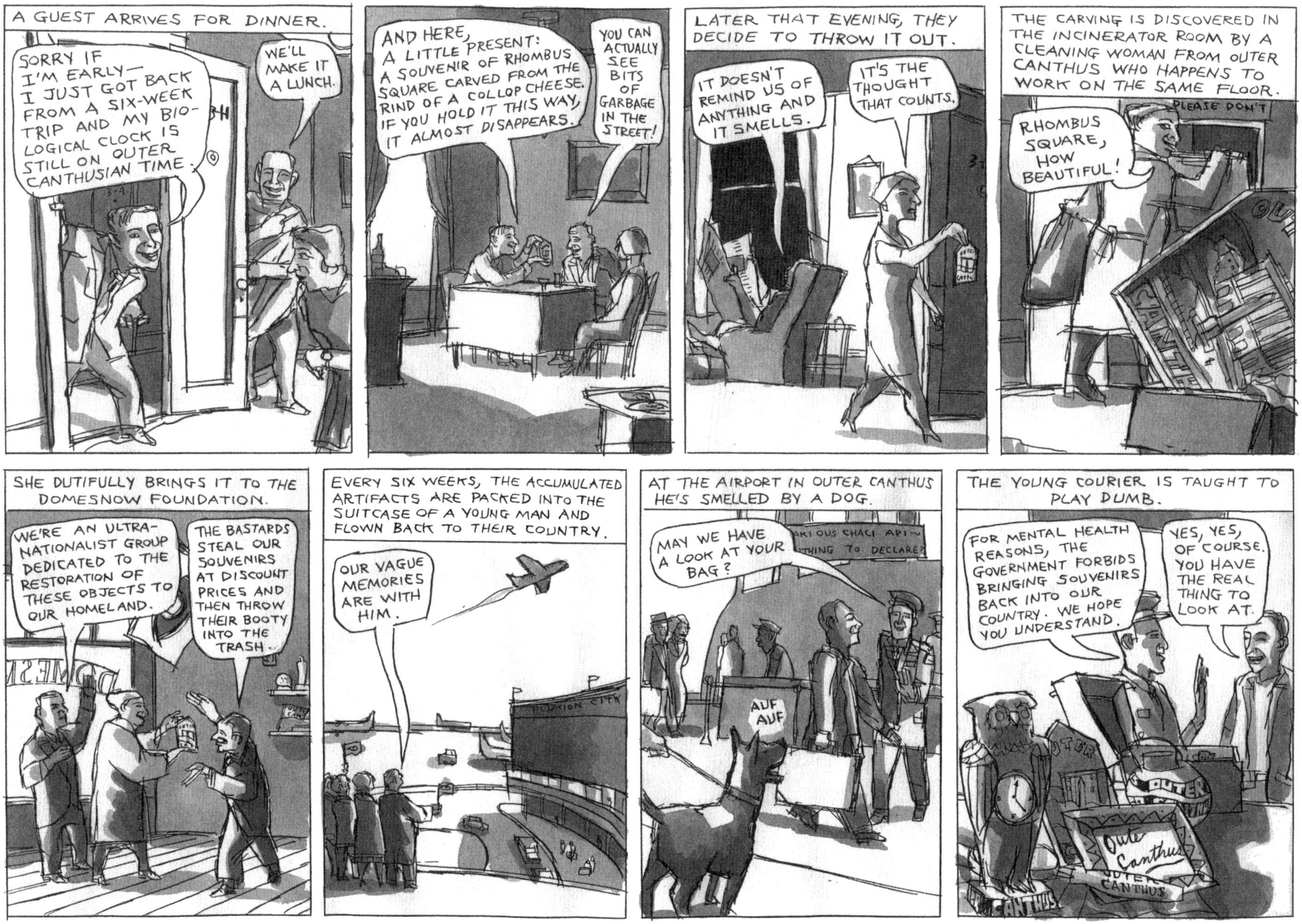
A GUEST ARRIVES FOR DINNER.
SORRY IF I'M EARLY— I JUST GOT BACK FROM A SIX-WEEK TRIP AND MY BIOLOGICAL CLOCK IS STILL ON OUTER CANTHUSIAN TIME.
WE'LL MAKE IT A LUNCH.
AND HERE, A LITTLE PRESENT: A SOUVENIR OF RHOMBUS SQUARE CARVED FROM THE RIND OF A COLLOP CHEESE. IF YOU HOLD IT THIS WAY, IT ALMOST DISAPPEARS.
YOU CAN ACTUALLY SEE BITS OF GARBAGE IN THE STREET!
LATER THAT EVENING, THEY DECIDE TO THROW IT OUT.
IT DOESN'T REMIND US OF ANYTHING AND IT SMELLS.
IT'S THE THOUGHT THAT COUNTS.
THE CARVING IS DISCOVERED IN THE INCINERATOR ROOM BY A CLEANING WOMAN FROM OUTER CANTHUS WHO HAPPENS TO WORK ON THE SAME FLOOR.
PLEASE DON'T
RHOMBUS SQUARE, HOW BEAUTIFUL!
SHE DUTIFULLY BRINGS IT TO THE DOMESNOW FOUNDATION.
WE'RE AN ULTRA-NATIONALIST GROUP DEDICATED TO THE RESTORATION OF THESE OBJECTS TO OUR HOMELAND.
THE BASTARDS STEAL OUR SOUVENIRS AT DISCOUNT PRICES AND THEN THROW THEIR BOOTY INTO THE TRASH.
EVERY SIX WEEKS, THE ACCUMULATED ARTIFACTS ARE PACKED INTO THE SUITCASE OF A YOUNG MAN AND FLOWN BACK TO THEIR COUNTRY.
OUR VAGUE MEMORIES ARE WITH HIM.
AT THE AIRPORT IN OUTER CANTHUS HE'S SMELLED BY A DOG.
MAY WE HAVE A LOOK AT YOUR BAG?
AUF AUF
THE YOUNG COURIER IS TAUGHT TO PLAY DUMB.
FOR MENTAL HEALTH REASONS, THE GOVERNMENT FORBIDS BRINGING SOUVENIRS BACK INTO OUR COUNTRY. WE HOPE YOU UNDERSTAND.
YES, YES, OF COURSE. YOU HAVE THE REAL THING TO LOOK AT.
Oute Canthus
OUTER CANTHUS

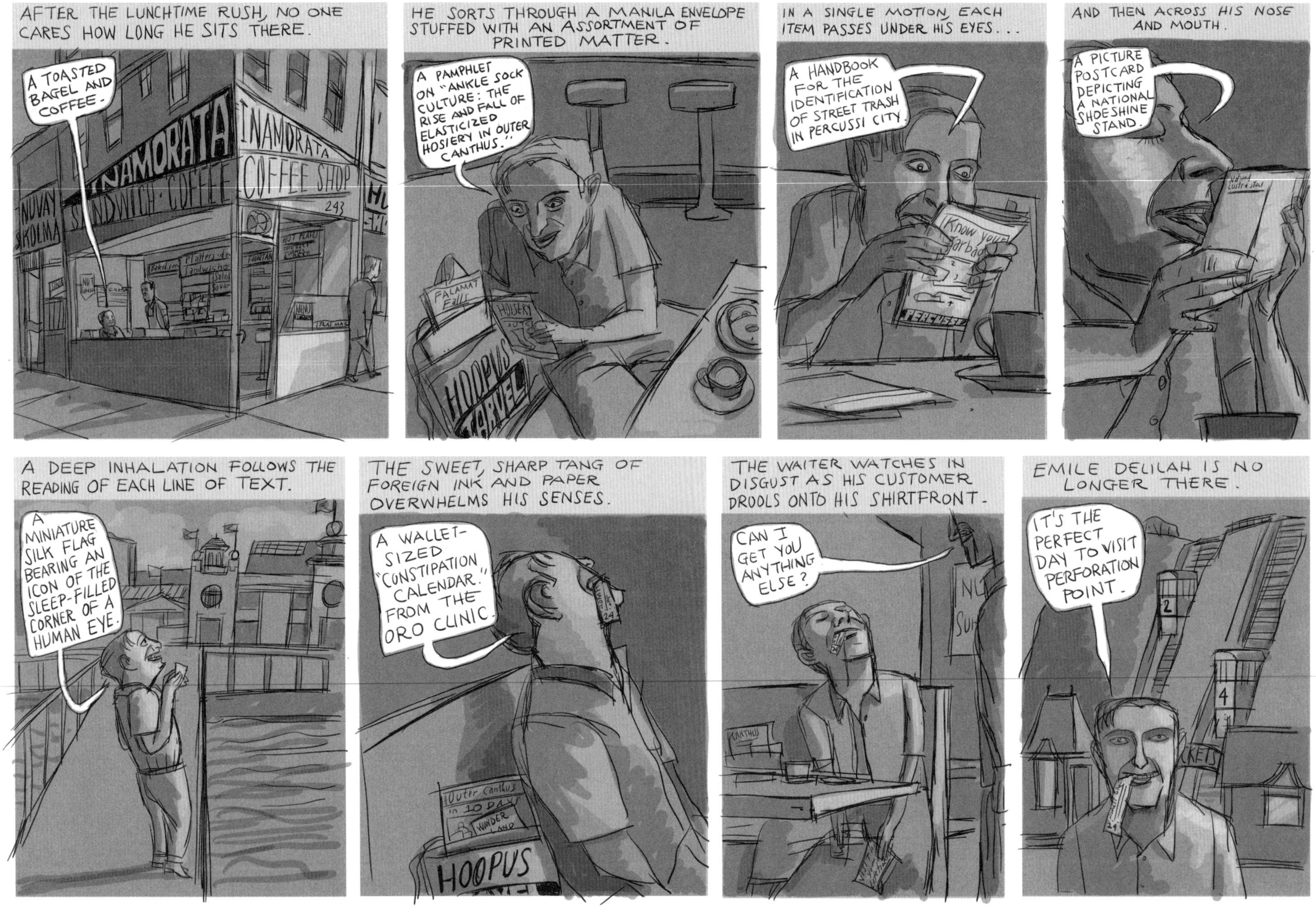
AFTER THE LUNCHTIME RUSH, NO ONE CARES HOW LONG HE SITS THERE.
A TOASTED BAGEL AND COFFEE.
INAMORATA
SANDWICH · COFFEE
INAMORATA COFFEE SHOP
243
HE SORTS THROUGH A MANILA ENVELOPE STUFFED WITH AN ASSORTMENT OF PRINTED MATTER.
A PAMPHLET ON "ANKLE SOCK CULTURE: THE RISE AND FALL OF ELASTICIZED HOSIERY IN OUTER CANTHUS."
HOSIERY
HOOPUS
IN A SINGLE MOTION, EACH ITEM PASSES UNDER HIS EYES . . .
A HANDBOOK FOR THE IDENTIFICATION OF STREET TRASH IN PERCUSSI CITY.
AND THEN ACROSS HIS NOSE AND MOUTH.
A PICTURE POSTCARD DEPICTING A NATIONAL SHOESHINE STAND.
A DEEP INHALATION FOLLOWS THE READING OF EACH LINE OF TEXT.
A MINIATURE SILK FLAG BEARING AN ICON OF THE SLEEP-FILLED CORNER OF A HUMAN EYE.
THE SWEET, SHARP TANG OF FOREIGN INK AND PAPER OVERWHELMS HIS SENSES.
A WALLET-SIZED "CONSTIPATION CALENDAR" FROM THE ORO CLINIC.
Outer Canthus in 10 DAYS
WONDER LAND
HOOPUS
THE WAITER WATCHES IN DISGUST AS HIS CUSTOMER DROOLS ONTO HIS SHIRTFRONT.
CAN I GET YOU ANYTHING ELSE?
EMILE DELILAH IS NO LONGER THERE.
IT'S THE PERFECT DAY TO VISIT PERFORATION POINT.
2
4

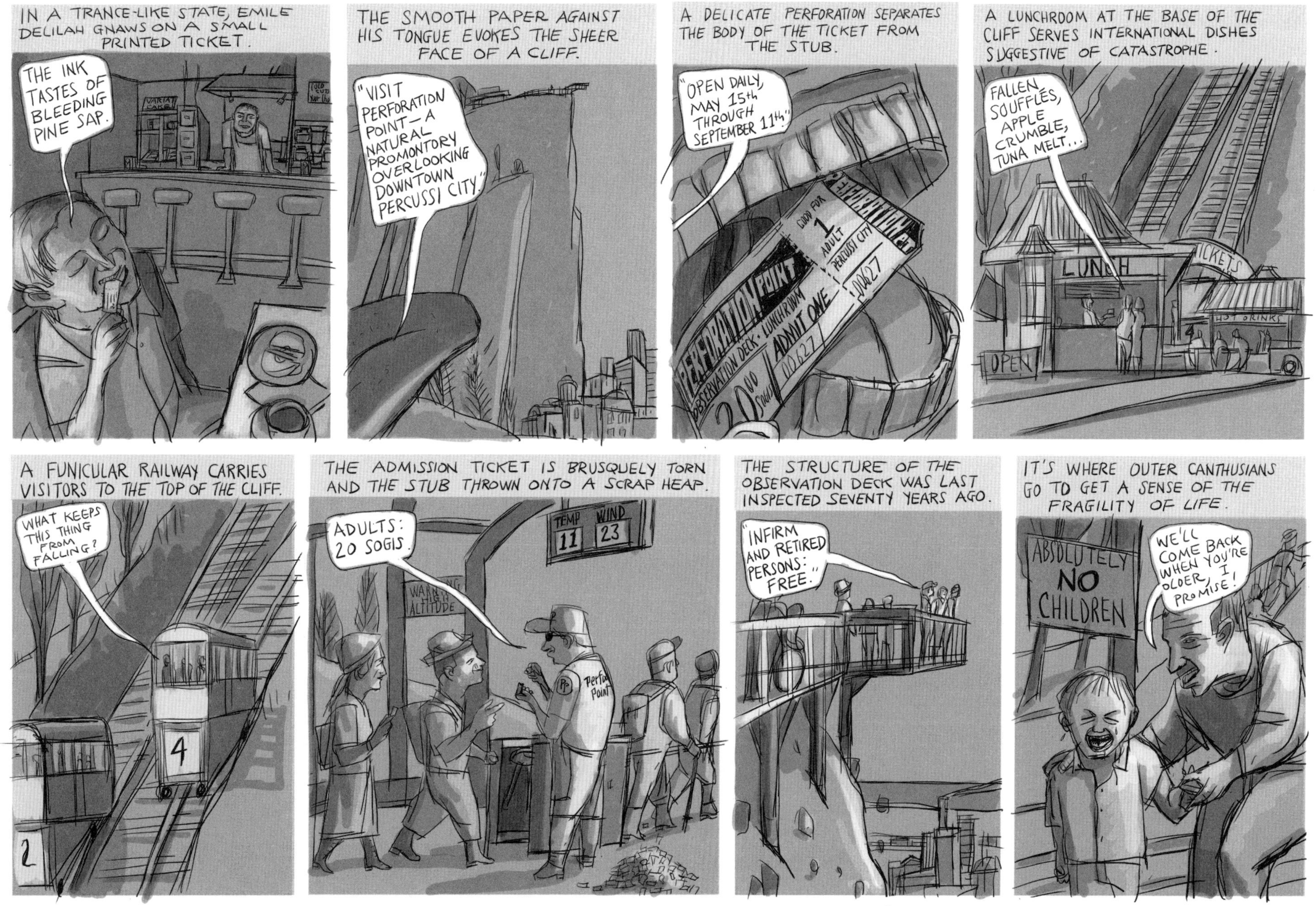
IN A TRANCE-LIKE STATE, EMILE DELILAH GNAWS ON A SMALL PRINTED TICKET.
THE INK TASTES OF BLEEDING PINE SAP.
THE SMOOTH PAPER AGAINST HIS TONGUE EVOKES THE SHEER FACE OF A CLIFF.
"VISIT PERFORATION POINT—A NATURAL PROMONTORY OVERLOOKING DOWNTOWN PERCUSSI CITY."
A DELICATE PERFORATION SEPARATES THE BODY OF THE TICKET FROM THE STUB.
"OPEN DAILY, MAY 15th THROUGH SEPTEMBER 11th."
PERFORATION POINT
OBSERVATION DECK · LUNCHROOM
ADMIT ONE
00627
GOOD FOR 1 ADULT
PERCUSSI CITY
00627
A LUNCHROOM AT THE BASE OF THE CLIFF SERVES INTERNATIONAL DISHES SUGGESTIVE OF CATASTROPHE.
FALLEN SOUFFLÉS, APPLE CRUMBLE, TUNA MELT...
LUNCH
TICKETS
HOT DRINKS
OPEN
A FUNICULAR RAILWAY CARRIES VISITORS TO THE TOP OF THE CLIFF.
WHAT KEEPS THIS THING FROM FALLING?
4
2
THE ADMISSION TICKET IS BRUSQUELY TORN AND THE STUB THROWN ONTO A SCRAP HEAP.
ADULTS: 20 SOGIS.
TEMP 11
WIND 23
THE STRUCTURE OF THE OBSERVATION DECK WAS LAST INSPECTED SEVENTY YEARS AGO.
"INFIRM AND RETIRED PERSONS: FREE."
IT'S WHERE OUTER CANTHUSIANS GO TO GET A SENSE OF THE FRAGILITY OF LIFE.
ABSOLUTELY NO CHILDREN
WE'LL COME BACK WHEN YOU'RE OLDER, I PROMISE!

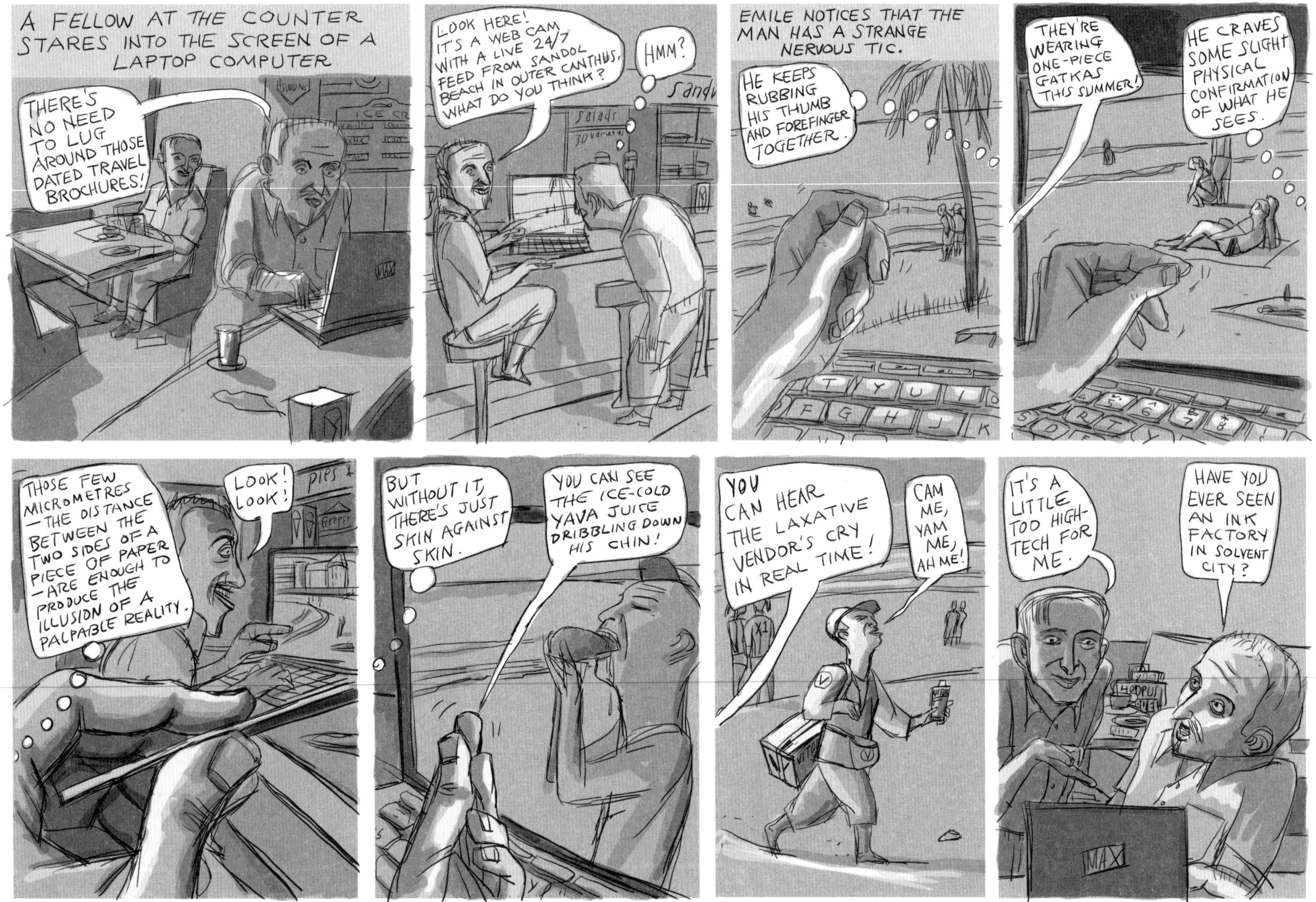
A FELLOW AT THE COUNTER STARES INTO THE SCREEN OF A LAPTOP COMPUTER
THERE'S NO NEED TO LUG AROUND THOSE DATED TRAVEL BROCHURES!
LOOK HERE! IT'S A WEB CAM WITH A LIVE 24/7 FEED FROM SANDOL BEACH IN OUTER CANTHUS. WHAT DO YOU THINK?
HMM?
EMILE NOTICES THAT THE MAN HAS A STRANGE NERVOUS TIC.
HE KEEPS RUBBING HIS THUMB AND FOREFINGER TOGETHER.
THEY'RE WEARING ONE-PIECE GATKAS THIS SUMMER!
HE CRAVES SOME SLIGHT PHYSICAL CONFIRMATION OF WHAT HE SEES.
THOSE FEW MICROMETRES —THE DISTANCE BETWEEN THE TWO SIDES OF A PIECE OF PAPER —ARE ENOUGH TO PRODUCE THE ILLUSION OF A PALPABLE REALITY.
LOOK! LOOK!
BUT WITHOUT IT, THERE'S JUST SKIN AGAINST SKIN.
YOU CAN SEE THE ICE-COLD YAVA JUICE DRIBBLING DOWN HIS CHIN!
YOU CAN HEAR THE LAXATIVE VENDOR'S CRY IN REAL TIME!
CAM ME, YAM ME, AH ME!
IT'S A LITTLE TOO HIGH-TECH FOR ME.
HAVE YOU EVER SEEN AN INK FACTORY IN SOLVENT CITY?

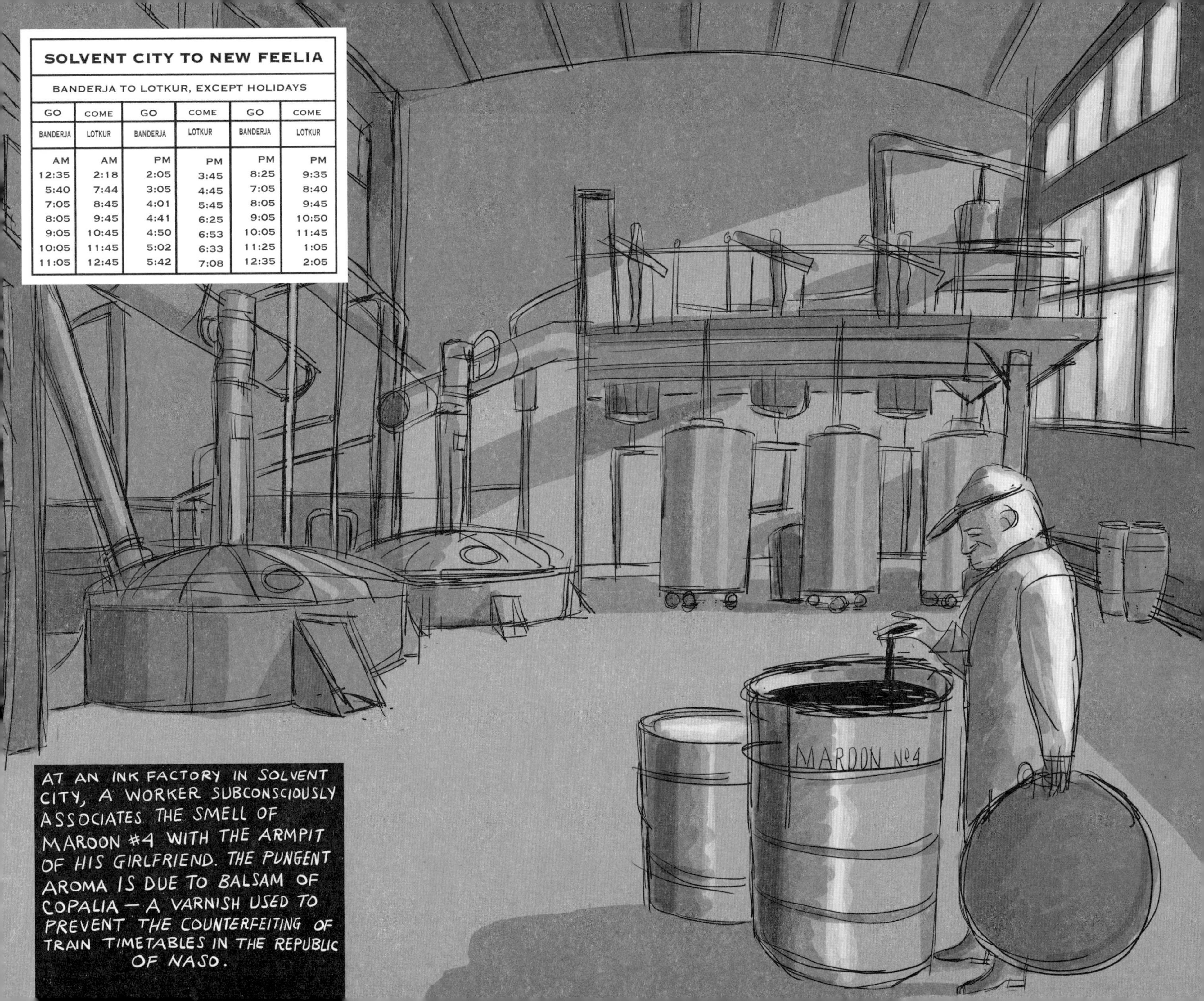

SOLVENT CITY TO NEW FEELIA					
BANDERJA TO LOTKUR, EXCEPT HOLIDAYS					
GO	COME	GO	COME	GO	COME
BANDERJA	LOTKUR	BANDERJA	LOTKUR	BANDERJA	LOTKUR
AM	AM	PM	PM	PM	PM
12:35	2:18	2:05	3:45	8:25	9:35
5:40	7:44	3:05	4:45	7:05	8:40
7:05	8:45	4:01	5:45	8:05	9:45
8:05	9:45	4:41	6:25	9:05	10:50
9:05	10:45	4:50	6:53	10:05	11:45
10:05	11:45	5:02	6:33	11:25	1:05
11:05	12:45	5:42	7:08	12:35	2:05

MARDON No4
AT AN INK FACTORY IN SOLVENT CITY, A WORKER SUBCONSCIOUSLY ASSOCIATES THE SMELL OF MAROON #4 WITH THE ARMPIT OF HIS GIRLFRIEND. THE PUNGENT AROMA IS DUE TO BALSAM OF COPALIA — A VARNISH USED TO PREVENT THE COUNTERFEITING OF TRAIN TIMETABLES IN THE REPUBLIC OF NASO.

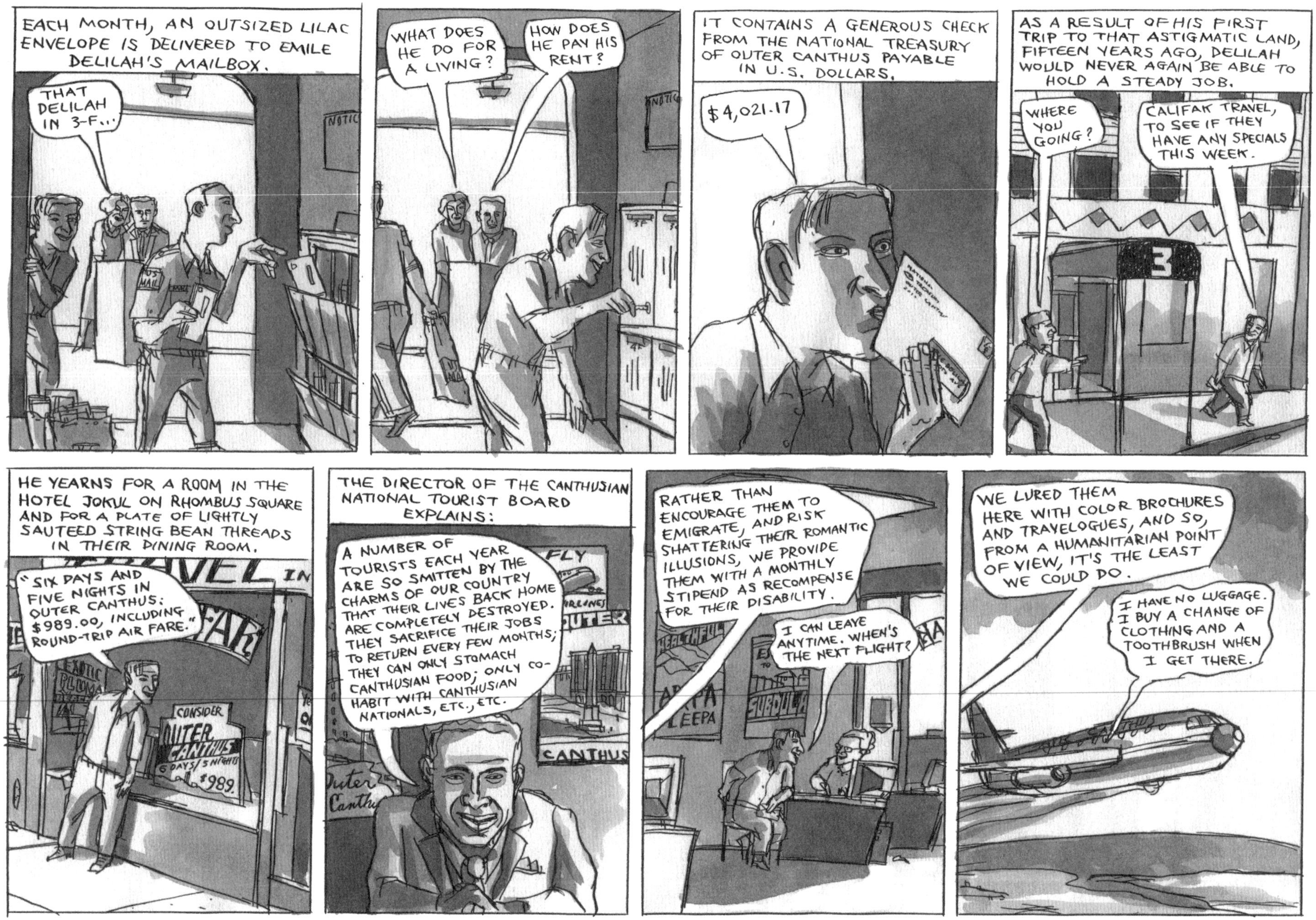
EACH MONTH, AN OUTSIZED LILAC ENVELOPE IS DELIVERED TO EMILE DELILAH'S MAILBOX.
THAT DELILAH IN 3-F...
WHAT DOES HE DO FOR A LIVING?
HOW DOES HE PAY HIS RENT?
IT CONTAINS A GENEROUS CHECK FROM THE NATIONAL TREASURY OF OUTER CANTHUS PAYABLE IN U.S. DOLLARS.
$4,021.17
AS A RESULT OF HIS FIRST TRIP TO THAT ASTIGMATIC LAND, FIFTEEN YEARS AGO, DELILAH WOULD NEVER AGAIN BE ABLE TO HOLD A STEADY JOB.
WHERE YOU GOING?
CALIFAK TRAVEL, TO SEE IF THEY HAVE ANY SPECIALS THIS WEEK.
HE YEARNS FOR A ROOM IN THE HOTEL JOKUL ON RHOMBUS SQUARE AND FOR A PLATE OF LIGHTLY SAUTEED STRING BEAN THREADS IN THEIR DINING ROOM.
"SIX DAYS AND FIVE NIGHTS IN OUTER CANTHUS: $989.00, INCLUDING ROUND-TRIP AIR FARE."
CONSIDER OUTER CANTHUS 6 DAYS/5 NIGHTS $989.
THE DIRECTOR OF THE CANTHUSIAN NATIONAL TOURIST BOARD EXPLAINS:
A NUMBER OF TOURISTS EACH YEAR ARE SO SMITTEN BY THE CHARMS OF OUR COUNTRY THAT THEIR LIVES BACK HOME ARE COMPLETELY DESTROYED. THEY SACRIFICE THEIR JOBS TO RETURN EVERY FEW MONTHS; THEY CAN ONLY STOMACH CANTHUSIAN FOOD; ONLY CO-HABIT WITH CANTHUSIAN NATIONALS, ETC., ETC.
CANTHUS
RATHER THAN ENCOURAGE THEM TO EMIGRATE, AND RISK SHATTERING THEIR ROMANTIC ILLUSIONS, WE PROVIDE THEM WITH A MONTHLY STIPEND AS RECOMPENSE FOR THEIR DISABILITY.
I CAN LEAVE ANYTIME. WHEN'S THE NEXT FLIGHT?
WE LURED THEM HERE WITH COLOR BROCHURES AND TRAVELOGUES, AND SO, FROM A HUMANITARIAN POINT OF VIEW, IT'S THE LEAST WE COULD DO.
I HAVE NO LUGGAGE. I BUY A CHANGE OF CLOTHING AND A TOOTHBRUSH WHEN I GET THERE.

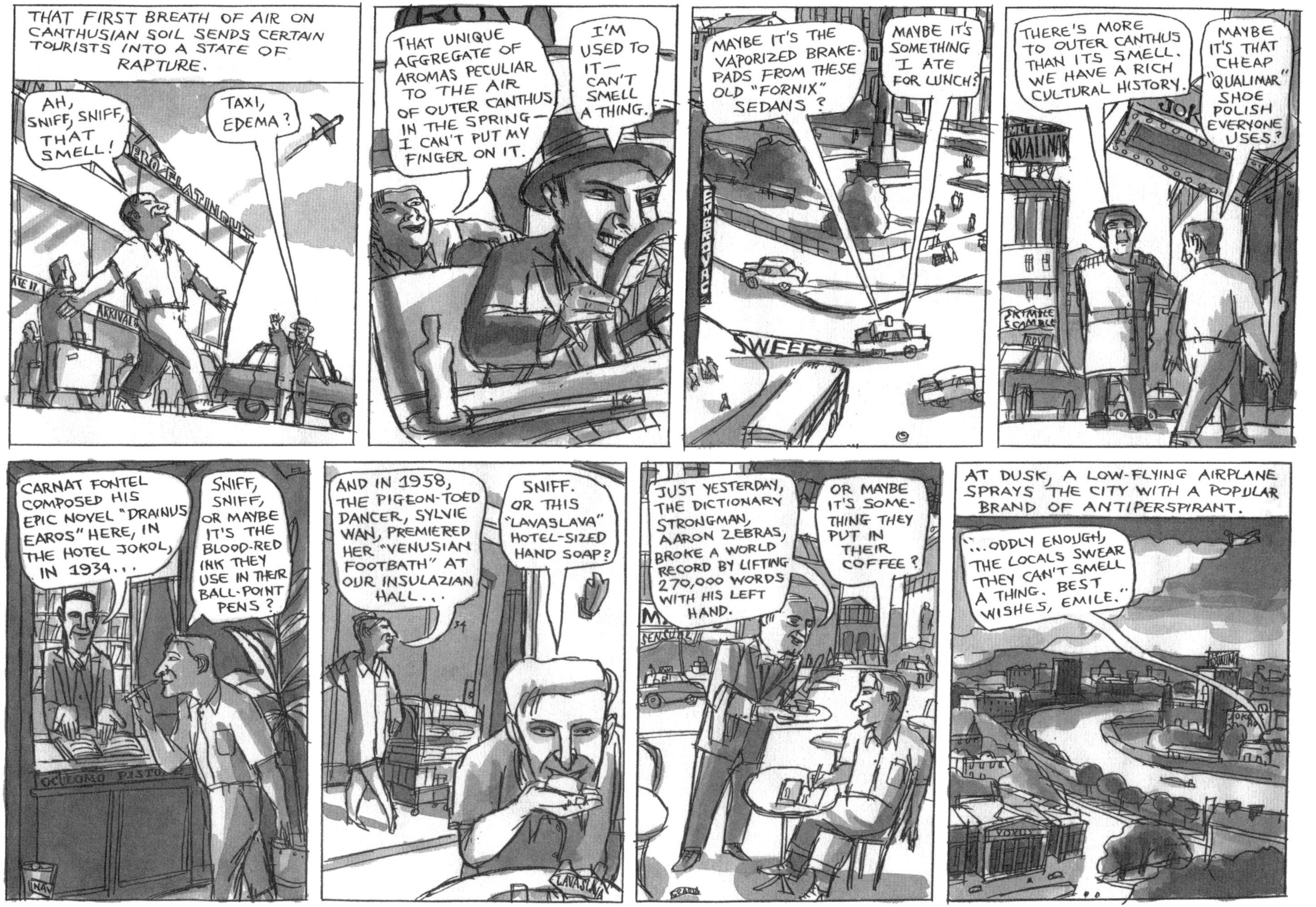

THAT FIRST BREATH OF AIR ON CANTHUSIAN SOIL SENDS CERTAIN TOURISTS INTO A STATE OF RAPTURE.
AH, SNIFF, SNIFF, THAT SMELL!
TAXI, EDEMA?
THAT UNIQUE AGGREGATE OF AROMAS PECULIAR TO THE AIR OF OUTER CANTHUS IN THE SPRING— I CAN'T PUT MY FINGER ON IT.
I'M USED TO IT— CAN'T SMELL A THING.
MAYBE IT'S THE VAPORIZED BRAKE-PADS FROM THESE OLD "FORNIX" SEDANS?
MAYBE IT'S SOMETHING I ATE FOR LUNCH?
SWEEEE
THERE'S MORE TO OUTER CANTHUS THAN ITS SMELL. WE HAVE A RICH CULTURAL HISTORY.
MAYBE IT'S THAT CHEAP "QUALIMAR" SHOE POLISH EVERYONE USES?
QUALIMAR
CARNAT FONTEL COMPOSED HIS EPIC NOVEL "DRAINUS EAROS" HERE, IN THE HOTEL JOKOL, IN 1934...
SNIFF, SNIFF, OR MAYBE IT'S THE BLOOD-RED INK THEY USE IN THEIR BALL-POINT PENS?
AND IN 1958, THE PIGEON-TOED DANCER, SYLVIE WAN, PREMIERED HER "VENUSIAN FOOTBATH" AT OUR INSULAZIAN HALL...
SNIFF. OR THIS "LAVASLAVA" HOTEL-SIZED HAND SOAP?
LAVASLAVA
JUST YESTERDAY, THE DICTIONARY STRONGMAN, AARON ZEBRAS, BROKE A WORLD RECORD BY LIFTING 270,000 WORDS WITH HIS LEFT HAND.
OR MAYBE IT'S SOMETHING THEY PUT IN THEIR COFFEE?
AT DUSK, A LOW-FLYING AIRPLANE SPRAYS THE CITY WITH A POPULAR BRAND OF ANTIPERSPIRANT.
"...ODDLY ENOUGH, THE LOCALS SWEAR THEY CAN'T SMELL A THING. BEST WISHES, EMILE."

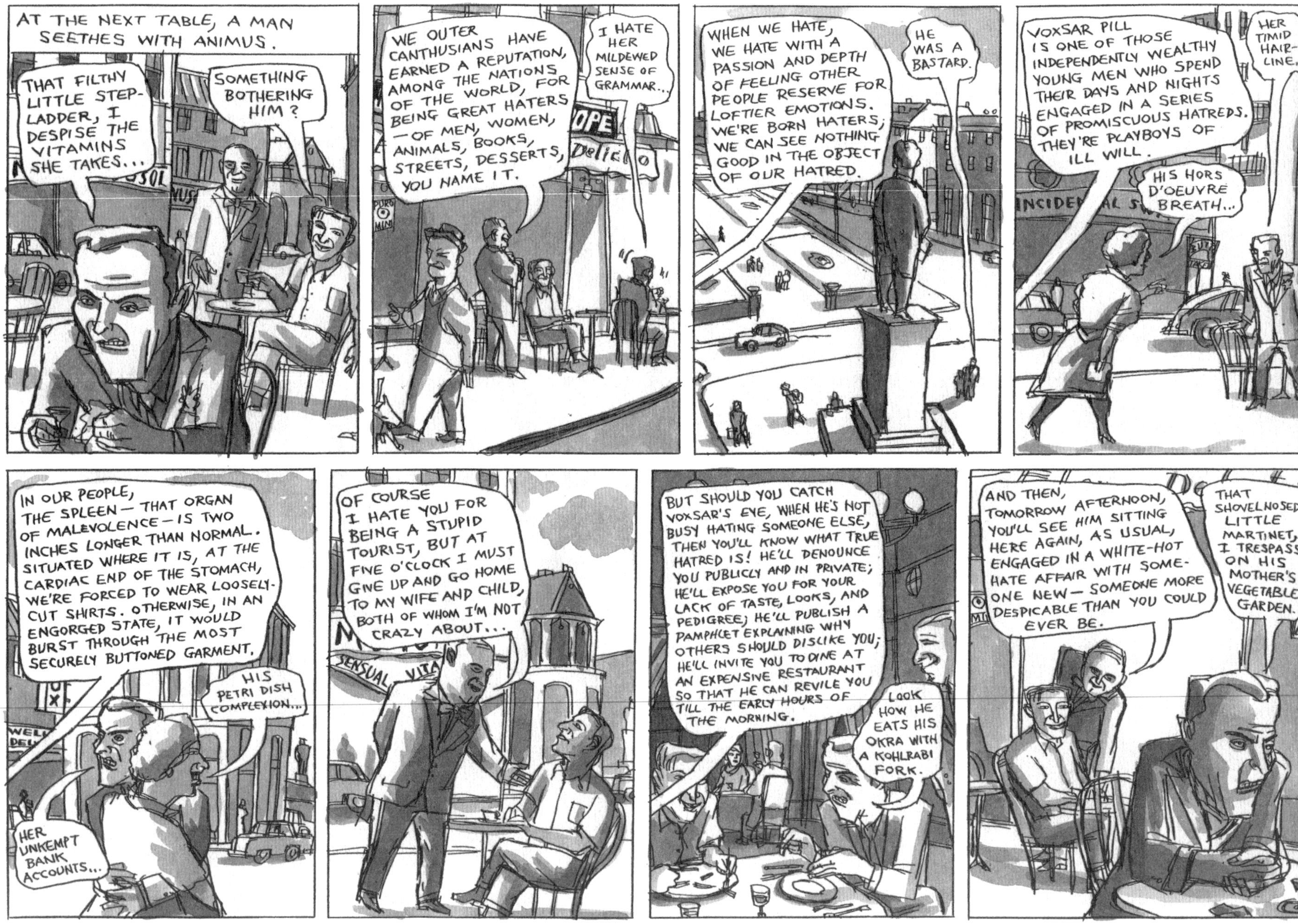
AT THE NEXT TABLE, A MAN SEETHES WITH ANIMUS.
THAT FILTHY LITTLE STEP-LADDER, I DESPISE THE VITAMINS SHE TAKES...
SOMETHING BOTHERING HIM?
WE OUTER CANTHUSIANS HAVE EARNED A REPUTATION, AMONG THE NATIONS OF THE WORLD, FOR BEING GREAT HATERS —OF MEN, WOMEN, ANIMALS, BOOKS, STREETS, DESSERTS, YOU NAME IT.
I HATE HER MILDEWED SENSE OF GRAMMAR...
WHEN WE HATE, WE HATE WITH A PASSION AND DEPTH OF FEELING OTHER PEOPLE RESERVE FOR LOFTIER EMOTIONS. WE'RE BORN HATERS; WE CAN SEE NOTHING GOOD IN THE OBJECT OF OUR HATRED.
HE WAS A BASTARD.
VOXSAR PILL IS ONE OF THOSE INDEPENDENTLY WEALTHY YOUNG MEN WHO SPEND THEIR DAYS AND NIGHTS ENGAGED IN A SERIES OF PROMISCUOUS HATREDS. THEY'RE PLAYBOYS OF ILL WILL.
HER TIMID HAIR-LINE...
HIS HORS D'OEUVRE BREATH...
IN OUR PEOPLE, THE SPLEEN — THAT ORGAN OF MALEVOLENCE — IS TWO INCHES LONGER THAN NORMAL. SITUATED WHERE IT IS, AT THE CARDIAC END OF THE STOMACH, WE'RE FORCED TO WEAR LOOSELY-CUT SHIRTS. OTHERWISE, IN AN ENGORGED STATE, IT WOULD BURST THROUGH THE MOST SECURELY BUTTONED GARMENT.
HIS PETRI DISH COMPLEXION...
HER UNKEMPT BANK ACCOUNTS...
OF COURSE I HATE YOU FOR BEING A STUPID TOURIST, BUT AT FIVE O'CLOCK I MUST GIVE UP AND GO HOME TO MY WIFE AND CHILD, BOTH OF WHOM I'M NOT CRAZY ABOUT...
BUT SHOULD YOU CATCH VOXSAR'S EYE, WHEN HE'S NOT BUSY HATING SOMEONE ELSE, THEN YOU'LL KNOW WHAT TRUE HATRED IS! HE'LL DENOUNCE YOU PUBLICLY AND IN PRIVATE; HE'LL EXPOSE YOU FOR YOUR LACK OF TASTE, LOOKS, AND PEDIGREE; HE'LL PUBLISH A PAMPHLET EXPLAINING WHY OTHERS SHOULD DISLIKE YOU; HE'LL INVITE YOU TO DINE AT AN EXPENSIVE RESTAURANT SO THAT HE CAN REVILE YOU TILL THE EARLY HOURS OF THE MORNING.
LOOK HOW HE EATS HIS OKRA WITH A KOHLRABI FORK.
AND THEN, TOMORROW AFTERNOON, YOU'LL SEE HIM SITTING HERE AGAIN, AS USUAL, ENGAGED IN A WHITE-HOT HATE AFFAIR WITH SOME-ONE NEW — SOMEONE MORE DESPICABLE THAN YOU COULD EVER BE.
THAT SHOVELNOSED LITTLE MARTINET, I TRESPASS ON HIS MOTHER'S VEGETABLE GARDEN.

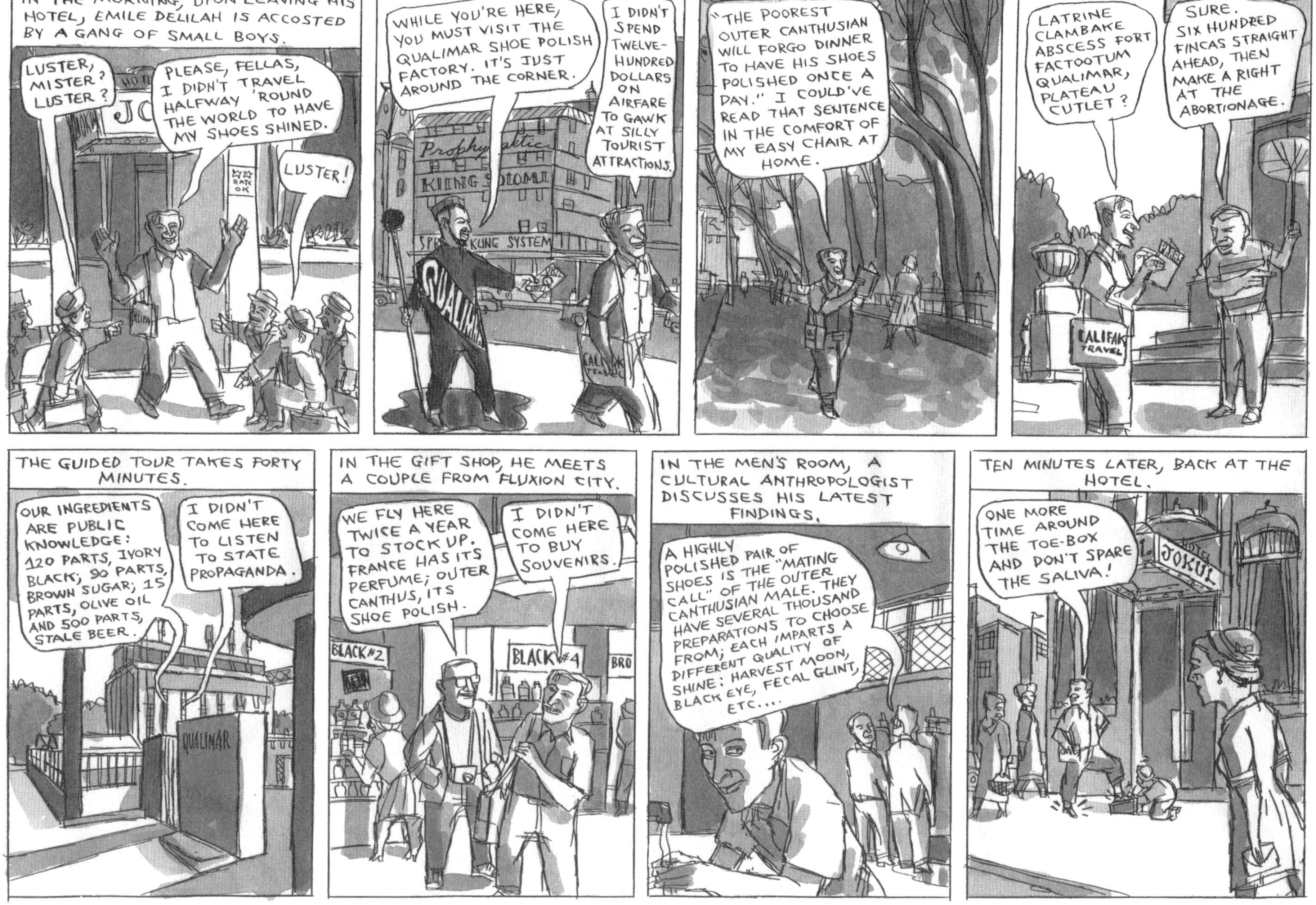
IN THE MORNING, UPON LEAVING HIS HOTEL, EMILE DELILAH IS ACCOSTED BY A GANG OF SMALL BOYS.
LUSTER, MISTER? LUSTER?
PLEASE, FELLAS, I DIDN'T TRAVEL HALFWAY 'ROUND THE WORLD TO HAVE MY SHOES SHINED.
LUSTER!
RATE OK
WHILE YOU'RE HERE, YOU MUST VISIT THE QUALIMAR SHOE POLISH FACTORY. IT'S JUST AROUND THE CORNER.
I DIDN'T SPEND TWELVE-HUNDRED DOLLARS ON AIRFARE TO GAWK AT SILLY TOURIST ATTRACTIONS.
Prophylactic
QUALIMAR
"THE POOREST OUTER CANTHUSIAN WILL FORGO DINNER TO HAVE HIS SHOES POLISHED ONCE A DAY." I COULD'VE READ THAT SENTENCE IN THE COMFORT OF MY EASY CHAIR AT HOME.
LATRINE CLAMBAKE ABSCESS FORT FACTOOTUM QUALIMAR, PLATEAU CUTLET?
SURE. SIX HUNDRED FINCAS STRAIGHT AHEAD, THEN MAKE A RIGHT AT THE ABORTIONAGE.
CALIFAK TRAVEL
THE GUIDED TOUR TAKES FORTY MINUTES.
OUR INGREDIENTS ARE PUBLIC KNOWLEDGE: 120 PARTS, IVORY BLACK; 90 PARTS, BROWN SUGAR; 15 PARTS, OLIVE OIL AND 500 PARTS, STALE BEER.
I DIDN'T COME HERE TO LISTEN TO STATE PROPAGANDA.
QUALIMAR
IN THE GIFT SHOP, HE MEETS A COUPLE FROM FLUXION CITY.
WE FLY HERE TWICE A YEAR TO STOCK UP. FRANCE HAS ITS PERFUME; OUTER CANTHUS, ITS SHOE POLISH.
I DIDN'T COME HERE TO BUY SOUVENIRS.
BLACK #2
BLACK #4
IN THE MEN'S ROOM, A CULTURAL ANTHROPOLOGIST DISCUSSES HIS LATEST FINDINGS.
A HIGHLY POLISHED PAIR OF SHOES IS THE "MATING CALL" OF THE OUTER CANTHUSIAN MALE. THEY HAVE SEVERAL THOUSAND PREPARATIONS TO CHOOSE FROM; EACH IMPARTS A DIFFERENT QUALITY OF SHINE: HARVEST MOON, BLACK EYE, FECAL GLINT, ETC....
TEN MINUTES LATER, BACK AT THE HOTEL.
ONE MORE TIME AROUND THE TOE-BOX AND DON'T SPARE THE SALIVA!
JOKUL

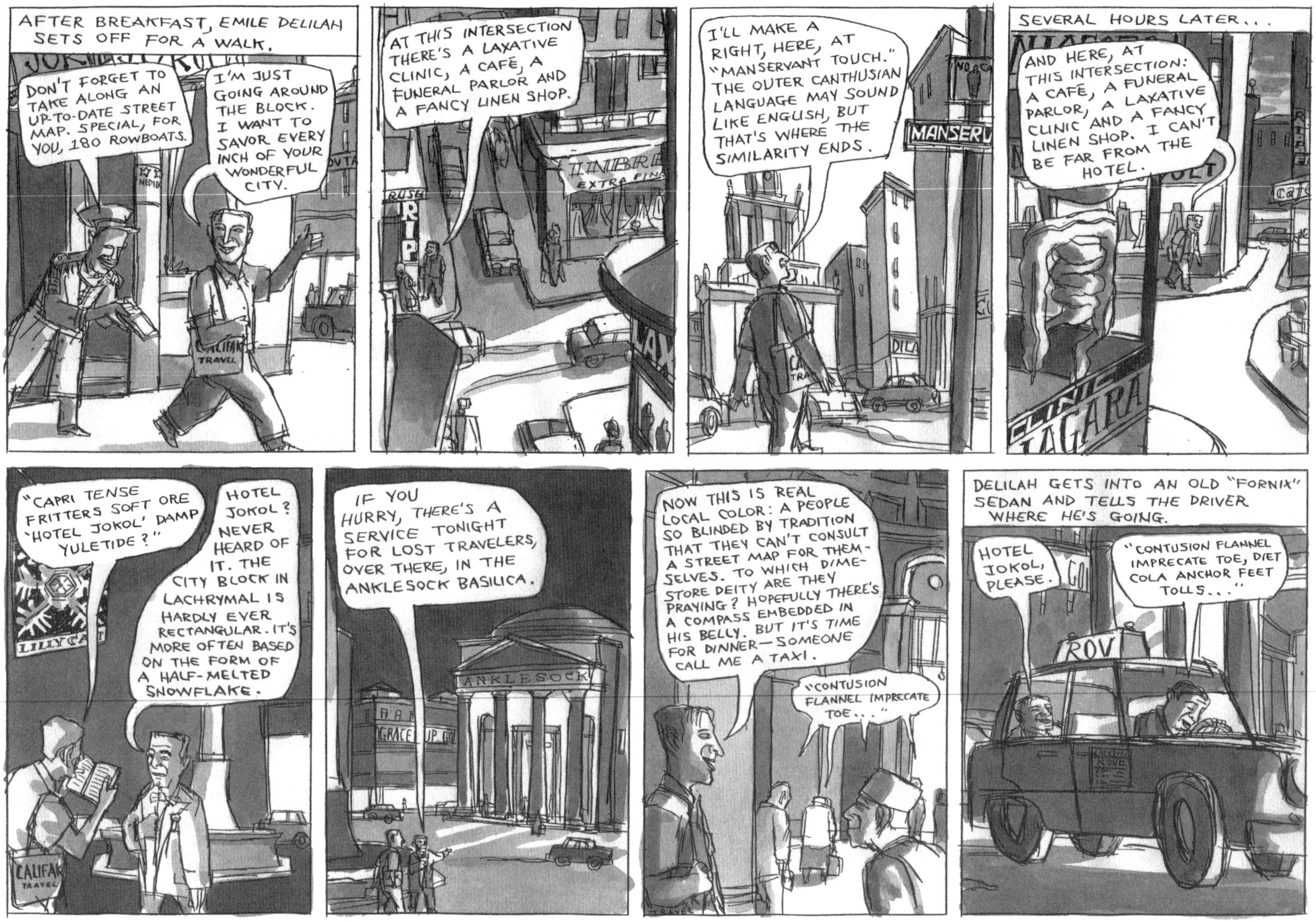
AFTER BREAKFAST, EMILE DELILAH SETS OFF FOR A WALK.
DON'T FORGET TO TAKE ALONG AN UP-TO-DATE STREET MAP. SPECIAL, FOR YOU, 180 ROWBOATS.
I'M JUST GOING AROUND THE BLOCK. I WANT TO SAVOR EVERY INCH OF YOUR WONDERFUL CITY.
CALIFAX TRAVEL
AT THIS INTERSECTION THERE'S A LAXATIVE CLINIC, A CAFÉ, A FUNERAL PARLOR AND A FANCY LINEN SHOP.
I'LL MAKE A RIGHT, HERE, AT "MANSERVANT TOUCH." THE OUTER CANTHUSIAN LANGUAGE MAY SOUND LIKE ENGLISH, BUT THAT'S WHERE THE SIMILARITY ENDS.
SEVERAL HOURS LATER...
AND HERE, AT THIS INTERSECTION: A CAFÉ, A FUNERAL PARLOR, A LAXATIVE CLINIC AND A FANCY LINEN SHOP. I CAN'T BE FAR FROM THE HOTEL.
"CAPRI TENSE FRITTERS SOFT ORE 'HOTEL JOKOL' DAMP YULETIDE?"
HOTEL JOKOL? NEVER HEARD OF IT. THE CITY BLOCK IN LACHRYMAL IS HARDLY EVER RECTANGULAR. IT'S MORE OFTEN BASED ON THE FORM OF A HALF-MELTED SNOWFLAKE.
LILLY CAT
CALIFAX TRAVEL
IF YOU HURRY, THERE'S A SERVICE TONIGHT FOR LOST TRAVELERS, OVER THERE, IN THE ANKLESOCK BASILICA.
ANKLESOCK
NOW THIS IS REAL LOCAL COLOR: A PEOPLE SO BLINDED BY TRADITION THAT THEY CAN'T CONSULT A STREET MAP FOR THEMSELVES. TO WHICH DIME-STORE DEITY ARE THEY PRAYING? HOPEFULLY THERE'S A COMPASS EMBEDDED IN HIS BELLY. BUT IT'S TIME FOR DINNER—SOMEONE CALL ME A TAXI.
"CONTUSION FLANNEL IMPRECATE TOE..."
DELILAH GETS INTO AN OLD "FORNIX" SEDAN AND TELLS THE DRIVER WHERE HE'S GOING.
HOTEL JOKOL, PLEASE.
"CONTUSION FLANNEL IMPRECATE TOE, DIET COLA ANCHOR FEET TOLLS..."

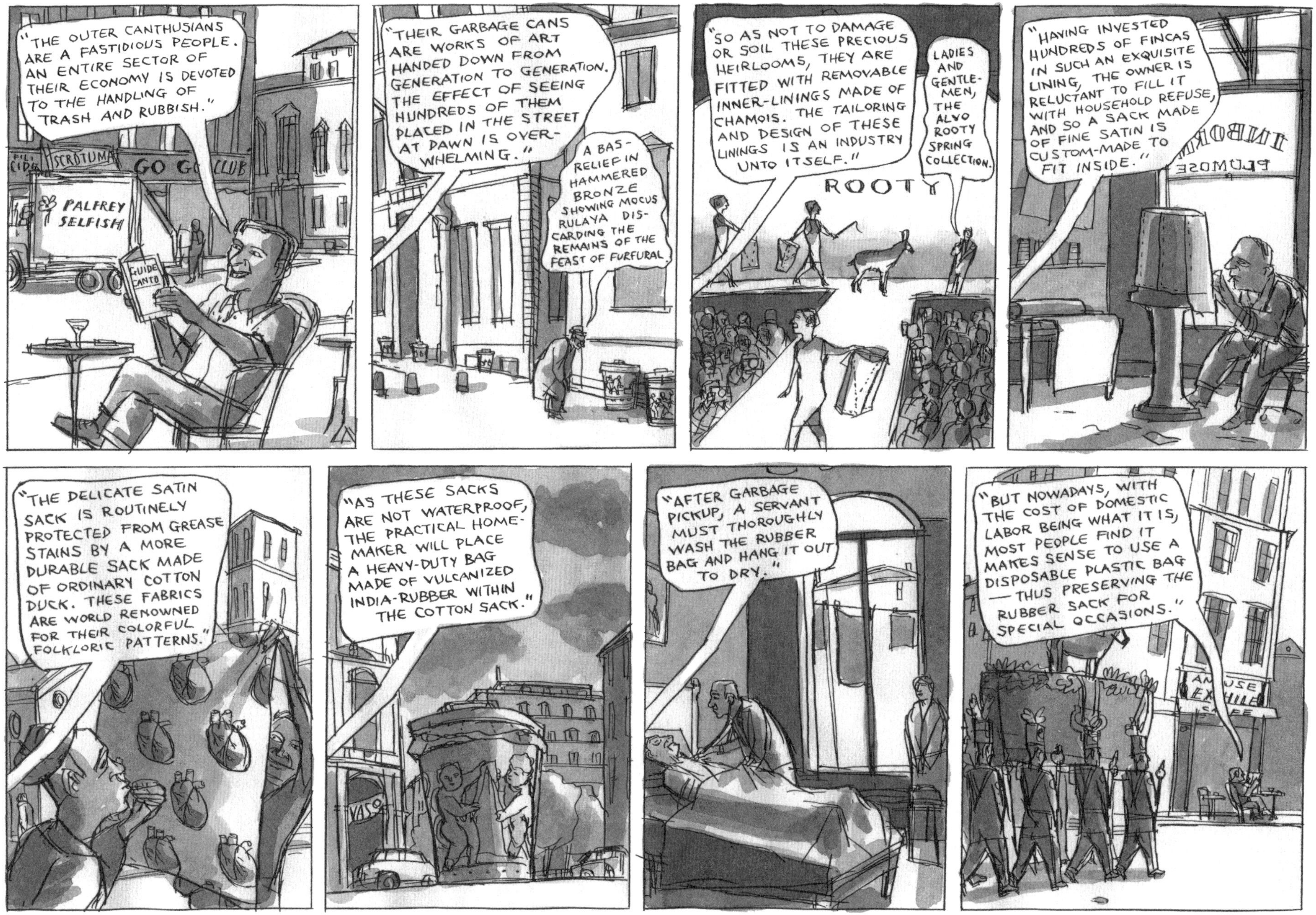
"THE OUTER CANTHUSIANS ARE A FASTIDIOUS PEOPLE. AN ENTIRE SECTOR OF THEIR ECONOMY IS DEVOTED TO THE HANDLING OF TRASH AND RUBBISH."
SCROTUMA
GO GO CLUB
PALFREY SELFISH
GUIDE CANTO
"THEIR GARBAGE CANS ARE WORKS OF ART HANDED DOWN FROM GENERATION TO GENERATION. THE EFFECT OF SEEING HUNDREDS OF THEM PLACED IN THE STREET AT DAWN IS OVER-WHELMING."
A BAS-RELIEF IN HAMMERED BRONZE SHOWING MOCUS RULAYA DIS-CARDING THE REMAINS OF THE FEAST OF FURFURAL.
"SO AS NOT TO DAMAGE OR SOIL THESE PRECIOUS HEIRLOOMS, THEY ARE FITTED WITH REMOVABLE INNER-LININGS MADE OF CHAMOIS. THE TAILORING AND DESIGN OF THESE LININGS IS AN INDUSTRY UNTO ITSELF."
LADIES AND GENTLE-MEN, THE ALVO ROOTY SPRING COLLECTION.
ROOTY
"HAVING INVESTED HUNDREDS OF FINCAS IN SUCH AN EXQUISITE LINING, THE OWNER IS RELUCTANT TO FILL IT WITH HOUSEHOLD REFUSE, AND SO A SACK MADE OF FINE SATIN IS CUSTOM-MADE TO FIT INSIDE."
"THE DELICATE SATIN SACK IS ROUTINELY PROTECTED FROM GREASE STAINS BY A MORE DURABLE SACK MADE OF ORDINARY COTTON DUCK. THESE FABRICS ARE WORLD RENOWNED FOR THEIR COLORFUL FOLKLORIC PATTERNS."
"AS THESE SACKS ARE NOT WATERPROOF, THE PRACTICAL HOME-MAKER WILL PLACE A HEAVY-DUTY BAG MADE OF VULCANIZED INDIA-RUBBER WITHIN THE COTTON SACK."
VASO
"AFTER GARBAGE PICKUP, A SERVANT MUST THOROUGHLY WASH THE RUBBER BAG AND HANG IT OUT TO DRY."
"BUT NOWADAYS, WITH THE COST OF DOMESTIC LABOR BEING WHAT IT IS, MOST PEOPLE FIND IT MAKES SENSE TO USE A DISPOSABLE PLASTIC BAG — THUS PRESERVING THE RUBBER SACK FOR SPECIAL OCCASIONS."

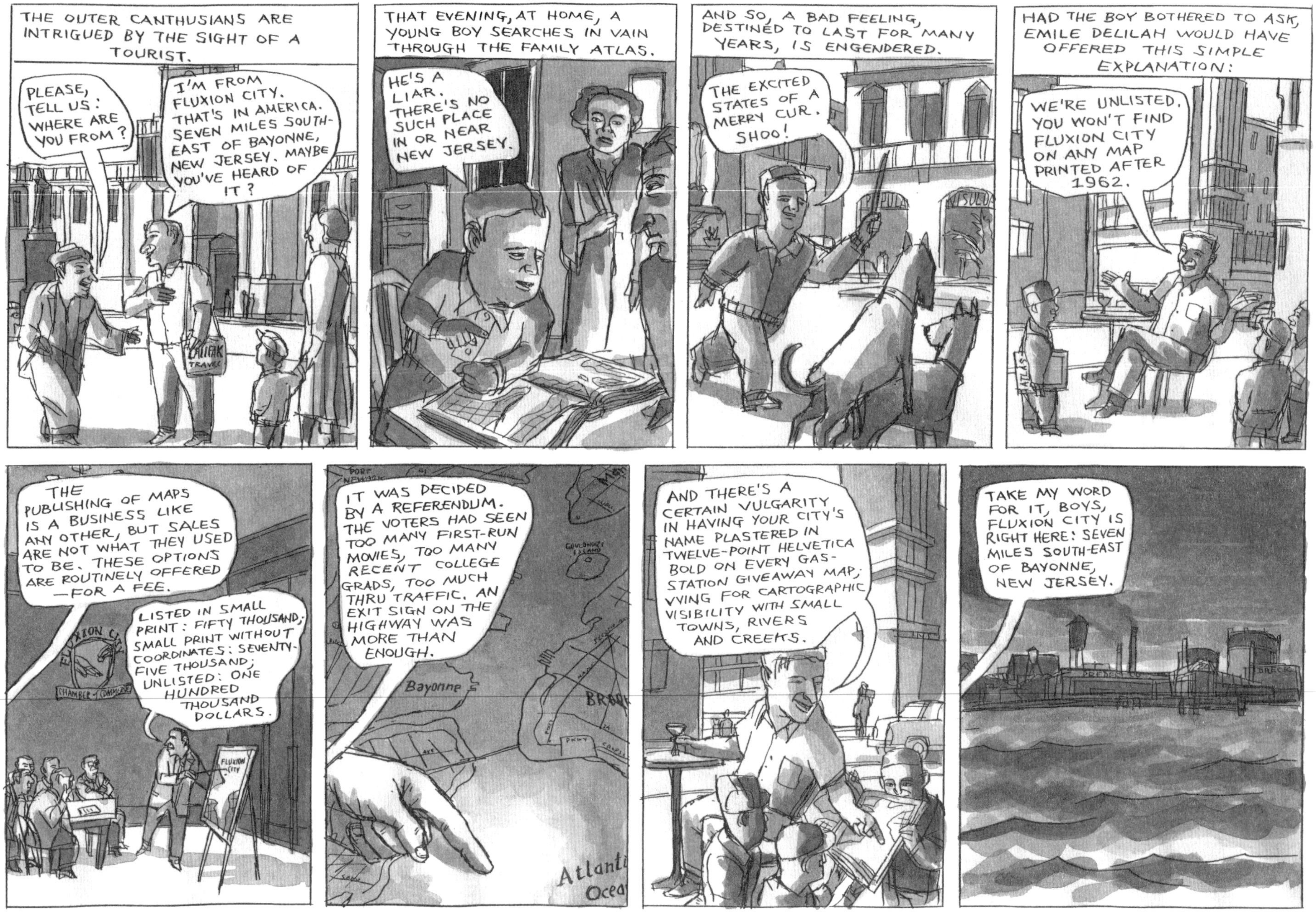
THE OUTER CANTHUSIANS ARE INTRIGUED BY THE SIGHT OF A TOURIST.
PLEASE, TELL US: WHERE ARE YOU FROM?
I'M FROM FLUXION CITY. THAT'S IN AMERICA. SEVEN MILES SOUTH-EAST OF BAYONNE, NEW JERSEY. MAYBE YOU'VE HEARD OF IT?
THAT EVENING, AT HOME, A YOUNG BOY SEARCHES IN VAIN THROUGH THE FAMILY ATLAS.
HE'S A LIAR. THERE'S NO SUCH PLACE IN OR NEAR NEW JERSEY.
AND SO, A BAD FEELING, DESTINED TO LAST FOR MANY YEARS, IS ENGENDERED.
THE EXCITED STATES OF A MERRY CUR. SHOO!
HAD THE BOY BOTHERED TO ASK, EMILE DELILAH WOULD HAVE OFFERED THIS SIMPLE EXPLANATION:
WE'RE UNLISTED. YOU WON'T FIND FLUXION CITY ON ANY MAP PRINTED AFTER 1962.
ATLAS
THE PUBLISHING OF MAPS IS A BUSINESS LIKE ANY OTHER, BUT SALES ARE NOT WHAT THEY USED TO BE. THESE OPTIONS ARE ROUTINELY OFFERED —FOR A FEE.
LISTED IN SMALL PRINT: FIFTY THOUSAND; SMALL PRINT WITHOUT COORDINATES: SEVENTY-FIVE THOUSAND; UNLISTED: ONE HUNDRED THOUSAND DOLLARS.
CHAMBER of COMMERCE
FLUXION CITY
IT WAS DECIDED BY A REFERENDUM. THE VOTERS HAD SEEN TOO MANY FIRST-RUN MOVIES, TOO MANY RECENT COLLEGE GRADS, TOO MUCH THRU TRAFFIC. AN EXIT SIGN ON THE HIGHWAY WAS MORE THAN ENOUGH.
Bayonne
AND THERE'S A CERTAIN VULGARITY IN HAVING YOUR CITY'S NAME PLASTERED IN TWELVE-POINT HELVETICA BOLD ON EVERY GAS-STATION GIVEAWAY MAP; VYING FOR CARTOGRAPHIC VISIBILITY WITH SMALL TOWNS, RIVERS AND CREEKS.
TAKE MY WORD FOR IT, BOYS, FLUXION CITY IS RIGHT HERE: SEVEN MILES SOUTH-EAST OF BAYONNE, NEW JERSEY.

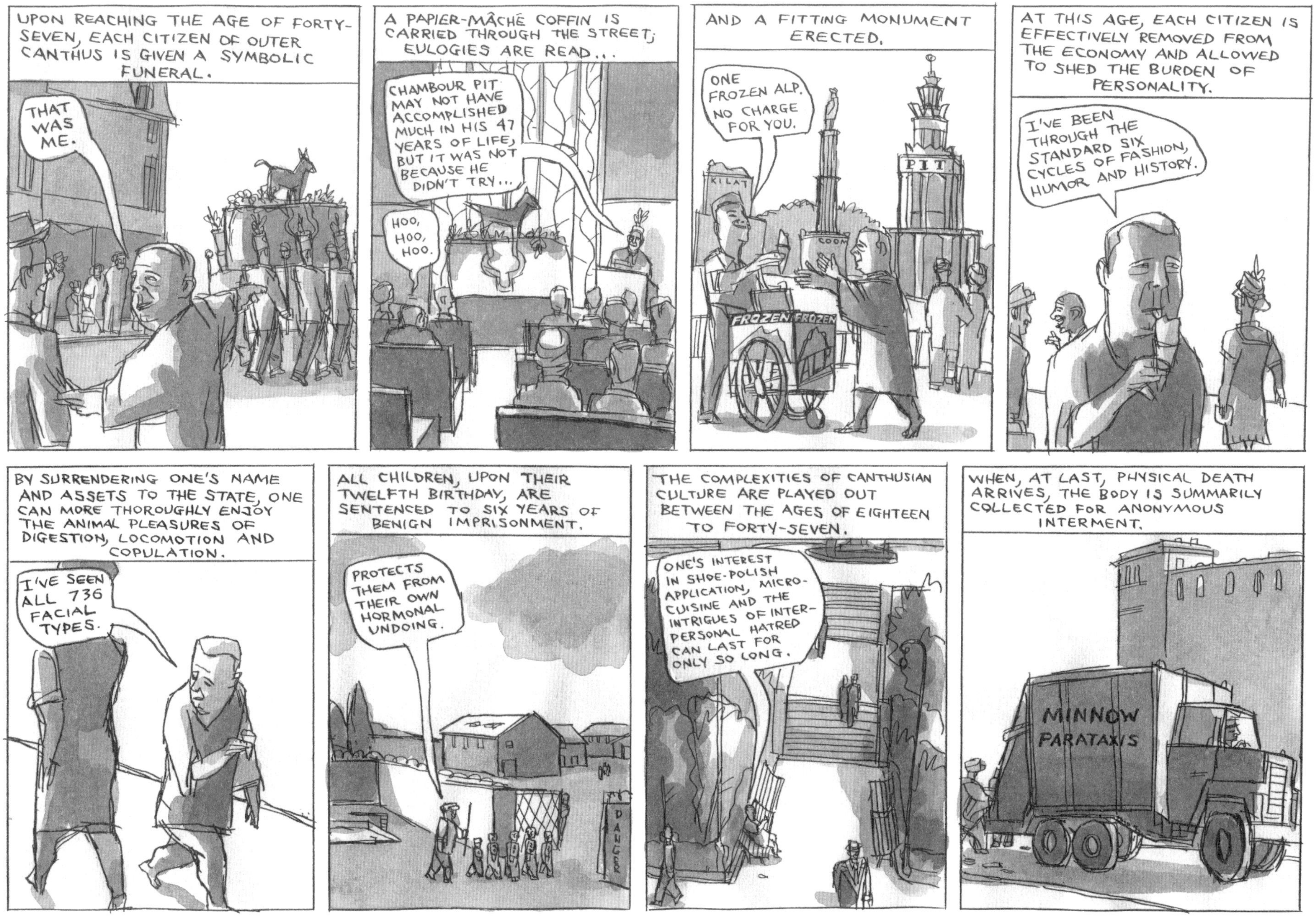
UPON REACHING THE AGE OF FORTY-SEVEN, EACH CITIZEN OF OUTER CANTHUS IS GIVEN A SYMBOLIC FUNERAL.
THAT WAS ME.
A PAPIER-MÂCHÉ COFFIN IS CARRIED THROUGH THE STREET; EULOGIES ARE READ...
CHAMBOUR PIT MAY NOT HAVE ACCOMPLISHED MUCH IN HIS 47 YEARS OF LIFE, BUT IT WAS NOT BECAUSE HE DIDN'T TRY...
HOO, HOO, HOO.
AND A FITTING MONUMENT ERECTED.
ONE FROZEN ALP. NO CHARGE FOR YOU.
PIT
FROZEN
FROZEN
AT THIS AGE, EACH CITIZEN IS EFFECTIVELY REMOVED FROM THE ECONOMY AND ALLOWED TO SHED THE BURDEN OF PERSONALITY.
I'VE BEEN THROUGH THE STANDARD SIX CYCLES OF FASHION, HUMOR AND HISTORY.
BY SURRENDERING ONE'S NAME AND ASSETS TO THE STATE, ONE CAN MORE THOROUGHLY ENJOY THE ANIMAL PLEASURES OF DIGESTION, LOCOMOTION AND COPULATION.
I'VE SEEN ALL 736 FACIAL TYPES.
ALL CHILDREN, UPON THEIR TWELFTH BIRTHDAY, ARE SENTENCED TO SIX YEARS OF BENIGN IMPRISONMENT.
PROTECTS THEM FROM THEIR OWN HORMONAL UNDOING.
DANGER
THE COMPLEXITIES OF CANTHUSIAN CULTURE ARE PLAYED OUT BETWEEN THE AGES OF EIGHTEEN TO FORTY-SEVEN.
ONE'S INTEREST IN SHOE-POLISH APPLICATION, MICRO-CUISINE AND THE INTRIGUES OF INTER-PERSONAL HATRED CAN LAST FOR ONLY SO LONG.
WHEN, AT LAST, PHYSICAL DEATH ARRIVES, THE BODY IS SUMMARILY COLLECTED FOR ANONYMOUS INTERMENT.
MINNOW PARATAXIS

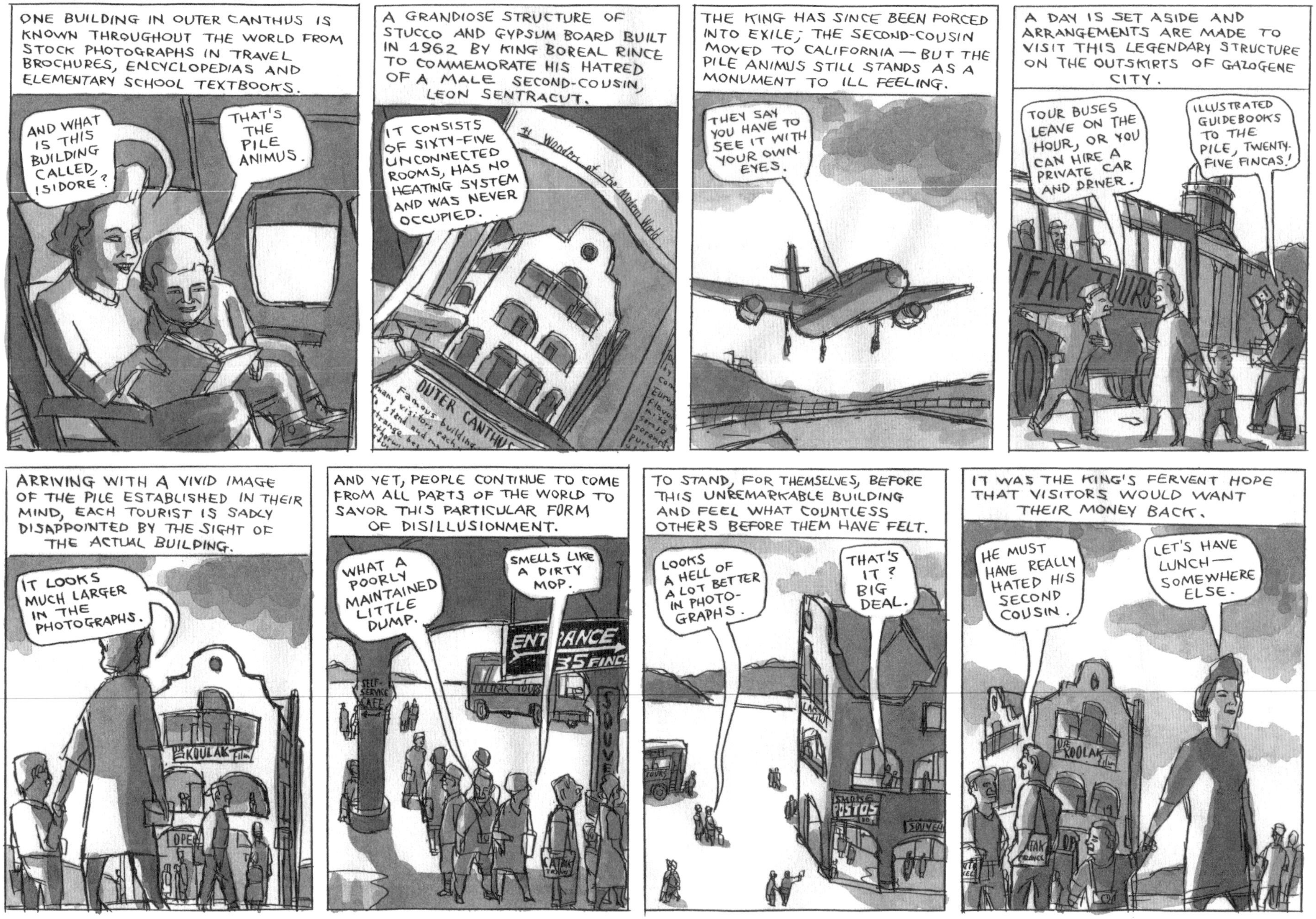
ONE BUILDING IN OUTER CANTHUS IS KNOWN THROUGHOUT THE WORLD FROM STOCK PHOTOGRAPHS IN TRAVEL BROCHURES, ENCYCLOPEDIAS AND ELEMENTARY SCHOOL TEXTBOOKS.
AND WHAT IS THIS BUILDING CALLED, ISIDORE?
THAT'S THE PILE ANIMUS.
A GRANDIOSE STRUCTURE OF STUCCO AND GYPSUM BOARD BUILT IN 1962 BY KING BOREAL RINCE TO COMMEMORATE HIS HATRED OF A MALE SECOND-COUSIN, LEON SENTRACUT.
IT CONSISTS OF SIXTY-FIVE UNCONNECTED ROOMS, HAS NO HEATING SYSTEM AND WAS NEVER OCCUPIED.
Wonders of The Modern World
OUTER CANTHUS
THE KING HAS SINCE BEEN FORCED INTO EXILE; THE SECOND-COUSIN MOVED TO CALIFORNIA — BUT THE PILE ANIMUS STILL STANDS AS A MONUMENT TO ILL FEELING.
THEY SAY YOU HAVE TO SEE IT WITH YOUR OWN EYES.
A DAY IS SET ASIDE AND ARRANGEMENTS ARE MADE TO VISIT THIS LEGENDARY STRUCTURE ON THE OUTSKIRTS OF GAZOGENE CITY.
TOUR BUSES LEAVE ON THE HOUR, OR YOU CAN HIRE A PRIVATE CAR AND DRIVER.
ILLUSTRATED GUIDEBOOKS TO THE PILE, TWENTY-FIVE FINCAS!
ARRIVING WITH A VIVID IMAGE OF THE PILE ESTABLISHED IN THEIR MIND, EACH TOURIST IS SADLY DISAPPOINTED BY THE SIGHT OF THE ACTUAL BUILDING.
IT LOOKS MUCH LARGER IN THE PHOTOGRAPHS.
AND YET, PEOPLE CONTINUE TO COME FROM ALL PARTS OF THE WORLD TO SAVOR THIS PARTICULAR FORM OF DISILLUSIONMENT.
WHAT A POORLY MAINTAINED LITTLE DUMP.
SMELLS LIKE A DIRTY MOP.
SELF-SERVICE CAFE
TO STAND, FOR THEMSELVES, BEFORE THIS UNREMARKABLE BUILDING AND FEEL WHAT COUNTLESS OTHERS BEFORE THEM HAVE FELT.
LOOKS A HELL OF A LOT BETTER IN PHOTOGRAPHS.
THAT'S IT? BIG DEAL.
IT WAS THE KING'S FERVENT HOPE THAT VISITORS WOULD WANT THEIR MONEY BACK.
HE MUST HAVE REALLY HATED HIS SECOND COUSIN.
LET'S HAVE LUNCH — SOMEWHERE ELSE.

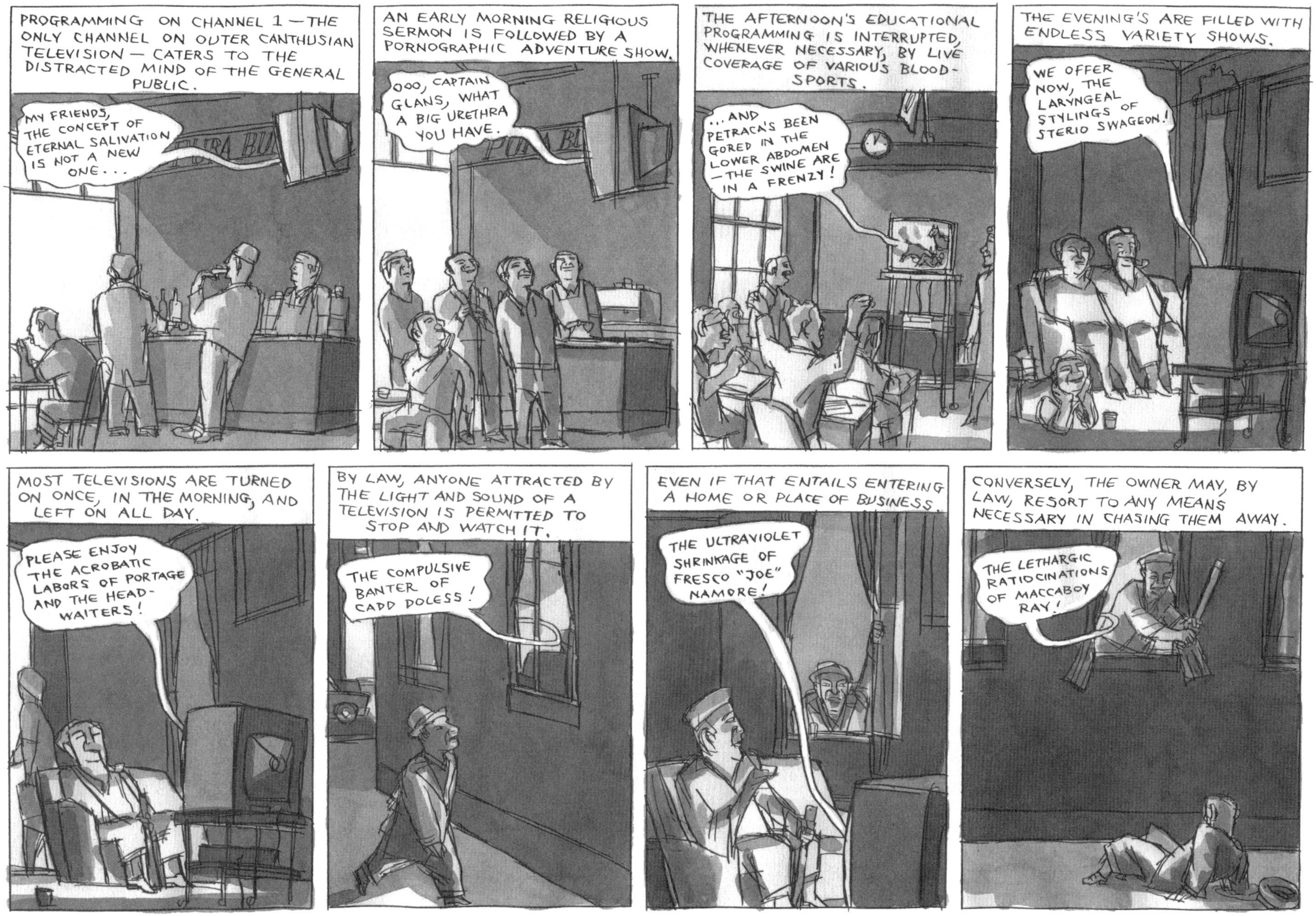
PROGRAMMING ON CHANNEL 1 — THE ONLY CHANNEL ON OUTER CANTHUSIAN TELEVISION — CATERS TO THE DISTRACTED MIND OF THE GENERAL PUBLIC.
MY FRIENDS, THE CONCEPT OF ETERNAL SALVATION IS NOT A NEW ONE...
AN EARLY MORNING RELIGIOUS SERMON IS FOLLOWED BY A PORNOGRAPHIC ADVENTURE SHOW.
OOO, CAPTAIN GLANS, WHAT A BIG URETHRA YOU HAVE.
THE AFTERNOON'S EDUCATIONAL PROGRAMMING IS INTERRUPTED, WHENEVER NECESSARY, BY LIVE COVERAGE OF VARIOUS BLOOD-SPORTS.
...AND PETRACA'S BEEN GORED IN THE LOWER ABDOMEN — THE SWINE ARE IN A FRENZY!
THE EVENING'S ARE FILLED WITH ENDLESS VARIETY SHOWS.
WE OFFER NOW, THE LARYNGEAL STYLINGS OF STERIO SWAGEON!
MOST TELEVISIONS ARE TURNED ON ONCE, IN THE MORNING, AND LEFT ON ALL DAY.
PLEASE ENJOY THE ACROBATIC LABORS OF PORTAGE AND THE HEAD-WAITERS!
BY LAW, ANYONE ATTRACTED BY THE LIGHT AND SOUND OF A TELEVISION IS PERMITTED TO STOP AND WATCH IT.
THE COMPULSIVE BANTER OF CADD DOLESS!
EVEN IF THAT ENTAILS ENTERING A HOME OR PLACE OF BUSINESS.
THE ULTRAVIOLET SHRINKAGE OF FRESCO "JOE" NAMORE!
CONVERSELY, THE OWNER MAY, BY LAW, RESORT TO ANY MEANS NECESSARY IN CHASING THEM AWAY.
THE LETHARGIC RATIOCINATIONS OF MACCABOY RAY!

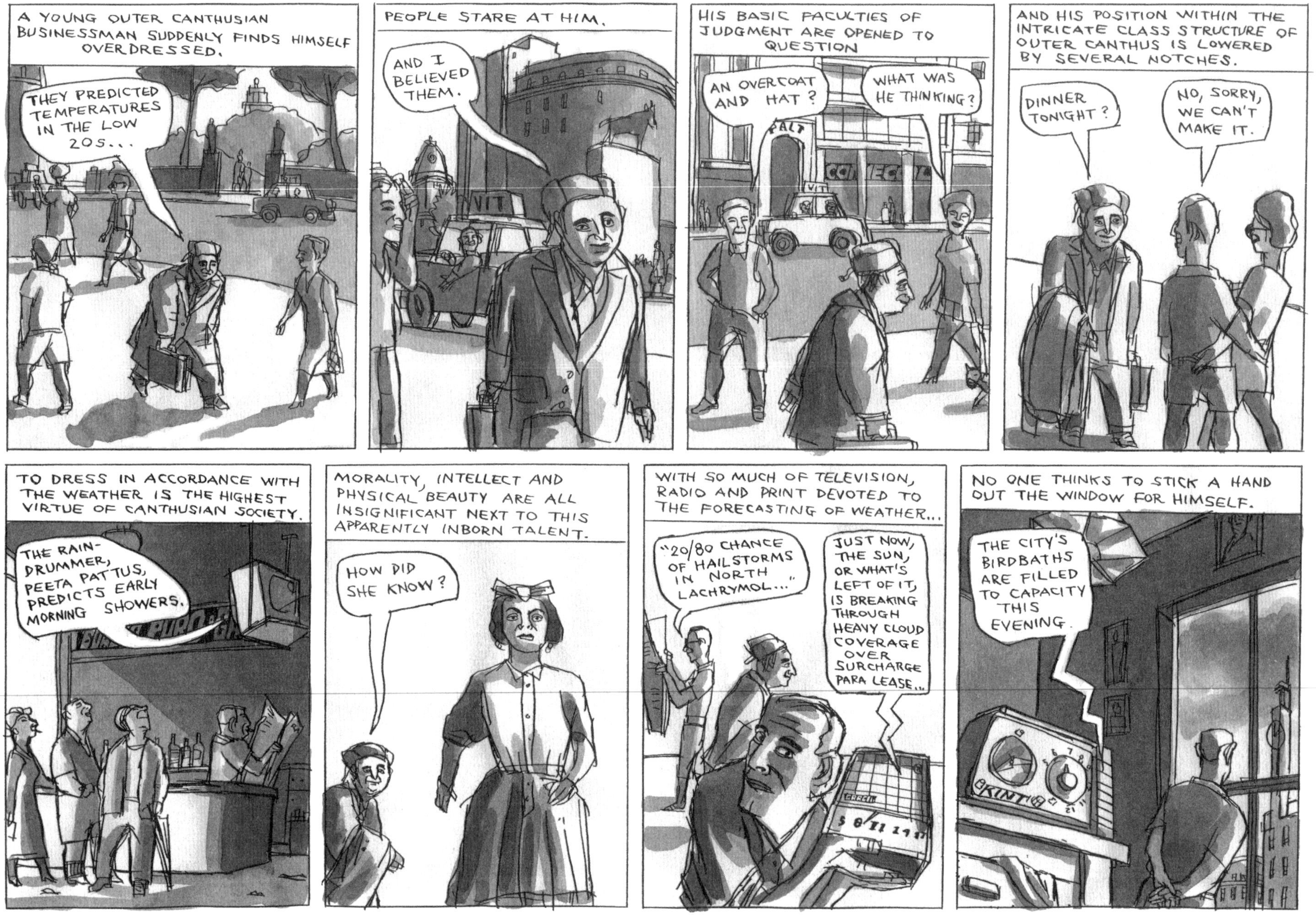

A YOUNG OUTER CANTHUSIAN BUSINESSMAN SUDDENLY FINDS HIMSELF OVERDRESSED.
THEY PREDICTED TEMPERATURES IN THE LOW 20S...
PEOPLE STARE AT HIM.
AND I BELIEVED THEM.
VIT
HIS BASIC FACULTIES OF JUDGMENT ARE OPENED TO QUESTION
AN OVERCOAT AND HAT?
WHAT WAS HE THINKING?
AND HIS POSITION WITHIN THE INTRICATE CLASS STRUCTURE OF OUTER CANTHUS IS LOWERED BY SEVERAL NOTCHES.
DINNER TONIGHT?
NO, SORRY, WE CAN'T MAKE IT.
TO DRESS IN ACCORDANCE WITH THE WEATHER IS THE HIGHEST VIRTUE OF CANTHUSIAN SOCIETY.
THE RAIN-DRUMMER, PEETA PATTUS, PREDICTS EARLY MORNING SHOWERS.
MORALITY, INTELLECT AND PHYSICAL BEAUTY ARE ALL INSIGNIFICANT NEXT TO THIS APPARENTLY INBORN TALENT.
HOW DID SHE KNOW?
WITH SO MUCH OF TELEVISION, RADIO AND PRINT DEVOTED TO THE FORECASTING OF WEATHER...
"20/80 CHANCE OF HAILSTORMS IN NORTH LACHRYMOL..."
JUST NOW, THE SUN, OR WHAT'S LEFT OF IT, IS BREAKING THROUGH HEAVY CLOUD COVERAGE OVER SURCHARGE PARA LEASE...
NO ONE THINKS TO STICK A HAND OUT THE WINDOW FOR HIMSELF.
THE CITY'S BIRDBATHS ARE FILLED TO CAPACITY THIS EVENING.
KINT

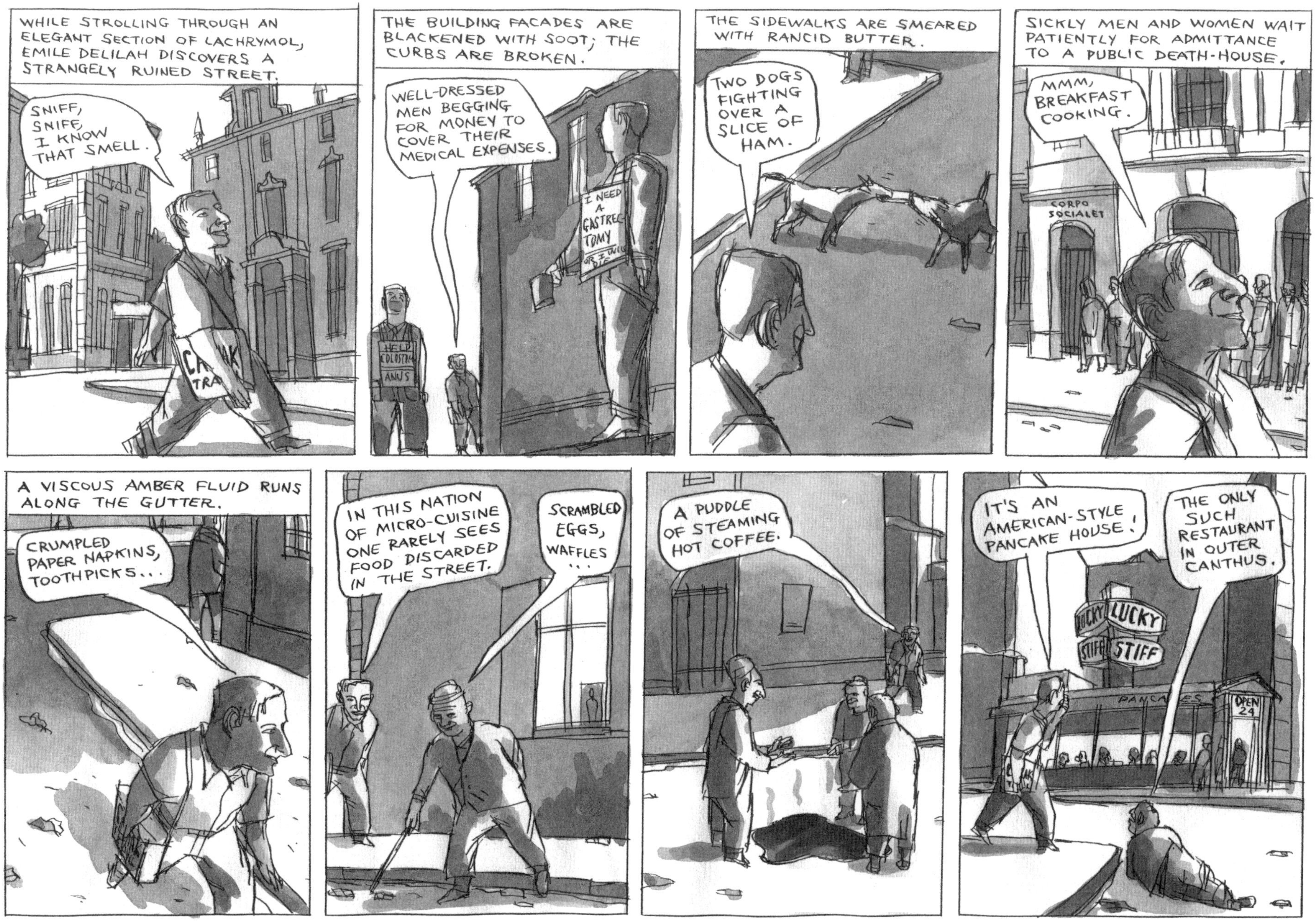
WHILE STROLLING THROUGH AN ELEGANT SECTION OF LACHRYMOL, EMILE DELILAH DISCOVERS A STRANGELY RUINED STREET.
SNIFF, SNIFF, I KNOW THAT SMELL.
THE BUILDING FACADES ARE BLACKENED WITH SOOT; THE CURBS ARE BROKEN.
WELL-DRESSED MEN BEGGING FOR MONEY TO COVER THEIR MEDICAL EXPENSES.
I NEED A GASTREC-TOMY
THE SIDEWALKS ARE SMEARED WITH RANCID BUTTER.
TWO DOGS FIGHTING OVER A SLICE OF HAM.
SICKLY MEN AND WOMEN WAIT PATIENTLY FOR ADMITTANCE TO A PUBLIC DEATH-HOUSE.
MMM, BREAKFAST COOKING.
CORPO SOCIALET
A VISCOUS AMBER FLUID RUNS ALONG THE GUTTER.
CRUMPLED PAPER NAPKINS, TOOTHPICKS...
IN THIS NATION OF MICRO-CUISINE ONE RARELY SEES FOOD DISCARDED IN THE STREET.
SCRAMBLED EGGS, WAFFLES ...
A PUDDLE OF STEAMING HOT COFFEE.
IT'S AN AMERICAN-STYLE PANCAKE HOUSE!
THE ONLY SUCH RESTAURANT IN OUTER CANTHUS.
LUCKY STIFF
OPEN 24

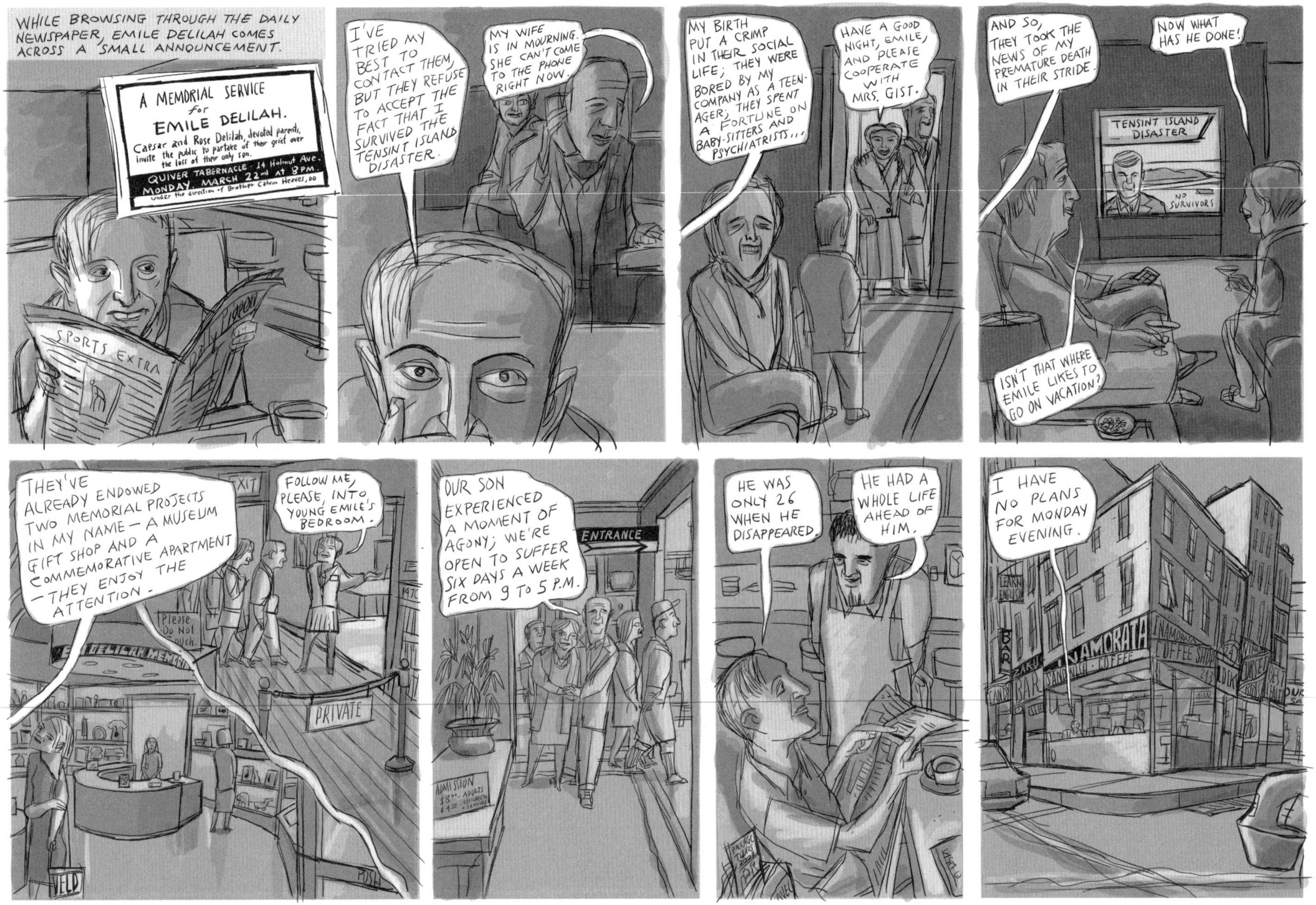
WHILE BROWSING THROUGH THE DAILY NEWSPAPER, EMILE DELILAH COMES ACROSS A SMALL ANNOUNCEMENT.
A MEMORIAL SERVICE for EMILE DELILAH.
Caesar and Rose Delilah, devoted parents, invite the public to partake of their grief over the loss of their only son.
QUIVER TABERNACLE · 14 Holmut Ave. MONDAY, MARCH 22nd AT 8PM.
under the direction of Brother Calvin Heaves, DD
SPORTS EXTRA
I'VE TRIED MY BEST TO CONTACT THEM, BUT THEY REFUSE TO ACCEPT THE FACT THAT I SURVIVED THE TENSINT ISLAND DISASTER.
MY WIFE IS IN MOURNING. SHE CAN'T COME TO THE PHONE RIGHT NOW.
MY BIRTH PUT A CRIMP IN THEIR SOCIAL LIFE; THEY WERE BORED BY MY COMPANY AS A TEEN-AGER; THEY SPENT A FORTUNE ON BABY-SITTERS AND PSYCHIATRISTS...
HAVE A GOOD NIGHT, EMILE, AND PLEASE COOPERATE WITH MRS. GIST.
AND SO, THEY TOOK THE NEWS OF MY PREMATURE DEATH IN THEIR STRIDE.
NOW WHAT HAS HE DONE!
TENSINT ISLAND DISASTER
NO SURVIVORS
ISN'T THAT WHERE EMILE LIKES TO GO ON VACATION?
THEY'VE ALREADY ENDOWED TWO MEMORIAL PROJECTS IN MY NAME — A MUSEUM GIFT SHOP AND A COMMEMORATIVE APARTMENT — THEY ENJOY THE ATTENTION.
FOLLOW ME, PLEASE, INTO YOUNG EMILE'S BEDROOM.
EXIT
PRIVATE
OUR SON EXPERIENCED A MOMENT OF AGONY; WE'RE OPEN TO SUFFER SIX DAYS A WEEK FROM 9 TO 5 P.M.
ENTRANCE
HE WAS ONLY 26 WHEN HE DISAPPEARED.
HE HAD A WHOLE LIFE AHEAD OF HIM.
I HAVE NO PLANS FOR MONDAY EVENING.
COFFEE SHOP

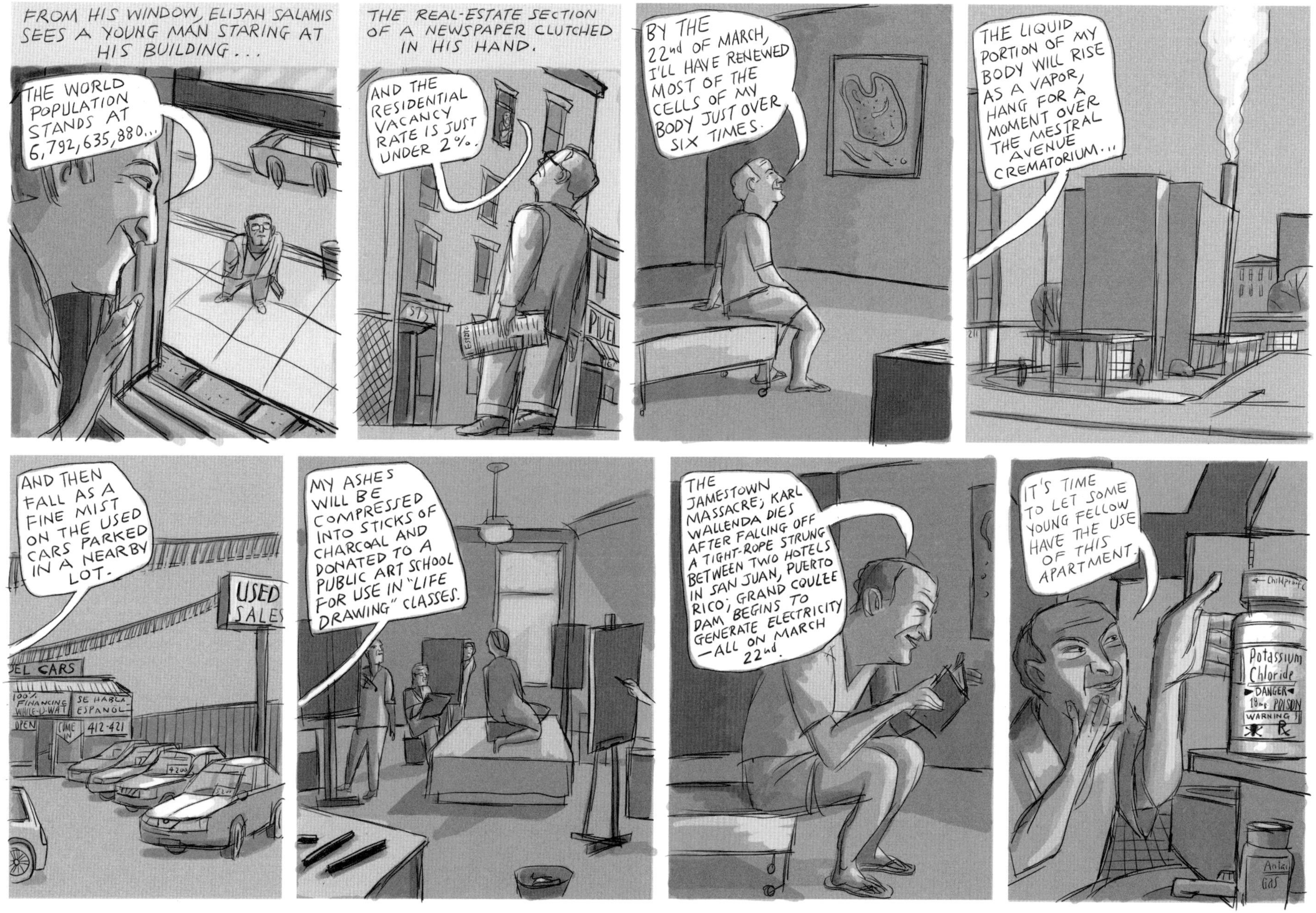
FROM HIS WINDOW, ELIJAH SALAMIS SEES A YOUNG MAN STARING AT HIS BUILDING...
THE WORLD POPULATION STANDS AT 6,792,635,880...
THE REAL-ESTATE SECTION OF A NEWSPAPER CLUTCHED IN HIS HAND.
AND THE RESIDENTIAL VACANCY RATE IS JUST UNDER 2%.
575
BY THE 22nd OF MARCH, I'LL HAVE RENEWED MOST OF THE CELLS OF MY BODY JUST OVER SIX TIMES.
THE LIQUID PORTION OF MY BODY WILL RISE AS A VAPOR, HANG FOR A MOMENT OVER THE MESTRAL AVENUE CREMATORIUM...
AND THEN FALL AS A FINE MIST ON THE USED CARS PARKED IN A NEARBY LOT.
USED SALES
100% FINANCING WHILE-U-WAIT
SE HABLA ESPANOL
OPEN
COME IN
412-421
MY ASHES WILL BE COMPRESSED INTO STICKS OF CHARCOAL AND DONATED TO A PUBLIC ART SCHOOL FOR USE IN "LIFE DRAWING" CLASSES.
THE JAMESTOWN MASSACRE; KARL WALLENDA DIES AFTER FALLING OFF A TIGHT-ROPE STRUNG BETWEEN TWO HOTELS IN SAN JUAN, PUERTO RICO; GRAND COULEE DAM BEGINS TO GENERATE ELECTRICITY —ALL ON MARCH 22nd.
IT'S TIME TO LET SOME YOUNG FELLOW HAVE THE USE OF THIS APARTMENT.
Potassium Chloride
DANGER
POISON
WARNING

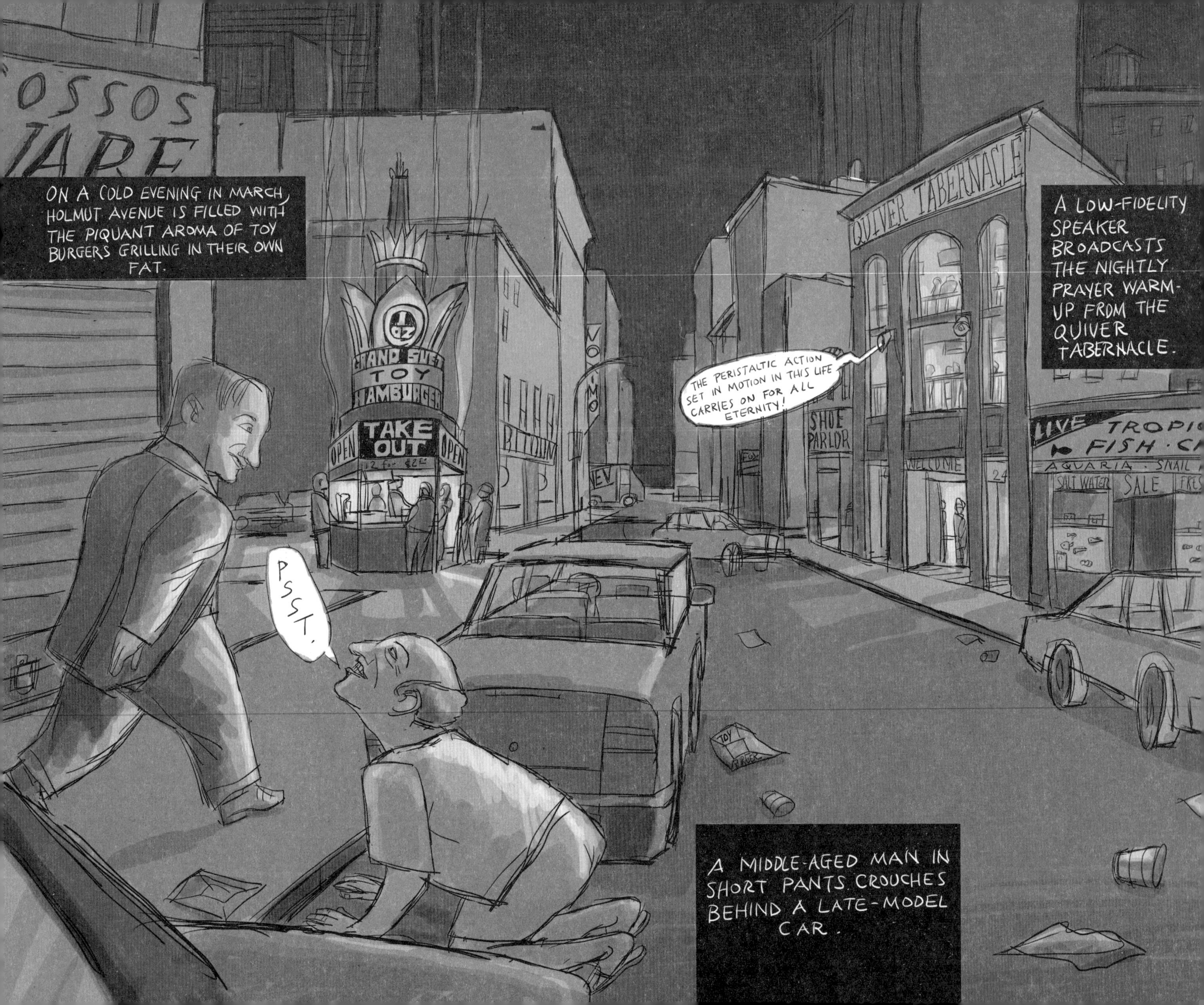
ON A COLD EVENING IN MARCH, HOLMUT AVENUE IS FILLED WITH THE PIQUANT AROMA OF TOY BURGERS GRILLING IN THEIR OWN FAT.
GRAND SUET TOY HAMBURGER
TAKE OUT
OPEN
OPEN
A LOW-FIDELITY SPEAKER BROADCASTS THE NIGHTLY PRAYER WARM-UP FROM THE QUIVER TABERNACLE.
QUIVER TABERNACLE
THE PERISTALTIC ACTION SET IN MOTION IN THIS LIFE CARRIES ON FOR ALL ETERNITY!
SHOE PARLOR
LIVE TROPIC FISH
AQUARIA · SNAIL
SALT WATER
SALE
PSST.
A MIDDLE-AGED MAN IN SHORT PANTS CROUCHES BEHIND A LATE-MODEL CAR.

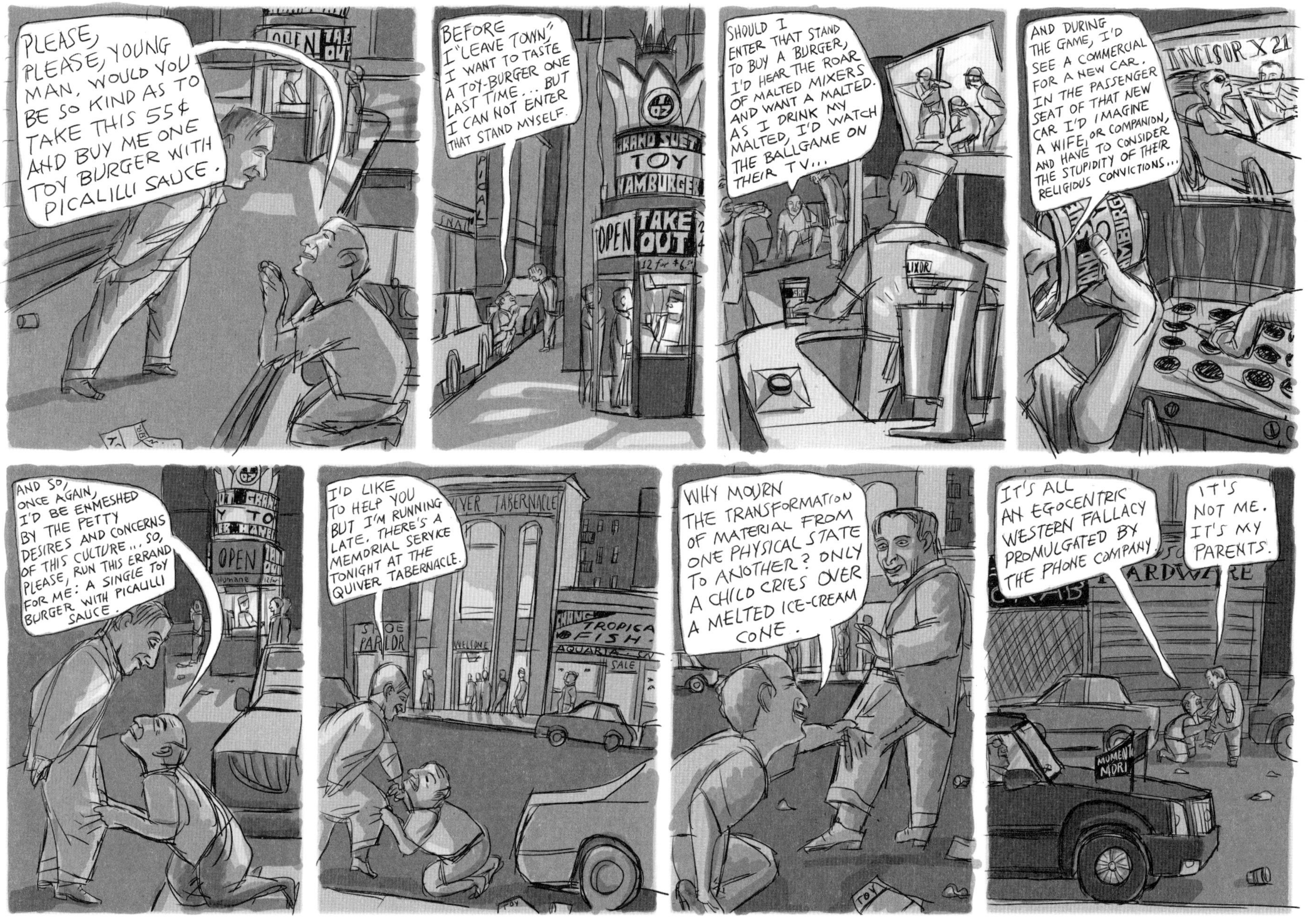
PLEASE, PLEASE, YOUNG MAN, WOULD YOU BE SO KIND AS TO TAKE THIS 55¢ AND BUY ME ONE TOY BURGER WITH PICALILLI SAUCE.
BEFORE I "LEAVE TOWN," I WANT TO TASTE A TOY-BURGER ONE LAST TIME... BUT I CAN NOT ENTER THAT STAND MYSELF.
TOY
HAMBURGER
OPEN
TAKE OUT
12 for $6.
SHOULD I ENTER THAT STAND TO BUY A BURGER, I'D HEAR THE ROAR OF MALTED MIXERS AND WANT A MALTED. AS I DRINK MY MALTED, I'D WATCH THE BALLGAME ON THEIR TV...
AND DURING THE GAME, I'D SEE A COMMERCIAL FOR A NEW CAR. IN THE PASSENGER SEAT OF THAT NEW CAR I'D IMAGINE A WIFE, OR COMPANION, AND HAVE TO CONSIDER THE STUPIDITY OF THEIR RELIGIOUS CONVICTIONS...
INCISOR X21
AND SO, ONCE AGAIN, I'D BE ENMESHED BY THE PETTY DESIRES AND CONCERNS OF THIS CULTURE... SO, PLEASE, RUN THIS ERRAND FOR ME: A SINGLE TOY BURGER WITH PICALILLI SAUCE.
OPEN
I'D LIKE TO HELP YOU BUT I'M RUNNING LATE. THERE'S A MEMORIAL SERVICE TONIGHT AT THE QUIVER TABERNACLE.
TROPICAL FISH
AQUARIA
SALE
WHY MOURN THE TRANSFORMATION OF MATERIAL FROM ONE PHYSICAL STATE TO ANOTHER? ONLY A CHILD CRIES OVER A MELTED ICE-CREAM CONE.
TOY
IT'S ALL AN EGOCENTRIC WESTERN FALLACY PROMULGATED BY THE PHONE COMPANY.
IT'S NOT ME. IT'S MY PARENTS.
MEMENTO MORI

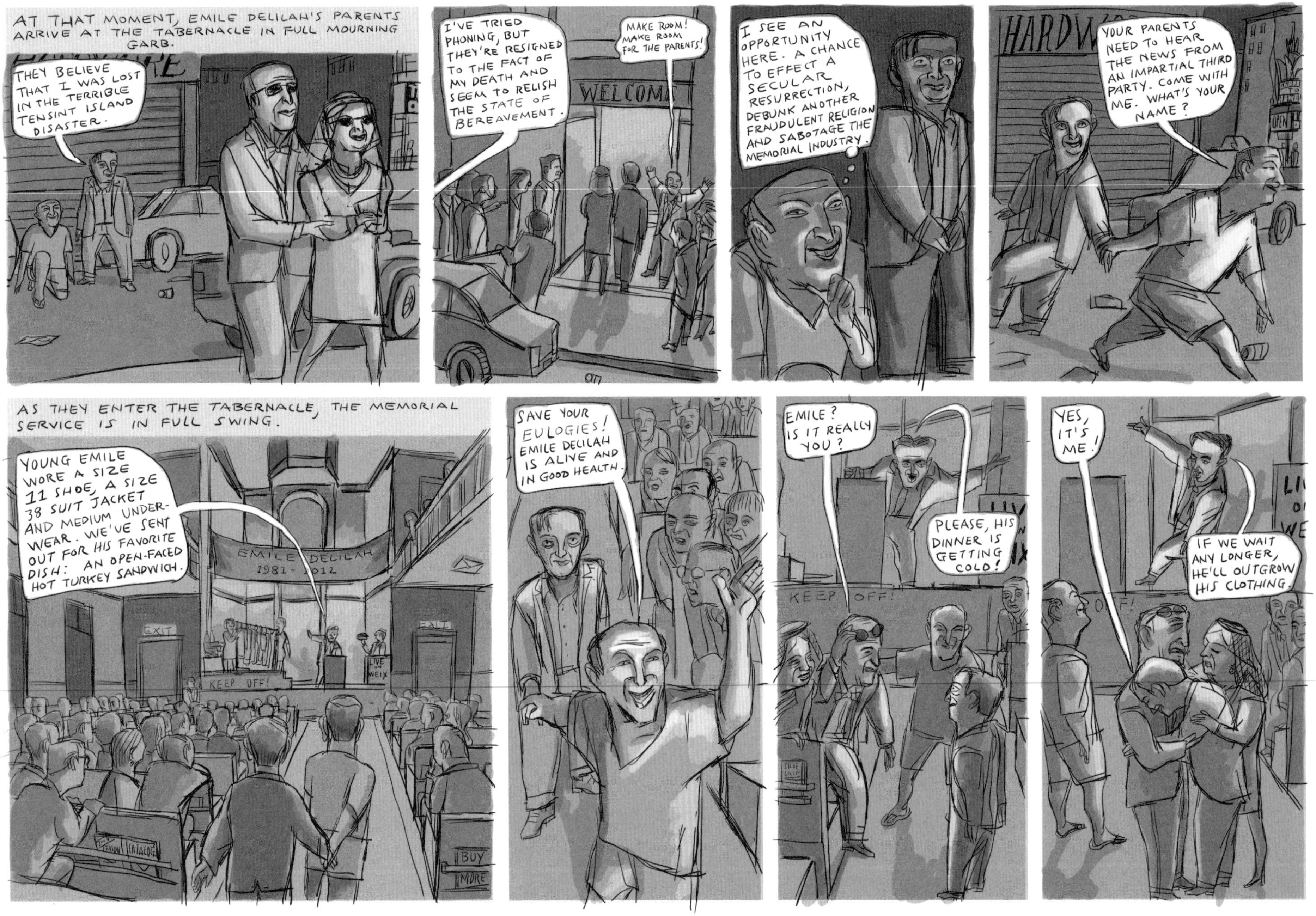
AT THAT MOMENT, EMILE DELILAH'S PARENTS ARRIVE AT THE TABERNACLE IN FULL MOURNING GARB.
THEY BELIEVE THAT I WAS LOST IN THE TERRIBLE TENSINT ISLAND DISASTER.
I'VE TRIED PHONING, BUT THEY'RE RESIGNED TO THE FACT OF MY DEATH AND SEEM TO RELISH THE STATE OF BEREAVEMENT.
MAKE ROOM! MAKE ROOM FOR THE PARENTS!
WELCOME
I SEE AN OPPORTUNITY HERE. A CHANCE TO EFFECT A SECULAR RESURRECTION, DEBUNK ANOTHER FRAUDULENT RELIGION AND SABOTAGE THE MEMORIAL INDUSTRY.
HARDW
YOUR PARENTS NEED TO HEAR THE NEWS FROM AN IMPARTIAL THIRD PARTY. COME WITH ME. WHAT'S YOUR NAME?
AS THEY ENTER THE TABERNACLE, THE MEMORIAL SERVICE IS IN FULL SWING.
YOUNG EMILE WORE A SIZE 11 SHOE, A SIZE 38 SUIT JACKET AND MEDIUM UNDERWEAR. WE'VE SENT OUT FOR HIS FAVORITE DISH: AN OPEN-FACED HOT TURKEY SANDWICH.
EMILE DELILAH
1981-2012
EXIT
EXIT
LIVE ON WEIX
KEEP OFF!
BUY MORE
SAVE YOUR EULOGIES! EMILE DELILAH IS ALIVE AND IN GOOD HEALTH.
EMILE? IS IT REALLY YOU?
PLEASE, HIS DINNER IS GETTING COLD!
KEEP OFF!
YES, IT'S ME!
IF WE WAIT ANY LONGER, HE'LL OUTGROW HIS CLOTHING.

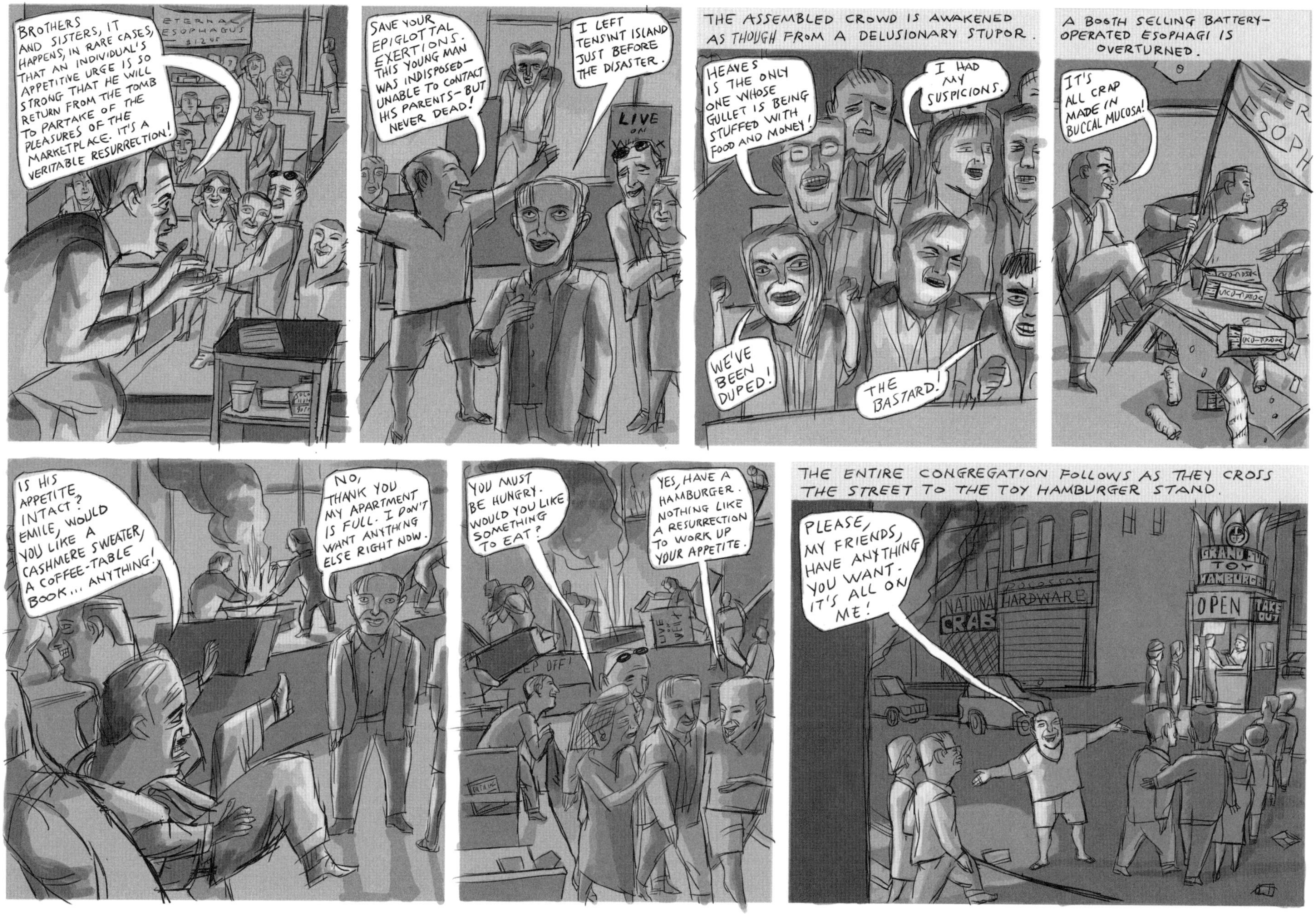

ETERNAL ESOPHAGUS $1245
BROTHERS AND SISTERS, IT HAPPENS, IN RARE CASES, THAT AN INDIVIDUAL'S APPETITIVE URGE IS SO STRONG THAT HE WILL RETURN FROM THE TOMB TO PARTAKE OF THE PLEASURES OF THE MARKETPLACE. IT'S A VERITABLE RESURRECTION!
SAVE YOUR EPIGLOTTAL EXERTIONS. THIS YOUNG MAN WAS INDISPOSED—UNABLE TO CONTACT HIS PARENTS—BUT NEVER DEAD!
I LEFT TENSINT ISLAND JUST BEFORE THE DISASTER.
LIVE ON
THE ASSEMBLED CROWD IS AWAKENED AS THOUGH FROM A DELUSIONARY STUPOR.
HEAVES IS THE ONLY ONE WHOSE GULLET IS BEING STUFFED WITH FOOD AND MONEY!
I HAD MY SUSPICIONS.
WE'VE BEEN DUPED!
THE BASTARD!
A BOOTH SELLING BATTERY-OPERATED ESOPHAGI IS OVERTURNED.
IT'S ALL CRAP MADE IN BUCCAL MUCOSA!
IS HIS APPETITE INTACT? EMILE, WOULD YOU LIKE A CASHMERE SWEATER, A COFFEE-TABLE BOOK... ANYTHING!
NO, THANK YOU MY APARTMENT IS FULL. I DON'T WANT ANYTHING ELSE RIGHT NOW.
YOU MUST BE HUNGRY. WOULD YOU LIKE SOMETHING TO EAT?
YES, HAVE A HAMBURGER. NOTHING LIKE A RESURRECTION TO WORK UP YOUR APPETITE.
THE ENTIRE CONGREGATION FOLLOWS AS THEY CROSS THE STREET TO THE TOY HAMBURGER STAND.
PLEASE, MY FRIENDS, HAVE ANYTHING YOU WANT. IT'S ALL ON ME!
NATIONAL CRAB
HARDWARE
GRAND TOY HAMBURGER
OPEN
TAKE OUT

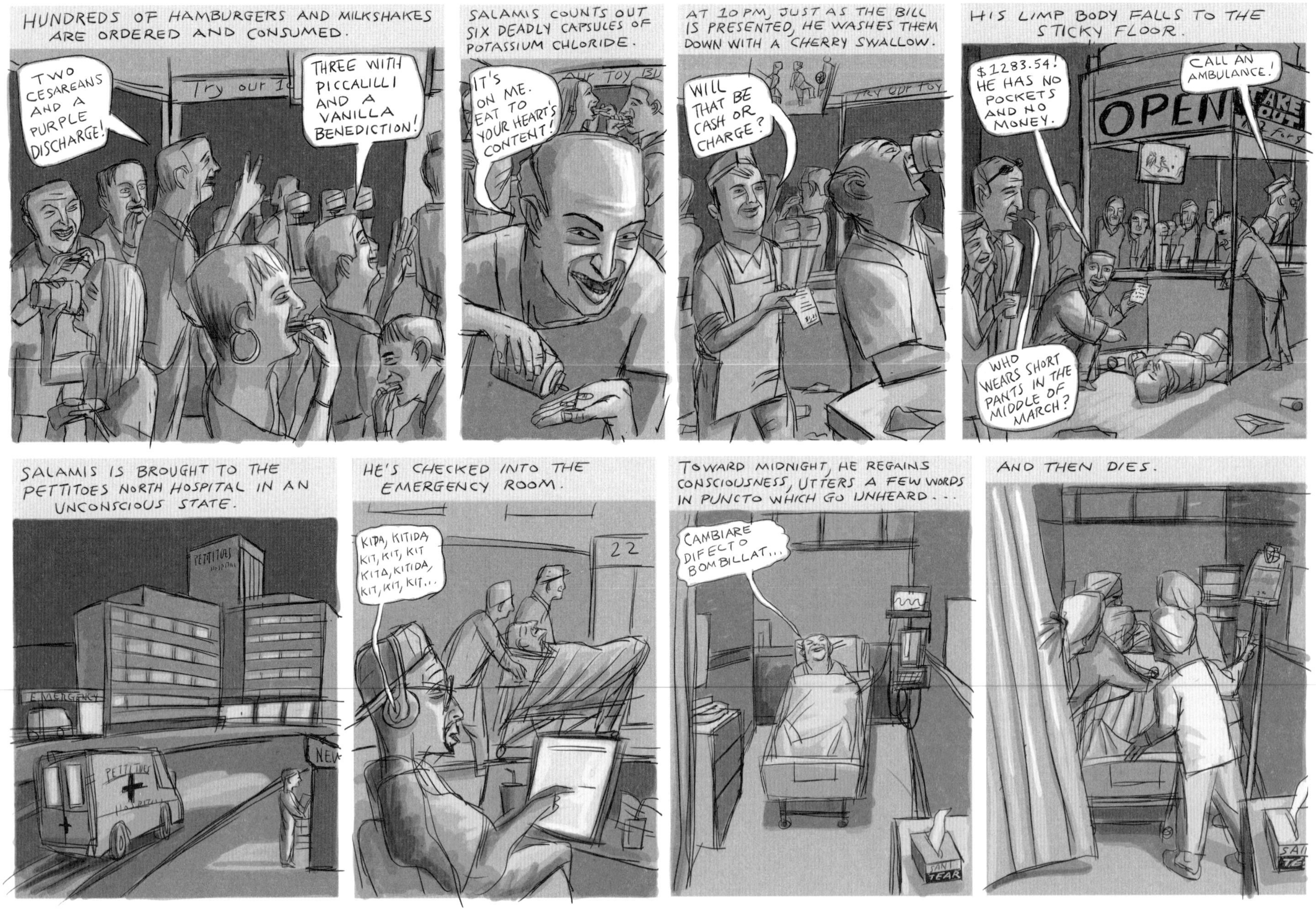
HUNDREDS OF HAMBURGERS AND MILKSHAKES ARE ORDERED AND CONSUMED.
TWO CESAREANS AND A PURPLE DISCHARGE!
THREE WITH PICCALILLI AND A VANILLA BENEDICTION!
SALAMIS COUNTS OUT SIX DEADLY CAPSULES OF POTASSIUM CHLORIDE.
IT'S ON ME. EAT TO YOUR HEART'S CONTENT!
AT 10 PM, JUST AS THE BILL IS PRESENTED, HE WASHES THEM DOWN WITH A CHERRY SWALLOW.
WILL THAT BE CASH OR CHARGE?
HIS LIMP BODY FALLS TO THE STICKY FLOOR.
$1283.54! HE HAS NO POCKETS AND NO MONEY.
CALL AN AMBULANCE!
OPEN
WHO WEARS SHORT PANTS IN THE MIDDLE OF MARCH?
SALAMIS IS BROUGHT TO THE PETTITOES NORTH HOSPITAL IN AN UNCONSCIOUS STATE.
PETTITOES
HE'S CHECKED INTO THE EMERGENCY ROOM.
KIDA, KITIDA KIT, KIT, KIT KITA, KITIDA, KIT, KIT, KIT...
22
TOWARD MIDNIGHT, HE REGAINS CONSCIOUSNESS, UTTERS A FEW WORDS IN PUNCTO WHICH GO UNHEARD...
CAMBIARE DIFECTO BOMBILLAT...
SANI TEAR
AND THEN DIES.

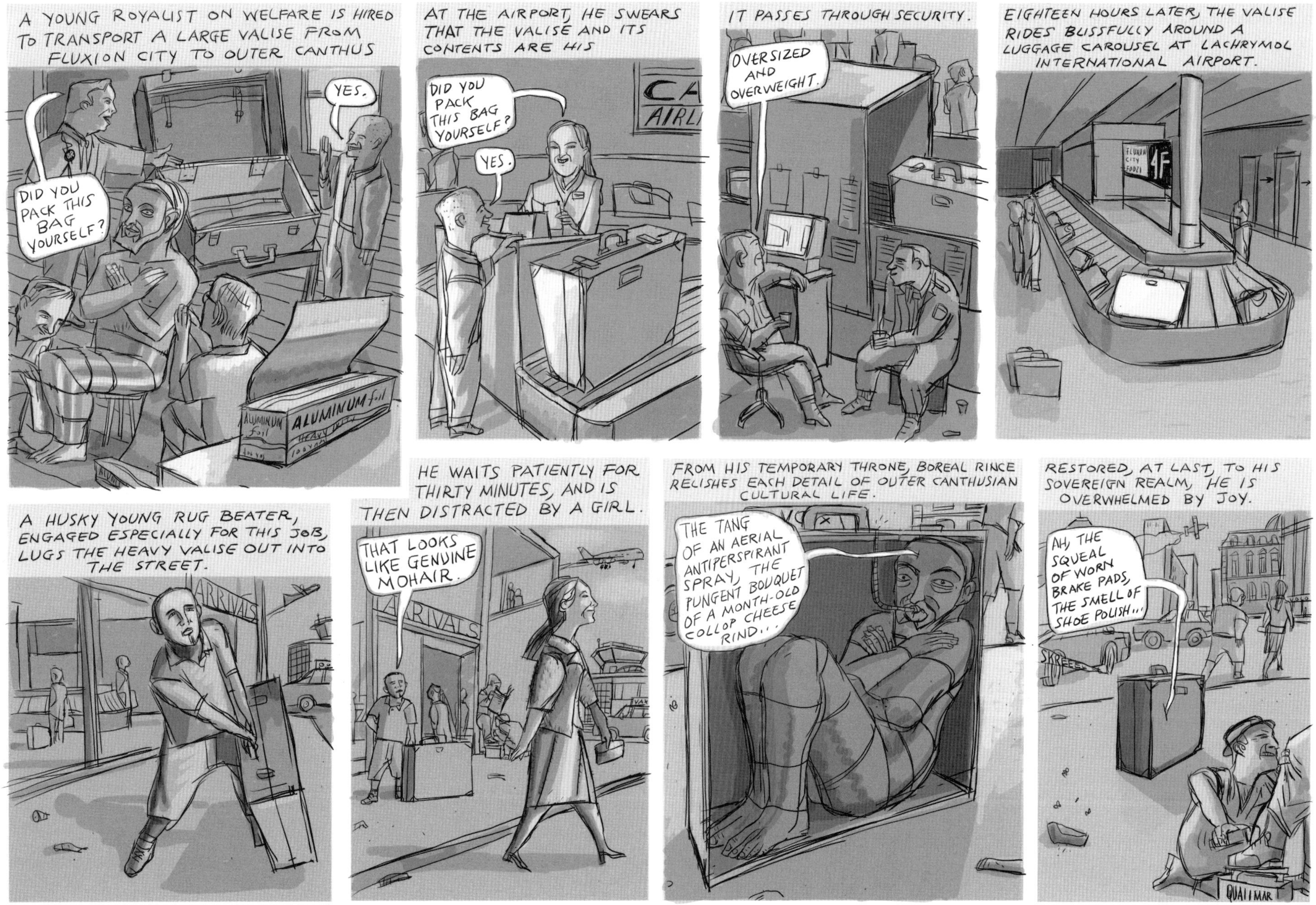

A YOUNG ROYALIST ON WELFARE IS HIRED TO TRANSPORT A LARGE VALISE FROM FLUXION CITY TO OUTER CANTHUS
YES.
DID YOU PACK THIS BAG YOURSELF?
ALUMINUM foil
AT THE AIRPORT, HE SWEARS THAT THE VALISE AND ITS CONTENTS ARE HIS
DID YOU PACK THIS BAG YOURSELF?
YES.
IT PASSES THROUGH SECURITY.
OVERSIZED AND OVERWEIGHT.
EIGHTEEN HOURS LATER, THE VALISE RIDES BLISSFULLY AROUND A LUGGAGE CAROUSEL AT LACHRYMOL INTERNATIONAL AIRPORT.
4F
A HUSKY YOUNG RUG BEATER, ENGAGED ESPECIALLY FOR THIS JOB, LUGS THE HEAVY VALISE OUT INTO THE STREET.
ARRIVALS
HE WAITS PATIENTLY FOR THIRTY MINUTES, AND IS THEN DISTRACTED BY A GIRL.
THAT LOOKS LIKE GENUINE MOHAIR.
ARRIVALS
FROM HIS TEMPORARY THRONE, BOREAL RINCE RELISHES EACH DETAIL OF OUTER CANTHUSIAN CULTURAL LIFE.
THE TANG OF AN AERIAL ANTIPERSPIRANT SPRAY, THE PUNGENT BOUQUET OF A MONTH-OLD COLLOP CHEESE RIND...
RESTORED, AT LAST, TO HIS SOVEREIGN REALM, HE IS OVERWHELMED BY JOY.
AH, THE SQUEAL OF WORN BRAKE PADS, THE SMELL OF SHOE POLISH...
SKREEE

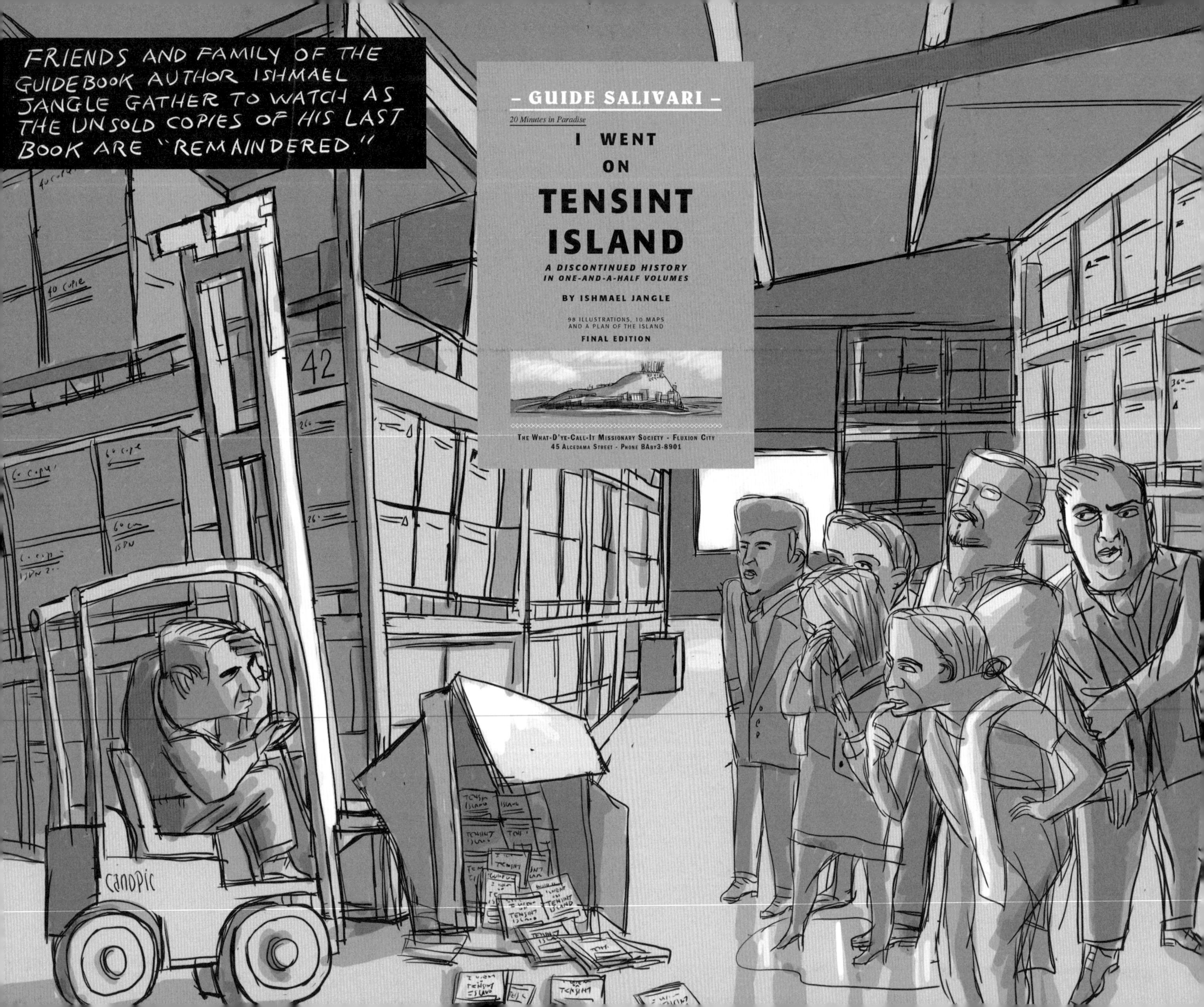
FRIENDS AND FAMILY OF THE GUIDEBOOK AUTHOR ISHMAEL JANGLE GATHER TO WATCH AS THE UNSOLD COPIES OF HIS LAST BOOK ARE "REMAINDERED."
– GUIDE SALIVARI –
20 Minutes in Paradise
I WENT ON TENSINT ISLAND
A DISCONTINUED HISTORY IN ONE-AND-A-HALF VOLUMES
BY ISHMAEL JANGLE
98 ILLUSTRATIONS, 10 MAPS AND A PLAN OF THE ISLAND
FINAL EDITION
THE WHAT-D'YE-CALL-IT MISSIONARY SOCIETY - FLUXION CITY
45 ALCEDAMA STREET - PHONE BAY3-8901
42